War and Peace in Asia

War and Peace in Asia

International Law and Politics in Armed Conflicts

Kriangsak Kittichaisaree

NUS PRESS
SINGAPORE

Published by:

NUS Press
National University of Singapore
AS3-01-02, 3 Arts Link
Singapore 117569

Fax: (65) 6774-0652
E-mail: nusbooks@nus.edu.sg
Website: http://nuspress.nus.edu.sg

ISBN: 978-981-325-325-4 (paperback, Asia only)
ISBN: 978-981-325-330-8 (casewrap)
ISBN: 978-981-325-326-1 (ePDF)

Source of globe: https://www.pngegg.com/en/png-ngqga#

Typeset by: Westchester Publishing Services UK
Printed by: Integrated Books International

Contents

Preface vii

Abbreviations and Acronyms ix

Introduction 1

1. Asian Perspectives on the International Legal Order 8

2. International Law Regulating the Use of Force 28

3. Sovereignty Disputes 54

4. Insurgency and Self-Determination 119

5. Annexation 157

6. Humanitarian Intervention and the Responsibility to Protect (R2P) Doctrine 168

7. Terrorism and Self-Defence against Non-state Actors 195

8. Intervention by Invitation 209

9. Present and Future Directions of War and Peace in Asia 231

Epilogue 265

Bibliography 267

Index 293

Preface

This book is intended for a professional audience, of diplomats, policy-makers, commentators, lawyers, scholars and students who will want to understand actions by parties to armed conflict in Asia, think through alternative responses and endeavour to find mutually acceptable solutions. It aims to shift the frame of discussion of the use of force, which is one of the most controversial subdisciplines within international law and relations, from a Western-centric perspective to a more broad-based one. However, the author does not go as far as endorsing all the views propagated by the followers of the Third World Approach to International Law (TWAIL), which opposes "the unjust global order" with its international norms and institutions that subordinate non-Europeans to Europeans as well as create and perpetuate Western hegemony to serve Western interests.[1] Instead, the book proceeds to identify the common legal principles and rules universally accepted by the international community of nations around the globe, while identifying points of contention, or "grey areas", that owing to power asymmetry have been abused to serve relatively more powerful nation states to the disadvantage of their less powerful Asian counterparts and the positions taken by the Asian states concerned. For this purpose, the views of as many Asian international lawyers as possible are duly taken into consideration.

[1] As lucidly explained in David P. Fidler, "Revolt against or from within the West—TWAIL, the Developing World, and the Future Direction of International Law", *Chinese Journal of International Law* 2 (2003): 29; Antony Anghie and B.S. Chimni, "Third World Approaches to International Law and Individual Responsibility in Internal Conflicts", *Chinese Journal of International Law* 2 (2003): 77; B.S. Chimni, "Customary International Law: A Third World Perspective", *American Society of International Law* 112 (2018): 1; and Antony Anghie, "Rethinking International Law: A TWAIL Retrospective", *European Journal of International Law* 34 (2023): 7.

Unlike most of this author's other writings, this book avoids using too many footnotes so as not to overburden readers with excessive citation sources. Publications that may be representative of the respective arguments will be selected and referenced. Having served as a diplomat and negotiator involved in some of the armed conflicts dealt with in this book, the author approaches the relevant aspects of international politics from a practitioner's perspective rather than relying on political theories.

As an international judge, arbitrator and conciliator, the author has to avoid discussing disputes between certain states that have come or may come before him.

This book would not have seen the light of day without the invaluable assistance and guidance from Peter Schoppert and Lena Qua of NUS Press as well as Julie Willis and Estelle Lloyd of Westchester Publishing Services UK, and my proofreader, Peter Moorby, to whom I hereby express my sincerest appreciation.

All the webpages referred to in this book are accessible as of 1 November 2025.

Abbreviations and Acronyms

ACT	Accountability, Coherence and Transparency Group
AP I	1977 Protocol Additional to the Geneva Conventions of 12 August 1949, and relating to the Protection of Victims of International Armed Conflicts
AP II	1977 Protocol Additional to the Geneva Conventions of 12 August 1949, and relating to the Protection of Victims of Non-International Armed Conflicts
APEC	Asia-Pacific Economic Cooperation
AQAP	Al Qaeda in the Arabian Peninsula
ARSIWA	Articles on Responsibility of States for Internationally Wrongful Acts
Art.	Article
ASEAN	Association of Southeast Asian Nations
ATT	2013 Arms Trade Treaty
BERSATU	United Front for the Independence of Pattani
BRICS	an international bloc initiated by Brazil, Russia, India, China and South Africa
BRN	Berisan Revolusi Nasional
CAVR	Commission for Reception, Truth, and Reconciliation in East Timor
CBM	confidence-building measure
CCG	Chinese Coast Guard
ch.	chapter
CIA	Central Intelligence Agency
COC	Code of Conduct in the South China Sea/East Sea
DOC	2002 Declaration on the Conduct of Parties in the South China Sea/East Sea
DR Congo	Democratic Republic of the Congo

EPF	European Peace Facility
EU	European Union
FRETILIN	Revolutionary Front for an Independent East Timor
GA	United Nations General Assembly
GCC	Gulf Cooperation Council
GID	Syria's General Intelligence Directorate
GMIP	Geragan Mujahideen Islam Pattani
GSI	Global Security Initiative
HRC	United Nations Human Rights Council
ICC	International Criminal Court
ICCPR	1966 International Covenant on Civil and Political Rights
ICESCR	1966 International Covenant on Economic, Social and Cultural Rights
ICJ	International Court of Justice
ICRC	International Committee of the Red Cross
ICT	information and communications technologies
ICTY	International Criminal Tribunal for the former Yugoslavia
IGN	Inter-Governmental Negotiations on Security Council Reform
IHL	international humanitarian law
ILA	International Law Association
ILC	United Nations International Law Commission
ISIL	Islamic State in Iraq and the Levant
ISSG	International Syria Support Group
ITLOS	International Tribunal for the Law of the Sea
JeM	Jaish-e-Mohammed
KLA	Kosovo Liberation Army
KPP-HAM	Commission of Inquiry into Human Rights Violations in East Timor
KSC	Kosovo Specialist Chambers
LTTE	Liberation Tigers of Tamil Eelam
MILF	Moro Islamic Liberation Front
MLC	Movement for the Liberation of the Congo
MNLF	Moro National Liberation Front
mtg(s)	meeting(s)
NAM	Non-Aligned Movement
NATO	North Atlantic Treaty Organization
NGO	non-governmental organization
NUG	National Unity Government (Myanmar)
OAU	Organisation of African Unity

OIC	Organisation of Islamic Cooperation
P5	the five permanent members of the United Nations Security Council
PCA	Permanent Court of Arbitration
PKK	Kurdistan Workers' Party
PRC	People's Republic of China
PRK	People's Republic of Kampuchea
PULO	Pattani United Liberation Organization
Quad	Quadrilateral Security Dialogue
R2P	responsibility to protect
Rep.	Reports
Res.	Resolution
R.I.A.A.	Reports of International Arbitral Awards
RKK	Runda Kampulan Kecil
RMN	Royal Malaysian Navy
RP	Responsible Protection
SCO	Shanghai Cooperation Organisation
SDF	Syrian Democratic Forces
Sess.	Session
SOC	Syrian Opposition Council
STC	Southern Transitional Council
SWV	South Warriors of Valaya
TNI-AL	Indonesian Navy
TPLF	Tigray People's Liberation Front
UAE	United Arab Emirates
UN	United Nations
UNCLOS	1982 United Nations Convention on the Law of the Sea
UNESCO	United Nations Educational, Scientific and Cultural Organization
UNGA	United Nations General Assembly
UN GAOR	United Nations General Assembly Official Records
UNROCA	United Nations Register of Conventional Arms
UNSC	United Nations Security Council
UNTAC	UN Transitional Authority in Cambodia
UNTAET	United Nations Transitional Authority for East Timor
UPR	Universal Periodic Review
WTO	World Trade Organization
YPG	Kurdish People's Protection Units (aka Kurdish People's Defence Units)

Introduction

The aims and scope of this book are to deal with war and peace in Asia after the adoption of the Charter of the United Nations and the establishment of the United Nations in 1945. It analyses, from the perspective of international law and that of international relations, the justifications invoked to wage war and how peace is restored or is attempted to be restored in each case, if at all, through a bilateral or multilateral political settlement that may or may not comply with international law, as well as future implications for international law and international relations.

The term "war" is commonly used by laypersons including policymakers of nation states in different contexts and with different meanings.[1] A state of war is relevant for certain reasons. For example, national law may require a formal state of war to prosecute certain crimes such as treason or trading with the enemy, and a state of war may have legal implications on enforcement of private contractual obligations. As another example, the term "war" is stipulated in international treaties so as to trigger the rights or obligations thereunder, as in the case of the four Geneva Conventions of 12 August 1949 that established international rules for humanitarian treatment in war[2] and their first[3] and third

[1] See Andrew Clapham, *War* (Oxford: Oxford University Press, 2021), pp. xiv–xix and ch. 1.

[2] Convention for the Amelioration of the Condition of the Wounded and Sick in Armed Forces in the Field (75 *United Nations Treaty Series* 31); Convention for the Amelioration of the Condition of the Wounded, Sick and Shipwrecked Members of Armed Forces at Sea (75 *United Nations Treaty Series* 85); Convention Relative to the Treatment of Prisoners of War (75 *United Nations Treaty Series* 135); and Convention Relative to the Protection of Civilian Persons in Time of War (75 *United Nations Treaty Series* 287). All of them entered into force on 21 Oct. 1950.

[3] Protocol Additional to the Geneva Conventions of 12 Aug. 1949, and relating to the Protection of Victims of International Armed Conflicts, 1125 *United Nations Treaty Series* 3, in force on 7 Dec. 1978.

protocols,[4] which apply to all cases of declared war irrespective of the existence or non-existence of fighting or violence.[5]

For the purpose of this book, "war" means an "armed conflict" and this includes declared and undeclared war as well.

The *Final Report on the Meaning of Armed Conflicts in International Law* (2010) by the International Law Association (ILA)[6] finds that the term "armed conflict" has become especially significant since the adoption of the UN Charter in 1945, while the term "war" has declined in importance. However, neither the UN Charter nor any other important treaty currently defines "armed conflict". After extensive research into hundreds of violent situations since 1945, the ILA concludes that as a matter of customary international law a situation of armed conflict depends on the satisfaction of two essential minimum criteria, namely: the existence of organised armed groups *and* the groups' engagement in fighting of some intensity. Declarations of war or armed conflict, national legislation, expressions of subjective intent by parties to a conflict and the like may have evidentiary value but such expressions do not alone create a de jure state of war or armed conflict. The accurate identification of a situation of armed conflict has significant and wide-ranging implications, including an impact on treaty obligations, on UN operations, on asylum rights and duties, on arms control obligations, and on the law of neutrality, among others. Perhaps most importantly, only in armed conflict may states claim belligerent rights permitting them to undertake certain acts that they would not otherwise be entitled to in situations of peace since these acts may violate fundamental human rights. For example, during armed conflict states have expanded rights to kill without warning, detain without trial, and suspend or derogate from treaties and other obligations.[7]

---

[4] Protocol Additional to the Geneva Conventions of 12 Aug. 1949, and relating to the Adoption of an Additional Distinctive Emblem, 2404 *United Nations Treaty Series* 261, in force on 14 Jan. 2007.

[5] Clapham, *War*, pp. 7, 31–8.

[6] The ILA is a private and independent academic think tank founded in Brussels in 1873, whose objectives are "the study, clarification and development of international law, both public and private, and the furtherance of international understanding and respect for international law". The ILA has consultative status, as an international non-governmental organisation, with a number of the UN specialised agencies. It currently has approximately 4,500 members around the world and the focal point of its activities is the series of biennial conferences.

[7] ILA, "Final Report on the Meaning of Armed Conflict in International Law", in *Report of the Seventy-Fourth Conference* (The Hague: ILA, 2010), pp. 805–48.

It has now been well established that an armed conflict is a resort to armed force between nation states or protracted armed violence between governmental authorities and organised armed groups or between such groups within a nation state.[8] Intrastate protracted armed violence excludes situations of internal disturbances and tensions that do not reach that threshold, such as riots, isolated and sporadic acts of violence or other acts of a similar nature.[9]

"Peace" as understood in this book may be a permanent peace, a truce or a reasonably long period of cessation of armed conflict, especially when the parties in question are engaged in negotiations to end the fighting once and for all. It could be the "general close of military operations" in armed conflicts between nation states and a "lasting pacification" in internal armed conflict not involving a foreign nation state.[10] It does not, however, go as far as the concept of "positive peace", which focuses on building a just, equitable and harmonious society.

The geographical scope covered by the book is the entire Asian continent except for countries in Oceania and those members of the Commonwealth of Independent States that have come into existence since the dissolution of the Soviet Union in 1991 that are geographically situated in Asia.

According to the Stockholm International Peace Research Institute, the fighting in Asia and Oceania in 2021 comprised major internationalised civil wars; low-intensity, combined interstate border and subnational armed conflicts; high-intensity, combined interstate border and subnational armed conflicts; and the various threats and conflicts falling within the broad terrorism/counterterrorism rubric, involving both states and non-state actors.[11]

---

[8] *Prosecutor v. Dusko Tadic*, Decision on the Defence Motion for Interlocutory Appeal on Jurisdiction, International Criminal Tribunal for the former Yugoslavia (ICTY) Appeals Chamber, Judgment of 2 Oct. 1995, para. 70, followed by the International Criminal Court in *Prosecutor v. Jean-Pierre Bemba Gombo*, ICC-01/05-01/08, Pre-Trial Chamber II, Judgment of 15 June 2009, para. 229. See also Rogier Bartels, "The Classification of Armed Conflicts by International Criminal Courts and Tribunals", *International Criminal Law Review* 20 (2020): 595.

[9] Art. 8(3) of the Rome Statute of the International Criminal Court (2187 *United Nations Treaty Series* 3, in force 1 July 2002).

[10] International Committee of the Red Cross, *International Humanitarian Law and the Challenges of Contemporary Armed Conflicts* (Geneva: ICRC, 2015), pp. 8–10; Jann Kleffner, "Scope of Application of International Humanitarian Law", in *The Handbook of International Humanitarian Law*, ed. Dieter Fleck (3rd ed., Oxford: Oxford University Press, 2013), pp. 43, 61–2.

[11] Stockholm International Peace Research Institute, *SIPRI Yearbook 2022: Armaments, Disarmament and International Security Summary* (Stockholm: SIPRI, 2022), p. 5.

Data from the Peace Research Institute Oslo shows that the year 2023 recorded the highest number of state-based conflicts since 1946. A state-based conflict is "contested incompatibility over government and/or territory, where at least one party is a State and the use of armed force results in at least 25 battle-related deaths within a calendar year". In 2023, Africa remained the region with the most state-based conflicts per year (28), followed by Asia (17), the Middle East (10), Europe (3) and the Americas (1).[12]

As of May 2024, seven of the world's top ten largest armies are in Asia. Vietnam ranks first (with 5.8 million military personnel), India second (5.1 million), South Korea third (3.8 million), China fifth (3.2 million), North Korea eighth (2 million), Pakistan ninth (1.7 million) and Iran tenth (1.2 million). In between are Russia, which ranks fourth with 3.6 million military personnel; Ukraine sixth, with 2.2 million military personnel; and the United States seventh, with 2.1 million military personnel.[13]

Incidents of use of force by one Asian state against another make international news headlines all year round. Here are just a few examples. In January 2024, Iran and Pakistan carried out cross-border missile attacks against one another, targeting what both sides called "terrorist" groups in the regions around their mutual border. Fortunately, the foreign ministers of both countries agreed in their telephone conversation soon after the incident to de-escalate the tension and resume good neighbourly relations. On 1 April 2024, Israel was believed to be behind the airstrike against the Iranian embassy complex in Damascus, killing 16 people including eight officers of Iran's Islamic Revolutionary Guard Corps. Iran responded on 13 April 2024 by launching missiles and drone attacks against military targets in Israel and the Israeli-occupied Golan Heights. These mutual attacks by Israel and Iran did not escalate into a full-scale war, apparently because both sides realised it would be catastrophic for them and the Middle East region as a whole. Above all, the full-scale war between Hamas and Israel that started on 7 October 2023 has not come to an end at the time of writing.

Since the list of past and ongoing armed conflicts in Asia is very long even after confining the geographical scope of coverage as mentioned above,[14] the au-

[12] Peace Research Institute Oslo, *Conflict Trends: A Global Overview, 1946–2023* (Oslo: PRIO, 2024).

[13] Bruno Venditti, "Mapped: The World's Largest Armies in 2024", *Visual Capitalist* (1 June 2024), https://www.visualcapitalist.com/mapped-the-worlds-largest-armies-in-2024/.

[14] See, for example, https://en.m.wikipedia.org/wiki/List_of_conflicts_in_Asia; Asia Foundation, *The State of Conflict and Violence in Asia 2021: Identity-Based Conflict and Extremism* (2nd ed., San Francisco: Asia Foundation, 2021).

thor has to be selective, using a thematic approach and focusing on armed conflicts of international concern whose analysis can be managed in discrete chapters.

Chapter 1 examines Asian perspectives on international legal order. Chapter 2 analyses the basic rules of international law against the threat or use of force under Article 2(4) and the right to self-defence under Article 51 of the UN Charter and customary international law, as well as the grey area as regards nuclear weapons. Sovereignty disputes over borders and territories are covered in Chapter 3, insurgencies/conflicts arising from groups seeking self-determination in Chapter 4, annexations of one state's territory by another state in Chapter 5, conflicts under the guise of "humanitarian interventions" and the responsibility to protect doctrine in Chapter 6, self-defence against terrorists and non-state actors who are driven by ideology and not self-determination in Chapter 7, and armed intervention by invitation in Chapter 8. The final chapter (Chapter 9) will sum up the lessons learned from the preceding chapters and try to make constructive suggestions for the future world order under the international rule of law.

Each chapter of the book proceeds to, first of all, identify the justifications to engage in armed conflicts in each case study without going into historical details. "Facts" are usually disputed by the opposing parties and this is a field where intelligence information and official secrets are not accessible to the general public. Thus, this book will only rely on information about the parties' positions that is in the public domain, and it will not determine which party's position is justified under international law—the respective positions are identified merely for the purpose of serving as bases for international legal and political analyses. The chapter then explores how peace is restored or attempted to be restored, if ever, be it by bilateral or multilateral means.

Throughout this book, in discussing a use of force, "legitimacy" is distinguished from "legality" or "lawfulness", the former connoting justification, political or otherwise, to resort to the use of force, whereas the latter signifies lawfulness in the sense of conformity with international law regulating the use of force. The author aims to show not only the operation of the principles of law of armed conflicts but how international law interacts with international politics and how legality/lawfulness of the justification in the use of force helps build legitimacy or acceptability in the eyes of the international community of nations.

Legitimacy in the use of force is often influenced by the international perception of whether the entity using force duly observes international humanitarian law (IHL or *jus in bello*), which regulates conducts during an armed conflict[15] and international human rights law.[16] The focus of this book is on the international law on the use of force (*jus ad bellum*), although the other two branches of international law may be referred to insofar as they have a bearing on the legitimacy or otherwise of the use of armed forces in question. For example, mistakes in war causing unintentional deaths, injuries or destructions abound[17] and can undermine just causes for the war. As another example, one of the hottest topics in international humanitarian law is the use of autonomous weapons, such as "drones" or "remotely piloted aircraft" or "unmanned aerial vehicles", which may violate the IHL principles of distinction, proportionality and precaution, owing primarily to a lack of sufficiently advanced artificial intelligence and contextual awareness, unlike the psychological processes in human judgement that are necessary to assess proportionality and so forth.[18] Reports of

[15] International Committee of the Red Cross, *How Is the Term "Armed Conflict" Defined in International Humanitarian Law?* (Geneva: ICRC Opinion Paper 2024). See also Yoram Dinstein and Arne Willy Dahl, *Oslo Manual on Select Topics of the Law of Armed Conflict: Rules and Commentary* (Cham: Springer, 2020); Gal Cohen, "Mixing Oil and Water? The Interaction between *Jus ad Bellum* and *Jus in Bello* during Armed Conflicts", *Journal on the Use of Force & International Law* 9 (2022): 352; Keiichiro Okimoto, "The Cumulative Requirements of *Jus ad Bellum* and *Jus in Bello* in the Context of Self-Defence", *Chinese Journal of International Law* 11 (2012): 45.

[16] See, for example, Christian Schaller, "Using Force Against Terrorists 'Outside' Areas of Active Hostilities–The Obama Approach and the Bin Laden Raid Revisited", *Journal of Conflict & Security Law* 20 (2015): 195, 209–26; Ka Lok Yip, *The Use of Force against Individuals in War under International Law: A Social Ontological Approach* (Oxford: Oxford University Press, 2022), pp. 105–37, 214–32; Emma Lush, "The View through a Different Lens: Increasing Respect for International Humanitarian Law through the Use of International Human Rights Law Framework", *Journal of International Humanitarian Legal Studies* 14 (2023): 95; Terry D. Gill and Kinga Tibori-Szabó, *The Use of Force and the International Legal System* (Cambridge: Cambridge University Press, 2023), pp. 315–46; Yuval Shanny, "Human Rights Norms Applicable in the Situation of Armed Conflict: Beyond the *Lex Generalis/Lex Specialis* Framework", *Japanese Yearbook of International Law* 66 (2023): 3.

[17] Oona A. Hathaway and Azmat Khan, "'Mistakes' in War", *University of Pennsylvania Law Review* 173 (2024): 1.

[18] Elliot Winter, "The Compatibility of Autonomous Weapons with the Principles of International Humanitarian Law", *Journal of Conflict & Security Law* 27 (2022): 1. See also Tim McFarland, "Minimum Levels of Human Intervention in Autonomous Attacks", *Journal of Conflict & Security Law* 27 (2022): 387; Peter Bergen and A.G. Sims, "America's Drone Wars Outside of Conventional War Zones", in *Routledge Handbook of U.S. Counterterrorism and Irregular Warfare Operations*, ed. Michael A. Sheehan, Erich Marquardt and Liam Collins (Abingdon: Routledge, 2022), pp. 460–76; Jaemin Lee, *Artificial Intelligence and*

collateral damage resulting from their use can tarnish and have tarnished the legitimacy of the use of force by a foreign state in the territory of another state, irrespective of the lawfulness or otherwise of the former's use of force under the law on the use of force.

International Law (Singapore: Springer, 2022), pp. 191–210; Diego Mauri, *Autonomous Weapons Systems and the Protection of the Human Person: An International Law Analysis* (Cheltenham: Edward Elgar Publishing, 2022), pp. 118–75; Bérénice Boutin, "State Responsibility in Relation to Military Applications of Artificial Intelligence", *Leiden Journal of International Law* 36 (2023): 133.

CHAPTER 1

Asian Perspectives on the International Legal Order

Asian Contributions to the International Legal Order

A new international legal regime, the archipelagic state doctrine, has come into existence thanks mostly to an Asian perspective. The Philippines and Indonesia took the lead in espousing, and succeeded in getting, the international recognition of the right of any state constituted wholly by one or more archipelagos, to draw straight baselines, or "archipelagic baselines", joining the outermost points of the outermost islands and drying reefs of the archipelago. Satya Nanda, a Fijian diplomat, played an important role in this regard. Part IV of the 1982 UN Convention on the Law of the Sea, which has 170 states parties at the time of writing, concretises this Asian perspective.[1] Twenty states purport to claim this archipelagic state status, half of which are in the Asia-Pacific region: Antigua and Barbuda, the Bahamas, Cabo Verde, Comoros, the Dominican Republic, Fiji, Indonesia, Jamaica, Kiribati, the Maldives, the Marshall Islands, Papua New Guinea, the Philippines, Saint Vincent and the Grenadines, São Tomé and Príncipe, the Seychelles, the Solomon Islands, Trinidad and Tobago, Tuvalu and Vanuatu.[2] Asian perspectives on the international legal order regu-

[1] Charlotte Ku, "The Archipelagic States Concept and Regional Stability in Southeast Asia", *Case Western Reserve Journal of International Law* 23 (1991): 463, 467–71; Tommy Koh, *Building a New Legal Order for the Oceans* (Singapore: NUS Press, 2020), pp. 251–64.
[2] Office of the Staff Judge Advocate (USA), "Archipelagic States", *International Law Studies* 97 (2021): 12.

lating war and peace, however, may not be as universally accepted as the Asian archipelagic state doctrine.

Wars have been waged in Asia from time immemorial. Sun Tsu's *The Art of War* was an ancient Chinese military manual written around the fifth century BCE.[3] The Islamic Quran lays down clear guidelines as to when war is just, as well as how such a war should be conducted.[4] Ancient Hindu texts taught about rules of armed conflicts and preached fair and humane conduct in battle as well as compassion on behalf of both combatants and non-combatants.[5] The *Arthashastra*—an ancient Indian Sanskrit treatise on statecraft, political science, economic policy and military strategy—was written, expanded and redacted between the second century BCE and the third century CE.[6] Military rule and the martial tradition of the samurai dominated Japanese culture for more than eight centuries, with their own code of battle.[7]

Although several principles of these Asian peoples have been shared by other civilisations of the present days, especially in the realm of humane conduct of war, the modern law of use of force (*jus ad bellum*), as opposed to international humanitarian law (*jus in bello*), has been formulated mostly in the West, especially by nations with colonies in Asia, Africa and the Americas. For centuries, the Westphalian system, in which each state has exclusive sovereignty over its territory, developed in Europe after the Peace of Westphalia in 1648,[8] remained somewhat at odds with Asian models based on the tributary

[3] See also Rue Xue, "Humanitarianism in Chinese Traditional Military Ethics and International Humanitarian Law Training in the People's Liberation Army", in *Asia-Pacific Perspectives on International Humanitarian Law*, ed. Suzannah Linton, Tim McCormack and Sandesh Sivakumaran (Cambridge: Cambridge University Press, 2020), pp. 94–8.

[4] See, for example, Brigadier General S.K. Malik, *The Quranic Concept of War* (New Delhi: Himalayan Books, 1986); Patchrathanyarasm Salamat, "The Quranic Concept of Peace and Humanity", *Manusya, Journal of Humanities* 11 (2008): 1.

[5] Raj Balkaran and A. Walter Dorn, "Charting Hinduism's Rules of Armed Conflicts: Indian Sacred Texts and International Humanitarian Law", *International Review of the Red Cross* 104, no. 920–21 (Nov. 2022): 1762–97.

[6] Carl Landauer, "C.H. Alexandrowicz's India and the Kautilyan Moment", *Asian Journal of International Law* 15 (2024): 107–32.

[7] Thomas Cleary, *The Japanese Art of War: Understanding the Culture of Strategy* (Boulder, CO: Shambhala Classics, 2005); Thomas Conlan, "The Nature of Warfare in Fourteenth Century Japan: The Record of Nomoto Tomoyuki", *Journal of Japanese Studies* 25 (1999): 299.

[8] The Peace of Westphalia was a series of peace treaties signed between May and Oct. 1648 in the Westphalian cities of Osnabrück and Münster to end the Thirty Years' War in Central Europe between 1618 and 1648 and the Eighty Years' War, or Dutch War of Independence (1568–1648), against the political and religious hegemony of King Philip II of Spain. The

system under imperial China[9] and several other ancient Asian kingdoms as well as the system of governance by princely states in the Indian subcontinent before British colonisation. Western colonisation of Asia, Africa and the Americas proved that the Westphalian paradigm did not apply outside Europe. Sovereign equality, cherished by Western nations, did not necessarily apply to Asian nations or peoples.

Here is one example. Japan, under the Tokugawa Shogunate, imposed a seclusionist or isolationist policy between 1639 and 1854. In 1853, the US and other great powers demanded that it "open up", even, in some cases, with the threat of force. In 1858, Japan had to conclude a series of unequal treaties of commerce with the great powers, such as the United States, Britain, the Netherlands, France and Russia. Under these treaties, the great powers had extraterritorial jurisdiction in their respective designated areas in Japan and Japan also lost its tariff autonomy. At the end of the Tokugawa Shogunate, Japan sent people to Europe, including the Netherlands, to study international law and in the Meiji era (25 January 1868–30 July 1912), which brought about the modernisation and Westernisation of the country, many authoritative textbooks of international law in the Western world were translated into Japanese. Nevertheless, Japan harboured the idea that international law was useless and too weak to bind states, especially the great powers. For Japan, international law was regarded as "a political bargaining chip" that could be taken advantage of solely by "civilised nations", which meant European or Western nations.[10]

Japan, with China's support, failed at the Versailles Peace Conference in 1919 after the First World War to have racial equality included in the Covenant of the League of Nations, alongside non-discrimination, either in law or in fact, of aliens on account of their race or nationality.[11] This proposal was rejected by

---

Peace of Westphalia recognised, among other things, the exclusive sovereignty of each party over its territories after territorial adjustments under the treaties and right to decide its own destiny. For an argument that the "Westphalian system" could be traced back to the ideas of 18th-century diplomats, politicians and intellectuals, see Christoph Kampmann, "The Treaty of Westphalia as Peace Settlement and Political Concept", in *International Law and Peace Settlement*, ed. Marc Weller, Mark Retter and Andrea Varga (Cambridge: Cambridge University Press, 2022), pp. 64–85.

[9] See John King Fairbank, ed., *The Chinese World Order: Traditional China's Foreign Relations* (Cambridge, MA: Harvard University Press, 1968).

[10] Atsuko Kanehara, "Double Aspects of Being a Sovereign State: Positive and Passive Aspects", https://cigs.canon/en/article/20240611_8159.html, pp. 4–8.

[11] Naoko Shimazu, *Japan, Race and Equality: The Racial Equality Proposal of 1919* (Abingdon: Routledge, 1998).

the United States, Great Britain and Australia. For its part, China was the only delegation at the Conference that refused to sign the Treaty of Versailles at the signing ceremony on 28 June 1919, feeling betrayed by the Conference's hand-over to Japan of the German-leased territory in China, which covered an area of 552 square kilometres.

Asia is also the only place where nuclear bombs have ever been used—on Hiroshima and Nagasaki in Japan on 6 August and 9 August 1945, respectively, to end the Second World War. The justifications therefore remain highly controversial to the present day.[12]

It has been rightly pointed out that, by 1914, after numerous colonial wars, virtually all the territories of Asia, Africa and the Pacific had been colonised by the major European states and this resulted in the assimilation of all these non-European peoples into a system of international law that was fundamentally European in that it derived from European thought and experience.[13] For instance, the Chinese Foreign Ministry found it necessary to study and use Henry Wheaton's *Elements of International Law*, first published in the United States in 1836 and translated into Chinese in 1864, to defend its interests against European states.[14]

The Permanent Court of International Justice, the predecessor of the International Court of Justice (ICJ), was established by the Covenant of the League of Nations. It held its inaugural sitting in 1922 and was dissolved in 1946. The court had judges from the Republic of China and Japan, including Mineichiro Adachi from Japan, who served as its president from 1931 to 1933. Nevertheless, there is no record to show how these Asian judges interpreted international law in a unique, Asian, way different from the rest of their peers.

An Asian perspective of international law from an international judge from Asia was first observed at the International Military Tribunal for the Far East, or the Tokyo War Crimes Tribunal, convened on 29 April 1946 to try leaders of the Japanese Empire for their crimes against peace, conventional war crimes and crimes against humanity, leading up to and during the Second World War. There

[12] See, for example, Philip Nobile, ed., *Judgment at the Smithsonian: The Bombing of Hiroshima and Nagasaki* (Boston, MA: Da Capo Press, 1995); J. Samuel Walker, "Recent Literature on Truman's Atomic Bomb Decision: A Search for Middle Ground", *Diplomatic History* 29 (2005): 311.

[13] Antony Anghie, *Imperialism, Sovereignty and the Making of International Law* (Cambridge: Cambridge University Press, 2005), ch. 2.

[14] Sze Hong Lam, "The Gentle Civilizer of the Far East—A Re-Examination of the Encounter between 'China' and 'International Law'", *Journal of the History of International Law* 26 (2024): 1, 36.

were 11 judges of the tribunal, appointed by US General Douglas MacArthur, supreme commander of the Allied powers. The three Asian judges were Radhabinod Pal from India, Mei Ju-ao from the Republic of China and Delfín Jaranilla y Jebución from the Philippines. The judgment and sentences were rendered in December 1948. The judge from the Philippines disagreed with the penalties imposed by the tribunal as being too lenient, not exemplary and deterrent, and not commensurate with the gravity of the offence or offences committed. It was Judge Pal from India who showed an "Asian perspective" of the international legal order. Pal was the only judge in favour of the acquittal of all of the defendants. He dismissed the legitimacy of the tribunal as victors' justice, referring to the exclusion of Western colonialism and the atomic bombings of Hiroshima and Nagasaki from the list of crimes and the absence on the bench of judges from the vanquished nations. He also found insufficient evidence to convict those accused of conspiracy to commit an act of aggressive war or atrocities during the notorious massacre in Nanking, China. In any case, conspiracy to wage aggressive war was not illegal in 1937, or at any time up to the date of the judgment. Unlike the Japanese military and civilian leadership who stood trial before the tribunal, he found overwhelming evidence of atrocities perpetrated by the members of the Japanese armed forces against the civilian population of some of the territories occupied by them, and against the prisoners of war.

Fifty nations not allied with the vanquished Axis powers during the Second World War met at the San Francisco Conference from 25 April 1945 to 26 June 1945 to draft the UN Charter. The participants from Asia were from China, Iran, Iraq, Lebanon, Saudi Arabia, Syria, "the British Raj" (that is, the rule of the British Crown over the Indian subcontinent) and the Commonwealth of the Philippines, which was an unincorporated territory and commonwealth of the United States from 1935 to 1946. Each part of the UN Charter required a two-thirds majority for its adoption. Thirty-one states represented at the San Francisco Conference that formed the most important bloc were the 20 Latin American states, China, Egypt, Ethiopia, Iran, Iraq, Lebanon, Liberia, Philippines, Saudi Arabia, Syria and Turkey. This group of states pressed for the inclusion in the UN Charter of the end of colonialism, while Latin American states wanted the rules of sovereignty and non-intervention in internal affairs to be subordinated to international law.[15] The norm of the use of force and its self-defence exception, by then already established in the West, were not chal-

[15] Kathryn Sikkink, *Evidence for Hope: Making Human Rights Work in the 21st Century* (Princeton, NJ: Princeton University Press, 2017), pp. 55–93.

lenged, although the UN Charter gives extraordinary power in this regard to the five permanent members of the UN Security Council (UNSC)—China, France, Russia, the United Kingdom and the United States—as the pillars of collective security for world peace.

Now the UN has 193 member states, 53 of which are members of the Asia-Pacific Group. Asian nation states of the present day try to assert perspectives on the international order that are somewhat different from the West and non-Asian countries.[16]

Before China was forced by Western powers to open its doors in the 1840s, it considered itself the centre of the world, with the basic assumption that the international order should be based on China's cultural superiority and tribute system for its neighbouring countries. The traditional Chinese preference for consultation, mediation and conciliation over formal methods of dispute resolution has its origins in Confucian philosophy, which views social conflicts as shameful aberrations from the natural order of social life, where a person would know the difference between right and wrong and a court of law (*fayuan*) is a place to mete out severe punishment instead of a venue to seek justice. In September 1972, the People's Republic of China (PRC) informed the UN secretary-general that China did not recognise the declaration made by the Kuomintang government (the former Chinese government) in October 1946 accepting the compulsory jurisdiction of the ICJ and considered it defunct. Yet the PRC has accepted third-party settlement of its international disputes in the economic and trading fields, including the World Trade Organization dispute resolution mechanisms.[17] According to ICJ Judge Xue Hanqin from China, modern-day China attaches great importance to the role of international law, believing it will contribute to peace, stability and development, and in its international relations China strongly upholds the principle of sovereignty, because it believes in diversity and mutual respect in international political life. This position rests both upon China's historical past and its vision of the future world order, based upon the Five Principles of Peaceful Coexistence as proclaimed by China together with some other Asian countries in the 1950s, namely mutual respect for each other's territorial integrity and sovereignty, mutual non-aggression, mutual non-interference in each other's internal affairs, equality

[16] Xue Hanqin, "Meaningful Dialogue through a Common Discourse: Law and Values in a Multi-Polar World", *Asian Journal of International Law* 1 (2011): 13.

[17] Junwu Pan, "Chinese Philosophy and International Law", *Asian Journal of International Law* 1 (2011): 233, 235, 236, 237, 239, 245. See also Xue Hanqin, "China's Open Policy and International Law", *Chinese Journal of International Law* 4 (2005): 133.

and mutual benefit, and peaceful coexistence. This position has never been changed in China's foreign relations.[18] These five principles contain many elements that basically reflect the common aspirations of small and weak countries for equality and justice in international relations, especially with regard to the principles of sovereignty, sovereign equality and non-interference.[19]

With respect to India, its foreign policy and attitude towards international law have been based on its enthusiasm to stay clear of the power politics of states' rival alliances; establish peace, harmony and cooperation; and protect fiercely its own independence. India played a major and active role in the decade-long intense negotiations between the West, the East and the Third World that culminated in the consensual adoption in 1970 by the UN General Assembly (UNGA) of the Declaration on Principles of International Law concerning Friendly Relations and Cooperation among States in accordance with the Charter of the United Nations (hereinafter "the 1970 Declaration on Friendly Relations"),[20] embodying formulations of seven principles of modern international law, namely the prohibition of the use of force, non-intervention, the peaceful settlement of international disputes, international cooperation, equal rights and self-determination, sovereign equality, and fulfilment in good faith of international obligations.[21]

On 29 April 1954, China and India signed an Agreement on Trade and Communications between the Tibet region of China and India, based on the Five Principles of Peaceful Coexistence. On 28 June 1954, these principles were confirmed in a joint communiqué of the two countries. According to former UN secretary-general Boutros Boutros-Ghali, these five principles, with the exception of the last one, are not new and have been enshrined in various instruments including the UN Charter. In his view, the Asian-African Conference held in Bandung, Indonesia, in April 1955 accepted the Five Principles even though they were not mentioned in the final communiqué, being replaced by the "Ten Principles", namely respect for fundamental human rights and for the purposes and the principles of the UN Charter; respect for the sovereignty and territorial in-

[18] Xue Hanqin, "Chinese Observations on International Law", *Chinese Journal of International Law* 6 (2007): 83, 85, 86.

[19] Xue Hanqin, "Chinese Contemporary Perspectives on International Law: History, Culture and International Law", *Collected Courses of the Hague Academy of International Law* 355 (2011): 41, 68–9, 95; Xue, "Chinese Observations on International Law", 86.

[20] GA Res. 2625 (XXV), A/8028 (1970), 121.

[21] V.S. Mani, "An Indian Perspective on the Evolution of International Law on the Threshold of the Third Millennium", *Asian Yearbook of International Law* 9 (2004): 31, 66, 69–70.

tegrity of all nations; recognition of the equality of all races and of the equality of all nations large and small; abstention from intervention or interference in the internal affairs of another country; respect for the right of each nation to defend itself singly or collectively, in conformity with the UN Charter; abstention from the use of arrangements of collective defence to serve the particular interests of any of the big powers as well as abstention by any country from exerting pressures on other countries; refraining from acts or threats of aggression or the use of force against the territorial integrity or political independence of any country; settlement of all international disputes by peaceful means, such as negotiation, conciliation, arbitration or judicial settlement as well as other peaceful means of the parties' own choice, in conformity with the UN Charter; promotion of mutual interests and cooperation; and respect for justice and international obligations. China's Prime Minister Zhou En-lai considered the Ten Principles merely an extension and development of the Five Principles of Peaceful Coexistence, insofar as the Ten Principles can be said to focus essentially on political self-determination, mutual respect for sovereignty, non-aggression, non-interference in internal affairs and equality in international relations. Thirty countries and territories participated in the Bandung Conference, with 22 coming from Asia: Afghanistan, Burma, Cambodia, Ceylon (Sri Lanka), India, Indonesia, Iran, Iraq, Japan, Jordan, Laos, Lebanon, Nepal, Pakistan, the Philippines, the PRC, Saudi Arabia, Syria, Thailand, North Vietnam, South Vietnam and Yemen.[22] At Bandung, the Asian and African states, in effect, endorsed the Five Principles both as a protection against the hegemonic intervention of the then two superpowers—the United States and the Soviet Union—and as a standard for good international conduct between all states. Peaceful coexistence became the main objective of the policy of non-alignment, replacing the Cold War between the Western world and the Eastern bloc led by the Soviet Union by a policy of peaceful coexistence and helping non-aligned countries to avoid involvement in the Cold War. The advocates of non-alignment aspire to promote a world in which weaker nations can live unmolested by powerful nations and can choose their own ideologies and develop their own political and economic system, in accordance with their traditions, needs and potentials.[23]

[22] The participants from outside Asia were pre-independence Cyprus, Egypt, Ethiopia, Gold Coast (now Ghana), Liberia, Libya, pre-independence Sudan and Turkey.

[23] Boutros Boutros-Ghali, "The Five Principles", *Chinese Journal of International Law* 3 (2004): 373–8. See also Xue, "Meaningful Dialogue through a Common Discourse", 14; Edward McWhinney, "The Renewed Vitality of the International Law Principles of Peaceful Coexistence in the Post-Iraq Invasion Era: The 50th Anniversary of the China/India Pancha Shila Agreement of 1954", *Chinese Journal of International Law* 3 (2004): 379.

Ironically, the emphasis on the principles of sovereign equality, mutual non-interference and formal equality of states propounded by these Asian states mirrors the 1648 Peace of Westphalia to such an extent that Asia may be considered to be propagating its own "Eastphalian" world order to counter Western dominance in international law and relations.[24]

The Ten Principles of the Bandung Conference in 1955 were reaffirmed by the Asian-African Conference held in Indonesia in 2005 to commemorate the fiftieth anniversary of the Bandung Conference. The "Bandung Message" issued by the Asian-African Conference held in Indonesia in 2015 to commemorate the sixtieth anniversary of the Bandung Conference states, inter alia, that the participating countries remain committed to the principle of self-determination as set forth by the 1955 Bandung Conference; reiterate the central role of the United Nations in the maintenance of international peace and security, in particular those relating to the respect for territorial integrity, sovereignty and political independence of states, refraining from the threat or use of force against the independence and territorial integrity of states and interference in their domestic affairs; and resolve to strengthen the role and capacity of regional and subregional organisations in the two continents in the peaceful settlement of disputes, conflict prevention and resolution, as well as promoting political stability.

The Ministry of Foreign Affairs of the PRC and the Chinese Society of International Law jointly held a colloquium on international law on 27 May 2014 to commemorate the sixtieth anniversary of the Five Principles of Peaceful Coexistence.[25] It was noted that the Five Principles have been incorporated into the Ten Principles of Bandung in 1955, the UNGA's Resolution 1236 of 1957 on Peaceful and Neighbourly Relations among States, the 1970 Declaration on Friendly Relations and the Resolution on the Charter of Economic Rights and Duties of States in 1974, as well as a large number of bilateral treaties and other instruments. At present, as the multipolarisation of the world and economic globalisation intensify and global challenges and non-

---

[24] For an analysis on this point, see Tom Ginsburg, "Eastphalia as the Perfection of Westphalia", *Indian Journal of Global Legal Studies* 17 (2010): 27.

[25] More than 70 participants came from China, India, Myanmar, Indonesia, Pakistan, Russia, Bangladesh, Brunei, Cambodia, Laos, Nepal, Thailand, the UN Secretariat, the ICJ, the Asian-African Legal Consultative Organization, the Asian Society of International Law, the African Institute of International Law, the American Society of International Law, the European Society of International Law, the International Committee of the Red Cross, the Asian-Pacific Space Cooperation Organization and the Chinese Society of Space Law, among others.

conventional threats grow, it is of practical significance to further apply and develop the Five Principles as follows.

First, regarding the principle of mutual respect for sovereignty and territorial integrity, states have the right to participate in the making of, interpreting and applying international law on an equal footing, and the obligation to comply with international law in good faith, promote international equality and justice, and apply international law on the basis of the purposes and principles of the UN Charter in a coherent and consistent manner. States shall, in accordance with the UN Charter and other international treaties, respect, protect and promote individual and collective human rights, including safeguarding the right to development. Peoples who remain under colonial domination and foreign occupation have the right to self-determination in accordance with international law. States have the right to take lawful measures within their own territory to defend their territorial integrity and to provide for their preservation and prosperity.

Second, on the principle of non-aggression, which is a fundamental guarantee for international peace and security, unless authorised by the UNSC or in the exercise of the right of self-defence, all states shall refrain, in their international relations, from the threat or use of force, in particular any form of aggression, against the sovereignty, territorial integrity or political independence of any state, or in any other manner inconsistent with the purposes of the United Nations. States shall lend their full support to the system of collective security where the UNSC plays the central role. The international community may take collective action, through the UNSC, in accordance with the UN Charter on a case-by-case basis, to protect populations from genocide, war crimes, ethnic cleansing and crimes against humanity.

Third, with respect to the principle of non-interference in each other's internal affairs, no state or group of states has the right to intervene, directly or indirectly, for any reason whatever, in the internal or external affairs of any other state. No state shall organise, assist, foment, finance, incite or tolerate subversive, terrorist or armed activities directed towards the violent overthrow of the regime of another state or interfere in civil strife in another state. All states, in fighting against terrorism, shall comply with international law and refrain from applying double standards. Every state shall refrain from any action aimed at the partial or total disruption of the national unity and territorial integrity of any other state or country. It is not against the principle of non-interference in each other's internal affairs that states and international organisations, with the authorisation of the UNSC in accordance with the UN Charter or with the consent of a state, intervene in the affairs of that state.

Fourth, pursuant to the principle of equality and mutual benefit interests, states should pay due regard to the interests of other states and protect and promote the common interests of the international community, and seek mutual benefit with a win–win approach. States should strengthen international cooperation in all fields, especially under the framework of the United Nations and regional arrangements. States should also improve international mechanisms and legislations in common response to global challenges and non-conventional security threats, in particular regarding cyberspace, polar regions, the seabed and ocean floor and subsoil thereof beyond the limits of national jurisdiction, outer space and climate change, with a view to promoting sustainable development.

Fifth, the principle of peaceful coexistence is necessary for a stable international order and smooth cooperation. States shall settle international disputes by peaceful means in accordance with international law, commit themselves to settling disputes relating to state sovereignty and security, including issues left over from history, through negotiations and consultations, and mutually respect each other's free choice of peaceful means for dispute settlement. States shall uphold the central role of the United Nations in maintaining international peace and security and safeguarding economic and social stability and development. As a necessary supplement, states are encouraged to establish rule-based regional arrangements. States should discard "zero-sum game" thinking or a "rising power seeking hegemony" mindset.

The Beijing colloquium considers that these Five Principles, together with the other principles of the United Nations, with all their universal applicability and vitality, will continue to evolve and adapt to the ever-changing circumstances.[26]

The principle of peaceful coexistence was stressed three times in the Chinese foreign minister's speech at the Symposium on the International Situation and China's Foreign Relations, held in Beijing on 25 December 2022.

On the whole, the aforesaid Five Principles and Ten Principles are ideal aspirations among Asian states, the actual implementation of which has much to desire. For instance, during the Cultural Revolution in China (1966–76), the PRC cultivated ties with insurgent communist parties in Thailand, Malaysia, the Philippines, Indonesia and Burma and endorsed their calls for armed struggles against the respective central governments—a flagrant interference in

---

[26] Xu Hong, "The Chair's Summary of the Colloquium on the Five Principles of Peaceful Coexistence and the Development of International Law Held in Beijing on May 27, 2014", *Chinese Journal of International Law* 13 (2014): 501–6.

internal affairs of these countries.[27] More shortcomings in the application of these principles will be explained in the following chapters of this book.

On 21 February 2023 the Chinese government published a concept paper on the Global Security Initiative (GSI).[28] The GSI comprises six interconnected core concepts and principles: (1) commitment to the vision of common, comprehensive, cooperative and sustainable security; (2) commitment to respecting the sovereignty and territorial integrity of all countries; (3) commitment to abiding by the purposes and principles of the UN Charter; (4) commitment to taking the legitimate security concerns of all countries seriously; (5) commitment to peacefully resolving differences and disputes between countries through dialogue and consultation; and (6) commitment to maintaining security in both traditional and non-traditional domains. Regarding the second one, sovereign equality and non-interference in internal affairs are basic principles of international law and the most fundamental norms governing contemporary international relations. The third one means true multilateralism, firm respect for the international system with the UN at its core, the international order underpinned by international law and the basic norms of international relations underpinned by the UN Charter, and upholding the authority of the UN and its status as the main platform for global security governance.

There are 20 priorities for cooperation under the GSI. The following are of direct relevance to this book. The first priority area identified by the GSI is active participation in formulating a "new agenda for peace" and other proposals put forth in the *Our Common Agenda* report by the UN secretary-general in 2021, in particular by supporting UN efforts to enhance conflict prevention and fully harnessing the peacebuilding architecture to assist post-conflict states in peacebuilding. The UN secretary-general's Peace and Security Sub-fund of the China-UN Peace and Development Trust Fund is to be further leveraged. A bigger UN role in global security affairs and enhancing the capacity for implementing UN peacekeeping mandates are to be supported. The second priority is to promote coordination and sound interaction among "major countries" and build a major-country relationship featuring peaceful coexistence, overall stability and balanced development. It calls on major countries to lead by example in honouring equality, good faith, cooperation and the rule of law, and in complying with the UN Charter and international law as well as adhering to mutual respect, peaceful coexistence

[27] William R. Heaton, "China and the Southeast Asian Communist Movements: The Decline of Dual Track Diplomacy", *Asian Survey* 22 (1982): 779.

[28] https://en.chinadiplomacy.org.cn/pdf/The_Global_Security_Initiative_Concept_Paper.pdf.

and win–win cooperation, sticking to the bottom line of no conflict and no confrontation, seeking common ground while reserving differences, and managing differences. Another priority area is the promotion of political settlement of international and regional hotspot issues, such as the "Ukraine crisis" after the start of the full-scale Russia–Ukraine war in February 2022, through candid dialogue and communication/negotiation, with the international community's support in constructively participating in the political settlement of hotspots, under the premise of non-interference in internal affairs, mainly through the means of facilitating peace talks, with fairness and practicality as the main attitude, and mainly following the approach of addressing both symptoms and root causes. The GSI identifies as a priority area the support and improvement of the regional security cooperation mechanism and architecture centred around the Association of Southeast Asian Nations (ASEAN), and adherence to the ASEAN way of consensus-building and accommodating each other's comfort level to further strengthen security dialogue and cooperation among regional countries. With respect to the Middle East, the GSI supports the five-point proposal on realising peace and stability in the Middle East, including advocating mutual respect, upholding equity and justice, realising non-proliferation, jointly fostering collective security, and accelerating development cooperation, so as to jointly establish a new security framework in the Middle East, with the League of Arab States and other regional organisations playing a constructive role in this regard. The GSI aims to strengthen maritime dialogue and exchange and practical cooperation, as well as properly handling maritime differences. The GSI also supports strengthening the UN's role as the central coordinator in the global fight against terrorism.

Regarding the platforms and mechanisms of cooperation, the GSI will engage in wide-ranging discussions and communication on peace and security at the UNGA, relevant UN committees, the UNSC, relevant institutions, and other international and regional organisations based on their respective mandates, and put forward common initiatives and propositions to forge consensus in the international community to address security challenges. The GSI will also leverage the roles of the Shanghai Cooperation Organisation (SCO), the Conference on Interaction and Confidence Building Measures in Asia, and relevant mechanisms of East Asian cooperation, and carry out security cooperation incrementally to achieve similar or the same goals. It will establish a multilateral dialogue platform in the Gulf region and give play to the role of coordinating and cooperative mechanisms to promote regional and global peace and stability. High-level conferences on the GSI will strengthen policy communication in the field of security, promote intergovernmental dialogue and cooperation, and further foster synergy in the international community to address security challenges. Other security forums, such as the Middle East Security Forum and other international dialogue platforms contributing to deepening exchange and cooperation on security, will be used to solicit support for the GSI.

On 24 February 2023, the first anniversary of the start of the Russia–Ukraine war, China released its 12-point Position on the Political Settlement of the Ukraine Crisis: respecting the sovereignty of all countries; abandoning the Cold War mentality; ceasing hostilities; resuming peace talks; resolving the humanitarian crisis; protecting civilians and prisoners of war; keeping nuclear power plants safe; reducing strategic risks; facilitating grain exports; stopping unilateral sanctions; keeping industrial and supply chains stable; and promoting post-conflict reconstruction.[29] The first two of these points clearly echo China's entrenched stance as regards the international order. On 21 March 2023, President Xi and Russian president Putin issued a joint statement after their meeting in Moscow. On the Ukraine issue, the two sides believe that the purposes and principles of the UN Charter must be observed and international law must be respected. They "oppose the practice by any country or group of countries to seek advantages in the military, political and other areas to the detriment of the legitimate security interests of other countries". The Russian side reaffirms its commitment to the resumption of peace talks as soon as possible and welcomes China's willingness to play a positive role for the political and diplomatic settlement of the Ukraine crisis, including "the constructive proposals" set forth in China's Position on the Political Settlement of the Ukraine Crisis. The two sides point out that, to settle the Ukraine crisis, "the legitimate security concerns of all countries must be respected, bloc confrontation should be prevented and fanning the flames avoided". The two sides stress that "responsible dialogue" is the best way for appropriate solutions, with the international community providing support to the relevant constructive efforts. The two sides also "call for stopping all moves that lead to tensions and the protraction of fighting to prevent the crisis from getting worse or even out of control". The two sides oppose any unilateral sanctions unauthorised by the UNSC.

Japan, another Asian state, is currently the world's fourth largest economy, after the United States, China and Germany. Japan has been playing important roles in the international order for centuries but since the Second World War its focus has been on national defence, avoiding military adventurism and staying under the US nuclear umbrella to protect Japan from threats or use of nuclear weapons. Japan's constitution allows it to maintain its Self-Defence Forces exclusively for the purpose of national defence. In 2007, Japan's prime minister

---

[29]https://www.aljazeera.com/news/2023/3/20/full-text-chinas-position-on-settling-the-ukraine-crisis.

initiated the Quadrilateral Security Dialogue (or the Quad), a strategic security dialogue with Australia, India and the United States, to counter China militarily and diplomatically in the Indo-Pacific region, particularly in the South China Sea. The Quad was terminated after Australia's withdrawal in 2008 but it was revived in 2017. To counter unilateral changes to the status quo by force and to ensure its security, Japan reinforces collaboration with as many countries as possible, while also promoting multilateral and multilayered defence cooperation and exchanges, taking into account characteristics of the Asia-Pacific region as well as the situation of each country. Japan is also careful to pay attention to communication with China and Russia so as to avoid any misunderstanding that may lead to armed confrontation.[30]

Asian Regional Organisations

Asia does not have a military alliance organisation like the North Atlantic Treaty Organization (NATO), set up to protect the defence interests of the United States, Canada and its European member states.

All Muslim-majority states in Asia are members of the Organisation of Islamic Cooperation (OIC), although Syria was suspended from the OIC from 14/15 August 2012 to 7 March 2025. The OIC Charter lists among the OIC's objectives the respect for the right of self-determination and non-interference in the domestic affairs and the respect for sovereignty, independence and territorial integrity of each member state; and support for the restoration of complete sovereignty and territorial integrity of any member state under occupation, as a result of aggression, on the basis of international law and cooperation with the relevant international and regional organisations. To attain these objectives, all OIC member states shall commit themselves to the purposes and principles of the UN Charter; settle their disputes through peaceful means and refrain from the use or threat of use of force in their relations; undertake to respect the national sovereignty, independence and territorial integrity of other member states; refrain from interfering in the internal affairs of others; undertake to contribute to the maintenance of international peace and security; and refrain from interfering in each other's internal affairs as enshrined in the OIC Charter, the UN Charter, international law and international humanitarian law. However, the OIC member

---

[30] See Japan's *National Security, National Defense Strategy, and Defense Buildup Program (Outline)*, Dec. 2023, https://www.mod.go.jp/en/d_act/d_policy/pdf/overview-202409.pdf.

states failed to collectively oppose the Soviet invasion of Afghanistan in 1979 and the Iraqi invasion of Iran in 1980, among others.[31]

As for the Gulf Cooperation Council (GCC), its members are also members of the League of Arab States. The GCC Charter does not mention security explicitly, although since its establishment the GCC has been primarily seeking to achieve full and effective cooperation in terms of security. Article V of the Arab League Charter prohibits the use of force to settle a dispute and empowers the Arab League Council to mediate or arbitrate a dispute, delivering a binding decision by a majority vote. Nonetheless, the GCC and Arab League's judicial and quasi-judicial dispute settlement mechanisms have to date been bypassed, allegedly because their members prefer a diplomatic settlement (including by a border demarcation agreement of 1996 to end a military confrontation between Qatar and Saudi Arabia that had resulted in three casualties) and because Article V of the Arab League Charter excludes disputes relating to sovereignty, that is, national security.[32]

The Association of Southeast Asian Nations (ASEAN) was set up on 8 August 1967 by Indonesia, Malaysia, the Philippines, Singapore and Thailand, motivated by their common fear of the spread of communism into Southeast Asia. After the end of the Vietnam War, ASEAN expanded to include Brunei Darussalam on 7 January 1984 (a few days after its independence from Great Britain), Vietnam on 28 July 1995, Laos and Myanmar both on 23 July 1997 and Cambodia on 30 April 1999, with ASEAN agreeing in principle in November 2022 to admit Timor-Leste as the eleventh ASEAN Member State. Yet ASEAN is not a military alliance. The 1976 Treaty of Amity and Cooperation in Southeast Asia, to which all ASEAN member states are parties and which is open to accession by other states,[33] enumerates in Article 2 the following principles guiding the relations between its contracting parties: (1) mutual respect for the independence, sovereignty, equality, territorial integrity and national iden-

[31] Salim Farrar, "The Organisation of Islamic Cooperation: Forever on the Periphery of Public International Law", *Chinese Journal of International Law* 13 (2014): 787, 794.

[32] Abdulmalik Altamimi, "An Appraisal of the Gulf Cooperation Council's Mechanisms for Co-operation and the Settlement of Disputes", *Asian Journal of International Law* 10 (2020): 321.

[33] At the time of writing, there are 57 contracting parties to the Treaty, including China and the other four permanent members of the UNSC (France, Russia, United Kingdom and United States) as well as the European Union. The other contracting parties from Asia are India, Japan, Pakistan, Bahrain, South Korea, Timor-Leste, Bangladesh, Sri Lanka, North Korea, Mongolia, Iran, Oman, Qatar, UAE, Papua New Guinea, Saudi Arabia and Kuwait.

tity of all nations; (2) the right of every state to lead its national existence free from external interference, subversion or coercion;[34] (3) non-interference in the internal affairs of one another; (4) the settlement of differences or disputes by peaceful means; (5) the renunciation of the threat or use of force; and (6) effective cooperation among themselves. These principles largely mirror the Five Principles of Peaceful Existence.

Although the SCO, set up by China and Russia together with certain states from the former Soviet Union, has been cooperating in the field of common regional security concerns, such as counterterrorism, to counterbalance the United States' influence within Eurasia, it is not a military alliance like NATO.[35]

In June 2009, the leaders of Brazil, Russia, India and China met in Yekaterinburg in Russia to discuss how to improve global economic situations, reform financial institutions and enhance future cooperation among them. In 2010, South Africa joined the grouping, which is now called "BRICS". BRICS incorporates from the Five Principles of Peaceful Coexistence the principles of non-interference, equality and win–win (mutual benefit).[36] Egypt, Ethiopia, Iran and the United Arab Emirates joined this "BRICS" bloc on 1 January 2024, as did Indonesia on 6 January 2025. Belarus, Bolivia, Kazakhstan, Cuba, Malaysia, Nigeria, Thailand, Uganda and Uzbekistan officially became BRICS partners in January 2025. BRICS is seen as trying to build an alternative world order, in which the Global South has greater geopolitical, economic and diplomatic clout. It has evolved to become a geopolitical bloc against Western dominance in the international order.

Asian States and Third-Party Dispute Settlement Mechanisms

As regards dispute settlement mechanisms, international courts or tribunals have "compulsory" jurisdiction over disputes based on bilateral or multilateral trea-

[34] On coercion, see Marko Milanovic, "Revisiting Coercion as an Element of Prohibited Intervention in International Law", *American Journal of International Law* 117 (2023): 601.

[35] Michael Salter and Yinan Yin, "Analysing Regionalism within International Law and Relations: The Shanghai Cooperation Organisation as a *Grossraum*", *Chinese Journal of International Law* 13 (2014): 819.

[36] Gutemberg P. Lopes, Jr., "The Sino-Brazilian Principles in a Latin American and BRICS Context: The Case for Comparative Public Budgeting Legal Research", *Wisconsin International Law Journal* 33 (2015): 1.

ties referring disputes thereunder to these courts or tribunals. States may, on an "optional" basis, declare their conditional or unconditional acceptance of the jurisdiction of an international court or tribunal.

To date, only 74 states have made declarations accepting the compulsory jurisdiction of the ICJ to settle international disputes to which they are parties. The United Kingdom is the only permanent member of the UNSC that has done so. So have very few Asian states covered by this book, namely Timor-Leste, Japan, Cambodia, India, Iran, the Philippines and Pakistan.

Japan's declaration of 2015 has excluded any dispute arising out of, concerning, or relating to research on, or conservation, management or exploitation of, living resources of the sea from Japan's acceptance of the ICJ's compulsory jurisdiction.

Among the disputes excluded by India in its declaration of 27 September 2019 accepting the ICJ's compulsory jurisdiction are disputes relating to or connected with facts or situations of hostilities, armed conflicts, individual or collective actions taken in self-defence, resistance to aggression, fulfilment of obligations imposed by international bodies, and other similar or related acts, measures or situations in which India is, has been or may in future be involved, including the measures taken for protection of national security and ensuring national defence. Also excluded are disputes with India concerning or relating to: (1) the status of its territory or the modification or delimitation of its frontiers or any other matter concerning boundaries; (2) the territorial sea, the continental shelf and the margins, the exclusive fishery zone, the exclusive economic zone, and other zones of national maritime jurisdiction including for the regulation and control of marine pollution and the conduct of scientific research by foreign vessels; (3) the condition and status of its islands, bays and gulfs and that of the bays and gulfs that for historical reasons belong to it; (4) the airspace superjacent to its land and maritime territory; and (5) the determination and delimitation of its maritime boundaries.

With respect to Pakistan, its declaration of 29 March 2017 accepting the ICJ's compulsory jurisdiction excludes, inter alia, disputes relating to or connected with any aspect of hostilities, armed conflicts, individual or collective self-defence or the discharge of any functions pursuant to any decision or recommendation of international bodies, the deployment of armed forces abroad, as well as action relating and ancillary thereto in which Pakistan is, has been or may in future be involved; all matters related to Pakistan's national security; and any dispute about the delimitation of maritime zones, including the territorial sea, the exclusive economic zone, the continental shelf, the exclusive fishery zone and other zones of national maritime jurisdiction or the exploitation of any disputed area adjacent to any such maritime zone.

The Philippines' declaration of 1972 excludes from the ICJ's compulsory jurisdiction disputes arising out of or concerning jurisdiction or rights claimed or exercised by the Philippines; in respect of the natural resources, including living organisms belonging to sedentary species, of the seabed and subsoil of the continental shelf of the Philippines or its analogue in an archipelago; or in respect of the territory of the Philippines, including its territorial seas and inland waters.

Iran's declaration of 25 June 2023 accepts the ICJ's compulsory jurisdiction only in relation to the following disputes: (1) the jurisdictional immunities of the state and state property; and (2) immunity from measures of constraint against state or state property. Except as provided for in (1) and/or (2), no other dispute shall be entertained by the ICJ, in particular: (1) disputes relating to questions that fall essentially within Iran's domestic jurisdiction; (2) disputes relating to sovereignty, sovereign rights or jurisdiction over land or maritime areas; and (3) disputes with any state not recognised by Iran. Two days later, on 27 June 2023, Iran instituted before the ICJ an application concerning the violations by Canada of Iran's jurisdictional immunity and immunity from measures of constraint under customary international law arising from a series of legislative, executive and judicial measures adopted by Canada against Iran and its property since 2012. Iran's declaration was thus specifically tailor-made for this case it has brought against Canada.

With respect to the 1982 UN Convention on the Law of the Sea (UNCLOS), which has 170 states parties at the date of writing, its Article 298(1) permits its parties to declare that they exclude from the compulsory dispute settlement regime under UNCLOS the following categories of disputes: (1) disputes relating to sea boundary delimitations or those involving historic bays or titles, including any dispute that necessarily involves the concurrent consideration of any unsettled dispute concerning sovereignty or other rights over continental or insular land territory; (2) disputes concerning military activities; (3) disputes in respect of which the UNSC is exercising the functions assigned to it by the UN Charter, unless the UNSC decides to remove the matter from its agenda or calls upon the parties to settle it by the means provided for in UNCLOS. China, South Korea and Thailand have declared that they do not accept compulsory dispute settlement for these three categories. The declarations by Singapore and by Indonesia exclude category (1) from the compulsory dispute settlement regime under UNCLOS.

Preliminary Conclusions

The Asian perspectives examined above show how Asian states, having suffered from Western colonialism and discriminatory treatment in the past, want the international order to be cognisant of their national interests, not subject to foreign domination or interference.

Noble principles are also applied with strategic interests in mind. For example, with China expanding its role and leverage in the international order, India has been trying to counter China's international political influence by joining the Quadrilateral Security Dialogue. According to one analysis, India has been increasingly asserting its role in the South China Sea by enhancing its military and diplomatic engagement with states such as the Philippines and Vietnam that have territorial disputes with China over geographical features in the South China Sea. There are several probable reasons for this. First, India may have attempted to increase its presence in the South China Sea to prevent tensions from spilling into the Indian Ocean, India's traditional sphere of influence. Second, India may perceive the South China Sea as a foothold to push forward Indian prime minister Modi's "Act East Policy" and leverage to balance China's expansions in the Indian Ocean and its offensives along the disputed China–India border. Third, since half of its foreign trade passes through the Malacca Strait, free and secure navigation in the South China Sea is the key to India's trade security.[37]

As will be seen in the following chapters, when their national interests are threatened, these Asian states rarely hesitate to interpret grey areas in international law to serve their own interests, notwithstanding their repeated pledge to uphold noble principles, such as the Five Principles of Peaceful Coexistence. Most disputes giving rise to the use of force between Asian states are not subject to any mandatory international dispute settlement mechanisms. Therefore, diplomacy is a major avenue for the disputing parties to attain a lasting peace.

The next chapter will analyse how the Asian perspectives have been put to the test within the overall framework of the international law regulating the use of force.

---

[37] Nian Peng, "India's Involvement in the South China Sea Disputes", *The Diplomat*, 10 Nov. 2023, https://thediplomat.com/2023/11/indias-growing-involvement-in-the-south-china-sea-disputes/.

CHAPTER 2

International Law Regulating the Use of Force

The International Regime

Pursuant to Article 24(1) of the UN Charter, the UN Security Council (UNSC) has primary responsibility over the maintenance of international peace and security. By virtue of Article 25 of the Charter, UN members agree to accept and carry out the decisions of the UNSC in accordance with the Charter. The International Court of Justice (ICJ) has explained that the answer to the question of whether a resolution by the UNSC imposes any legal duty on any state or legally affects any right of any state can be found in the language of the resolution in each case, having regard to the terms of the resolution to be interpreted, the discussions leading to it, the UN Charter provisions invoked and, in general, all the circumstances that might assist in determining the legal consequences of the UNSC's resolution.[1]

The UNSC is composed of five permanent members (China, France, Russia, the United Kingdom and the United States), or the P5, and the other ten non-permanent members, which are elected to serve for a two-year term. Although each UNSC member has one vote, Article 27(3) of the Charter gives each member of the P5 a veto power over non-procedural matters.

The collective security system under the UN Charter is stipulated in Chapter VII (Actions with Respect to Threats to the Peace, Breaches of the Peace

[1] *Legal Consequences for States of the Continued Presence of South Africa in Namibia (South West Africa) notwithstanding Security Council Resolution 276 (1970)*, Advisory Opinion, ICJ Rep. 1971, p. 16 at p. 53 [114].

and Acts of Aggression). It was built on the premise that the "unity of purpose", based on the recognition of common interests especially among the five principal Allied powers fighting the Axis during the Second World War, would serve as the linchpin of world peace after the adoption of the Charter in 1945.[2] Article 39 of the Charter stipulates that the UNSC shall determine the existence of any threat to the peace, breach of the peace or act of aggression and shall make recommendations, or decide what measures shall be taken in accordance with Articles 41 (measures not involving the use of armed force) and 42 (such action by air, sea or land forces as may be necessary and may include demonstrations, blockades and other operations by air, sea or land forces of UN members) to maintain or restore international peace and security. Pursuant to Article 48, the action required to carry out the UNSC's decisions for the maintenance of international peace and security shall be taken by all the members of the United Nations or by some of them, as the UNSC may determine. Such decisions shall be carried out by the UN members directly and through their action in the appropriate international agencies of which they are members. By virtue of Article 49, the members of the United Nations shall join in affording mutual assistance in carrying out the measures decided upon by the UNSC.

Neither the UN Charter nor the Statute of the International Court of Justice provides for judicial review of UNSC decisions. As of now, judicial review of UNSC resolutions remains controversial and it is rather unclear whether such power really exists.[3]

Article 2(4) of the UN Charter requires UN members to refrain from the threat or use of force "against the territorial integrity or political independence of any State, or in any other manner inconsistent with the purposes of the United Nations". By virtue of Article 51 of the Charter, nothing in the Charter shall impair "the inherent right of individual or collective self-defence if an armed attack occurs" against a UN member, until the UNSC has taken the measures necessary to maintain international peace and security. Measures taken by members in the exercise of this right of self-defence shall be immediately reported to the UNSC and shall not in any way affect the UNSC's authority and responsi-

---

[2] Hisashi Owada, "The United Nations and the Maintenance of International Peace and Security—The Current Debate in the Light of Reform Proposals", *Japanese Annual of International Law* 48 (2005): 1, 3. See also Laurie Blank, *International Conflict and Security Law* (Cheltenham: Edward Elgar Publishing, 2023), pp. 11–34.

[3] Josef Mrázek, "The International Court of Justice and Its Power of Judicial Review of the United Nations Security Council Resolutions", *Lawyer Quarterly* 12 (2022): 393. See also Dagmar Richter, "Judicial Review of Security Council Decisions—A Modern Vision of the Administration of Justice?", *Polish Yearbook of International Law* 32 (2012): 271.

bility under the UN Charter to take at any time such action as it deems necessary in order to maintain or restore international peace and security.

Provision of military aid and/or assistance by one state to another may arguably, if certain conditions are met, reach the threshold of a use of force, albeit an indirect one, by the former against the latter under Article 2(4) of the UN Charter. These include an intent by the supporting state to contribute to the supported state's direct use of force; the timing of aid or assistance relative to the consequences of its use by the supported state; the direct causal nexus between aid or assistance and the supported state's direct use of force; the nature of the aid and assistance that directly contributes to the use of force by the supported state; the geopolitical context in which the support is rendered; and the impact of military aid or assistance on the direct use of force by the supported state.[4]

The ICJ explained in *Military and Paramilitary Activities in and against Nicaragua (Nicaragua v. USA)* that the regulation of the use of force under the UN Charter by no means covers the whole area of the regulation of the use of force in international relations. Article 51 of the Charter refers to the "inherent right" of individual or collective self-defence, which "nothing in the present Charter shall impair" and which applies in the event of an armed attack. The Charter, having itself recognised the existence of this inherent right, does not go on to regulate directly all aspects of its content. For example, it does not contain any specific rule whereby self-defence would warrant only measures that are *proportional* to the armed attack and *necessary* to respond to it, a rule well established in customary international law. Moreover, a definition of an "armed attack" that, if found to exist, authorises the exercise of the "inherent right" of self-defence is not provided in the UN Charter itself and is not part of treaty law. Therefore, customary international law continues to exist alongside the UN Charter. The areas governed by the two sources of law thus do not overlap exactly, and the rules do not have the same content. This could also be demonstrated for other subjects, in particular for the principle of non-intervention.[5]

The ICJ in *Nicaragua* distinguished between "the most grave forms of the use of force (those constituting an armed attack)" and "other less grave forms". In determining the legal rule that applies to these latter forms, the ICJ draws on the 1970 Declaration on Friendly Relations, whose adoption by states affords an indication of their legal conviction (*opinio juris*) as to customary international law on the question. Alongside certain descriptions that may refer to aggression,

---

[4] Michael N. Schmitt and W. Casey Biggerstaff, "Aid and Assistance as a 'Use of Force' under the *Jus ad Bellum*", 100 *International Law Studies* (2023): 186.

[5] ICJ Rep. 1986, p. 14 at p. 94 [176].

this text includes others that refer only to "less grave forms of the use of force". In particular, according to the 1970 Declaration:

> Every State has the duty to refrain from the threat or use of force to violate the existing international boundaries of another State or as a means of solving international disputes, including territorial disputes and problems concerning frontiers of States.
>
> . . .
>
> States have a duty to refrain from acts of reprisal involving the use of force.
>
> . . .
>
> Every State has the duty to refrain from any forcible action which deprives peoples referred to in the elaboration of the principle of equal rights and self-determination of that right to self-determination and freedom and independence.
>
> Every State has the duty to refrain from organizing or encouraging the organization of irregular forces or armed bands, including mercenaries, for incursion into the territory of another State.
>
> Every State has the duty to refrain from organizing, instigating, assisting or participating in acts of civil strife or terrorist acts in another State or acquiescing in organized activities within its territory directed towards the commission of such acts, when the acts referred to in the present paragraph involve a threat or use of force.[6]

Moreover, in the part of this 1970 declaration devoted to the principle of non-intervention in matters within the national jurisdiction of states, a very similar rule is found: "Also, no State shall organize, assist, foment, finance, incite or tolerate subversive, terrorist or armed activities directed towards the violent overthrow of the régime of another State, or interfere in civil strife in another State".[7]

In *Nicaragua*, the ICJ laid down some criteria to determine whether an "armed attack" has occurred. Relying on the 1974 General Assembly's Definition of Aggression,[8] which reflects customary international law, the ICJ ruled that an armed attack can be an action by regular armed forces in the traditional sense or the sending by or on behalf of a state of armed bands, groups, irregulars or mercenaries that carry out acts of armed force against another state, "if such an operation, because of its *scale and effects*, would have been classified *as*

[6] Ibid., p. 101 [191].
[7] Ibid., p. 102 [192].
[8] GA Res. 3314 (XXIX).

an armed attack rather than as a mere frontier incident had it been carried out by regular armed forces".[9] The ICJ clarified that there is no rule in customary international law permitting another state to exercise the right of collective self-defence on the basis of its own assessment of the situation, and that, where collective self-defence is invoked, it is to be expected that the state for whose benefit this right is used will have declared itself to be the victim of an armed attack.[10] Whether the response to the attack is lawful depends on observance of the criteria of the *necessity* and the *proportionality* of the measures taken in self-defence.[11]

The ICJ in *Nicaragua* found it unnecessary in that case to express its view on the issue of the lawfulness of a response to "the imminent threat of armed attack", since neither party had raised it in that case.[12] A frequently cited authority on this issue is the *Caroline* incident, in which Canadian loyalist forces entered United States territory to attack a ship, the *Caroline*, supplying Canadian rebels. According to the *Caroline* test, there must be "a necessity of self-defence, instant, overwhelming, leaving no choice of means, and no moment for deliberation".[13]

As Shi Jiuyong, a former president of the ICJ from China, pointed out in 2018,[14] where states use force, the nucleus of the dispute in many cases is the factual circumstances, not the legal justification, and that, as the ICJ noted in *Nicaragua* with regard to the prohibition on the use of force, states often affirm the rule as they attempt to defend their actions. Hence, despite frequent and unfortunate breaches of the rule, the rule remains robust. In Judge Shi's opinion, the inclusion of the final words "or in any other manner inconsistent with the purposes of the United Nations" are heavily indicative of a broad prohibition with limited exceptions, particularly when read in combination with the fore-

[9] ICJ Rep. 1986, p. 103 [195] (emphasis added).

[10] Ibid., p. 104 [195]. However, James A. Green [*Collective Self-Defence in International Law* (Cambridge: Cambridge University Press, 2024), pp. 140–68] argues that state practice and *opinio juris* do not substantiate the requirement that the state that has been attacked must "declare" that it has been so attacked.

[11] ICJ Rep. 1986, p. 103 [194].

[12] Ibid.

[13] Daniel Webster, Letter to Henry Stephen Fox, in *The Papers of Daniel Webster: Diplomatic Papers*, ed. K.E. Shewmaker, vol. 1, 1841–43 (Hanover, NH: University Press of New England, 1983), p. 62.

[14] Shi Jiuyong, "Prohibition of Use of Force in International Law", *Chinese Journal of International Law* 17 (2018): 1.

most purpose of the United Nations—the maintenance of international peace and security and the very principle of sovereign equality of states.

Nonetheless, Judge Shi found that, in drafting Article 51 of the UN Charter, the United States delegation, which took the lead in inserting the requirement of an "armed attack", had no intention of allowing anticipatory self-defence—the "inherent right" of self-defence is activated only "if an armed attack occurs". In his view, a real possibility of widening the scope of self-defence to anticipatory acts would do little more than license the use of force in all circumstances, since recent history has shown that states do not always have accurate perceptions of the threats that other countries pose. There appears to be an uncomfortably wide scope for abuse in the concept of anticipatory self-defence, whereas one of the great virtues of the "armed attack" criterion is that it lends some objectivity to what might otherwise be a murky and subjective exception. Judge Shi cited some subsequent practice invoked in support of anticipatory self-defence, which appeared to go well beyond the *Caroline* standard. For example, Israel claimed anticipatory self-defence in its 1967 attack against Egypt, its 1975 attack against Palestinian camps in Lebanon and its 1981 strike against the Osiraq nuclear reactor in Iraq.[15] This practice has further broadened to become part of the so-called "Bush Doctrine" of "pre-emptive self-defence" in the aftermath of the 11 September 2001 terrorist attacks on US soil, which has not yet met with states' widespread approval. Given such predominantly negative responses by the international community, it is difficult to believe that any principle of anticipatory self-defence exists. The ICJ itself stated in *Armed Activities on the Territory of the Congo (DR Congo v. Uganda)* that "Article 51 of the Charter may justify a use of force in self-defence only within the strict confines there laid down. It does not allow the use of force by a State to protect perceived security interests beyond these parameters"—other means being available to a concerned state, including, in particular, recourse to the UNSC.[16]

Judge Shi added that the conditions of necessity and proportionality are usually considered together and are, to a certain extent, intertwined and mutually reinforcing. The test for necessity is, as the ICJ notes in *Oil Platforms (Iran v. USA)*, "strict and objective, leaving no room for any 'measure of discretion'".[17] Often this will be a question of fact in the particular circumstances of a case, and not a principle amenable to exhaustive legal definition and the pres-

[15] See also Michael Wood, "International Law and the Use of Force: What Happens in Practice?", *Indian Journal of International Law* 53 (2013): 345, 357–9.
[16] ICJ Rep. 2005, p. 168 at pp. 223–4 [148].
[17] ICJ Rep. 2003, p. 161 at p. 196 [73].

ence of equally effective alternatives will tend to undermine a claim to necessity. However, the more common situation—in which diplomacy is a possibility but one unlikely to bear fruit—may give rise to more difficult questions. Necessity also points to the requirement that the use of force for self-defence be adequately linked to the armed attack. In *Nicaragua*, a significant lapse of time following an attack, during which that attack was largely repulsed, tended to lead to the conclusion that there was no necessity. Likewise, in *Oil Platforms*, the ICJ was sceptical of the link between the Iranian oil platforms and the attacks on US ships. Without such a link, necessity could not be established. Necessity is a crucial factor that distinguishes self-defence from what might otherwise simply be armed reprisals or punitive acts, which are prohibited by international law as unequivocally stipulated in the 1970 Declaration on Friendly Relations.

Also pertinent is the requirement of proportionality in self-defence, which in most cases is also treated as a question of fact. Judge Shi explains that the ICJ has tended to consider the nature of the targets may be relevant to both necessity and proportionality. The *Oil Platforms* judgment strongly suggests that a proportionate response will be one that is directed at legitimate military targets, not targets of economic opportunity. In *DR Congo v. Uganda*, the ICJ noted that the taking of airports and towns many hundreds of kilometres from Uganda's border would not seem proportionate to the series of transborder attacks Uganda claimed had given rise to the right of self-defence, nor to be necessary to that end.[18] Finally, there is the most obvious indicator of proportionality, which is the scale of the attacks. The ICJ in *Nicaragua* noted that the impugned US activities were considerably more substantial than those about which the US complained.

Therefore, the US air strikes on 25 February 2021 against infrastructure at a Syria–Iraq border crossing that, the Biden administration claimed, were being used by Iranian-backed militant groups, killing 22 militiamen, have been considered by certain commentators to be an unlawful use of force. In support of its military action, the US government reportedly cited the rocket attack on the airport in Erbil, Iraq, on 15 February 2021 that killed a Filipino contractor, wounded four US contractors and wounded a US soldier, which was not of sufficient gravity to constitute an "armed attack" giving rise to the right to self-defence. Furthermore, Article 51 of the UN Charter requires that an armed attack is actually physically occurring or its effects are still being felt or manifesting themselves, as in the situation of an invasion and subsequent occupation

[18] ICJ Rep. 2005, p. 223 [147].

of territory, making it necessary to act in self-defence to secure immediate protection to the state concerned. But there was no ongoing or imminent armed attack against the United States satisfying any requisite threshold of gravity for it to invoke the right to self-defence. Non-military options to resolve the perceived threat posed by the militia groups were also available, including having recourse to the UNSC, diplomacy or cooperation with either the Syrian or Iraqi government to contain the threat. A proportionality assessment goes beyond the quantitative and teleological models to also include the sovereignty and territorial integrity of Syria and wider impacts of the US action on regional and international peace and security, including the deterioration of the US government's already-volatile relationship with Iran, accused of being behind the non-state actors carrying out the 15 February 2021 rocket attack. Above all, the right to self-defence cannot be exercised to "punish" past attacks, to "deter" future attacks or threats thereof or to further the national security and foreign policy interests of the state invoking the right to self-defence.[19]

Japan is the only Asian nation whose government has formally adopted its policy on collective self-defence. According to the Cabinet Decision of 1 July 2014, Japan may exercise the right of collective self-defence under international law not only when an armed attack against Japan occurs but also when an armed attack against a foreign country that is in a close relationship with Japan occurs and as a result threatens Japan's survival and poses a clear danger to fundamentally overturn the Japanese people's right to life, liberty and pursuit of happiness, and when there is no other appropriate means available to repel the attack and ensure Japan's survival and protect its people. In answering a question in Parliament in 2015 as to whether the exercise of self-defence must terminate when the UNSC has taken measures, the Japanese government replied that it depends on concrete circumstances of each case, and according to the interpretation of the UN Charter, and that it is not always necessary to stop such an exercise of the right of self-defence.[20]

---

[19] Christian Henderson, "The 25 February 2021 Military Strikes and the 'Armed Attack' Requirement of Self-Defence: From '*sina qua non*' to the Point of Vanishing?", *Journal on the Use of Force & International Law* 9 (2022): 55, 60–1, 64, 68; Chris O'Meara, "February 2021 American Airstrikes in Syria: Necessary and Proportionate Acts of Self-Defence or Unlawful Armed Reprisals?", *Journal on the Use of Force & International Law* 9 (2022): 78.

[20] Tadashi Mori, "Collective Self-Defence in International Law and in the New Japanese Legislation for Peace and Security (2015)", *Japanese Yearbook of International Law* 60 (2017): 158–70. See also Shunji Yanai, "New Japanese Legislation for Peace and Security: Its Background and Salient Points", *Japanese Yearbook of International Law* 60 (2017): 136, 150–1.

The International Law Association (ILA) published its *Final Report on Aggression and the Use of Force* in 2018.[21] The report was prepared by a committee of 38 world-renowned international lawyers, most of whom were from the West, with two Japanese and one South Korean international law professors being the only ILA members from Asia. The ILA concluded that the UN Charter's goal of collective peace and security depends upon strict adherence to the international law on the use of force, and that what is needed are not new rules on the use of force but political will on the part of states, including members of the UNSC, which must use the UNSC's powers proactively, positively and with clarity. Overall, current international law on the use of force, properly interpreted and applied, remains a solid "cornerstone" for international peace and security. Specifically, there is general agreement that Article 2(4) of the Charter is generally accepted as referring only to the use of "armed" or "physical" force; the prohibition on the use of force in Article 2(4) is not limited by the words "against the territorial integrity or political independence of any State"; the UNSC's powers have long been accepted as including the power to authorise states, or in some cases international organisations, to use force; it is desirable to have as much clarity as possible when the UNSC authorises the use of force, and the fact that the UNSC takes action to restore or maintain international peace and security after an unlawful (or questionable) use of force cannot in itself be seen as an endorsement of the original use of force. State practice indicates that small-scale border attacks involving the use of lethal force are not excluded from the concept of "armed attack" and may give rise to the right of self-defence. Overall, the determining criteria seem to be centred upon questions of "scale and effects" of the attack. However, the ILA finds that in practice it appears that the gravity threshold attached to armed attacks is not markedly high,[22] and would include most uses of force likely to cause casualties or significant property damage. As such, if there is a gap between "use of force" under Article 2(4) and "armed attack" under Article 51, it would be relatively narrow. The gravity of the attack would nevertheless be a crucial factor in assessing the necessity and proportionality of a forcible response. On the issue of accumulation of small-scale attacks as justification for the right to self-defence,

[21] See the summary in Noam Lubell and Michael Wood, "The ILA's 2018 Report on Aggression and the Use of Force", *Journal on the Use of Force & International Law* 6 (2019): 4.

[22] According to Judge Shi, although there is some minimum requirement as to the seriousness or gravity of the attack, thus far the case law has indicated that the threshold is relatively low. He cites the examples of *Nicaragua*, where the activities of armed bands sufficed, and *Oil Platforms*, where the ICJ noted that a single ship striking a naval mine could potentially constitute an armed attack (Shi, "Prohibition of Use of Force in International Law", 6).

the ILA considers it is unclear whether this justification has been widely accepted. The accumulation of smaller attacks may, however, be relevant insofar as these incidents might in some circumstances support the case for likelihood of an imminent attack. They could also affect the modalities of self-defence when assessing the necessity and proportionality of the force being used.

Contrary to Judge Shi's view, the ILA found increasing support for the view that the right to self-defence does exist in relation to manifestly imminent attacks, narrowly construed. Although the matter remains unsettled, there may be reason to accept that, when faced with a specific imminent armed attack based on objectively verifiable indicators, states may engage in measures to defend themselves in order to prevent the attack. Any such measures would have to conform to all the earlier stated requirements of armed attack, necessity and proportionality, which will further constrain the anticipatory use of force, and must give primacy to effective measures by the UNSC.

In reality, the right to self-defence against manifestly imminent armed attacks may be invoked only by a state with military capabilities that are superior or at least equal to another state against whom this right is invoked. Otherwise, the former state will likely suffer deleterious consequences when the latter responds with counterattacks. From the perspective of Asian states whose military capabilities are relatively limited, Judge Shi's view is to be preferred.

In the ILA's view, there is growing recognition—including through state practice—that there are certain circumstances in which a state may have a right of self-defence against non-state actors operating extraterritorially and whose attacks cannot be attributed to the state on whose territory they are based. The military operations by numerous states from a variety of regions on Syrian territory against the so-called Islamic State in Iraq and the Levant (ISIL) since 2015 have, in particular, demonstrated the readiness of a considerable number of states to invoke Article 51 of the UN Charter in the context of operations against a non-state actor. Nonetheless, the modalities of how self-defence might be carried out in this context do raise considerable challenges and continue to be debated. It must be noted, in this context, that the UNSC has the power to take action directed against threats to the peace by armed groups, and has taken measures of this nature in the past. By acting decisively in future situations of such type, the UNSC could reduce the risk of states taking matters into their own hands.

With regard to the right to self-defence against cyberattacks, the International Groups of Experts invited by the NATO Cooperative Cyber Defence Centre of Excellence have come up with a rule stipulating: "A State that is the target of a cyber operation that rises to the level of an armed attack may exercise its inherent right of self-defence" and "[w]hether a cyber operation constitutes an armed attack depends on its scale and effects".[23] This conclusion is in accordance with the ICJ's Advisory Opinion in *Legality of the Threat or Use of Nuclear Weapons* that the prohibition of the use of force under the UN Charter does not refer to specific weapons—it applies to any use of force, regardless of the weapons employed.[24] The countries, mostly from the West, that have adopted this approach include Canada, Estonia, Germany, Italy, the Netherlands, New Zealand, Norway, the United Kingdom, the United States and NATO. Nevertheless, other countries are more cautious, as evident from the summary of the chairperson of the Open-Ended Working Group on Developments in the Field of Information and Telecommunications in the Context of International Security, convened by the United Nations on 8–12 March 2021. The chairperson pointed out that for some states the international legal issues that have yet to be fully clarified include the kind of cyber-related activity that might be a threat or use of force under Article 2(4) of the UN Charter or that might entitle a state to invoke the right to self-defence under Article 51 of the Charter.[25] In the Final Substantive Report of the Working Group, states reaffirm that international law, particularly the UN Charter, is applicable and essential to maintaining peace and stability and promoting an open, secure, stable, accessible and peaceful environment for information and communications technologies (ICTs), and that, in this regard, states are called upon to avoid and refrain from taking any measures not in accordance with international law, in particular the UN Charter. Paradoxically, they find it necessary to develop common understandings on *how* international law applies to states' use of ICTs,[26] and they will continue to further study and discuss this matter within future UN processes.[27]

The ICJ's ruling in *Legality of the Threat or Use of Nuclear Weapons* in 1996, in response to the request for an advisory opinion made by the UN General Assembly (UNGA), has left a lot of uncertainty as regards the legality of the use of nuclear weapons.[28]

---

[23] Michael N. Schmitt, ed., *Tallinn Manual 2.0 on the International Law Applicable to Cyber Operations* (Cambridge: Cambridge University Press, 2017), pp. 339–48. See also Kriangsak Kittichaisaree, *Public International Law of Cyberspace* (Cham: Springer, 2017), pp. 166–75.

[24] ICJ Rep. 1996, p. 226 at p. 244 [39].

[25] Chair's summary, third substantive session, A/AC.290/2021/CRP.3 (10 Mar. 2021).

[26] A/AC.290/2021/CRP.2 (10 Mar. 2021), para. 34.

[27] Ibid., para. 40.

[28] See also Laurence Boisson de Charzournes and Philippe Sands, eds., *International Law, the International Court of Justice and Nuclear Weapons* (Cambridge: Cambridge University Press, 1999).

There were three ICJ judges from Asia in that case. The ICJ opined, unanimously, that there is no specific authorisation, in either customary or conventional international law, for the threat or use of nuclear weapons. By 11 votes to three, with Judge Weeramantry from Sri Lanka being one of the dissentients, the ICJ opined that customary and conventional international law also has no comprehensive and universal prohibition as such of the threat or use of nuclear weapons. Unanimously, the ICJ opined that a threat or use of force by means of nuclear weapons that is contrary to Article 2(4) of the UN Charter and that fails to meet all the requirements of Article 51 is unlawful. Also unanimously, the ICJ ruled that a threat or use of nuclear weapons should also be compatible with the requirements of the international law applicable in armed conflict, particularly those of the principles and rules of international humanitarian law, as well as with specific obligations under treaties and other undertakings that expressly deal with nuclear weapons. Most controversial of all is subparagraph E of the operative clause of the Advisory Opinion, where the ICJ opined, by seven votes to seven, with the casting vote of ICJ president Judge Bedjaoui from Algeria, that it follows from the above-mentioned requirements that the threat or use of nuclear weapons would generally be contrary to the rules of international law applicable in armed conflict, and in particular the principles and rules of humanitarian law; however, "in view of the current state of international law, and of the elements of fact at its disposal, the [ICJ] cannot conclude definitively whether the threat or use of nuclear weapons would be lawful or unlawful in an extreme circumstance of self-defence, in which the very survival of a State would be at stake". Judge Oda from Japan and the Sri Lankan judge were among the seven judges voting against this conclusion, while Judge Shi from China was among those seven judges voting in favour. The ICJ then concluded, unanimously, that there exists an obligation to pursue in good faith and bring to a conclusion negotiations leading to nuclear disarmament in all its aspects under strict and effective international control.[29]

Judge Shi explained that he had voted in favour of the operative paragraphs of the advisory opinion although he had reservations with regard to the role that the ICJ assigns to the policy of deterrence in determining the existence of a customary rule on the use of nuclear weapons. In his view, "nuclear deterrence" is an instrument of policy to which certain nuclear-weapon states, supported by those states accepting nuclear umbrella protection, adhere in their relations with other states. This practice is within the realm of international politics. Also, leaving aside the nature of the policy of deterrence, states adhering to the policy of

[29] ICJ Rep. 1996, pp. 266–7.

deterrence, though important and powerful members of the international community and playing an important role on the stage of international politics, by no means constitute a large proportion of the membership of the international community. Further, the structure of the community of states is built on the principle of sovereign equality. The ICJ cannot view these nuclear-weapon states and their allies in terms of material power but rather should have regard of them from the standpoint of international law. Any undue emphasis on the practice of these materially powerful states, constituting merely a fraction of the membership of the community of states, would not only be contrary to the principle of sovereign equality of states but also make it more difficult to give an accurate and proper view of the existence of a customary rule on the use of nuclear weapons.

Japanese Judge Oda explained that he had voted against part of the ICJ's Advisory Opinion because the ICJ should have exercised its discretionary power to refrain from rendering an opinion in response to the request by the UNGA, which was prepared and drafted with highly political motives—not in order to ascertain the status of existing international law on the subject but to try to promote the total elimination of nuclear weapons. He noted that, as the five nuclear-weapon states have repeatedly given assurances to the non-nuclear-weapon states of their intention not to use nuclear weapons against them, there is almost no probability of any use of nuclear weapons given the current doctrine of nuclear deterrence. Judge Oda concluded by stressing his earnest hope that nuclear weapons will be eliminated from the world but that the decision on this matter is a function of political negotiations among states in Geneva (the Conference on Disarmament) or New York (the United Nations) but not one that concerns the ICJ. He voted against subparagraph E as the equivocations contained therein serve, in his view, to confirm his point that it would have been prudent for the ICJ to decline from the outset to give any opinion at all in the present case.

Judge Weeramantry's dissenting opinion, which runs to 127 pages, is based on the proposition that the use or threat of use of nuclear weapons is illegal in any circumstances whatsoever. First, it violates the fundamental principles of international law, and represents the very negation of the humanitarian concerns that underlie the structure of humanitarian law, including the prohibition against causing unnecessary suffering, the principle of proportionality, the principle of discrimination between combatants and civilians, the principle against causing damage to neutral states, the prohibition against causing serious and lasting damage to the environment, the prohibition against genocide, and the basic principles of human rights law. Second, it offends treaty provisions and, in particular, the Geneva Gas Protocol of 1925 and Article 23(a) of the Hague Regulations of 1907, which were clearly applicable to nuclear weapons, as they prohibited the use of poison. Third, it contradicts the fundamental principle of the dignity and worth of the human person, on which all law depends. Fourth, it endangers the human environment in a manner that threatens the entirety of life on the planet. His opinion also draws attention to the multicultural and ancient origins of the laws of war, referring to the recognition of its basic rules in Hindu, Buddhist, Chinese, Judaic, Islamic, African and modern European cultural traditions. As such, the humanitarian rules of warfare were not to be regarded as a new sentiment, invented in the 19th century and which may be lightly overridden. From philosophical perspectives, no credible legal system could contain a rule within itself that rendered legitimate an act that could destroy the entire civilisation of which that legal system formed a part. On nuclear deterrence, one of the dangers of the possession of nuclear weapons for purposes of deterrence is the blurring of this distinction and the use of the power the nuclear weapon gives for purposes of deterring unwelcome actions on the part of another state. Since what is necessary for deterrence is assured destruction of the enemy, deterrence thus comes within the ambit of that which goes beyond the purposes of war. Moreover, in the split-second response to an armed attack, the finely graded use of appropriate strategic nuclear missiles or "clean" weapons that cause minimal damage does not seem a credible possibility. In terms of sovereign equality, either all nations have the right to self-defence with any particular weapon or none of them can have it and there is no reason why nuclear weapons should be subject to a different regime.

Reports to the United Nations Security Council

Article 51 of the UN Charter requires that measures taken by UN members in the exercise of this right of self-defence shall be immediately reported to the UNSC. However, there are no codified rules or guidelines on the format of the report.

One study identifies a total of 311 such reports to the UNSC between 1958 and 2019, with states in Asia outside the Middle East submitting 24 (or 15 per cent) and states in the Middle East submitting 58 (or 37 per cent) thereof.

From the 158 reports analysed by the author of that study, almost half of the reports mentioned, in some way, the date the measures in self-defence took place, whereas the other half of the reports did not do so or left it ambiguous. More than 80 per cent of the reports (58) that mentioned the date of the measures in self-defence were submitted to the UNSC within a week, of which 20 per cent (14) were submitted on the same day that the measure took place. A fraction of the reports were submitted more than two weeks after the measures in self-defence took place, with some outliers, like the reports submitted by Eritrea concerning its conflict with Ethiopia, submitted 7 and 11 months after the measures took place. The majority of reports analysed referred to measures taken ex post facto, though a small number of reports could be considered to be pre-emptive, referring to measures that were going to be pursued instead of already taken. Pre-emptive reports included language indicating that the respective state actor would or might be forced to exercise its right to self-defence or was taking measures. This study finds that only 26 reports—less than 20 per cent of the total reports analysed—could be labelled as being pre-emptive in nature. However, an increase in the use of pre-emptive reporting was observable during the measures against ISIL in Syria by Western states. That author considers pre-emptive reports to be problematic since, first, it is unclear if their submissions constitute a report of measures already taken as required under Article 51, as opposed to measures to be taken, and, second, the object and purpose of Article 51 is to enable the UNSC to respond to threats to and breaches of the peace, and the UNSC needs to be immediately informed on measures taken so as to place the use of force under the scrutiny of the international community and for the UNSC to react accordingly. Significantly, the reporting states interpreted the meaning of "armed attack" under Article 51 in different ways based on a variety of justifications behind their use of force. Some reports included references to other concepts related to self-defence such as necessity, proportionality or other legal concepts. The reports from 1958 until the beginning of 2019 showed that states referred even less frequently to proportionality than to necessity in their reports: only 29 out of 158 reports did so. Nearly all reports only mentioned the fact that measures taken were (or would be) proportionate but did not provide factual or legal substantiation on how and why these measures were considered proportionate. A small fraction of the reports (11 per cent) mentioned other legal obligations or restrictions to the measures taken in self-defence, as in, for example, the report by Australia following the invocation of collective self-defence after the 11 September 2001 terrorist attacks on US soil, in which Australia stated that it would "scrupulously abide by its obligations under international humanitarian law". Slightly fewer than half of the reports submitted to the UNSC did not have a description of the measures taken in self-defence. Together with the reports that had a vague description, these accounted for the vast majority of the reports submitted: 67 per cent. In addition, there was a strong connection between reports that had no description or a vague description of the measures taken and reports that were pre-emptive in nature.[30]

The inconsistency in the reports submitted to the UNSC pursuant to Article 51 of the UN Charter has led Mexico to propose that there be standard requirements concerning the information to be included; the level of detail to be expected; how Article 51 should be interpreted with regard to attacks perpetrated by non-state actors, particularly, but not exclusively, terrorist attacks; and whether, under Article 51 of the Charter, self-defence can be invoked in respect of another state when that state is considered to lack the capacity or the will to address an armed attack. Procedurally, there should be a reasonable time frame for the submission of a report under Article 51 following an armed attack, and it has to be settled whether such a report may be submitted before the use of force in self-defence or whether it can be submitted afterwards. Given the gravity of the use of force and the importance these instances have for all UN member states, a question is asked whether it would be desirable and necessary for the UNSC to regularly discuss, examine and consider such reports, and the UNSC's inaction following receipt of such reports should be interpreted. The proposal also seeks more transparency, publicity and access to the reports.[31]

One study of 45 conflict situations between 1990 and 2014 (after the end of the Cold War) that resulted in no fewer than 25 battle-related deaths (in at least one year of the conflict), reaches the following conclusions. There were three cases that did not invoke international law, 19 cases involving uncontroversial armed interventions, seven cases that invoked unestablished rules of international law and 16 that invoked established rules of international law. Even in cases in which the armed intervention was almost unanimously considered by the international community to be illegal, states advanced legal arguments to justify their action, as in the Iraqi invasion of Kuwait in 1990. All of the 19 uncontroversial armed invitations relied on the doctrine of intervention by invitation to target internal terrorists. Of these 19, two concerned the Asian region covered by this book, namely the Indian armed intervention to help suppress the Liberation Tigers of Tamil Eelam armed group in Sri Lanka in 1990 and the United States'

---

[30] Nick van der Steenhoven, "Conduct and Subsequent Practice by States in the Application of the Requirement to Report under UN Charter Article 51", *Journal on the Use of Force & International Law* 6 (2019): 242.

[31] Report of the Special Committee on the Charter of the United Nations and on the Strengthening of the Role of the Organization, A/76/33 (25 Feb. 2021), summarised in Patrick M. Butchard and Jasmin Johurun Nessa, "Digest of State Practice: 1 January–30 June 2021", *Journal on the Use of Force & International Law* 8 (2021): 343, 394–6.

intervention to help suppress Al Qaeda in the Arabian Peninsula in Yemen in 2009–14, although Iran has criticised the latter.[32]

Legal Effects of Silence regarding the Use of Force

Asian states are relatively silent in their reaction to the use of force unless they are directly and adversely affected as victims.

A study by Harvard Law School[33] has comprehensively analysed the legal effects of such silence. The study finds that international law does not offer clear general guidance on what could or should be inferred from apparent silence or inaction. Silence will convey consent only if the circumstances must be such as call for some reaction, within a reasonable period, on the part of the authorities of the state concerned, if they wish to disagree with the fact or act in question or have any serious question to raise in regard to it. They did not do so, either then or for many years, and thereby must be held to have acquiesced if all of the following conditions are established: where it refers to facts that are, or ought to be, known by the acquiescing state (*notoriety* or *awareness*); where such facts are of direct interest for the acquiescing state (*interest*); when these facts have existed for a significant period (*lapse of time*) without significant change of context and the meaning conveyed (*consistency*); and in cases in which the conduct is attributable to a relevant representative of the state (*provenance*). Acquiescence and estoppel are often considered to be entangled. The crucial element concerning estoppel in international law consists of evidence that the state in question has openly relied on a certain situation of fact, and that a change of that state's position thereof would lead to undue prejudice (or an unjustified benefit for the other state). The study argues that, at least in relation to international law regulating the use of force (*jus ad bellum*), only certain forms of *qualified silence*—whether of states or of the UNSC—may be capable of contributing to legal effects. Owing in part to the nature

---

[32] Christian Marxsen, "Violation and Confirmation of the Law: The Intricate Effects of the Invocation of the Law in Armed Conflict", *Journal on the Use of Force & International Law* 5 (2018): 8.

[33] Dustin A. Lewis, Naz K. Modirzadeh and Gabriella Blum, "Quantum of Silence: Inaction and *Jus ad Bellum*", in *Annex HLS PILAC Catalogue of Communications to the Security Council of Measures Taken by United Nations Member States in Purported Exercise of the Right of Self-Defense: October 24, 1945 through December 31, 2018* (Cambridge, MA: Harvard Law School, 2019). See also Danae Azaria, *State Silence as Acceptance: A Presumption and an Exception* (University College London Faculty of Laws: Research Paper Series No. 15/2023, 2023).

and status of the norms underlying this field, those forms of qualified silence ought not to be lightly presumed. Arguably, there is a strong, if rebuttable, presumption that silence alone does not constitute acceptance of a *jus ad bellum* claim. Still, states and other international actors should be aware of the possible role that their silence could play in the identification and development of *jus ad bellum*.

The study catalogues more than 400 communications made from the founding of the United Nations in late October 1945 up to 2018. These communications reflect the views of the submitting state(s) on the scope of the right to use force on the purported basis of self-defence. Notably, UN members are apparently not made aware of such statements on the use of force as a matter of routine practice. This means that, at least in some instances, states might fail to comment on or otherwise react to other states' positions on the use of force, not as a deliberate choice but for lack of awareness. Therefore, only qualified silence is to be accorded potential legal significance: if states are unaware of practices or positions forwarded by other states, it is difficult to see how the silence of those unaware states can carry normative value. Besides, especially in the *jus ad bellum* field, the fact that states are not routinely made aware contemporaneously of self-defence communications made to the UNSC under Article 51 of the UN Charter is a significant concern that ought to be addressed as a matter of priority.

Indeed, at an open-ended informal meeting of the UNSC on 24 February 2021, most UN member states participating in the meeting considered that silence from the international community should not be interpreted as acquiescence in self-defence claims.[34]

As former ICJ president Shi Jiuyong from China has wisely summed up, the way the UNSC and the UNGA respond can be useful indicators of how states view the law. For example, condemnation of a state in these forums can be a good indicator that those states view the act as illegal. However, lack of condemnation in the UNSC or the UNGA may be owing to political reasons rather than legal ones, particularly in the use of the veto in the UNSC since the UNSC usually avoids direct attribution of blame. He concludes that "[i]n this

---

[34] The participants in the meeting included the P5, India, Iran, Pakistan, Qatar, Syria, Sri Lanka, Vietnam, Ireland, Norway, Tunisia, Kenya, Estonia, Saint Vincent and the Grenadines, Liechtenstein, Ecuador, Armenia, Denmark, Peru, Austria, Finland, Türkiye, Brazil, Azerbaijan, Netherlands, Georgia, Australia, Ukraine and Belgium. Reported in Butchard and Nessa, "Digest of State Practice: 1 January–30 June 2021", 396–7.

complex milieu, care should be taken to avoid equating a failure to condemn with an outright affirmation of legality".[35]

Any deviation from generally accepted international law regulating the use of force must satisfy an extremely high standard of endorsement by the international community for it to be accepted as lawful. This is because the prohibition of aggression in violation of the law of the UN Charter or customary international law concerning the prohibition of the use of force is a peremptory norm of international law (*jus cogens*) that reflects and protects fundamental values of the international community. That norm is universally applicable and hierarchically superior to other rules of international law, having been accepted and recognised by the international community of states as a whole as a norm from which no derogation is permitted and which can be modified only by a subsequent norm of general international law having the same character. The phrase "international community of states as a whole" does not require the acceptance and recognition of all states but does require the acceptance and recognition of a very large and representative majority. With regard to consequences of serious breaches of *jus cogens*, states shall cooperate to bring to an end through lawful means any serious breach by a state of an obligation arising under *jus cogens*, and no state shall recognise as lawful a situation created by a serious breach by a state of an obligation arising under *jus cogens*, nor render aid or assistance in maintaining that situation. A breach of an obligation arising under *jus cogens* is serious if it involves a gross or systematic failure by the responsible state to fulfil that obligation. This conclusion is without prejudice to the other consequences that any breach by a state of an obligation arising under *jus cogens* may entail under international law.[36]

Deadlocks in the United Nations Security Council

What if the UNSC is deadlocked or stalled because of a (potential) veto by one of its permanent members who is either directly involved in the armed conflict in question or whose ally is so involved? On 3 November 1950, after the Soviet Union's veto since August 1950 of all UNSC resolutions to deal with the then ongoing crisis in the Korean Peninsula after North Korea's armed invasion of

[35] Shi, "Prohibition of Use of Force in International Law", 3.

[36] UN International Law Commission, "Peremptory Norms of General International Law (*jus cogens*)", A/77/10 (2022). See also Paulina Starski, "Silence within the Process of Normative Change and Evolution of the Prohibition on the Use of Force: Normative Volatility and Legislative Responsibility", *Journal on the Use of Force & International Law* 4 (2017): 14, esp. at 43–4.

South Korea on 25 June 1950, the UNGA adopted the "Uniting for Peace Resolution" by 52 votes to 5 (those voting against were Byelorussian SSR, Czechoslovakia, Poland, the Soviet Union and Ukrainian SSR), with two abstentions (Argentina and India). This resolution reads in its pertinent part as follows:

> *Resolves* that if the Security Council, because of lack of unanimity of the permanent members, fails to exercise its primary responsibility for the maintenance of international peace and security in any case where there appears to be a threat to the peace, breach of the peace, or act of aggression, the General Assembly shall consider the matter immediately with a view to making *appropriate recommendations to Members for collective measures, including* in the case of a breach of the peace or act of aggression *the use of armed force when necessary*, to maintain or restore international peace and security. If not in session at the time, the General Assembly may meet in emergency special session within twenty-four hours of the request therefor. Such emergency special session shall be called if requested by the Security Council on the vote of any seven members, or by a majority of the Members of the United Nations.[37]

However, the UNGA's decisions or resolutions, unlike those of the UNSC's, are not legally binding. Article 11(2) of the UN Charter provides that the UNGA "may discuss any questions relating to the maintenance of international peace and security brought before it", but any such question on which action is necessary shall be referred to the UNSC by the UNGA either before or after discussion. The ICJ's Advisory Opinion in the *Certain Expenses* case defines "action" under this provision as "coercive or enforcement action".[38]

Practice subsequent to the Uniting for Peace Resolution is quite limited and the relevant subsequent UNGA resolutions do not always cite the Uniting for Peace Resolution. In the Korean War context itself, UNGA Resolution 498(V) of 1 February 1951 did not refer specifically to the Uniting for Peace Resolution but noted in its preamble that the lack of unanimity among the UNSC permanent members had led to the failure of the UNSC to exercise its primary responsibility for the maintenance of international peace and secu-

---

[37] A/RES/377 (3 Nov. 1950), emphasis added.

[38] *Certain Expenses of the United Nations (Article 17, Paragraph 2, of the Charter)*, Advisory Opinion, ICJ Rep. 1962, p. 151 at pp. 164–5. See also Andrew J. Carswell, "Unblocking the UN Security Council: The Uniting for Peace Resolution", *Journal of Conflict & Security Law* 18 (2013): 453, 463–79.

rity. UNGA Resolution 498(V) then proceeded to, inter alia, find that the People's Republic of China engaged in aggression in Korea and to call on all states and authorities to continue to render every assistance to the UN's action in Korea.[39] Since the Uniting for Peace Resolution, at the time of writing, 11 emergency special sessions have been convened according to the conditions laid down in that resolution, the first being on the occasion of the 1956 war between Israel and Egypt and the British–French attack on the Suez Canal zone.[40] The tenth special session, which deals with the Israeli occupation of Palestinian territory, first convened in 1997, has not yet come to an end at the time of writing. On 2 March 2022, following Russia's "special military operation" against Ukraine and Russia's veto in the UNSC against the UNSC adopting resolution on the situation, the UNSC, by majority vote, decided to call an emergency special session of the UNGA on the ground that Russia's veto had "prevented it from exercising its primary responsibility for the maintenance of international peace and security", invoking the Uniting for Peace Resolution. The UNGA adopted (by a vote of 141 in favour, 5 against[41] and 35 abstentions,[42] with 12 being absent) Resolution ES 11/1 (Aggression against Ukraine) the operative paragraphs of which, inter alia, "deplored in the strongest terms the aggression by the Russian Federation against Ukraine in violation of Article 2(4) of the UN Charter" and demanded that Russia cease its use of force against Ukraine as well as immediately, completely and unconditionally withdraw all of its military forces from the territory of Ukraine within its internationally recognised borders.[43]

On 26 April 2022, the UNGA adopted, by consensus, a resolution titled "Standing mandate for a General Assembly debate when a veto is cast in the Security Council",[44] or the "Veto Initiative", to hold the P5 accountable for their use of veto. Pursuant to this resolution, the president of the UNGA shall convene a formal meeting of the UNGA within ten working days of the casting of a veto by one or more permanent members of the UNSC, to hold a debate on the situation as to which the veto was cast, provided that the UNGA does not

---

[39] A/RES/498(V) (1 Feb. 1951).

[40] See Table 1 in Gabriel Anich, "A New Life for Uniting for Peace?", *Revista Tribuna Internacional* 12 (2023): 43, 48.

[41] Belarus, Eritrea, North Korea, Russia and Syria.

[42] The abstaining Asian states were Bangladesh, China, India, Iran, Iraq, Laos, Mongolia, Pakistan, Sri Lanka and Vietnam.

[43] See also Michael P. Scharf, "Power Shift: The Return of the Uniting for Peace Resolution", *Case Western Reserve Journal of International Law* 55 (2023): 217.

[44] A/RES/76/262 (26 Apr. 2022).

meet in an emergency special session on the same situation. It invites the UNSC to submit a special report on the use of the veto in question to the UNGA at least 72 hours before the relevant discussion in the UNGA.[45] The Veto Initiative was first activated to enable the UNGA to meet on 8 June 2022 to address the vetoes cast by China and Russia in the UNSC against a draft resolution to condemn North Korea for its unprecedented series of ballistic missile tests with increasingly versatile systems across all ranges, including intercontinental ballistic missiles, the latest of which were launched on 5 June 2022, together with the evidence of ongoing nuclear activities, in flagrant breaches of its obligations under many relevant UNSC resolutions. The Veto Initiative has been invoked several times since then, including in response to vetoes in the UNSC on draft resolutions on the Israel/Hamas war in Gaza, which started on 7 October 2023.

Countermeasures in Response to the Use of Force below the "Armed Attack" Threshold

With regard to the use of force below the threshold of "armed attack", states may respond by resorting to "countermeasures not involving the use of force". The ICJ in *Gabčíkovo-Magymaros Project (Hungary/Slovakia)* has elaborated three conditions for a justifiable countermeasure. First, it must be taken in response to a previous international wrongful act of another state and must be directed against that state. Second, the injured state must have called upon the state committing the wrongful act to discontinue its wrongful conduct or to make reparation for it. Third, the effects of a countermeasure must be commensurate with the injury suffered, taking account of the rights in question.[46]

Case Study: Vietnam's Invasion of Cambodia

A notorious case study of the alleged exercise of the right self-defence in Asia is the Vietnamese full-scale invasion of Cambodia on 25 December 1978, overrunning and taking control of the country in just two weeks. On 8 January 1979,

[45] See also Oona A. Hathaway, Maggie M. Mills and Heather Zimmerman, "Crisis and Change at the United Nations: Non-amendment Reform and Institutional Evolution", *Michigan Journal of International Law* 46 (2025): 1, 53–7.

[46] ICJ Rep. 1997, p. 7, at pp. 55–6 [83]–[5]. See also Daniel Franchini, "Extraterritorial Sanctions in Response to Global Security Challenges: Countermeasures as Gap-Fillers in the United Nations Collective Security System", *Cambridge International Law Journal* 12 (2023): 129.

Vietnam put in power Cambodia's pro-Vietnamese government, which renamed the country the People's Republic of Kampuchea (PRK). In a letter to the UNSC, Vietnam accused the Khmer Rouge regime, which was governing Cambodia at the time of the Vietnamese invasion, of having attacked Vietnam, and that, "[i]nstigated and supported by the Peking authorities, the [Khmer Rouge regime had] waged a large-scale war of aggression along Vietnam's southwestern border, committing extremely barbarous crimes against the Vietnamese people".[47] Vietnam was a Soviet Union ally and a foe of China, which supported the Khmer Rouge regime. The Vietnamese invasion, even if undertaken in self-defence, was clearly in violation of international law since it flagrantly failed the proportionality requirement for self-defence. The majority of states condemned Vietnam's invasion as unlawful.[48]

On 17 February 1979, China invaded Vietnam. In a letter to the UNSC, China accused Vietnam of "[i]gnoring China's repeated warnings", having "of late continually sent armed forces to encroach on Chinese territory and attack Chinese frontier guards and inhabitants, causing a rapid deterioration of the situation and seriously threatening the peace and security of China's frontiers".[49] In response, Vietnam accused China of continued occupation of Vietnamese territory by Chinese troops, despite statements otherwise, and that, "[s]ince 17 February 1979, the Chinese rulers [had] mobilized over half a million troops to wage a war of aggression against Vietnam, an independent and sovereign country".[50] This 27-day Sino-Vietnamese armed conflict was apparently China's teaching Vietnam a lesson and it forced Vietnam to station a large number of Vietnamese troops along its border with China, thereby diverting Vietnamese military resources from venturing militarily further afield beyond Cambodia.

---

[47] S/13011 (8 Jan. 1979).

[48] See, for example, *United Nations Security Council Official Records*, 34th year, 2109th mtg, para. 18 (Norway); *United Nations Security Council Official Records*, 34th year, 2109th mtg, para. 36 (France); *United Nations Security Council Official Records*, 34th year, 2110th mtg, para. 49 (Singapore); *United Nations Security Council Official Records*, 34th year, 2110th mtg, paras 27–9 (Portugal); *United Nations Security Council Official Records*, 34th year, 2110th mtg, para. 58 (New Zealand). Cited in Mohammad Taghi Karoubi, "Unilateral Use of Armed Forces and the Challenge of Humanitarian Intervention in International Law", *Asian Yearbook of International Law* 10 (2005): 95, 120. Only the Soviet Union and Czechoslovakia supported Vietnam's action.

[49] S/13094 (17 Feb. 1979).

[50] S/13022 (4 Apr. 1979).

Soon after the Vietnamese got control of the Cambodian capital city in January 1979, representatives of the ousted Khmer Rouge regime called for a meeting of the UNSC. A draft resolution calling for a ceasefire and withdrawal of all foreign forces from Cambodia was vetoed by the Soviet Union. Those opposed to the Vietnamese invasion opted not to recognise the PRK, which was denied its seat at the United Nations, and they imposed economic and financial sanctions on Vietnam. The PRK was recognised only by India and countries in the Soviet bloc, except Romania. ASEAN—then comprising Indonesia, Malaysia, the Philippines, Singapore and Thailand—took a leading role in response to the Vietnamese invasion. Despite the notoriously heinous and nationwide human rights violations by the Khmer Rouge regime, those opposed to the Vietnamese invasion were more concerned with the "domino effect" theory—that, after the fall of South Vietnam and Cambodia to Communist North Vietnam, Thailand would be the next in line to fall to Communism. Thailand reportedly harboured armed resistance groups to fight the Vietnamese forces in Cambodia and there were fighting spillovers into Thailand. For instance, in July 1980, Thailand sent a letter to the UNSC accusing Vietnamese troops of entering Thailand, and that "[t]he allegation that Thai troops intruded into [Cambodia] [was] therefore a distortion aimed at creating tension" since "Thailand was only acting in self-defence when it took action to repulse Vietnamese forces which intruded into Thailand".[51] In January 1983, Thailand sent another letter to the UNSC accusing the Vietnamese forces in Cambodia of engaging in "indiscriminate shelling over the Thai-[Cambodian] border" that resulted in the deaths of four children at a village approximately seven kilometres inside the border until "Thai forces, stationed inside Thai territory, in exercise of the legitimate right to self-defence, returned fire".[52]

In order to have a government in Cambodia that was not seen as a Vietnamese puppet, Cambodians negotiated among themselves to find a mutually acceptable solution. The late 1980s witnessed the waning of the Soviet Union, with Mikhail Gorbachev at the helm. He ensured the withdrawal of Soviet troops from Afghanistan, the end of the Cold War and, eventually, the formal dissolution of the Soviet Union on 26 December 1991. Without Soviet support as in the past and hamstrung by international sanctions that severely crippled its economy, Vietnam officially withdrew its troops from Cambodia in September 1989. On 23 October 1991, the Paris Peace Agreements to restore

[51] S/14072 (25 July 1980).
[52] S/15559 (12 Jan. 1983).

peace in Cambodia were signed by Vietnam, both political factions in Cambodia, the six ASEAN member states (with Brunei as a member of ASEAN since January 1984), Australia, Canada, China, France, India, Japan, Laos, the Soviet Union, the United Kingdom, the United States and Yugoslavia. Pursuant to the Paris Agreements, the UN Transitional Authority in Cambodia (UNTAC) was set up in accordance with UNSC Resolution 745, adopted unanimously on 28 February 1992. Forty-six countries, including all five permanent members of the UNSC, participated in UNTAC by providing military observers, police and troops. In addition to the PRC, the other participating Asian countries were Japan, India, Pakistan, Bangladesh, Jordan, Fiji, Nepal and all the ASEAN member states except Singapore. It was the first time that the United Nations had taken over the administration of an independent nation state. UNTAC had a broad mandate to supervise the main policies and administration of Cambodia as well as organise and run elections until a Cambodian government was democratically elected in 1993.

Thailand's foreign policy under the new Thai government, which came into office in August 1988, dramatically changed. It abandoned its predecessors' hard-line policy towards Indochina and instead immediately initiated a new policy that essentially involved befriending Vietnam and the Phnom Penh government in its efforts to "turn Indochina from a battlefield to a marketplace". The impending end of the Cold War made this new policy practicable. The Thai government succeeded in convincing its ASEAN allies as well as China and the United States that, from the perspective of Thailand, the frontline state bordering Indochina, the new policy was a continuation of the efforts to bring peace to the region, consistent with ASEAN's interest.[53] Vietnam joined ASEAN on 28 July 1995, followed by Cambodia on 30 April 1999.

On the whole, although there was no international court or tribunal with compulsory jurisdiction to rule on the lawfulness or otherwise of Vietnam's alleged exercise of the right to self-defence against Cambodia and its subsequent military occupation of the latter country, international law did provide the basis for the international community's response to the Vietnamese actions. Geopolitics and diplomacy played crucial roles in the final outcome of this war.

A lesson from this episode is that a full-scale invasion of another country, especially when followed by its occupation, is too costly economically and politically for the invading state. Military superiority does not necessarily translate into a speedy and comprehensive military conquest over another state that is not

[53] Salinee Phonprapai, *Battlefield to Marketplace: Responses to Thailand's Major Foreign Policy Change* (Bangkok: International Studies Center, 2021).

as well-equipped militarily. The Latin aphorism *inter arma silente leges* (among arms, laws are silent) does not necessarily hold true.

The next chapter will examine how international law and politics interact as regards one of the most sensitive issues in international relations, namely sovereignty disputes.

CHAPTER 3

Sovereignty Disputes

Sovereignty disputes are disputes over the exact location of the boundary lines dividing land territories or maritime areas of two or more states ("border disputes") or disputes over the entitlement to a piece of land territory of any size or dimension or a maritime geographical feature ("territorial disputes").

Border and territorial disputes have caused numerous armed conflicts in Asia. The disputes can be categorised as ones caused by different interpretations of treaty provisions concerning sovereignty over a territory, divergent interpretations of facts underlying the claims to entitlement over the territory or different interpretations of the exact location of an interstate boundary. An example is the dispute between Iran and the UAE over the territorial sovereignty over Greater Tunb, Lesser Tunb and Abu Musa—three islands in the Strait of Hormuz that Iran seized by force in November 1971 with a few casualties on both sides after the withdrawal by Britain as a colonial power in the Persian Gulf. Iran claims the islands had been part of the Persian Empire since the sixth century BCE, whereas the UAE claims that Arabs had maintained control and sovereignty of the islands since the seventh century BCE. There is no surviving documentation from precolonial times regarding the sovereignty of these islands, though. While the UAE reportedly wants to submit the territorial dispute to the International Court of Justice (ICJ), Iran does not consent to this.

Borders connect political, social, economic, technological, cultural and psychological processes in space, in time and at the level of everyday life. Borders are inherently political as they divide territorial sovereignty, and they have become complex sociopolitical arenas where issues related to identity, security and mobility, among others, are entangled. It is traditionally assumed that borders are necessary to secure national unity and territorial integrity. However, there is overwhelming evidence that border securitisation does not make states more secure. The artificiality of the postcolonial borders has led to social, economic and, in some cases, political conflict and generated countless hardships for local populations, particularly those living in border communities. In a context of security-led rebordering and resurgent nationalism, borders are widely mobilised in populist discourses and authoritarian postures that seek to reinforce and legitimise their role in protecting a secure and familiar "inside" from a dangerous and chaotic "outside".[1]

The case studies in this chapter are the dispute between India and Pakistan over Kashmir, the one between China and India regarding the McMahon Line, the one between Laos and Thailand over Ban Romklao, the dispute between Cambodia and Thailand over Preah Vihear/Phra Viharn, and the disputed sovereignty over maritime geographical features in the Paracels (or Xisha Islands in Chinese) and the Spratlys (or Nansha Islands in Chinese) in the South China Sea.

The root causes of most of the boundary and territorial disputes in Asia can be traced back to the days of Western colonialism, when the colonial rulers divided areas and regions to serve their selfish objectives (such as to get as much territory as possible under their sovereignty or to divide areas into different administrative regions to serve their interests) or out of sheer ignorance of local cultures, religious faiths and traditions. This happened, for instance, in the case of the Radcliffe Line dividing Punjab Province which was declared a boundary between India and Pakistan on 17 August 1947 upon the partition of British India into India and Pakistan. The British based the line on flawed colonial cartography; the boundary had no physical existence on the ground, and the criteria used to draw the line were deeply misguided, with the line being drawn between contiguous Muslim- and non-Muslim-majority areas in spite of the fact that religion did not play a prominent role as an identity in Punjab, where caste, class and linguistic criteria were far stronger markers of identity. The line did not take into account local interests, and it split up farmlands and homes, villages and towns, industries, spiritual communities, irrigation networks and infrastructure. By cutting through Punjab Province solely on religious criteria, the line disrupted its pre-existing syncretic identity and provided the ideological ground for communalism. Communal killings in Punjab began almost immediately after the line was announced and continued well into the following months. Prior to partition, the western territories of Punjab had a 29.1 per cent

[1] James W. Scott, ed., *A Research Agenda for Border Studies* (Cheltenham: Edward Elgar Publishing, 2020).

Hindu population and a 14.9 per cent Sikh population that, through migration, reduced to zero by 1951, while the Muslim population of the eastern territories shrank from 35 per cent to 2 per cent in the aftermath of partition.[2]

Kashmir: India v. Pakistan

The same problem arises in relation to Kashmir, which has been subject to a territorial dispute and armed conflict between India and Pakistan.

According to *Encyclopaedia Britannica*, Kashmir is a region of the north-western Indian subcontinent with a total area of 222,200 square kilometres, bounded by China's Xinjiang Autonomous Region to the north-east and China's Tibet Autonomous Region to the east, by the Indian states of Himachal Pradesh and Punjab to the south, by Pakistan to the west and by Afghanistan to the north-west.

Fear of Hindu domination among the Muslim population of India forced the partition of the country in 1947 into India and Pakistan. Partition left various issues of Muslim-dominated communities such as Hyderabad, Kutch and Kashmir unresolved.[3] Jammu and Kashmir, situated in the southern portion of the larger Kashmir region, formed a state that, prior to the transfer of power by the British to India and Pakistan, was in treaty relations with the British Crown, which controlled its foreign relations and was responsible for its defence. At the time of partition, the ruler of the state of Jammu and Kashmir, who was a Hindu, delayed making a decision about the future of his state. India and Pakistan fought two wars over Kashmir, from October 1947 to 1 January 1949 and in August/September 1965.

On 1 January 1948, India sent a letter to the president of the UN Security Council (UNSC) in connection with the defence of "the people of Kashmir" against the hostile activities of certain tribesmen from the territory of Pakistan and later against activities of Pakistan's troops in Kashmir. India said that, after the raids by Pakistan into the state of Jammu and Kashmir, India was informally approached by the ruler of that state to accept the state's accession into the Indian Dominion. On 25 October 1947, the ruler of the state appealed urgently

---

[2] Vanshaj Ravi Jain, "Broken Boundaries: Border and Identity Formation in Post-Colonial Punjab", *Asian Journal of International Law* 10 (2020): 261, 274–92.

[3] Joshua Castellino, "The Secession of Bangladesh in International Law: Setting New Standards?" *Asian Yearbook of International Law* 7 (2000): 83, 86; Shaiba Rather, "Falling through the Cracks: Kashmir's Resistance against Settler Colonialism and the Limits of International Law", *Harvard International Law Journal Online* 63 (2022): 1, 4–22.

to the Indian government for military help and requested that the state be allowed to accede to the Indian Dominion. The Indian government also simultaneously received an appeal for help from the largest popular organisation in Kashmir, the National Conference, which further strongly supported the request for the state's accession to the Indian Dominion. The Indian government was thus approached, not only officially by the state authorities but also on behalf of "the people of Kashmir", both for military aid and for the accession of the state to the Indian Dominion. The Indian government felt it had to respond to the appeal for armed assistance because India could not let a neighbouring and friendly state to be compelled by force to determine either its internal affairs or external relations, and the accession of the state of Jammu and Kashmir to the Indian Dominion made India responsible for the defence of that state. India also assured the UNSC that "once the soil of the State had been cleared of the invaders and normal conditions restored, its people would be free to decide their future by the recognized democratic method of a plebiscite or referendum which, in order to ensure complete impartiality, might be held under international auspices".[4]

Pakistan insists that the issue of sovereignty over Kashmir is still unresolved under international law and demands that the people of Kashmir be able to exercise their right to self-determination and to hold a referendum on the status of Kashmir.[5] In its earliest armed clashes with India, Pakistan accused India of not only having mounted its offensive but also having subsequently continued to move on to other areas, occupying certain portions and rapidly advancing towards Pakistan's border, as a result of which the Pakistani armed forces went, so far as Kashmir was concerned, "in aid of the freedom of the people, in order to enable them to hold what territory was left to them against the Indian advance", so as "to avoid the imminent danger that threatened the security of Pakistan and the economy of Pakistan".[6]

The UNSC adopted Resolution 39 on 20 January 1948 to set up the UN Commission for India and Pakistan to mediate between India and Pakistan to bring about a cessation of fighting in Kashmir and to make arrangements for a popular plebiscite.[7] Both countries eventually agreed on a

---

[4] S/628 (1 Jan. 1948).

[5] Christian Marxsen, "Violation and Confirmation of the Law: The Intricate Effects of the Invocation of the Law in Armed Conflict." *Journal of the Use of Force & International Law* 5, (2018): 8, 16–17.

[6] S/PV.464 (8 Feb. 1950).

[7] S/RES/39 (1948).

ceasefire, effective as of 1 January 1949. The UNSC has since adopted several resolutions on Kashmir calling for prompt cessation of hostilities and initiated many measures to resolve the issue.[8] The UNSC's position is that "the final disposition of the State of Jammu and Kashmir will be made in accordance with the will of the people expressed through the democratic method of a free and impartial plebiscite conducted under the auspices of the United Nations".[9]

The elections held in the Indian-controlled Jammu and Kashmir in 1951 supported the state's accession to India. India considers that this result makes a referendum pointless, whereas Pakistan insists that a referendum needs to take into consideration the opinions of all voters in Jammu and Kashmir, including people in Pakistan-controlled parts. India has continued to oppose the proposal to conduct a plebiscite in Kashmir for want of a neutral atmosphere that could be ensured only by the withdrawal of tribesmen and Pakistani soldiers/nationals who had entered the state for the purpose of fighting, the possible repercussion of the religion-based plebiscite on the secular structure of the Indian polity, the need to protect the interests of Hindus and Buddhists in Kashmir, and the vital economic interests at stake because of the huge Indian expenditure for the benefit of Kashmir.[10] Coming into force in October 1949, Article 370 of the Indian Constitution granted autonomous status to the state of Jammu and Kashmir, allowing it to make its own laws in all matters except finance, defence, foreign affairs and communications. This was to provide space in matters of governance to the people of Jammu and Kashmir, who have always felt vulnerable about their identity and insecure about the future. Since 1957, however, the constitution of Indian-administrated Jammu and Kashmir has defined Jammu and Kashmir as being an integral part of India.

In August 1965, Pakistan launched a military operation code-named "Operation Gibraltar" to infiltrate forces into Jammu and Kashmir to precipitate an insurgency against rule by India, and India retaliated by launching a full-scale military attack on West Pakistan. The 17-day war caused heavy casualties on both sides, with both sides using armoured vehicles and tanks in the battles. The hostilities formally ended after a ceasefire was declared in September 1965

[8] See Venkatachala G. Hegde, "India and International Settlement of Disputes", *Indian Journal of International Law* 56 (2016): 1, 12–13.

[9] For example, UNSC Resolution S/3779 (1957), adopted by 10 to 0, with the Soviet Union abstaining. For discussion on the draft resolution, see *United Nations Security Council Official Records*, 765th Meeting, 24 Jan. 1957.

[10] P.I. Bhat, "Peaceful Resolution of International Disputes: Drawing Lessons from the Indian Experiences", *Indian Journal of International Law* 59 (2021): 1, 37.

following diplomatic intervention by the Soviet Union and United States and the subsequent issuance of the Tashkent Declaration on 10 January 1966, which stated that, no later than 25 February 1966, the Indian military and the Pakistani military would pull back to their pre-conflict positions, their pre-August 1965 lines; neither nation would interfere in each other's internal affairs; economic and diplomatic relations would be restored; there would be an orderly transfer of prisoners of war; and both leaders would work towards improving bilateral relations.[11]

At the end of the Indo-Pakistani war of 1971 in which India assisted East Pakistan to secede from Pakistan to become a newly independent nation called Bangladesh, India and Pakistan concluded the Simla Agreement in 1972. The agreement provides, inter alia, that both countries will settle their differences by peaceful means through bilateral negotiations. India has since maintained that the Kashmir dispute is a bilateral issue that must be settled through bilateral negotiations as stipulated in the 1972 agreement, without any third-party intervention, even by the United Nations. The 1972 agreement converted the ceasefire line of 17 December 1971 into the "Line of Control" between India and Pakistan and it was agreed that "neither side shall seek to alter it unilaterally, irrespective of mutual differences and legal interpretations". As a result of this Line of Control, the northern and western portions of Kashmir are administered by Pakistan and comprise three areas—Azad Kashmir, Gilgit and Baltistan, whereas India administers the southern and south-eastern portions—Jammu and Kashmir and Ladakh.

India and Pakistan often accuse one another in the UNSC of conducting a series of armed attacks and occupation across the Line of Control.[12] From May to July 1999, India and Pakistan engaged in armed conflicts in the Kargil district of Jammu and Kashmir and elsewhere along the Line of Control. On 26 July 1999, the "Kargil War" officially ended with the Indian Army announcing the complete withdrawal of Pakistani irregular and regular forces from the Indian side of the Line of Control. India counted 591 violations by Pakistan in January and February 2021, while Pakistan accused Indian forces of violating the Line of Control no fewer than 175 times during that same period. Pakistan wrote to the UNSC in February 2021 to reiterate its allegations against India and what Pakistan considers to be India's illegal occupation and violations of international law in Jammu and Kashmir, and India's conduct at their shared border. However, on 25 February 2021, India's and Pakistan's directors general

[11] UNSC Doc. S/7221 (25 Mar. 1966).

[12] See, for example, S/2014/730 (13 Oct. 2014).

of military operations released a joint statement on the situation at their shared border and the Line of Control, stating that, in the interest of achieving mutually beneficial and sustainable peace along the borders, the two directors general had agreed to address each other's core issues and concerns, which had the propensity to disturb peace and lead to violence. Both sides agreed to abide strictly by all agreements, understandings and ceasefires along the Line of Control and all other sectors with effect from midnight on 24/25 February 2021. Both sides also reiterated that existing mechanisms of hotline contact and border personnel meetings would be utilised to resolve any unforeseen situation or misunderstanding. Pakistan referred to this agreement in another complaint to the United Nations in June 2021, alleging that India had "vitiated the prospects for a dialogue through its illegal and unilateral actions" in Kashmir. Pakistan therefore requested that the UNSC fulfil its obligation to ensure the full implementation of its resolutions guaranteeing the exercise of Kashmiris' right to self-determination, call upon India to "end its campaign of repression in the Indian illegally occupied Jammu and Kashmir and reverse all its illegal actions, including those initiated on and after 5 August 2019, and to cease and desist from imposing any additional unilateral changes in the occupied territory".[13]

Despite India's assurance to the UNSC in January 1948 that it would recognise the result of a plebiscite or referendum on the future of Kashmir, India has consistently rejected the right of self-determination of peoples. For instance, in its judgment of 12 April 1960 in *Case Concerning Right of Passage over Indian Territory (Portugal v. India)*, the ICJ noted India's unhesitant declaration made on 6 September 1955 that "in the event of the populations concerned opting in favour of the maintenance of Portuguese sovereignty [over Dadra and Nagar-Aveli, the two Portuguese enclaves surrounded by India's territory], India would not be disposed to tolerate this", which constitutes the very negation of the right of self-determination of peoples.[14] India has also declared that the right of self-determination under Common Article 1 of the 1966 International Covenant on Civil and Political Rights and the 1966 International Covenant on Economic, Social and Cultural Rights applies only to the peoples under foreign domination, and does not apply to sovereign independent states or to a

[13] Patrick M. Butchard and Jasmin Johurun Nessa, "Digest of State Practice: 1 January–30 June 2021." *Journal of Use of Force & International Law* 8 (2021): 343, 388–9.
[14] ICJ Rep. 1960, p. 6 at p. 16.

section of a people or nation—which is the essence of national integrity.[15] Pakistan has objected to the Indian declarations because, in its view, the right of self-determination as enshrined in the UN Charter and as embodied in the 1966 Covenants applies to all peoples under *foreign occupation* and alien domination.

In 2019 the right-wing Bharatiya Janata Party federal government repealed Article 370 of the Indian Constitution, thereby revoking the autonomy of the state of Jammu and Kashmir, claiming it would eradicate armed rebellion in the disputed region. The Jammu and Kashmir Reorganisation Act, in force as of 31 October 2019, reconstitutes the state of Jammu and Kashmir into two Indian-administered union territories called the Union Territory of Jammu and Kashmir and the Union Territory of Ladakh. Jammu and Kashmir has three distinct areas: the overwhelmingly Muslim-majority Kashmir Valley (95 per cent Muslim), with a population of nearly 7 million people; the Hindu-majority Jammu (66 per cent Hindu and 30 per cent Muslim), with a population of approximately 5.35 million people; and Ladakh, which has a population of 287,000 people, 46 per cent of whom are Muslims, 40 per cent of whom are Buddhists and 12 per cent of whom are Hindus. Pursuant to the Act of 2019, the Union Territory of Jammu and Kashmir has a legislature but the Union Territory of Ladakh does not. In December 2023, the five-judge constitutional bench of the Indian Supreme Court upheld the 2019 decision of the Indian government to repeal Article 370 of the Indian Constitution, ruling that Jammu and Kashmir are to be restored to the same statehood as any other Indian state, with no separate autonomy rights, as soon as possible since Article 370 was merely an interim arrangement owing to war conditions in Kashmir at that time.

Pakistan considers India's repeal of Article 370 a flagrant human rights violation. The prime minister of Pakistan has consistently maintained that talks with India to solve the Kashmir dispute can only happen once the revocation of Article 370 is reversed, and that the settlement of this dispute must be in accordance with the UN resolutions and the aspirations of the people of Jammu and Kashmir.

These situations will persist as long as the dispute is not settled by an international court or tribunal agreed upon by the two countries. This is evidenced, more recently at the time of writing, by the four-day armed conflict between the two nations in May 2025 in the wake of the killing of 26 Indian

---

[15] See further, Prabhakar Singh, "Indian before and after the *Right of Passage* Case", *Asian Journal of International Law* 5 (2015): 176, 199.

civilians in Indian-administered Jammu and Kashmir on 22 April 2025, which India attributed to a certain terrorist organisation allegedly supported by Pakistan.

McMahon Line: China v. India

India also has had armed clashes with China as a result of their border dispute.

China has land boundaries of approximately 22,000 kilometres long and borders 14 states. When the People's Republic of China (PRC) was founded in 1949, there was no single boundary that was clearly demarcated and free of disputes with the neighbouring countries. According to Xue Hanqin, now an ICJ judge from China, as a result of the two Opium Wars fought in the mid-19th century between China and Britain and between China, on the one side, and Britain and France, on the other, respectively, China was forced to conclude several "unequal treaties" with other countries. Because of these unequal treaties, China had to pay exorbitant war damages as well as cede Hong Kong, Taiwan and the Shandong Peninsula to the United Kingdom, Japan and Germany, respectively, while, up in the north, large pieces of land were ceded to Russia. When the PRC was founded, it was considered that a new China was born. Regarding treaties concluded by the previous Chinese governments, the PRC decided to review them one by one, and then in light of their content determine whether to recognise, annul, amend or replace them.[16] Before that review was done, China would not accept any claims from foreign states on the basis of these treaties.[17] At the Asian-African Conference in Bandung, Indonesia, in 1955 Chinese premier Zhou Enlai solemnly declared that the PRC wanted to settle boundary issues with its neighbouring countries through peaceful negotiations. In the spirit of mutual understanding and compromise, the PRC concluded its first boundary treaty with Burma in 1960,[18] followed subsequently by boundary treaties with Nepal, Mongolia, Pakistan and Afghanistan, which covered nearly half of China's boundaries. From the 1990s to the early 2000s, China settled almost all of its land boundary disputes with

---

[16] Hanqin Xue, "China's Open Policy and International Law", *Chinese Journal of International Law* 4 (2005): 135.

[17] Hanqin Xue, "Chinese Contemporary Perspectives on International Law: History, Culture and International Law", *Collected Courses of the Hague Academy of International Law* 355 (2011): 64–5.

[18] The agreement uses the "unequal treaties" with the demarcation line suggested by Britain (Junwu Pan, "Chinese Philosophy and International Law", *Asian Journal of International Law* 1 (2011): 233, 242).

its neighbouring countries—with Laos in 1991, Vietnam in 1999, and Russia in 1991, 1994 and 2004. Following the dissolution of the Soviet Union, in the 1990s China concluded boundary treaties with three new states that had previously been part of the Soviet Union: Kazakhstan, Kyrgyzstan and Tajikistan. During boundary negotiations, China has frequently referred to "the established international norms" and "general rules and principles of international law" as the guiding principles to achieve equitable and reasonable solutions in the interest of peace and good neighbourliness. By 2011, China had successfully resolved border issues and concluded boundary treaties and agreements with 12 neighbours, settling 90 per cent of its land boundaries. As for maritime boundary delimitations, China concluded its first treaty with Vietnam on the delimitation of the territorial sea, exclusive economic zone and continental shelf in the Beibu Gulf on 25 December 2000.[19]

Geopolitics certainly play a crucial role in settling China's border disputes with its neighbours. China and Vietnam had a series of armed clashes over their border disputes from 1979 until 1988, peaking in the years 1984–85. By the early 1990s, after the Vietnamese withdrawal from Cambodia in 1990, as explained in Chapter 2, and the dissolution of the Soviet Union, which was Vietnam's staunch ally, in 1991, the bilateral relationship between China and Vietnam gradually improved. After the two countries officially proclaimed the normalisation of their diplomatic relations in November 1991, they developed a system of talks at the expert, governmental and high levels to deal with the tensions and with the border issues as such.[20]

With regard to the border conflict between China and India, British India, China and Tibet participated in a trilateral conference in Simla, northern India, in March–April 1914, which ended in a draft tripartite agreement. Disputes then arose concerning the borders between China and Tibet and the degree and nature of Chinese "suzerainty" over the Tibetan government. Suzerainty signifies the rights and obligations of one sovereign state to control a vassal state's foreign policy and relations while allowing the latter internal autonomy. After the Chinese delegation's walk-out, the other parties signed the tripartite Simla Convention on 3 July 1914 without China. China has not

[19] Xue, "Chinese Contemporary Perspectives on International Law", 82–5. See also Xinjun Zhang and Xidi Chen, "China and the Settlement of Territorial Disputes", in *The Handbook of China and International Law*, ed. Ignacio de la Rasilla and Congyan Cai (Cambridge: Cambridge University Press, 2024), pp. 522–47.

[20] Ramses Amer and Nguyen Hong Thao, "Vietnam's Border Disputes: Legal and Conflict Management Dimensions", *Asian Yearbook of International Law* 12 (2007): 111, 117, 125.

accepted the validity of the Simla Convention, which also laid down the frontiers between Tibet and India in the east, named the "McMahon Line" after Sir Arthur Henry McMahon, chief delegate of the British India delegation and chairman of the tripartite Simla conference in 1914. China claims that it did not sign the Simla Convention and that Tibet had no right to conclude treaties on its own.

In 1954, seven years after its independence, India concluded a treaty with China on trade and pilgrimage in Tibet, then already under China's sovereignty, without referring to the 1914 Simla Convention or the McMahon Line.[21] In 1962, Chinese troops crossed the McMahon Line in the east, leading to a four-week war between India and China. With the good offices of the representatives of six Asian and African nations who met in Colombo, Ceylon (now Sri Lanka), in December 1962 to develop peace proposals for India and China, a temporary truce was agreed, with China withdrawing 20 kilometres from the "Line of Actual Control" of 7 November 1959 that separates Indian-controlled territory from Chinese-controlled territory in the Sino-Indian border dispute. The 1993 Border Peace and Tranquility Agreement between the two countries acknowledges their differences and declares that the two sides shall jointly check and determine the segments of the Line of Actual Control where they have different views on its alignments.[22]

An author has described the current border dispute between China and India as being situated in the Himalayan Galwan River Valley, 17,000 feet above sea level, and comprising the westerly 1,000-kilometre stretch of a loosely defined 4,057-kilometre Line of Actual Control, which is a truncated line that is interrupted in central portions by Nepal and Bhutan. The eastern extension of the Line of Actual Control forms the disputed portion of the border (the McMahon Line) separating Tibet and Arunachal Pradesh, the 90,000-square-kilometre Indian-controlled state that is claimed in its entirety by China. The western extension of the Line separates eastern Ladakh from the 33,000-square-kilometre Chinese-controlled territory of Aksai Chin, historically claimed by India. It leads to more contested land north-east of Pakistan-controlled areas of Kashmir,

---

[21] Nirmal C. Sinha, "The Simla Convention 1914: A Chinese Puzzle", *Presidency College Magazine: Diamond Jubilee Number* (Calcutta, 1974): 35–9. One author argues that in 1907 Russia and Britain acknowledged Chinese suzerainty over Tibet, and that Britain maintained this position until 2008 (Yuan Yi Zhu, "Suzerainty, Semi-Sovereignty, and International Legal Hierarchies on China's Borderlands", *Asian Journal of International Law* 10 (2020): 293, 298–9, 304, 307, 311).

[22] See also Christopher Rossi, "Interstitial Space and the High Himalayan Dispute between China and India", *Harvard International Law Journal* 62 (2021): 429, 453–60.

which Pakistan ceded to China in the 1963 Sino-Pakistani Agreement establishing a border between these two countries in the disputed Kashmir region, and which India claims belongs to it (namely, the Shaksgam Valley/Trans-Karakoram Tract). China has effective control over Aksai Chin and Shaksgam Valley, whereas India effectively controls Ladakh and the territory in the eastern sector of Arunachal Pradesh.[23]

The Sino-Indian Confidence-Building Measures (CBM) Agreement in 1996 requires, inter alia, the parties to respect the Line of Actual Control and work for maintenance of peace and tranquillity pending the solution of the boundary dispute; restraints on the number of soldiers guarding the line; non-use of force in face-to-face encounters; measures in case of intrusions; and regular meetings between their border personnel and regular meetings on border issues. In 2013, both sides concluded the Border Defence Cooperation Agreement.

As the 1996 CBM Agreement bans firearms and explosives in the disputed region, in the clashes between the two sides that took place in June 2020 their soldiers used bare fists and weapons such as clubs spiked with nails and wrapped with barbed wire. India disclosed that 20 Indian soldiers were killed and 76 injured, while China admitted the Chinese side suffered "minor injuries". The defence ministers of the two countries met bilaterally to defuse the situation on 4 September 2020 in Moscow, on the sidelines of the Joint Meeting of the Heads of Defence Ministries of the Shanghai Cooperation Organisation, Commonwealth of Independent States and Collective Security Treaty Organization member countries. On 10 September 2020, the foreign ministers of China and India issued a joint statement after their bilateral meeting in Moscow, on the sidelines of the Shanghai Cooperation Organisation meeting, on the developments in the India–China border areas as well as on India–China relations. They agreed that both sides should take guidance from the series of consensus of the leaders on developing India–China relations, including not allowing differences to become disputes, and that the current situation in the border areas was not in the interest of either side. They agreed therefore that the border troops of both sides should continue their dialogue, quickly disengage, maintain proper distance and ease tensions; both sides were to abide by all the existing agreements and protocol on China–India boundary affairs, maintain peace and tranquillity in the border areas and avoid any action that could escalate matters. The two sides also agreed to continue to have dialogue and communication through the special representative mechanism on the India–China boundary question.

---

[23] Ibid., 429–30, 464.

They also agreed in this context that the Working Mechanism for Consultation and Coordination on India–China Border Affairs should also continue its meetings and that, as the situation eased, the two sides should expedite work to conclude new CBMs to maintain and enhance peace and tranquillity in the border areas.

Despite frequent talks between the two sides in 2020, clashes on the border between India and China spilled over into the start of 2021. On 20 January 2021, Indian and Chinese forces fought on the Himalayan border on the eastern tip of India's northern territory, but India labelled the incident a "minor face-off", while China did not immediately acknowledge what happened. In February 2021, India and China released a joint statement of the tenth round of China–India Corps Commander-Level Meeting detailing the disengagement of troops at the border in the Pangong Lake area as a significant step forward that provided a good basis for resolution of other remaining issues along the Line of Actual Control in the western sector. They agreed to follow the important consensus of their countries' leaders, continue their communication and dialogue, stabilise and control the situation on the ground, and push for a mutually acceptable resolution of the remaining issues in a steady and orderly manner, so as to jointly maintain peace and tranquillity in the border areas.[24]

Nevertheless, on 9 December 2022 the two sides were involved in an armed clash at the north-eastern tip of India, in the Tawang sector of India's Arunachal Pradesh State, which China calls southern Tibet, with a few soldiers suffering minor injuries. Tawang, a pilgrimage site for Tibetan Buddhists and home to India's largest Buddhist monastery, is situated just 35 kilometres to the south of China's Tibet. Both sides immediately disengaged from the area, and their commanders held a meeting on 11 December 2022 to restore peace and tranquillity. India took up the matter with China through diplomatic channels concerning what India described as Chinese troops' encroachment into Indian territory and unilateral attempt to change the status quo along the disputed border.[25] The Chinese foreign minister, addressing the Symposium on the International Situation and China's Foreign Relations held in Beijing on 25 December 2022, stated that China and India had maintained communication through the diplomatic and military-to-military

[24] Bhat, "Peaceful Resolution of International Disputes", 35–7; Butchard and Nessa, "Digest of State Practice: 1 January–30 June 2021", 385–6.

[25] "India and China Troops Clash on Arunachal Pradesh Mountain Border", BBC, 13 Dec. 2022, https://www.bbc.com/news/world-asia-63953400.

channels, and both countries were committed to upholding stability in the border areas. To continue this momentum of peaceful dialogue, on the sidelines of the G20 meeting in New Delhi on 2 March 2023, the foreign ministers of the two countries met to discuss how to alleviate this border conflict. Yet the latest edition of "China Standard Map", published by China's Natural Resources Ministry in August 2023, includes Arunachal Pradesh as part of China, immediately prompting a strong diplomatic protest from India. At the BRICS summit held in Russia in October 2024, where they met for the first time in five years, Chinese president Xi and Indian prime minister Modi agreed to a patrol arrangement to reduce tension along their disputed Himalayan border and said they would continue discussions on resolving the issue.

Ban Romklao: Laos v. Thailand

Thailand has had armed conflicts with Laos and Cambodia on the issue of territorial sovereignty over land territories caused by ambiguous provisions of treaties Thailand (then called Siam) concluded with France, which then colonised Laos and Cambodia. At the time of the armed conflict with Laos, Laos was not yet a member state of ASEAN but Cambodia was already an ASEAN member state during its armed conflict with Thailand.

In 1984, Thailand and Laos had a minor shooting incident due to their dispute over the territorial sovereignty of the 19-square-kilometre piece of land inhabited by three border villages. There was a more serious armed conflict over the territorial sovereignty of a 72-square-kilometre border area that Thailand calls Ban Romklao. The "Battle of Ban Romklao" between Laos and Thailand lasted 264 days, from 31 May 1987 until 19 February 1988.

Laos and Thailand have diverging views on the interpretation of the boundary maps annexed to the 1907 Franco-Siamese Treaty. According to Thailand, on 31 May 1987, 15 Laotian soldiers intruded into Thai territory at Chart Trakarn District, Phitsanulok Province, killing an innocent Thai labourer and destroying three tractors owned by a Thai company that had been granted a timber concession in the area. For its part, Laos demanded that Thailand recognise that Thai citizens had intruded to carry out illegal logging in Laos's territory and cease supporting non-state armed groups fighting the Laotian government.

The situation escalated into full-scale armed attacks to "recover" the disputed territory from November 1987 onwards. On 25 December 1987, Laos sent an official note to the UN secretary-general accusing Thailand of violation of the UN Charter and international law, although Laos was trying to start a negotiation to peacefully settle the dispute. On 31 December 1987, the UN secretary-general sent a telegram to the Thai foreign minister asking Thailand to settle its dispute with Laos by peaceful means. On 15 January 1988, Thailand informed the UNSC that it was exercising the right to self-defence, and Thailand also claimed that Laos had sent troops into Thailand to plant a large number of land mines and occupy the strategic Hill 1428 inside Thailand. The fighting intensified, including with the use of airstrikes by the Thai Air Force. Vietnam also sent troops to assist Laos. There were rumours in Thailand that Russian and Cuban troops were also seen helping Laos fight Thailand. The Soviet Union was Laos's close political ally, whereas Thailand had the United States as its ally. Therefore, the UNSC would not be able to hold either Laos or Thailand in violation of the UN Charter and international law owing to the potential veto by the Soviet Union or the United States in support of their respective allies. Going to the ICJ to settle this dispute would not be acceptable, at least for Thailand, whose memory of losing the *Temple of Preah Vihear* case to Cambodia in 1962, as will be explained in due course, was still coming back to haunt Thais, convinced that treaties concluded between Siam and France had severely placed Thailand in an unfair position as regards land boundaries with France's former colonies.

It was a combination of personal connections between certain government and military leaders of both countries and the looming demise of the Soviet Union that were instrumental in bringing the two sides together for talks to end the conflict. De-escalation of the war began with the agreement on mutual troop withdrawals three kilometres from the Hill 1428 battleground and a ceasefire, to be followed by political dialogues to find a mutually agreed and lasting solution. According to unofficial reports, some 700 Laotian and Thai soldiers were killed during this dispute. In 1996, they set up a joint boundary commission to demarcate their common land boundary. By May 2002, both countries had erected 136 land boundary pillars, extending 545 kilometres or 72 per cent of their 702-kilometre common land boundary.[26] Both Thailand and Laos have agreed to maintain the status quo in the three villages and Ban Romklao before their armed clashes, without prejudice to their respective legal positions on the sovereignty over these territories.[27]

---

[26] *Keesing's Contemporary Archives* 34 (Nov. 1988): 26292; Payan Eumsin, "Problems in International Relations from the Perspective of Thai Military Leaders Who Negotiated the Ban Romklao-Botaen Ceasefire Agreement of 1988", *Journal of Social Sciences* 51 (2021): 75–98.

[27] Press statement by the Ministry of Foreign Affairs of Thailand on 6 Oct. 2006.

Preah Vihear/Phra Viharn: Cambodia v. Thailand

The armed conflicts between Cambodia and Thailand during the years 2008–11 were in the vicinity of the mountain called Preah Vihear in Cambodian and Phra Viharn in Thai.

The ancient Hindu temple on the mountain top of Preah Vihear/Phra Viharn ("the Temple") has considerable artistic and archaeological interest, and is still used as a place of pilgrimage, although it was already partially in ruins as of 1962. It stands on a promontory of the same name, belonging to the eastern sector of the Dangrek range of mountains, which generally constitutes the boundary between the two countries in this region, Cambodia to the south and Thailand to the north. Considerable portions of this range consist of a high cliff-like escarpment rising abruptly above the Cambodian plain. This is the situation at Preah Vihear/Phra Viharn itself, where the main Temple buildings stand in the apex of a triangular piece of high ground jutting out into the plain. From the edge of the escarpment, the general inclination of the ground in the northerly directions is downwards to Nam Moun River, which is in Thailand.[28]

The 1904 treaty between France, then Cambodia's colonial power, and Siam set up a joint commission to demarcate the Cambodian–Siamese land border according to a watershed, which placed the Temple in Siamese territory. However, a 1907 map (the "Annex I map") drawn by French authorities relocated the boundary without explanation, placing the Temple in Cambodian territory. In 1959 Cambodia instituted proceedings against Thailand in the ICJ with regard to the territorial sovereignty over the Temple. The ICJ ruled in 1961 that it had jurisdiction over this dispute thanks to Cambodia's acceptance of the ICJ's compulsory jurisdiction and a declaration made by Thailand on 20 May 1950 with the legal effect of accepting the ICJ's compulsory jurisdiction.[29] In its judgment on the merits of 1962, the ICJ held that in 1908 "the Parties at that time adopted an interpretation of the treaty settlement which caused the map line, in so far as it may have departed from the line of the watershed, to prevail over the relevant clause of the treaty".[30] The ICJ proceeded to rule, inter alia, that the Temple is situated in territory under the sovereignty of Cambodia, and that "Thailand is under an obligation to withdraw any

---

[28] *Temple of Preah Vihear (Cambodia v. Thailand)*, ICJ Rep. 1962, p. 6, at p. 15.

[29] *Case concerning the Temple of Preah Vihear (Cambodia v. Thailand)*, Preliminary Objections, ICJ Rep. 1961, p. 1.

[30] ICJ Rep. 1962, p. 34.

military or police forces, or other guards or keepers, stationed by her at the Temple, or in its vicinity on Cambodian territory".[31]

In 2006 Cambodia asked the United Nations Educational, Scientific and Cultural Organization (UNESCO) to inscribe the site of the Temple on the UNESCO World Heritage List. Cambodia included as part of a buffer zone to complete the inscription a portion of territory adjacent to the Temple, which Thailand also claims as its territory. The maps submitted to UNESCO by Cambodia and Thailand showed an overlapping area of approximately 4.6 square kilometres claimed by each side as its own. Cambodia's map encompassed not only the entire promontory of Preah Vihear/Phra Viharn but also the hill of Phnom Trap, which appears as Thai territory in Thailand's map. Thailand also objected to Cambodia's use of the Annex I map, which Cambodia had claimed in the ICJ as representing the frontier between the two states. Phrased differently, Cambodia and Thailand disagreed on the meaning of "vicinity" under that ICJ judgment of 1962 and accused one another of illegal intrusion into the other state's territory and use of firearms against soldiers of that other state.

On 8 July 2008, UNESCO decided to inscribe the Temple as a World Heritage site. Tensions skyrocketed and both sides sent troops to the area, leading to the two armies exchanging gunfire on 3 August 2008. Their fighting recurred in October 2008, April 2010 and January 2011, with the most serious events taking place between 4 and 7 February 2010 and from 22 April to 3 May 2011.[32] Examples of the accusations by each side can be found in the following letters to the UNSC. In its letter to the UNSC on 15 October 2008, Cambodia accused Thai troops of firing guns on Cambodian soldiers in Cambodian territory.[33] In its letter sent to the UNSC two days later, Thailand said that, while conducting a routine patrol near the area called Phu Ma Khua in Thai territory, Thai soldiers came under hostile attack by Cambodian soldiers using rocket-propelled grenades and submachine guns. Thailand added that at Pha Mor I Dang, in Thai territory, another group of Cambodian soldiers also opened fire—using recoilless guns, rocket-propelled grenades, mortars and rifles—on Thai soldiers, with the first incident lasting five minutes and the second about 35 minutes.[34] In its letter to the UNSC on 7 February 2011, Cambodia alleged that

---

[31] Ibid., pp. 36–7. See also Thamil Venthan Ananthavinayagan, "Breaking Bad Customs: Involving the Idea of *Opinio Juris Communis* in Asian State Practice", *Asian Yearbook of International Law* 24 (2018): 24, 28–9.

[32] Hao Duy Phan, "Institutional Design and Its Constraints: Explaining ASEAN's Role in the Temple of Preah Vihear Dispute", *Asian Journal of International Law* 5 (2015): 7, 8.

[33] S/2008/653 (15 Oct. 2008).

[34] S/2008/657 (17 Oct. 2008).

approximately 300 Thai troops had entered Cambodian territory and attacked Cambodian troops at three locations, followed by the firing of many 130 mm and 155 mm artillery shells, which reached as far as about 20 kilometres inside Cambodian territory and caused much serious damage to the Temple, a UNESCO World Heritage site, as well as the death and injury of more than ten Cambodian troops and villagers. It added that Thai armed forces fired a number of 105 mm artillery shells at Phnom Trap hill, which lasted for about 20 minutes.[35] Thailand replied on the same day, accusing Cambodian troops of having opened fire at a Thai military post at Phu Ma Khua in Thai territory, using heavy weapons such as mortars, rocket-propelled grenades, recoilless rifles, long-range artillery and multi-launcher rockets. It added that Cambodian troops also opened fire from the area of the Temple at a Thai military post at Pha Mor I Dang in Thai territory and that, in between the two incidents, several artillery shells were fired by Cambodian troops into a village in Thailand's Si Sa Ket Province, located about five kilometres away from the border area, and Cambodian troops once again opened fire using weapons such as AK-47 rifles, mortars, rocket-propelled grenades, grenade launchers and recoilless rifles at Thai troops stationed in the area of Phu Ma Khua in Thai territory.[36]

ASEAN, of which both Cambodia and Thailand are member states, initially took a hands-off position in accordance with its tradition of non-interference in the internal affairs of ASEAN member states. In late July 2008, Cambodia asked Singapore, the then chair of ASEAN, to set up an ASEAN inter-ministerial group consisting of the foreign ministers of Singapore, Indonesia, Vietnam and Laos to help find a peaceful solution to the conflict. However, Thailand insisted this was a bilateral issue between the two countries and it would be premature to involve ASEAN. Thailand then assumed the rotating ASEAN chair in August 2008 and insisted the issue was a bilateral one. Fighting recurred in August and October of that year. ASEAN under Vietnam's chairmanship took no action and it did not start to act until the heavy fighting by the two sides in February 2011 and the ASEAN chair passed on to Indonesia at that time. Indonesian foreign minister Marty Natalegawa conducted shuttle diplomacy between Phnom Penh and Bangkok to urge both sides to let ASEAN intervene and bring in a truce.[37] He also convinced an urgent meeting of the UNSC, convened at Cambodia's request, to refer the

[35] S/2011/56 (7 Feb. 2011).

[36] S/2011/57 (7 Feb. 2011). See also S/2011/65 (22 Apr. 2011).

[37] This was despite the fact that Natalegawa's wife is a Thai, whose father served and younger brother was serving in the Thai diplomatic service.

issue back to ASEAN. One week after the UNSC meeting, Indonesia hosted an urgent meeting of ASEAN foreign ministers on the crisis, resulting in ASEAN agreeing to let Indonesia send observers to the disputed area to observe and report on complaints of violations and submit their findings to each party through Indonesia, the then chair of ASEAN, bearing in mind that the next rotating chair of ASEAN would be Cambodia, one of the parties to the conflict. Yet negotiation between Cambodia and Thailand on the terms of reference for an observer mission did not make any progress when the conflict got worse in April 2011. The dispute was addressed at the highest level for the first time at the ASEAN Summit in May 2011 and a set of terms of reference was agreed upon by both parties, but Thailand subsequently said it was not able to abide by it.[38]

One commentator has identified loopholes in the ASEAN system in relation to the Cambodia–Thailand armed conflict as follows. Under the 1976 Treaty of Amity and Cooperation in Southeast Asia, to which all ASEAN member states are parties, a party to a dispute may bring the dispute to the High Council, comprising the foreign ministers of all ASEAN member states, provided that both parties to the dispute agree to use this procedure to resolve their dispute. There is no timeframe specified for the parties to submit their acceptance of this procedure. Even when both parties have agreed to let the High Council intervene, as a political body comprising all ASEAN member states, including the parties to the dispute, it is unlikely that the High Council could produce any definitive solution on a consensus basis. Even if a consensus is reached, disputing parties are not obliged to implement the decisions or recommendations by the High Council. Either of the disputing parties could bring the use of force as a violation of the ASEAN Charter to the dispute settlement mechanism established by the 2010 Protocol. Under the 2010 Protocol, once consultation does not succeed, any party may request an arbitral tribunal, provided that the other party agrees. In case the responding party does not agree, the complaining party may refer the dispute to the ASEAN Coordinating Council for a direction on how to resolve the dispute by good offices, mediation, conciliation or arbitration. As a body composed of all ASEAN member states, including the disputing parties, the ASEAN Coordinating Council is unlikely to reach a decision on consensus. Although the parties may then refer an unresolved dispute to the ASEAN Summit of Heads of State or Government, there is not much the summit could do at this stage except issue a statement calling upon the parties to continue to resolve their dispute by peaceful means. In practice, a dispute of a

[38] Phan, "Institutional Design and Its Constraints", 9–12.

political and security nature between two ASEAN member states is still viewed as a bilateral affair, and ASEAN's consensus rule essentially gives each ASEAN member state the power of veto.[39]

On 28 April 2011, Cambodia filed an application asking the ICJ to order provisional measures of protection and interpret the ICJ's 1962 judgment. In its 18 July 2011 order on Cambodia's request for provisional measures, the ICJ ordered both parties to immediately withdraw their military personnel then present in the provisional demilitarised zone around the area of the Temple as designated by the ICJ in this order, and refrain from any military presence within that zone and from any armed activity directed at that zone, without prejudice to normal administration, including the presence of non-military personnel necessary to ensure the security of persons and property. It ordered Thailand not to obstruct Cambodia's free access to the Temple or Cambodia's provision of fresh supplies to its non-military personnel in the Temple. Both parties were ordered to continue the cooperation that they had entered into within ASEAN and, in particular, allow the observers appointed by ASEAN to have access to the provisional demilitarised zone. Both parties were also ordered to refrain from any action that might aggravate or extend the dispute or make it more difficult to resolve, and each party was to inform the ICJ as to its compliance with the aforesaid provisional measures.[40]

On 11 November 2013, in its judgment on the merits, the ICJ held, by way of interpretation, that its judgment of 1962 decided that Cambodia had sovereignty over "the whole territory of the promontory of Preah Vihear, as defined in paragraph 98 of the present judgment" and that, in consequence, Thailand was under an obligation to withdraw from that territory the Thai military or police forces, or other guards or keepers, that were stationed there. Paragraph 98 of the 2013 judgment defines in detail "the limits of the promontory of Preah Vihear".[41]

The ICJ president summed up the ICJ's reasoning behind paragraph 98 of the 2013 judgment as follows.[42] The term "vicinity on Cambodian territory" had to be interpreted as extending at least to the area where, at the time of the

---

[39] Ibid., 12–4.

[40] *Request for Interpretation of the Judgment of 15 June 1962 in the Case concerning the Temple of Preah Vihear (Cambodia v. Thailand) (Cambodia v. Thailand)*, Provisional Measures, Order of 18 July 2011, ICJ Rep. 2011, p. 537.

[41] *Request for Interpretation of the Judgment of 15 June 1962 in the Case concerning the Temple of Preah Vihear (Cambodia v. Thailand) (Cambodia v. Thailand)*, Judgment, ICJ Rep. 2013, p. 281.

[42] Speech by ICJ president Peter Tomka to the 69th Session of the UNGA, 30 Oct. 2014.

original proceedings before the ICJ, a Thai police detachment was found to have been stationed. The neighbouring hill of Phnom Trap, a valley that itself drops away in the south to the Cambodian plain, was found by the ICJ to lie outside the disputed area and the 1962 judgment did not address the question whether it was situated in Thai or Cambodian territory. Therefore, the promontory of Preah Vihear/Phra Viharn terminated at the foot of the hill of Phnom Trap; that is, where the ground begins to rise from the valley. In the north, the ICJ ruled that the limit of the promontory is the Annex I map line, from a point to the north-east of the Temple where that line abuts the escarpment to a point in the north-west where the ground begins to rise from the valley, at the foot of the hill of Phnom Trap. The ICJ president also alluded to the ICJ's observation that the Temple is now listed by UNESCO as a World Heritage site. Article 6 of the 1972 Convention concerning the Protection of the World Cultural and Natural Heritage, to which both Cambodia and Thailand are parties, obligates states parties to cooperate between themselves and with the international community in the protection of the site as a World Heritage. In addition, each state shall not take any deliberate measure that might directly or indirectly damage such heritage. In the context of these obligations, the ICJ emphasised the significance of ensuring access to the Temple from the Cambodian plain.

One legal scholar has cogently summed up the fallacies of the ICJ's judgments in 1962 and 2013 as follows.[43] The 1962 judgment was controversial because it relied, at face value, on an unofficial, unsigned and inaccurate sketch map produced to only one side of the dispute and deduced Thai acquiescence from a single photograph of a brief meeting between a Thai prince and a minor French official in 1930 (and who were both deceased when the issue came to the ICJ in October 1959). The 2013 judgment reinforced the 1962 judgment, which was, in retrospect, evidentially weak. As the Temple ruins are located in inhospitable, mountainous and isolated terrain, neither Siamese nor French colonial officials acting on behalf of Indo-China had shown much interest in the Temple until decolonisation approached in the 1950s. There were few assertions of sovereignty by either Siam or Cambodia. Cambodia's archives had been lost and no one responsible for producing the Annex F map, drawn up for a Franco-Siamese boundary delimitation settlement in 1904, was alive when Cambodia instituted the case against Thailand in the ICJ in October 1959. The 2013 judgment explained that the ICJ was not going to address Thailand's argument

[43] Victor Kattan, "The Ghosts of the Temple of Preah Vihear/Phra Viharn in the 2013 Judgment", *Asian Journal of International Law* 5 (2015): 16.

about the Annex I map, which the 1962 judgment had relied on to allocate the Temple to Cambodia. Ironically, had the 1962 judgment ignored the Annex F map, as the ICJ chose to ignore it in 2013, and relied instead on the text of the 1904 treaty that followed the watershed, it would have had to conclude that the Temple is, in fact, not in Cambodia but in Thailand. As pointed out in the dissenting opinion of Chinese judge Wellington Koo in the 1962 judgment, the map was one of a set of 11, drawn on the scale of 1:200,000, with the ground between the alleged frontier line and the Temple represented by a width of only 2.5 millimetres. Since Siam could not have possibly known that the Annex I map had awarded the Temple to Cambodia, Siam could not have acquiesced or been expected to protest. Judge Koo was realistic enough to point out that the colonial conditions in Indo-China at the time meant Siam could not have been expected to protest in the period of colonial expansion, for otherwise France could have taken the Temple by force. In his dissenting opinion, Australian Judge Sir Percy Spender found no evidence to suggest Siam knew of the contents of any of the map sheets before they were delivered to its minister at the Thai Embassy in Paris. He also alluded to the fact that France did not consult Siam about the production of the map but presented it with a fait accompli. Judge Spender also supported Judge Koo's opinion that by protesting Siam would only have given the French an excuse to seize more territory. The 1962 judgment was not willing to recognise claims made by states that did not fit in with its understanding of traditional Western methods of displaying territorial sovereignty. This was despite the fact that local Siamese authorities collected taxes in the area, granted permits to cut timber, sent forestry officers on inspections, built a road to the foot of Mount Preah Vihear/Phra Viharn, and sent guardians to the Temple. The majority in the ICJ held that the evidence Thailand presented at the ICJ to show its exercise of sovereign authority (*effectivité*) in the area of the Temple was not clothed in a legal form with which the ICJ was familiar,[44] whereas the ICJ had no doubt that the French topographical officers who produced the Annex I map acted in complete good faith, used all their skill and fully believed that the watershed in the Preah Vihear region ran as indicated by the Annex I line. The 1962 judgment was not prepared to recognise or give effect to displays of authority by local Siamese officials or sympathise with Siam's lack of topographical and cartographical expertise. Conceivably, the dispute over the Temple could have been readily resolved if, as Judge Moreno Quintana from Argentina opined in his dissenting opinion, the ICJ had ignored the Annex I map altogether and instead interpreted Article I of the 1904 treaty ac-

[44] That is, the Westphalian system of exercise of sovereignty.

cording to its natural and ordinary meaning. Even British judge Fitzmaurice, one in the majority, conceded in his separate opinion that the Temple had originally been located in Siam as a result of an 1867 treaty between Siam and France.

Thailand could claim it won the case in 2013 in the sense that the ICJ ruled that the dispute area was a "small one", concerned only with sovereignty in the "region of the Temple of Preah Vihear" and the ICJ unequivocally rejected Cambodia's contention that the "vicinity" included not only the promontory of Preah Vihear but also the hill of Phnom Trap.[45] Contrary to Cambodia's submission, the ICJ kept itself strictly within the limits of the original judgment in 1962 and refrained from answering questions the ICJ did not decide in 1962.[46]

It was partly the change of government in Thailand in August 2011 that, to a certain extent, cooled down the nationalistic/patriotic/irredentist atmosphere that had led to the armed conflicts between Thailand and Cambodia. When Cambodia unilaterally requested UNESCO to inscribe the Temple on the UNESCO World Heritage List in 2006, Thailand opposed it, leading to the UNESCO World Heritage Committee's deferral of this application by Cambodia until 2008. In February 2008, five months before the Committee's meeting then scheduled for August 2008, the Thai foreign minister at that time met with the Cambodian delegation in Paris to ask Cambodia to leave their disputed area out of its application. On 18 June 2008, the two sides and UNESCO's assistant director-general for culture signed a joint communiqué drafted by UNESCO's representatives, without prejudice to the rights of Cambodia and Thailand on the demarcation works of the Joint Commission for Land Boundary of the two countries. The new sketch map used by Cambodia to identify the area of the proposed World Heritage site did not encompass their disputed 4.6-square-kilometre land territory. Back home in Thailand and against the background of ongoing political turmoil in the country, the foreign minister was accused of helping Cambodia succeed in getting the Temple inscribed as a UNESCO World Heritage site. After Thailand's Central Administrative Court ordered an interim injunction on 27 June 2008 against the use of the joint communiqué dated 18 June 2008, the Thai Foreign Ministry sent a diplomatic note to the Ministry of Foreign Affairs of Cambodia and UNESCO, with copies thereof to all members of the UNESCO World Heritage Committee, to suspend the effect of the joint communiqué. When the

[45] ICJ Rep. 2013, p. 309 [38] and pp. 314–5 [92]–[6].

[46] Ibid., p. 306 [66], p. 307 [71], p. 316 [101] and p. 317 [104].

Temple was inscribed as a World Heritage site on 7 July 2008, the decision to inscribe it expressly states that the joint communiqué "must be disregarded, following the decision of the Government of Thailand to suspend the effect of the Joint Communiqué, pursuant to the Thai Administrative Court's interim injunction on this issue".[47] Subsequently, the Thai Constitutional Court ruled on 8 August 2008 that the joint communiqué of 18 June 2008 did not bind Thailand because it was a treaty concerning territorial integrity of the country which needed to be approved by the Thai parliament prior to being signed by the Thai government, and this constitutional step was not followed. The Constitutional Court added, in passing, that the joint communiqué might make Thailand lose sovereignty over the land territory over which Cambodia also claimed. This ruling seemed to arouse nationalist/patriotic/irredentist sentiment among those Thais who still could not accept the ICJ's 1962 judgment and compel the Thai military to "defend" Thailand's sovereignty from Cambodia's encroachment at any cost. Two days after the judgment of the Thai Constitutional Court, the Thai foreign minister resigned.[48] On 25 August 2008, Thailand notified Cambodia that the joint communiqué was null and void and, in reply, Cambodia stated that the joint communiqué was not an international agreement or treaty at all. That foreign minister's political party left office on 17 December 2008 and returned to run the country once again in August 2011. Both the Thai and the Cambodian governments then played down the conflict, leaving their officers at the technical level to work out how to implement the ICJ's 2013 judgment. On 4 September 2015, after weighing all the evidence, the Thai Supreme Court's Criminal Division for Holders of Political Offices, by a majority of six to three, acquitted the said foreign minister of the charge of wrongful or dishonest exercise of official functions by signing the joint communiqué with Cambodia in 2008.

South China Sea Disputes

The legal status of the following disputed islands or maritime geographical features has been left indetermined, together with questions as to what extent prior historic claims have an enduring effect on contemporary territorial title: the Dokdo/Takeshima dispute between South Korea and Japan; the Diaoyu/Senkaku Islands dispute between China and Japan; the South Kuril Islands/

---

[47] World Heritage Committee, Decision 32 COM 8B.102, para. 5.

[48] See further, Puangthong R. Pawakapan, *State and Uncivil Society in Thailand at the Temple of Preah Vihear* (Singapore: ISEAS-Yusof Ishak Institute, 2013), pp. 37–98.

Hoppo Ryodo dispute between Russia and Japan; the Paracel (Xisha) Islands dispute between China and Vietnam; and the Spratly (Nansha) Islands disputes among Brunei, Malaysia, China, Vietnam and the Philippines.[49]

This chapter will focus on the disputes in the South China Sea, which Vietnam calls the East Sea, since they have generated the most international concerns. Some of the world's busiest and most strategic sea lines of communication are in the South China Sea, eight of the world's ten busiest container ports are in the Asia-Pacific region, almost one-third of the world's maritime trade transits the South China Sea each year, over half of the world's annual merchant fleet tonnage passes through the South China Sea annually, and approximately US$5.3 trillion in shipborne trade (US$1.2 trillion bound for the United States) transits through the South China Sea annually. Each year, about two-thirds of the world's oil shipments transit through the Indian Ocean to the Pacific Ocean through the South China Sea.[50]

Vietnam claims it has maintained effective occupation of both the Paracel and Spratly Islands since at least the 17th century.[51]

China has argued that the "nine-dash line", which it drew to assert its claims over the South China Sea including "islands" therein, has been established and developed in the long process of history without protests from foreign states for a long time. Several Chinese scholars contend that the maritime geographical features, which China calls "islands", in the South China Sea were first discovered by China's Western Han dynasty as early as the second century BCE, more than two millennia ago, and that their discovery was reinforced by a Chinese mission in the third century CE to Cambodia, which made accounts of the Paracels and Spratlys, and between the tenth and 14th centuries, during the period of the Song and Yuan dynasties, many official and unofficial Chinese accounts

[49] Hitoshi Nasu and Donald R. Rothwell, "Re-evaluating the Role of International Law in Territorial and Maritime Disputes in East Asia", *Asian Journal of International Law* 4 (2014): 55, 57–61. See also Christian Schultheiss, *Ocean Governance and Conflict in the East and South China Sea: Negotiating Natural Resources, Institutions and Power* (Amsterdam: Amsterdam University Press 2024).

[50] Raul (Pete) Pedrozo, "Is a South China Sea Code of Conduct Viable?", *International Law Studies* 97 (2021): 937, 952–3. For an interdisciplinary analysis combining international law and international relations to address the South China Sea dispute, see Youngmin Seo, *The South China Sea Dispute as International Law and Politics: Discovering the Role of Law in Times of Power Shift* (Leiden: Brill, 2024).

[51] See also Raul (Pete) Pedrozo, "Vietnam's Indisputable Sovereignty over the Paracel Islands", in *Peaceful Management of Maritime Disputes*, ed. James Kraska and Heecheol Yang, pp. 193–213 (Abingdon: Routledge, 2023).

show the South China Sea to be within China's national boundaries.[52] Taiwan, which is recognised by some states as the Republic of China but which the People's Republic of China considers to be part of mainland China, apparently relies on this legal argument to maintain its claims in the South China Sea, while also trying to justify it in light of relevant legal principles stipulated in the 1982 United Nations Convention on the Law of the Sea (UNCLOS), to which the PRC, but not Taiwan, is party.[53]

In August 2023, China's Natural Resources Ministry published the latest edition of "China Standard Map", which reaffirms China's claim in the South China Sea and which has been immediately denounced by the other claimants.

Chinese international lawyers rely on the rule of "intertemporal law" in support of its claim that China's "nine-dash line" is based on historic rights that can and do continue to coexist alongside and independent from modern rules of international law, including UNCLOS.[54] As Max Huber, sole arbitrator, noted in the *Island of Palmas Case (Netherlands v. USA)*, "international law underwent profound modifications between the end of the Middle-Ages and the end of the nineteenth century, as regards the rights of discovery and acquisition of uninhabited regions or regions inhabited by savages or semi-civilised peoples", and "a juridical fact must be appreciated in the light of the law contemporary with it, and not of the law in force at the time when a dispute in regard to it arises or falls to be settled".[55] This has been followed by the ICJ in, for example, *Land and Maritime Boundary between Cameroon and Nigeria*

---

[52] Chinese Society of International Law, "The South China Sea Arbitration Awards: A Critical Study", *Chinese Journal of International Law* 17 (2018): 207, 455–65; Taisaku Ikeshima, "China's Dashed Line in the South China Sea: Legal Limits and Future Prospects", *Waseda Global Forum* 10 (2013): 17.

[53] Frédéric Lasserre, "Maritime Borders in the South China Sea: Dynamics of Claims and Legal Basis", in *Assessing Maritime Disputes in East Asia: Political and Legal Perspectives*, ed. Barthélémy Courmont and Frédéric Lasserre (Abingdon: Routledge, 2017), p. 122 at pp. 128–30. See also Bill Hayton, "Claim-Making in the Paracel Islands 1802–1936" in *Peaceful Management of Maritime Disputes*, ch. 8.

[54] National Institute of South China Sea Studies, "A Legal Critique of the Award of the Arbitral Tribunal in the *Matter of the South China Sea Arbitration*", *Asian Yearbook of International Law* 24 (2018): 151, 155–77; Chris Whomersley, "The Award on the Merits in the Case Brought by the Philippines against China relating to the South China Sea: A Critique", *Chinese Journal of International Law* 17 (2018): 387, 388–92. See also Nasu and Rothwell, "Re-evaluating the Role of International Law in Territorial and Maritime Disputes in East Asia", 64–5.

[55] Award of 4 Apr. 1928, 2 R.I.A.A. 829 at 856.

(Cameroon v. Nigeria: Equatorial Guinea intervening), where the ICJ held that, "even if [a] mode of acquisition does not reflect current international law, the principle of intertemporal law requires that the legal consequences of the [acts] at that time . . . be given effect today, in the present dispute".[56] It has also been pointed out that when China was unable to exercise any form of effective exercise of sovereign authority over its frontier regions it was able to secure its future sovereignty over Tibet and Mongolia through the principle of suzerainty or political hegemony over vassal entities, a concept widely used in 19th-century international law as an imperial legal technique to describe the political and legal identities of territories on the periphery of non-Western imperial state systems. In fact, as Western contacts with China increased, and as it became necessary to define the boundaries between China and Asian territories under Western influence or control, suzerainty was increasingly used in the West to denote China's relationships with territories within its periphery during the second part of the 19th century.[57]

Invoking the intertemporal law of discovery of unoccupied territories to support China's legal position in this matter is somewhat at odds with the understanding of the much-later international law governing acquisition of territories, which requires more than mere discovery of the territories in question. For instance, in *Territorial and Maritime Dispute (Nicaragua v. Colombia)* the ICJ found that neither Nicaragua nor Colombia had established that it had title to the disputed maritime features by virtue of *uti possidetis juris* (the principle that, upon independence, new states inherit the territories and boundaries of the former colonial provinces), because nothing clearly indicated whether these features were attributed to the colonial provinces of Nicaragua or of Colombia. The ICJ then ruled that Colombia has sovereignty over the maritime features in dispute since Colombia has continuously and consistently exercised its sovereign authority (*à titre de souverain*) in respect of both the maritime area surrounding the disputed features and the maritime features themselves for many decades. This exercise of sovereign authority was public and there is no evidence that it met with any protest from Nicaragua prior to the critical date. Moreover, the evidence of Colombia's acts of admin-

---

[56] ICJ Rep. 2002, p. 303, at p. 405 [205].

[57] Yuan, "Suzerainty, Semi-Sovereignty", 296, 302–4. See also David Ong, "Discerning the International Legal Threshold for Sovereignty over Islands: Implications for Judicial Settlement of International Disputes", in *Peaceful Management of Maritime Disputes*, ch. 1.

istration with respect to the islands contrasts with the absence of any evidence of acts *à titre de souverain* on the part of Nicaragua.[58]

Some Chinese legal scholars contend that China does not have much motivation to abide by those principles of customary international law it considers discriminatory because customary international law was created and developed by the West and China was deprived of the chance to play a role in the process of international norm creation[59] and the law, which was based on Western legal order, was unfairly imposed upon the Chinese.[60] This may be how the legal basis for China's territorial claim over maritime geographical features in the South China Sea seems to differ from rules of international law on acquisition of territories developed in the Western world during eras of colonisation, requiring effective occupation and exercise of sovereign authority over no man's land (terra nullius). China did not seem to have ever accomplished this over such maritime geographical features.[61] However, it is equally arguable that Western nations did not faithfully fulfil these conditions for the purpose of colonising territories abroad, starting from the Papal Bull of 1493 dividing the "new world" between Spain and Portugal and the Congress of Berlin concerning the Congo in 1884–85 that adopted the General Act to split Africa into spheres of influences among the then European states grabbing territories in Africa.[62] As one distinguished Chinese professor of international law points out, weak though the burdens of "effective occupation" as imposed under the

---

[58] ICJ Rep. 2012, p. 624 at pp. 655 [81] and 657 [84].

[59] For example, Pan, "Chinese Philosophy and International Law", 241. See also Isaac B. Kardon, *China's Law of the Sea: The New Rules of Maritime Order* (New Haven, CT: Yale University Press, 2023), pp. 41–72, 257–70.

[60] Xue, "China's Open Policy and International Law", 134.

[61] It should be noted that China commenced its underwater archaeological excavations in the South China Sea in the 1990s to find historical evidence of China's ancient activities in the South China Sea and on 18 Feb. 2023 a centre was officially set up for this purpose in China's southern island province of Hainan ("South China Sea Archaeology Centre to Boost Beijing's Claims", *Bangkok Post*, 23 Feb. 2023, https://www.bangkokpost.com/world/2511704/south-china-sea-archaeology-centre-aims-to-boost-beijings-claims). The excavations from 2023 to 2024 reportedly retrieved more than 900 pieces of cultural relics from two ancient shipwrecks discovered in the South China Sea dating to the Ming Dynasty (1368–1644). The Chinese authorities stated that this discovery provided evidence that Chinese ancestors developed, utilised and travelled to and from the South China Sea to trade and engage in cultural exchanges along the ancient Maritime Silk Road (Xinhua, "Over 900 Pieces of Relics Retrieved from Shipwrecks in South China Sea", 13 June 2024, https://english.news.cn/20240613/60116daccfb74c65a764ae5f500f20a9/c.html).

[62] General Act of the Conference of Berlin concerning the Congo, Chapter VI, *American Journal of International Law Supplement* 1 (1909): 7, 24. See also Henan Hu, "The Doctrine

General Act were, they still gave rise to various ways to circumvent them, or to lower them further, to the extent that they became almost non-existent, by claiming a "sphere of influence", where a European power claimed by declaration or agreement a sphere of influence (that is, political dominion) over a defined area usually adjoining an area under its sovereignty or protection, with or without intent to occupy it but definitely without having to shoulder any of the burdens of effective occupation. Another method was the theory of the hinterland, where a power having established a base on the coast claimed the right of priority over the vast area of the related hinterland to the limits of the navigable rivers, and so on, again without having to shoulder any burdens. Still another method was through leases granted to foreign states, usually under certain coercion.[63]

Following a series of provocations and reprisals starting in the summer of 1973, a briefly fought war broke out between China and South Vietnam on 19 January 1974 over the Paracels, located roughly equidistant between China and Vietnam. Before the battle, part of the Paracels was controlled by China and another part was controlled by South Vietnam. The battle lasted several hours. The Chinese navy sank one minesweeper, damaged three warships, killed or wounded over a hundred Vietnamese officers and sailors, captured 48 soldiers and seized three islands, bringing the entire Paracel archipelago under China's control. The South Vietnamese navy put one Chinese minesweeper out of action, shot up three other warships, killed 18 and wounded 67 other Chinese.[64] On 14 March 1988, an armed clash between the Chinese navy and the Vietnamese navy took place at Johnson South Reef in the Spratly Islands, close to the Vietnamese inhibited Sin Cowe Island and within the Philippines' claimed 200-nautical-mile exclusive economic zone. Sixty-four Vietnamese soldiers were reportedly killed and three Vietnamese naval vessels were lost. The Chinese succeeded in occupying the reef. The nine Vietnamese taken prisoner by the Chinese navy during the armed conflict were subsequently released on 2 September 1991. China and Vietnam started the first round of talks on the so-called "sea issues" in November 1995, followed by several rounds thereafter with very little progress due partly to disagreement

---

of Occupation: An Analysis of Its Invalidity under the Framework of International Legal Positivism", *Chinese Journal of International Law* 15 (2016): 75, 80, 103–38.

[63] Sienho Yee, "Territory in the Work of the Institut de Droit International", *Chinese Journal of International Law* 21 (2022): 219, 232.

[64] Toshi Yoshihara, "The 1974 Paracels Sea Battle: A Campaign Appraisal", *Naval War College Review* 69 (2016): 1.

over the issues to be included in the agenda, with Vietnam pushing for the inclusion of the issue of the Paracels while China insisted on excluding this topic.[65]

Brunei claims sovereignty over Louisa Reef, which lies atop its continental shelf. Louisa Reef is also claimed by China and Vietnam. Malaysia claims a portion of the South China Sea north of Borneo that is within the continental shelf proclaimed by Malaysia. This encompasses no fewer than 12 features in the Spratly Islands, including the Vietnamese-occupied Amboyna Cay and Barque Canada Reef, as well as the Philippine-occupied Commodore and Rizal Reefs. Malaysia also claims two low-tide elevations and three completely submerged reefs that are on its continental shelf. In 1978, the Philippines formally claimed certain maritime geographical features in the Spratlys called the Kalayan ("Freedom" in Filipino) Group, as no man's land (terra nullius) and based on their geographical location on the Philippine continental margin under the administrative control of its Palawan Province.[66] Since 2011, the Philippines has officially named the portion of the South China Sea claimed by it the West Philippine Sea.

On 22 January 2013, the Philippines instituted arbitral proceedings against China under Annex VII to UNCLOS. An Annex VII arbitral tribunal is the "default" or "residual" mechanism under UNCLOS where disputing parties have not chosen a means for the settlement of disputes under UNCLOS or do not agree on the same choice of dispute settlement forum. The arbitration concerned the role of historic rights and the source of maritime entitlements in the South China Sea, the status of certain maritime features in the South China Sea, and the lawfulness of certain actions by China in the South China Sea that the Philippines alleged to be in violation of UNCLOS. China adopted a position of non-acceptance and non-participation in the proceedings. The Permanent Court of Arbitration served as the registry in this arbitration. Because China has excluded sovereignty and maritime boundary disputes from the jurisdiction of the dispute settlement regime under UNCLOS, the Philippines emphasised it was not asking the tribunal to decide the question of sovereignty over maritime features in the South China Sea claimed by both the Philippines and China. Nor did the Philippines ask the tribunal to delimit any maritime boundary between the two states. On 29 October 2015 the Arbitral Tribunal ruled that it had jurisdiction over several of the Philippines' claims,

---

[65] Amer and Nguyen, "Vietnam's Border Disputes", 118.

[66] See also Jon Van Dyke and Mark Valencia, "How Valid Are the South China Sea Claims under the Law of the Sea Convention?", *Southeast Asian Affairs* 2000 at 47ff.

that China's decision not to participate in these proceedings did not deprive the tribunal of jurisdiction, and that the Philippines' decision to commence arbitration unilaterally was not an abuse of the dispute settlement procedures under UNCLOS.[67]

On 12 July 2016, the tribunal rendered its award on the merits.[68] On historic rights and the "nine-dash line", the tribunal concluded that UNCLOS comprehensively allocates rights to maritime areas, and that protections for pre-existing rights to resources were considered but not adopted by the Third UN Conference on the Law of the Sea, which negotiated UNCLOS. Therefore, to the extent China had historic rights to resources in the waters of the South China Sea, such rights were extinguished insofar as they were incompatible with the exclusive economic zones not extending beyond 200 nautical miles from the baselines from which the breadth of the territorial sea is measured where the coastal State has, inter alia, sovereign rights for the purpose of exploring and exploiting, conserving and managing the natural resources, whether living or non-living, of the waters superjacent to the seabed and of the seabed and its subsoil, and with regard to other activities for the economic exploitation and exploration of the zone, as provided for in UNCLOS.

The tribunal added that, although Chinese navigators and fishermen, as well as those of other states, had historically made use of the islands in the South China Sea, there was no evidence that China had historically exercised exclusive control over the waters or their resources; hence, China has no legal basis to claim historic rights to resources within the sea areas falling within the "nine-dash line".

The tribunal next considered entitlements to maritime areas and the status of the maritime geographical features within the "nine-dash line". Those features that are low-tide elevations cannot be appropriated, although a coastal state has sovereignty over low-tide elevations that are situated within its territorial sea, since it has sovereignty over the territorial sea itself. The tribunal

[67] *South China Sea Arbitration (Philippines v. China)*, Award on Jurisdiction and Admissibility, PCA Case Repository 2013–19 (PCA, 2015). For harsh criticisms of this decision on jurisdiction and admissibility, see "Special Issue on Jurisdiction and Admissibility of the South China Sea Arbitration", *Chinese Journal of International Law* 15 (2016): 217–487; Stefan Talmon, *The South China Sea Arbitration: Jurisdiction, Admissibility, Procedure* (Leiden: Brill, 2022). *Contra*: Alfredo C. Robles, Jr., *The Defaulting State and the South China Sea Arbitration* (Singapore: Palgrave Macmillan, 2023), pp. 79–188.

[68] *South China Sea Arbitration (Philippines v. China)*, Award, PCA Case Repository 2013–19 (PCA, 2016).

then proceeded to consider the other features. Article 121(1) of UNCLOS stipulates: "An island is a naturally formed area of land, surrounded by water, which is above water at high tide." Itu Aba, known as "Taiping Dao" in China and "Ligaw" in the Philippines, is the largest high-tide feature in the Spratly Islands, measuring approximately 1.4 kilometres in length and almost 400 metres at its widest point, with a surface area of approximately 0.43 square kilometres. Article 121(1) must be read conjunctively with Article 121(3) of UNCLOS. The latter provision stipulates that "[r]ocks which cannot sustain human habitation or economic life of their own shall have no exclusive economic zone or continental shelf". The tribunal noted that the Spratly Islands were historically used by small groups of fishermen and that several Japanese fishing and guano mining enterprises had been attempted. The tribunal concluded that such transient use does not constitute inhabitation by a stable community and that all of the historical economic activity had been extractive. Therefore, concluded the tribunal, none of the Spratly Islands fulfilled the conditions under Article 121(3) for it to be capable of generating extended maritime zones.[69] The tribunal also held that the Spratly Islands could not generate maritime zones collectively as a unit. Having ruled that none of the maritime features claimed by China was capable of generating an exclusive economic zone, the tribunal found that it could—without delimiting a boundary—declare that certain sea areas are within the exclusive economic zone of the Philippines, because those areas are not overlapped by any possible entitlement of China.

The tribunal further found that China had violated the Philippines' sovereign rights in the latter's exclusive economic zone by (1) interfering with Philippine fishing and petroleum exploration, (2) constructing artificial islands and (3) failing to prevent Chinese fishermen from fishing in the zone. The tribunal also ruled that fishermen from the Philippines (like those from China) had traditional fishing rights at Scarborough Shoal, an atoll situated in the north-east of the South China Sea approximately 116 nautical miles west of the Philippine island of Luzon and 448 nautical miles south of the Chinese mainland, which has been claimed by both the Philippines and China and which

[69] *Contra*: Myron H. Nordquist, "UNCLOS Article 121 and Itu Aba in the South China Sea Final Award: A Correct Interpretation?", in *The South China Sea Arbitration: The Legal Dimension*, ed. S. Jayakumar, Tommy Koh, Robert Beckman, Tara Davenport and Hao Duy Phan (Cheltenham: Edward Elgar Publishing, 2018), ch. 8. See also Malcolm D. Evans and Reese Lewis, *Islands, Law and Context: The Treatment of Islands in International Law* (Cheltenham: Edward Elgar Publishing, 2023), pp. 37–62.

has been under China's de facto control since 2012, and that China had interfered with these rights by restricting access thereto. The tribunal further held that Chinese law enforcement vessels had unlawfully created a serious risk of collision when they physically obstructed Philippine vessels. After considering the effect on the marine environment of China's recent large-scale land reclamation and construction of artificial islands at seven features in the Spratly Islands, the tribunal found that China had caused severe harm to the coral reef environment and violated its obligation to preserve and protect fragile ecosystems and the habitat of depleted, threatened or endangered species. The tribunal also found that Chinese authorities were aware that Chinese fishermen had harvested endangered sea turtles, coral and giant clams on a substantial scale in the South China Sea (using methods that inflict severe damage on the coral reef environment) and had not fulfilled their obligations to stop such activities. Finally, on the question of whether China's actions since the commencement of the arbitration had aggravated the dispute between the parties, the tribunal found that it lacked jurisdiction to consider the implications of a stand-off between Philippine marines and Chinese naval and law enforcement vessels at Second Thomas Shoal, or Ren'ai Jiao in Chinese, where a small Philippine military contingent was based on board a rusting Philippine naval vessel, the *Sierra Madre*, deliberately grounded atop the shoal by the Philippines in 1999 in an attempt to consolidate its claim to the shoal, because this dispute involved military activities that China had declared to be excluded from compulsory dispute settlement under UNCLOS. The tribunal found, however, that China's recent large-scale land reclamation and construction of artificial islands was incompatible with the obligations on a state during dispute resolution proceedings, insofar as China had inflicted irreparable harm to the marine environment, built a large artificial island in the Philippines' exclusive economic zone, and destroyed evidence of the natural condition of features in the South China Sea that formed part of the parties' dispute.[70]

---

[70] For harsh criticisms of this award, see National Institute of South China Sea Studies, "A Legal Critique of the Award of the Arbitral Tribunal in the *Matter of the South China Sea Arbitration*", 151–293; Chinese Society of International Law, "The South China Sea Arbitration Awards: A Critical Study", 207–784; *Journal of Boundaries & Ocean Studies–Selected Papers* 1(1) (Spring 2019): *passim*. See also Lingqun Li, *China's Policy towards the South China Sea: When Geopolitics Meets the Law of the Sea* (Abingdon: Routledge, 2019), ch. 7; Diane A. Desierto, "Enforcement Options and Paths to Compliance: Disputants and Global Stakeholders in *Philippines v. China*", *Asian Journal of International Law* 8 (2018): 64; Robles, Jr., *The Defaulting State and the South China Sea Arbitration*, pp. 189ff.

Although the tribunal in the *South China Sea Arbitration* clarified a number of legal issues pertaining to the South China Sea dispute, there remains considerable uncertainty pertaining to the sovereignty claims, the status of many maritime geographical features in the Spratly Islands not considered by the tribunal in that case and the effect of their location in relation to other Spratly Island features. This is the case of, for example, Whitsun Reef. The Philippines and Vietnam lodged diplomatic protests against China after the presence of more than 200 Chinese fishing vessels at the reef. Whitsun Reef is part of a larger reef formation known as Union Banks within the disputed Spratly Islands, which lies within the Philippines' 200-nautical-mile exclusive economic zone but within the territorial sea of islands subject to competing sovereignty claims of China, the Philippines and Vietnam.[71]

It should be noted that Article 293(1) of UNCLOS on applicable law wisely stipulates that a court or tribunal having jurisdiction thereunder "shall apply [UNCLOS] and other rules of international law not incompatible with [UNCLOS]". As one can see from the ongoing South China Sea disputes, "other rules of international law" can be resorted to so as to settle or manage the disputes, including the law of the UN Charter, customary international law, and international rules on the acquisition of territories, international cooperation and peaceful coexistence.

Rules of International Law in Favour of Non-use of Force to Settle Sovereignty Disputes

The 1970 Declaration on Friendly Relations, which the ICJ has held to reflect rules of customary international law, enunciates in this regard that "[e]very State has the duty to refrain from the threat or use of force to violate the existing international boundaries of another State or as a means of solving international disputes, including territorial disputes and problems concerning frontiers of States" and that "States have a duty to refrain from acts of reprisal involving the use of force".

Furthermore, pursuant to the rule of customary international law on *critical date*, rights and entitlements are frozen at the time when a dispute crystallises, after which date no acts attempting to improve the legal position of the party relying on them shall be of value to manifest, advance or affect that party's claim

---

71 Robert Beckman and Tara Davenport, "South China Sea Dispute: Whitsun Reef—Awash in a Sea of (Legal) Uncertainty", *Straits Times,* 13 Apr. 2021, https://www.straitstimes.com/opinion/whitsun-reef-awash-in-a-sea-of-legal-uncertainty.

in any way whatsoever.[72] This rule thus nullifies any act by a militarily stronger state in its attempt to consolidate its legal entitlement based on its political, military or other strength to the detriment of a weaker state.

Under customary international law, timely notification of *protests* against competing claims, coupled with reservation of rights through continued peaceful assertion of claims, suffices to rebut any presumption of acquiescence or estoppel in relation to the dispute in question.[73]

Restraint from engaging particular acts beyond a particular point in a disputed maritime area or general abstention from acting in relation thereto has been interpreted by international courts and tribunals in a positive light: the restraint is born out of a desire not to negatively influence the ongoing dispute by adding complications or extending its duration.[74]

One analyst has lucidly narrated how this has actually been happening in the disputed areas of South China Sea.[75] Chinese Coast Guard (CCG) vessels have repeatedly entered waters off the coast of Malaysia's Sabah and Sarawak and the waters north of Indonesia's Natuna Islands, which the latter two states claim as parts of their respective maritime zones but which intersect with China's "nine-dash line". The increasing intensity of the CCG's entry into these maritime areas has been probably motivated by the discovery of economically viable oil fields in Kasawari in 2011, located in Central Luconia off the coast of Sarawak, and Tuna Block in 2014, located in the northern part of the Natunas. China has demanded that both Malaysia and Indonesia cease their oil exploration and exploitation on the contested continental shelves. In response,

---

[72] *Sovereignty over Pulau Ligitan and Pulau Sipadan (Indonesia/Malaysia)*, ICJ Rep. 2002, p. 625 at p. 682 [135]; *Territorial and Maritime Dispute between Nicaragua and Honduras in the Caribbean Sea (Nicaragua v. Honduras)*, ICJ Rep. 2007, p. 659 at pp. 697–8 [117]; *Territorial and Maritime Dispute (Nicaragua v. Colombia)*, ICJ Rep. 2012, p. 624 at p. 652 [67].

[73] See, for example, *Island of Palmas Case*, p. 868; *Anglo-Norwegian Fisheries* case, ICJ Rep. 1951, p. 116 at pp. 138–9; *Land, Island and Maritime Frontier Dispute (El Salvador v. Honduras: Nicaragua intervening)*, ICJ Rep. 1992, p. 351, at p. 579 [368]; *Sovereignty over Pulau Ligitan and Pulau Sipadan*, p. 685 [148]; *Sovereignty over Pedra Branca/Pulau Batu Puteh, Middle Rocks and South Ledge (Malaysia/Singapore)*, ICJ Rep. 2008, p. 12 at p. 96 [276]; *Territorial and Maritime Dispute (Nicaragua v. Colombia)*, p. 657 [84].

[74] Youri van Logchem, *The Rights and Obligations of States in Disputed Maritime Areas* (Cambridge: Cambridge University Press, 2021), p. 72, citing *Territorial and Maritime Dispute between Nicaragua and Honduras in the Caribbean Sea* at pp. 735–6 [254]; *Sovereignty over Pulau Ligitan and Pulau Sipadan*, p. 664 [79].

[75] Emirza Adi Syailendra, "China, Indonesia, and Malaysia Waltzing around Oil Rigs", *The Diplomat*, 18 Aug. 2022, https://thediplomat.com/2022/08/china-indonesia-and-malaysia-waltzing-around-oil-rigs/.

the Royal Malaysian Navy (RMN) and the Indonesian Navy (TNI-AL) have adopted the practice of "shadowing" CCG vessels that enter the maritime zones claimed by each of them, rather than confronting and forcing the CCG vessels to leave the areas. Malaysia and Indonesia consider Chinese assertiveness something reactionary, as opposed to anticipatory, and believe that, for their economically beneficial relationships with China to deepen, Beijing should be afforded the room to express hostility within respectively agreeable red lines. When CCG vessels step forward, the RMN and TNI-AL step backwards, and vice-versa. The rule of engagement is "do not escalate first" and there is a need for both sides to save face. Significantly, Malaysia discouraged the United States and Australia from getting involved as the CCG and RMN engaged each other in the West Capella area in April 2020. Malaysia's red line is any physical interference with its natural resource exploitation activities. Malaysia has adopted the shadowing policy since 2009—the year when China became Malaysia's largest trading partner. Indonesia started this practice in 2017, with China's growing investments in and trading with Indonesia. In 2021, China became Indonesia's largest supplier of vaccines against COVID-19, accounting for more than 80 per cent of the vaccines available in Indonesia. Many policymakers in Jakarta have also recognised China's decision not to deploy military escorts to shield its survey ship, the Haiyang Dizhi, between August and September 2021, from the TNI-AL as a measure of restraint. This combination of factors made Indonesia willing to offer some room for China to enter the waters in the northern part of the Natuna Sea as long as this remained non-military in nature, and China refrained from physically interfering with Indonesia's oil exploration activities in the area. If China crosses the red lines, Malaysia and Indonesia are confident that the legality of their claim is undisputable and that they will be supported by the international community. When the red line is crossed, as when 16 Chinese military aircraft flew over disputed waters off Malaysia's Sarawak in April 2021, the Malaysian government lodged an official protest against China and the tension was resolved amicably behind the scenes.

On 6 June 2024, at the 37th Asia-Pacific Roundtable, hosted by the Institute of Strategic & International Studies (ISIS) Malaysia in Kuala Lumpur, the prime minister of Malaysia reportedly called for "aggressive" diplomatic engagement to resolve disputes in the South China Sea, pointing out that Malaysia itself had been "rather successful" in dealing with the South China Sea issue diplomatically, because it was "deemed and seemed to be really neutral in the engagement". Taking a question from a Philippine delegate on Malaysia's approach as the ASEAN chair for 2025 to address the Philippines' concerns in the

South China Sea, the prime minister said Malaysia would continue its active engagement within the ASEAN framework, and that the issue had to be resolved among ASEAN member countries and China, without the interference of external parties because it would be deemed to be more complex and complicate the matter.[76]

For its part, China's restraint is likely to be tested by the signing on 23 December 2022 by Indonesia and Vietnam of the agreement to delimit their exclusive economic zone within China's nine-dash line. The agreement was finalised after 12 years of negotiations between Indonesia and Vietnam.[77] On 2 January 2023 Indonesia announced its approval of the first plan of development for the Tuna offshore gas field, located in the South China Sea between Indonesia and Vietnam, with total estimated investment of US$3.07 billion up to the start of production. The Tuna field is expected to reach peak production of 115 million standard cubic feet per day in 2027, and natural gas from the field is expected to be exported to Vietnam starting in 2026. Of interest is the fact that China's CCG 5901, the world's largest coastguard vessel, left China's Sanya port in Hainan Island on 16 December 2022 and arrived in Indonesia's exclusive economic zone on 30 December 2022 and was observed sailing the Natuna Sea in early January 2023.

Also of special significance is Article 2(3) of the UN Charter, which obligates UN member states to settle disputes by peaceful means.

Asian states usually do not resort to third-party dispute settlement mechanisms, because of the Asian cultural sensitivity concerning losing face and honour should the judgment award the disputed territory or maritime area to another state. This is despite the fact that decisions of courts and tribunals can dispose of a troublesome issue when the resolution of a dispute is considered to be more important than the result, particularly when the dispute does not involve sensitive questions of sovereignty. Even for disputes involving sensitive questions of sovereignty, impartial decisions by internationally recognised judges that are based on recognised principles must be considered fair and neutral to the parties as well as to their national electorates. Moreover, litigation takes decision-making out of the hands of governments, thereby allowing governments

---

[76] Xinhua, "Malaysian PM Urges Diplomatic Engagement, Rejects External Interference on South China Sea", *China Daily*, 7 June 2024, https://www.chinadaily.com.cn/a/202406/07/WS6663083aa31082fc043cb88a.html.

[77] See also Nguyen Hong Thao, "Indonesia-Vietnam Maritime Delimitation: From a Single-Line to Double-Line", in *Asia and UNCLOS 30 Years' Implementation: An Assessment*, ed. Nguyen Hong Thao and Vu Hai Dang (Singapore: Springer, 2024), ch. 12.

to avoid one of the pitfalls of negotiations, namely the perception of national electorates that governments have given up too much—at the very least, there is an external third party that can be "blamed" for a decision that is not favourable to a disputing party. Also, resorting to binding dispute settlement mechanisms can facilitate negotiations towards an agreed settlement.[78] In several cases, the final judgments can be perceived as accommodating or reconciling the conflicting positions of the disputing parties.

The reluctance by Asian states to submit their border and territorial disputes to international litigation also derives from the significant weight accorded to the decisions or conducts of colonial powers by international courts and tribunals on territorial claims involving colonial territories, as in the ICJ's judgments in the territorial disputes between Qatar and Bahrain in 2001, between Nigeria and Cameroon in October 2002, and the Ligitan and Sipadan dispute of December 2002 between Indonesia and Malaysia, among others. It has been pointed out[79] that in the territorial dispute between Qatar and Bahrain, in recognising Bahrain's sovereignty over the Hawar Islands and Qatar's sovereignty over the Janan Island, the ICJ took into consideration as sole evidence the 1939 decision of the British government, which was the colonial power over the disputed area at the time.[80] Even in cases concerning territorial disputes of newly independent states, the decisions of the Western colonial powers that colonised the disputed areas were held to have absolute evidentiary value.[81] There is also trepidation with the virtual monopoly by Western international lawyers who argue cases before such courts and tribunals despite the fact that Asian international lawyers are no less qualified. According to this perception, the courts and tribunals hear mostly Western perspectives of international law, not a global one, and have to confine their decisions on the points of submission as formulated by these Western lawyers.

---

[78] Tara Davenport, "Southeast Asian Approaches to Maritime Boundaries", *Asian Journal of International Law* 4 (2014): 309, 349.

[79] Hee Eun Lee and Seokwoo Lee, "Positivism in International Law: State Sovereignty, Self-Determination, and Alternative Perspectives", *Asian Yearbook of International Law* 16 (2010): 1, 6.

[80] *Maritime Delimitation and Territorial Questions between Qatar and Bahrain (Qatar v. Bahrain)*, ICJ Rep. 2001, p. 40 at pp. 76–85 [113]–[148].

[81] For example, *Land and Maritime Boundary between Cameroon and Nigeria (Cameroon v. Nigeria: Equatorial Guinea intervening)*, ICJ Rep. 2002, p. 303; *Sovereignty over Pulau Ligitan and Pulau Sipadan*.

Accusations of "double standards" are often heard. For the Chinese, they often remind the international community of a few examples concerning the United States in this regard. In the *Nicaragua* case, after the ICJ had rejected the United States' challenge to the ICJ's jurisdiction in that case, the United States declined to participate in the merits phase of the case and refused to comply with the ICJ's judgment, in which, in spite of its non-appearance, the United States was deemed a party to the case. Article 94 of the UN Charter provides that each UN member undertakes to comply with the decision of the ICJ in any case to which it is a party, and that, if any party to a case fails to perform the obligations incumbent upon it under a judgment rendered by the ICJ, the other party may have recourse to the UNSC, which may, if it deems necessary, make recommendations or decide upon measures to be taken to give effect to the judgment. As a permanent member of the UNSC, the United States can get away with non-compliance with the ICJ's judgment legally binding upon it by casting a veto against any step to give effect to the judgment. The UN General Assembly (UNGA) passed a resolution on 3 November 1986, five months and one week after the ICJ's judgment in *Nicaragua*, in view of the continued financing by the United States of military and other activities in and against Nicaragua. The resolution "[u]rgently calls for full and immediate compliance" by the United States with the ICJ judgment "in conformity with the relevant provisions of the [UN Charter]".[82] As another example, on 9 December 2022 the World Trade Organization (WTO) circulated the dispute settlement panel reports in the cases brought by China, Norway, Switzerland and Türkiye in *United States—Certain Measures on Steel and Aluminium Products*, finding the US government in violation of WTO law by invoking, in 2018, national security concerns to justify imposing tariffs on steel and aluminium products from these countries.[83] In response, the US government strongly condemned the WTO panel's decision, which, in its view, was further proof that the WTO dispute settlement system was in need of fundamental reform. The US government would not remove the tariffs imposed owing to the United States' clear and unequivocal position, for over 70 years, that issues of national security cannot be reviewed in WTO dispute settlement and the WTO has no authority to second-guess the ability of a WTO member to respond to a wide range of threats to its security.

---

[82] A/RES/41/31 (3 Nov. 1986). Only El Salvador, Israel and the United States voted against this resolution.

[83] DS544, DS552, DS556 and DS564.

Decisions by states to have their territorial or border disputes settled by international litigation are not lightly taken. For example, it took Singapore and Malaysia 14 years to refer to the ICJ their dispute concerning the sovereignty over Pedra Branca/Pulau Batu Puteh as well as Middle Rocks and South Ledge, which are the two maritime features closest to Pedra Branca/Pulau Batu Puteh, after the dispute arose in 1980. Pedra Branca/Pulau Batu Puteh is a granite island, measuring 137 metres in length, with an average width of 60 metres and covering an area of about 8,560 square metres at low tide. It is situated at the eastern entrance of the Straits of Singapore, at the point where the Straits open up into the South China Sea. Middle Rocks is located 0.6 nautical miles to the south and consists of two clusters of small rocks about 250 metres apart that are permanently above water and stand 0.6 to 1.2 metres in height. South Ledge, at 2.2 nautical miles to the south-south-west of Pedra Branca/Pulau Batu Puteh, is a rock formation only visible at low tide.

Singapore's strategy was to persuade Malaysia that Singapore had a stronger legal case, including by disclosing unilaterally the documents Singapore had in support of Singapore's case. For its part, Malaysia's Royal Marine Police boats began to regularly intrude into Pedra Branca/Pulau Batu Puteh's waters, apparently in deliberate attempts to assert or build up a claim to sovereignty over this maritime feature and its surrounding waters, against which Singapore lodged protests at various levels while expressing Singapore's willingness to seek an amicable solution. The dispute also became a political issue in Malaysia, especially for Malaysia's Johor State because the feature was originally within the territory of the Johor Sultanate. With various Malaysian political parties urging the Malaysian government to staunchly defend Malaysia's interests, no Malaysian leader wanted to be seen as making any territorial concession to Singapore. Fortunately, the Malaysian leadership saw the need not to let the situation get out of control. In addition, Malaysia's legal advisers might have advised Malaysia that it had a plausible, even a good, case against Singapore. Owing to the political sensitivity and gravity of the dispute, the prime ministers of both countries discussed it when they met for bilateral discussions or on the sidelines at international conferences, followed by several rounds of bilateral consultations and exchanges of documents between their respective officials. On 6 September 1994, the prime ministers of both countries met and decided in principle to refer the dispute to a third party such as the ICJ. On 17 September 1994, Malaysia agreed in writing to refer the dispute to the ICJ. It took four years for both countries to negotiate a special agreement (*compromis*) to refer the case to the ICJ, specifying the details of the geographical scope of the dispute. However, Malaysia's proposed flexibility over territorial rights and interests of the losing party as a measure of saving "face" was rejected by Singapore for fear that it would invite the ICJ to come to a middle-way solution. It took another five years after 14 April 1998, when the text of the special agreement was finally settled, before it was eventually signed in February 2003. The dispute between Malaysia and Indonesia over Ligitan and Sipadan, two small islands off the east coast of Borneo, had been referred to the ICJ first, as the special agreement for that case had been signed in May 1997 and come into effect in May 1998. In December 2002, the ICJ delivered its judgment in the case between Malaysia and Indonesia, ruling that the sovereignty over Pulau Ligitan and Pulau Sipadan belongs to Malaysia.[84] With this victory at the ICJ that gave the Malaysians national pride, Malaysia began to show eagerness in getting the special agreement with Singapore signed and ratified.[85] In 2008, the ICJ ruled that the sovereignty over Pedra Branca/Pulau Batu Puteh belongs to Singapore, the sovereignty over Middle Rocks belongs to Malaysia, and the sovereignty over South Ledge belongs to the state in the territorial waters of which it is located.[86]

In the ICJ case between Indonesia and Malaysia, it was their need to exploit offshore oil deposits that led them to the ICJ. After their independence, Indonesia and Malaysia began to grant oil prospecting licences in waters off the east coast of Borneo during the 1960s. The dispute crystallised in 1969 in the context of discussions concerning the delimitation of the respective continental shelves of the two states. Following those negotiations a delimitation agreement was reached on 27 October 1969, coming into force on 7 November 1969. However, it did not cover the area lying to the east of Borneo. In October 1991 they set up a joint working group to study the situation of the islands of Ligitan and Sipadan, which failed to reach any agreement. The issue was subsequently entrusted to special emissaries of the two countries, which, in June 1996, recommended by mutual agreement that the dispute be referred to the ICJ. The special agreement to submit their dispute to the ICJ was signed on 31 May 1997.[87]

The territorial dispute between Bahrain and Qatar was mediated by the good offices of the king of Saudi Arabia with the agreement of the amirs of Bahrain and Qatar. As a consequence, a set of "Principles for the Framework for

---

[84] *Sovereignty over Pulau Ligitan and Pulau Sipadan*, ICJ Rep. 2002, p. 686 [150].

[85] Tommy Koh and S. Jayakumar, *Pedra Branca: The Road to the World Court* (Singapore: NUS Press, 2009), pp. 20–43.

[86] ICJ Rep. 2008, pp. 101–2 [300].

[87] ICJ Rep. 2002, p. 642 [31].

Reaching a Settlement" was approved during a tripartite meeting in March 1983. For the next few years, there was no progress towards a settlement of the dispute. The king of Saudi Arabia then sent the amirs of Qatar and Bahrain letters in identical terms dated 19 December 1987, in which he put forward new proposals. Those proposals were accepted by letters from the two heads of state, dated respectively 21 and 26 December 1987. The ICJ held that the exchanges of these letters and the document headed "Minutes" and signed at Doha on 25 December 1990 by the ministers for foreign affairs of Bahrain, Qatar and Saudi Arabia were international agreements creating rights and obligations for the parties. By the terms of those agreements, contrary to Bahrain's objection to the ICJ's jurisdiction in this case, the parties had undertaken to submit to the ICJ the whole of the dispute between them, as circumscribed by the Bahraini formula, which reads: "The Parties request the [ICJ] to decide any matter of territorial right or other title or interest which may be a matter of difference between them; and to draw a single maritime boundary between their respective maritime areas of seabed, subsoil and superjacent waters."[88]

With respect to India and Pakistan, the peaceful settlement of their *Rann of Kutch* dispute has been hailed as the most successful and major instance of dispute settlement by arbitration because of the unbegrudged acceptance of it by the parties and its swift implementation.[89] The "Rann of Kutch", meaning the desert or desolate place of Kutch, a district in India's state of Gujarat, comprises for the most part salt marshes but with some prospects for finding oil and natural gas. The "Great Rann of Kutch", the largest portion of the Rann, is conterminous between Sind province in Pakistan and India's Gujarat and spans 35,000 square miles. The boundary between India and Pakistan in this region remained unsettled after the partition of British India in 1947. The two countries engaged in armed clashes in April 1965 at the Rann of Kutch in Gujarat. On British prime minister Harold Wilson's intervention for reconciliation between the sides, a ceasefire was declared and an agreement was signed on 30 June 1965, with immediate troop withdrawal and the territorial dispute being referred to an international arbitral tribunal composed of one foreign nominee each from both sides and a chairman appointed by consensus. In 1968, the majority of the arbitrators awarded 90 per cent of the disputed territory to India,

---

[88] *Maritime Delimitation and Territorial Questions between Qatar and Bahrain, Jurisdiction and Admissibility*, Judgment, ICJ Rep. 1994, p. 112; *Maritime Delimitation and Territorial Questions between Qatar and Bahrain, Jurisdiction and Admissibility*, Judgment, ICJ Rep. 1995, p. 6.

[89] Bhat, "Peaceful Resolution of International Disputes", 14–26.

while the area awarded to Pakistan comprises almost all the elevated area above water all year round. The arbitration has, however, left unsettled the demarcation of the territory from the mouth of Sir Creek Channel, a 100-kilometre-long estuary in the salt marshes of the Rann of Kutch between Gujarat and Sind, to its top in Kutch area.[90]

The maritime boundary disputes in the Bay of Bengal between Bangladesh and Myanmar and between Bangladesh and India have been settled through international litigation. With the discovery of large reserves of natural gas in the Bay of Bengal, the three states bordering the bay tried to access the resources in their disputed maritime areas that often resulted in stand-offs between their navies or coastguards, such as the stand-off that lasted more than one week between the Bangladeshi navy and the Myanmar navy in November 2008 and the ones between the Bangladeshi navy and certain vessels flying the Indian flag in 1981 and 2008. In December 2008, Myanmar filed with the Commission on the Limits of the Continental Shelf, set up under UNCLOS to make recommendations to coastal states on matters related to the establishment of the outer limits of their continental shelf, preliminary information for Myanmar's extended continental shelf claim, followed by an update in 2009, which overlapped with Bangladesh's claim; this drew protests from both Bangladesh and India.[91] On 8 October 2009, Bangladesh submitted the dispute concerning the maritime boundary between Bangladesh and Myanmar to an Annex VII arbitral tribunal, which is a default mechanism under UNCLOS to which both countries are parties, because they had not chosen a means for the settlement of disputes under UNCLOS. In November 2009, Myanmar agreed to have this dispute settled by the International Tribunal for the Law of the Sea (ITLOS) and the case was transferred in December 2009 from the Annex VII arbitral tribunal to ITLOS. ITLOS rendered its judgment in March 2012, laying to rest once and for all the dispute between the two countries in the Bay of Bengal.[92] Also, on 8 October 2009, Bangladesh submitted its maritime boundary dispute with India to an Annex XII arbitral tribunal, separately from the

---

[90] J. Gillis Wetter, "The Rann of Kutch Arbitration", *American Journal of International Law* 65 (1971): 346; Mukund G. Untawale, "The Kutch-Sind Dispute", *International & Comparative Law Quarterly* 23 (1974): 818.

[91] Davenport, "Southeast Asian Approaches to Maritime Boundaries", 341; van Logchem, *The Rights and Obligations of States in Disputed Maritime Areas*, pp. 253–5.

[92] *Delimitation of the Maritime Boundary in the Bay of Bengal (Bangladesh/Myanmar)*, ITLOS Rep. 2012, p. 4.

case it was bringing against Myanmar. India subsequently agreed to this arbitration, which rendered its final award on 7 July 2014.[93]

Domestic politics has played a crucial role in the Philippines' position vis-à-vis China regarding their South China Sea disputes. It was the government of President Benigno Aquino III that instituted the arbitral tribunal proceedings against China in January 2013. Philippine president Rodrigo Duterte, who succeeded him on 30 June 2016, less than two weeks before the Arbitral Tribunal's award of 12 July 2016, was more conciliatory in his government's approach in this matter. As a pragmatist, Duterte hoped for closer economic ties with Beijing and sought a compromise in the South China Sea disputes since the Philippines' military was no match for China's. President Ferdinand R. Marcos, Jr., who became the Philippines' president on 30 June 2022, apparently tried to steer the middle ground between his two predecessors' instances in this regard, as will be shown below.

Mere Frontier Incidents or Armed Attacks Giving Rise to the Right to Self-Defence?

In *Nicaragua*, the ICJ distinguished between an "armed attack" and "mere frontier incidents", relying on the "scale and effects" of the attack[94] and the circumstances and motivations of the attack.[95] Yet, in *Oil Platforms* the ICJ "[did] not exclude the possibility that the mining of a *single military* vessel might suffice to bring into play the 'inherent right of self-defence'",[96] and in *Armed Activities on the Territory of the Congo* the ICJ opened up a possibility that a series of less grave forms of use of force considered cumulatively might meet the threshold of an "armed attack".[97]

A typical example of "mere frontier incidents" is the skirmish at the Afghanistan–Pakistan land border in December 2022. No fewer than six Pakistanis were killed and over a dozen were wounded on 11 December 2022 in what Pakistan alleged was unprovoked gunfire from Afghan forces near the southern border town of Chaman in Balochistan Province, whereas a Taliban member was killed and ten people were wounded on the Afghan side. A second round of shelling wounded no fewer than 16 Pakistani civilians on 15 December 2022.

---

[93] *Bay of Bengal Maritime Boundary Arbitration between Bangladesh and India (Bangladesh v. India)*, PCA Case Repository 2010–16 (PCA, 2014).

[94] ICJ Rep. 1986, pp. 103–4 [195].

[95] Ibid., pp. 119–20 [231].

[96] ICJ Rep. 2003, p. 195 [72] (emphasis added).

[97] ICJ Rep. 2005, pp. 222–3 [146].

The cause of the fighting was the construction of a border checkpoint by Pakistan along the land border between the two countries and Afghanistan has contested the British-era boundary demarcation, known as the Durand Line. Pakistan tried to cool down these incidents by lodging diplomatic protests against Afghanistan and prodded both sides to prevent the recurrence of these incidents. Afghanistan reportedly apologised to Pakistan for what happened.[98]

The domestic law of most states authorises its government agents to use force to repel encroachment upon their territory or maritime zones. For example, Article 22 of the Coast Guard Law of the People's Republic of China, adopted on 22 January 2021 and in force as of 1 February 2021,[99] provides: "When the sovereignty, sovereign rights and jurisdiction of the State face an imminent danger of unlawful infringement or unlawful violation by foreign organizations and individuals at sea, the China's Coast Guard Organization shall, in accordance with this Law and other laws or regulations, take all necessary measures, including the use of weapons." Although the law does not appear to allow the use of weapons against foreign warships and other government ships operated for non-commercial purposes that are entitled to sovereign immunity under Article 32 of UNCLOS, if they refuse to leave and cause serious harm or threat, then, by virtue of Article 21 of the law, the CCG "has the right to take measures such as forced eviction and forced towing".[100]

When government agents of state A confront what they consider to be an encroachment by government agents of state B into their territory or maritime zone, which is claimed by both states, both sides should exercise restraint and contact their superiors to discuss the matter urgently. If this fails, state A's agents should resort to "law enforcement measures" to apprehend or repel the agents of state B instead of entering into an armed conflict or, worse still, engaging in fighting of such "scale and effect" that make the skirmish an armed attack.

The distinction between the use of force in violation of Article 2(4) of the UN Charter and law enforcement short of such use of force was addressed by the Annex VII Arbitral Tribunal in *Guyana/Suriname Arbitration*.[101] The case

---

[98] "Pakistan Summons Afghan Diplomat over Border Shelling", *Al Jazeera,* 16 Dec. 2022, https://www.aljazeera.com/news/2022/12/16/pakistan-summons-afghan-diplomat-over-border-clashes.

[99] https://npcobserver.com/legislation/coast-guard-law/.

[100] Discussed in Alexander Lott, *Hybrid Threats and the Law of the Sea: Use of Force and Discriminatory Navigational Restrictions in Straits* (Leiden: Brill, 2022), pp. 112–13.

[101] Award of 17 Sept. 2007, 30 R.I.A.A. 1 (PCA, 2007), paras 401–46. See also the analysis of this distinction in Erin Pobjie, *Prohibited Force: The Meaning of "Use of Force" in International Law* (Cambridge: Cambridge University Press, 2024), pp. 180–9.

concerned the delimitation of Guyana's maritime boundary with Suriname and the alleged breaches of international law by Suriname in their disputed maritime area. The latter arose in relation to the activities of holders of oil concessions granted by Guyana in the maritime area claimed by both countries. An oil rig and a drill ship were ordered to leave and escorted from the area by the Surinamese navy in June 2000 and a similar incident followed in September 2000. The tribunal's award in this case affirmed the rule of customary international law that the use of force must be avoided as far as possible and, where force is unavoidable, it must not go beyond what is reasonable and necessary in the circumstances. The testimony of those involved in the incident clearly revealed that the rig was ordered to leave the area and, if this demand was not fulfilled, responsibility for unspecified consequences would be theirs. Although there was no common understanding among those involved in the incident as to what these "consequences" might have been, the order given to the rig constituted an explicit threat that force might be used if the order was not complied with. The question now arose as to whether this threat of the use of force breached UNCLOS, the UN Charter and general international law. The Arbitral Tribunal referred to the ICJ's case law that, if it is to be lawful, the declared readiness of a state to use force must be a use of force that is in conformity with the UN Charter,[102] and there is distinction between the most grave forms of the use of force (those constituting an armed attack) and other less grave forms.[103] The Arbitral Tribunal accepted the argument that in international law force may be used in law enforcement activities provided that such force is unavoidable, reasonable and necessary. However, in the circumstances of the case, the action mounted by Suriname on 3 June 2000 seemed more akin to a threat of military action than to mere law enforcement activity and, hence, a threat of the use of force in contravention of UNCLOS, the UN Charter and general international law. Suriname also argued that "should the Tribunal regard [its 3 June 2000] measures as contrary to international obligations owed by Suriname to Guyana, the measures were nevertheless lawful countermeasures since they were taken in response to an internationally wrongful act by Guyana in order to achieve cessation of that act". The Arbitral Tribunal ruled, however, that under a well-established principle of international law, countermeasures may not involve the use of force. Peaceful means of addressing Guyana's alleged breach of international law with respect to exploratory drilling were available to Suriname under UNCLOS, including by

[102] *Legality of the Threat or Use of Nuclear Weapons*, ICJ Rep. 1996, p. 246 [47].

[103] *Nicaragua*, ICJ Rep. 1986, p. 101 [191].

requesting ITLOS or an Annex VII arbitral tribunal to prescribe provisional measures of protection against irreparable damage or prejudice Suriname might suffer.

In the *Oil Platforms* case between the United States and Iran, the ICJ showed how the state using force is required to meticulously discharge a very high burden of proof to justify its use of force—the evidence must be *conclusive*, and not merely suggestive or circumstantial. The actions giving rise to both the claim and the counterclaim occurred in the context of the general events that took place in the Persian Gulf between 1980 and 1988, in particular the armed conflict between Iran and Iraq. In 1984, Iraq commenced attacks against ships in the Persian Gulf, notably tankers carrying Iranian oil. These were the first incidents of what later became known as the "Tanker War" between 1984 and 1988, when a number of commercial vessels and warships of various nationalities, including neutral vessels, were attacked by aircraft, helicopters, missiles or warships, or struck mines in the waters of the Persian Gulf. On 16 October 1987, the Kuwaiti tanker *Sea Isle City*, reflagged to the United States, was hit by a missile near Kuwait harbour. The United States attributed this attack to Iran and, three days later, on 19 October 1987, it attacked two Iranian offshore oil production installations in the Reshadat complex. On 14 April 1988, the warship USS *Samuel B. Roberts* struck a mine in international waters near Bahrain while returning from an escort mission; four days later the United States employed its naval forces to attack and destroy Iran's Nasr and Salman complexes simultaneously. The attacks on the *Sea Isle City* and the USS *Samuel B. Roberts* were invoked in support of the United States' claim to act in self-defence.

Having examined with great care the evidence and arguments presented on each side, the ICJ ruled that the United States had failed to discharge the burden of proof for its attack on 19 October 1987. As for the United States' attack on 18 April 1988, the ICJ noted that the attacks on the Salman and Nasr platforms were not an isolated operation, aimed simply at the oil installations, as had been the case with the attacks of 19 October 1987. They formed part of a much more extensive military action, designated "Operation Praying Mantis", conducted by the United States against what it regarded as "legitimate military targets"; armed force was used, and damage done to a number of targets, including the destruction of two Iranian frigates and other Iranian naval vessels and aircraft. Mines were being laid at the time by both belligerents in the Iran–Iraq war, so that evidence of other mine-laying operations by Iran was not conclusive as to responsibility of Iran for this particular mine that struck the USS *Samuel B. Roberts*. The discovery of moored mines in the same area, bearing serial numbers matching other Iranian mines, in particular those found aboard the vessel *Iran Ajr*, was highly suggestive, but not *conclusive*, as evidence. Furthermore, no attacks on US-flagged vessels (as distinct from US-owned vessels), additional to those cited as justification for the earlier attacks on the Reshadat platforms, had been brought to the ICJ's attention, other than the mining of the USS *Samuel B. Roberts* itself. The question was therefore whether that incident sufficed in itself to justify action in self-defence, as amounting to an "armed attack". Although the ICJ did not exclude the possibility that the mining of a single military vessel might be sufficient to bring into play the inherent right of self-defence, in light of all the circumstances, including the *inconclusiveness of the evidence* of Iran's responsibility for the mining of the USS *Samuel B. Roberts*, the ICJ is unable to hold that the attacks on the Salman and Nasr platforms were justifiably made in response to an "armed attack" on the United States by Iran, in the form of the mining of the USS *Samuel B. Roberts*. The ICJ was not sufficiently convinced that the evidence available supported the contentions of the United States as to the significance of the military presence and activity on the Reshadat oil platforms, and no such evidence was offered in respect of the Salman and Nasr complexes. However, even accepting those contentions, for the purposes of discussion, the ICJ was unable to hold that the attacks made on the platforms could have been justified as acts of self-defence. In the case of both the attack on the *Sea Isle City* and the mining of the USS *Samuel B. Roberts*, the ICJ was not satisfied that the attacks on the platforms were *necessary* to respond to these incidents. As to the requirement of *proportionality*, the attack of 19 October 1987 might, had the ICJ found that it was necessary in response to the *Sea Isle City* incident as an armed attack committed by Iran, have been considered proportionate. In the case of the attacks of 18 April 1988, however, they were conceived and executed as part of a more extensive operation entitled Operation Praying Mantis. As a response to the mining, by an unidentified agency, of a single United States warship, which was severely damaged but not sunk, and without loss of life, neither Operation Praying Mantis as a whole nor even that part of it that destroyed the Salman and Nasr platforms could be regarded, in the circumstances of this case, as a proportionate use of force in self-defence.

The ICJ has consistently upheld this evidentiary test for the state making the assertion to discharge its burden of proof that there is "conclusive evidence",[104] "a degree of certainty",[105] "inferences of fact [which] leave *no room* for reasonable

---

[104] *Corfu Channel*, ICJ Rep. 1949, p. 4 at p. 17.

[105] Ibid.

doubt",[106] "degree of certainty . . . supported by convincing evidence",[107] "clear evidence",[108] "[relevant facts] convincingly established by the evidence",[109] "evidence [that is] weighty and convincing"[110] and "evidence that is fully conclusive".[111]

It should be noted that states generally do not treat "accidental" uses of force as armed attacks giving rise to the right to self-defence. For instance, when the Chinese embassy in Belgrade was bombed accidentally by NATO in 1999, China did not claim it was a victim of an armed attack.

During an armed confrontation between parties to a territorial or border dispute, both sides need to have a "cooling-off" period to consider carefully how to prevent the situation from escalating into an armed conflict. They must not use sabre-rattling rhetoric to arouse patriotism, nationalism or irredentism. Prior personal interaction and connections among those responsible for management or containment of the dispute tend to ensure that actors on both sides see one another as human beings and not as mere pawns in a chess game of territorial conquest and resistance. Regional organisations to which they belong or any state or person which or who may use good offices to mediate their dispute should be approached.

With regard to "law enforcement" against encroachment by other states, law enforcement officers should abide by the 1990 UN Basic Principles on the Use of Force and Firearms by Law Enforcement Officials. As for law enforcement at sea, international law requires that the use of force must be avoided as far as possible and, where force is unavoidable, it must not go beyond what is reasonable and necessary in the circumstances. The normal practice used to stop a ship at sea is first to give an auditory or visual signal to stop, using internationally recognised signals. Where this does not succeed, a variety of actions may be taken, including the firing of shots across the bows of the ship. It is only after the appropriate actions fail that the pursuing vessel may, as a last resort, use force. Even then, appropriate warning must be issued to the ship and all efforts should

---

[106] Ibid., p. 18 (emphasis original).

[107] *Nicaragua*, ICJ Rep. 1986, pp. 24–5 [29].

[108] Ibid., p. 62 [109].

[109] *DR Congo v. Uganda*, ICJ Rep. 2005, p. 205 [72]. The ICJ in that case also used the term "convincing evidence" (ibid., p. 209 [91]).

[110] Ibid., p. 220 [136].

[111] *Application of the Convention on the Prevention and Punishment of the Crime of Genocide (Bosnia and Herzegovina v. Serbia and Montenegro)*, ICJ Rep. 2007, p. 43 at p. 129 [209].

be made to ensure that life is not endangered.[112] Nonetheless, where the area where the incident takes place is a disputed area, these principles must be considered in a different context—protests and self-restraints, as explained above, should suffice. The states concerned also need to pursue CBMs to maintain their good bilateral relations.

Confidence-Building Measures

According to the 1970 Declaration on Friendly Relations:

> Every State . . . has the duty to refrain from the threat or use of force to violate international lines of demarcation, such as armistice lines, established by or pursuant to an international agreement to which it is a party or which it is otherwise bound to respect. Nothing in the foregoing shall be construed as prejudicing the positions of the parties concerned with regard to the status and effects of such lines under their special regimes or as affecting their temporary character.

CBMs are promoted as a vital mechanism to prevent conflicts from worsening.

The Line of Control between India and Pakistan and the Line of Actual Control between China and India are two examples of CBMs whereby the disputing parties agree to the status quo without prejudice to their respective legal positions on the sovereignty disputes in question. Ways and means to manage or contain disputes over land territories, such as use of hotlines and regular meetings of border personnel, discussed above, are essential parts of CBMs.

In order to agree on CBMs to ease tension, the disputing parties need to come to an understanding of the nature and scope of activities they may either unilaterally or jointly undertake without prejudice to their respective claims.

Paragraph 9 of the joint statement from Vietnam's Communist Party chief Nguyen Phu Trong and Chinese president Xi Jinping issued on 2 November 2022 at the end of the official visit of the former to China touches extensively on conflicts in the South China Sea/East Sea. They considered that satisfactorily controlling disagreements and maintaining peace and stability in the South China/East Sea are extremely important, and they agreed to properly handle issues at sea, contributing to long-term peace and security in the region; discuss temporary, transitional solutions that do not affect stances and policies of each

[112] *M/V "SAIGA" (No. 2) (Saint Vincent and the Grenadines v. Guinea)*, ITLOS Rep. 1999, p. 10 at pp. 61–2.

side; and seek basic long-term solutions acceptable to both sides. They were willing to continue carrying out cooperation in less sensitive fields at sea and to discuss the expansion of cooperation at sea in the Tonkin Gulf on the basis of meeting practical benefit of both sides. They also agreed to continue to promote the full and effective implementation of the 2002 Declaration on the Conduct of Parties in the South China/East Sea between ASEAN and China and, on the basis of consultation, consensus, soon reach a substantive and effective code of conduct (COC) in the South China/East Sea in accordance with international law, including UNCLOS. In addition, they agreed to control disagreements at sea, without actions that complicate the situation and expand disputes, and maintain peace, stability in the South China/East Sea and promote cooperation at sea.[113]

Joint development by disputing states over a disputed land territory is generally not practicable because land territories are subject to states' territorial sovereignty and no state would recognise another state's sovereignty over the former's territory. At most, the state may grant a concession or licence to other states to utilise a piece of land, such as for mineral extraction. Unlike land territories, claims over maritime areas are of a more recent origin. With the advent of the regimes of territorial sea of up to 12 nautical miles from the coast, the continental shelf and the exclusive economic zone beyond the outer limit of the territorial sea, coastal states have asserted the limits of their respective maritime zones that often overlap with those of other states. In 1969, the ICJ laid down legal guidance that delimitation of the continental shelf was to be effected by agreement in accordance with applicable rules and principles of international law. If, after applying these rules and principles, "the delimitation leaves to the parties areas that overlap, these are to be divided between them in agreed proportions or, failing agreement, equally, unless they decide on a regime of joint jurisdiction, user, or exploitation of the zones of overlap or any part of them".[114] The same reasoning applies to other maritime zones that are not continental shelves.

Although there have been several suggestions about joint development over natural resources in the South China Sea, this has not materialised since no claimant state would recognise that another state or other states own(s) maritime geographical features in the South China Sea that generate the maritime area(s) in question. This is despite the fact that Chinese leaders from Deng Xiaoping to Hu Jintao and Wen Jiabao raised the idea of putting aside the dis-

[113] https://vietnamlawmagazine.vn/vietnam-china-issue-joint-statement-49135.html.
[114] *North Sea Continental Shelf Cases (Federal Republic of Germany/Denmark; Federal Republic of Germany/Netherlands)*, ICJ Rep. 1969, p. 3 at p. 53 [101(C)(2)].

pute over sovereignty in favour of joint development with their counterparts in Japan (regarding the dispute over the Diaoyu Islands), the Philippines, Malaysia and Brunei.[115] According to the June 2008 understanding between China and Japan on joint development, as the first step they would work on the following: (1) the block for joint development was to be the area bounded by straight lines joining the points specified in the understanding; and (2) the two sides would, through joint exploration, select by mutual agreement areas for joint development in the above-mentioned block under the principle of mutual benefit. Specific matters would be decided by the two sides through consultation. In order to carry out the joint development, the two sides would work to fulfil their respective domestic procedures and arrive at the necessary bilateral agreement at an early date, while also continuing to consult for the early realisation of joint development in other parts of the East China Sea.[116] The negotiations were suspended in 2010 when Sino-Japanese bilateral tensions rose in the aftermath of a Chinese trawler's collision with a Japan Coast Guard vessel. Above all, this understanding will never be implemented as long as both sides continue to insist on their respective positions concerning their disputed territories in the East China Sea[117] and unilaterally undertake hydrocarbon activities in the disputed area that might jeopardise or hamper the reaching of a final agreement based on the spirit of understanding and cooperation.[118] In October 2022, for example, Japan protested against China's unilateral extraction of natural gas in a contested area of the East China Sea, on the Chinese side of a Japanese-proposed median line separating the two countries' exclusive economic zones. Japan has accused China of building 18 drilling rigs on the Chinese side of the said median line, from where, fears Japan, gas on the Japanese side can also be extracted.

---

[115] Jianwei Li and Pingping Chen, "Joint Development in the South China Sea: Is the Time Ripe?", *Asian Yearbook of International Law* 22 (2016): 131, 137–43. According to one commentator, China's joint development proposal apparently tries to keep the South China Sea disputes below the threshold of active conflict while consolidating China's position in these disputes (Kardon, *China's Law of the Sea*, pp. 4–6).

[116] David M. Ong, "The International Legal Obligations of States in Disputed Maritime Jurisdiction Zones and Prospects for Co-operative Arrangements in the East China Sea Region", *Asian Yearbook of International Law* 22 (2016): 109, 129.

[117] Yann-huei Song, "Peaceful Proposals and Maritime Cooperation between Mainland China, Japan, and Taiwan in the East China Sea: Progress Made and Challenges Ahead", *Asian Yearbook of International Law* 22 (2016): 20, 45–6.

[118] Kentaro Nishimoto, "The Obligation of Self-Restraint in Undelimited Maritime Areas", *Japan Review* 3 (2019): 28, 38.

On 20 November 2018, the PRC and the Philippines signed a memorandum of understanding on cooperation on oil and gas development.[119] The memorandum refers to UNCLOS and the 2002 Declaration of Conduct in the South China Sea signed by ASEAN member states and the PRC. In accordance with the principles of "mutual respect, fairness and mutual benefit, flexibility and pragmatism and consensus", through equal and friendly consultation, the two governments have decided to negotiate, on an accelerated basis, arrangements to facilitate oil and gas exploration and exploitation in "relevant maritime areas" consistent with applicable rules of international law. An Inter-Governmental Steering Joint Committee co-chaired by their foreign ministers is set up for this purpose. The two governments have pledged to endeavour to agree on the cooperation arrangements within 12 months of this memorandum of understanding. This memorandum of understanding, along with all discussions, negotiations and activities of the two governments or their authorised enterprises under or pursuant to this memorandum of understanding, will be without prejudice to the respective legal positions of both governments. Finally, this memorandum of understanding does not create rights or obligations under international or domestic law. No agreement on the cooperation arrangements has been reached at the time of writing, however.

In November 2024, a joint statement issued during the newly elected Indonesian president Prabowo Subianto's official visit to Beijing, his first overseas visit since he assumed the presidency in October 2024, stated that both countries agreed to collaborate on maritime initiatives and "reached important common understanding on joint development in areas of overlapping claims". This seems to depart from Indonesia's long-standing policy of denying that China's nine-dash line in the South China Sea overlaps with Indonesia's exclusive economic zone in the North Natuna Sea. The Indonesian Foreign Ministry subsequently clarified that this cooperation had no impact on Indonesia's sovereignty, sovereign rights or the jurisdiction in the North Natuna Sea, reiterating Indonesia's position that Chinese claims in the South China Sea have no international legal basis. During that same visit, the two countries signed technical cooperation guidelines to implement the arrangement signed in September 2023 to cooperate on sustainable fisheries.

Instead of joint development of natural resources, projects such as joint marine scientific research and fish stock assessment have been proposed for

[119] https://www.mfa.gov.cn/eng/wjb/zzjg_663340/bianhaisi_eng_665278/bianhaixiangguanxinwen_665280/202406/t20240606_11405597.html.

disputed maritime areas, including in the South China Sea without prejudice to their respective legal entitlements, if any.[120]

Following China's occupation of Mischief Reef in the South China Sea in January 1995, ASEAN endorsed the idea of concluding a regional COC in the South China Sea as the foundation for long-term stability in the area and to foster understanding among claimant countries. In November 2002, ASEAN and China were able to agree on a non-binding Declaration on the Conduct of Parties in the South China Sea as an important first step towards setting the conditions for a peaceful and durable solution to the disputes in the South China Sea, and each party undertook to respect and take actions consistent with its provisions. They also "reaffirmed that a code of conduct in the South China Sea would further promote peace and stability in the region and agree to work, on the basis of consensus, towards the eventual attainment of this objective". As of this writing, no COC has been agreed upon.[121] ASEAN aims to conclude negotiations on the COC by 2026. China insists that the COC shall not be a legally binding instrument.

China prefers bilateral negotiations or dialogues with each of the other claimant states but the latter fear they will be overwhelmed by China's bargaining power and, therefore, prefer to pursue multilateral diplomacy to counterpoise China. Some non-claimant ASEAN member states are China's close allies and are unwilling to put too much pressure on China to yield, lest this would undermine their close relations, especially economic ones, with China. For its part, China perceives intervention by certain states outside the region in the South China Sea disputes as a thinly veiled attempt to stem the apparently unstoppable rise of China as one of the few economic, political and military superpowers of this century.[122] The Quadrilateral Security Dialogue (Quad) between

[120] See, for example, Yen-Chiang Chang, Sirong Xin and Xu (John) Zhang, "A Proposal for Joint Marine Scientific Research Activities in the Disputed Maritime Areas of the South China Sea", *Coastal Management* 50 (2022): 215; Lucio Blanco Pitlo III, "Duty to Cooperate and Practical Cooperation in the South China Sea", *China & US Focus*, 10 Aug. 2022, https://www.chinausfocus.com/peace-security/duty-to-cooperate-and-practical-cooperation-in-the-south-china-sea.

[121] For criticisms of the COC, see Pedrozo, "Is a South China Sea Code of Conduct Viable?", 938–52. On unilateral expansion of offshore outposts in this disputed maritime region, see the report released in January 2025 by the Asia Maritime Transparency Initiative of the Centre for Strategic and International Studies in Washington, DC, based on its findings from commercial satellite imagery at: https://www.csis.org/analysis/china-and-vietnam-are-driving-reef-destruction-south-china-sea.

[122] See also Ma Jianying, *The United States Involvement in the South China Sea Disputes* (New York: Peter Lang Publishing, 2022), pp. 59–146, 205–360; Gregory B. Poling, *On*

Australia, India, Japan and the United States, formed in 2007, aims to counter China militarily and diplomatically in the Indo-Pacific region, especially in the East China Sea and the South China Sea/East Sea. In the Quad Joint Leaders' Statement of 24 May 2022, the leaders of these four countries promised among themselves to "champion adherence to international law, particularly as reflected in UNCLOS, and the maintenance of freedom of navigation and overflight, to meet challenges to the maritime rules-based order, including in the East and South China Seas". They "strongly oppose any coercive, provocative or unilateral actions that seek to change the status quo and increase tensions in the area, such as the militarisation of disputed features, the dangerous use of coast guard vessels and maritime militia, and efforts to disrupt other countries' offshore resource exploitation activities".

What is worrisome from the perspective of war and peace is the existence of the Mutual Defence Treaty between Philippines and the United States of 30 August 1951.[123] By virtue of Article IV of the Treaty, "[e]ach Party recognizes that an armed attack in the Pacific area on either of the Parties would be dangerous to its own peace and safety and declares that it would act to meet the common dangers in accordance with its constitutional processes". The article adds that any such armed attack and all measures taken as a result thereof shall be immediately reported to the UNSC, and such measures shall be terminated when the UNSC has taken the measures necessary to restore and maintain international peace and security. Pursuant to Article V of the Treaty, "[f]or the purpose of Article IV, an armed attack on either of the Parties is deemed to include an armed attack on the metropolitan territory of either of the Parties, or on the Island territories under its jurisdiction in the Pacific Ocean, its armed forces, public vessels or aircraft in the Pacific". According to Article VI, this treaty does not affect and shall not be interpreted as affecting in any way the rights and obligations of the parties under the UN Charter or the responsibility of the United Nations for the maintenance of international peace and security. Pursuant to the United States and the Republic of the Philippines Bilateral Defence Guidelines, issued on 3 May 2023 during the Philippine president's visit to Washington, DC, an armed attack in the Pacific, including "anywhere in the South China Sea", on either Philippine or US armed forces—which includes both nations' coast guards—aircraft, or public vessels, would invoke mutual defence commitments under Article IV and Article V of the 1951

Dangerous Ground: America's Century in the South China Sea (New York: Oxford University Press, 2022).

[123] 177 *United Nations Treaty Series* 133, in force 27 Aug. 1952.

Treaty. The United States and the Philippines reaffirmed the importance of the 2016 Arbitral Award on the South China Sea, and that the two countries have a common interest in maintaining freedom of navigation and overflight and other lawful uses of the sea, as reflected in UNCLOS, as well as open sea lines of communication across the Indo-Pacific region. Modernising air defence capabilities and interoperability to defend Philippine and US sovereign airspace and to ensure freedom of overflight in the Indo-Pacific region remains an alliance priority.[124]

There is optimism that the Philippines will not invoke the 1951 Treaty for the United States to come to its aid against China. On 3–5 January 2023, the Philippines' president, Marcos, Jr., paid a state visit to China. In the joint statement issued after the visit, both sides had an in-depth and candid exchange of views on the situation in the South China Sea, emphasised that maritime issues do not comprise the sum total of relations between the two countries and agreed to appropriately manage differences through peaceful means. Both sides reaffirmed the importance of maintaining and promoting peace and stability in the region and the freedom of navigation in and overflight above the South China Sea, and reached consensus on the peaceful resolution of disputes on the basis of the 2002 Declaration, the UN Charter and UNCLOS. They concurred that CBMs would contribute to improving mutual trust and affirmed the importance of their foreign ministry consultations and the Bilateral Consultation Mechanism on the South China Sea. The two sides decided to establish a direct communication mechanism between the Department of Boundary and Ocean Affairs of the Ministry of Foreign Affairs of China and the Maritime and Ocean Affairs Office of the Department of Foreign Affairs of the Philippines. Both sides acknowledged the usefulness of practical cooperation between their coast guards and agreed to convene the annual defence security talks at a mutually convenient time.

On oil and gas cooperation, the presidents of both the PRC and the Philippines agreed to bear in mind the spirit of the 2018 memorandum of understanding on cooperation on oil and gas development and agreed to resume discussions on oil and gas development at an early date, building upon the outcomes of the previous talks, with a view to benefiting the two countries and their peoples.[125] According to the Philippine president, the only sticking point in this

---

[124] https://media.defense.gov/2023/May/03/2003214357/-1/-1/0/THE-UNITED-STATES-AND-THE-REPUBLIC-OF-THE-PHILIPPINES-BILATERAL-DEFENSE-GUIDELINES.PDF.

[125] https://english.news.cn/20230105/675b9a1034df4901b08c9cf4d9c3d7fb/c.html.

matter is simply whether the law of the Philippines or that of the PRC applies to their joint development regime in the South China Sea.[126] However, on 10 January 2023 the Philippine Supreme Court declared unconstitutional and void the 2005 Tripartite Agreement for Joint Marine Seismic Undertaking by and among the China National Offshore Oil Corporation, the Vietnam Oil and Gas Corporation and the Philippine National Oil Company involving an area in the South China Sea covering 142,886 square kilometres ("Agreement Area"). The court ruled that the Tripartite Agreement allowed wholly owned foreign corporations to participate in the exploration of the Philippines' natural resources without observing the safeguards provided in Section 2, Article XII of the 1987 Constitution of the Philippines, which mandates that the exploration, development and utilisation of natural resources shall be under the *full control* and supervision of the state. The court, noting that the term "exploration" pertains to a search or discovery of something in both its ordinary or technical sense, ruled that the Tripartite Agreement involves the exploration of the country's natural resources, particularly petroleum, with the clear purpose of determining if petroleum exists in the Agreement Area. That the parties designated the joint research as a "pre-exploration activity" did not detract from the fact that the intent and aim of the agreement was to discover petroleum which is tantamount to "exploration". This judgment is likely to impede the prospect of any joint development of hydrocarbon resources with the Philippines in the South China Sea.

Since that visit to China by President Marcos, Jr., there have been numerous incidents involving the CCG, on the one side, and Philippine fishermen and/or Coast Guard/Navy, on the other side at the Second Thomas Shoal, where Philippine troops are stationed on the naval vessel *Sierra Madre*, grounded atop the shoal, or while the latter were on the way to the Scarborough Shoal. Several protests have been lodged with the Chinese ambassador to the Philippines. The confrontation between the Philippines and China also spilled over to the Sabina Shoal in the Spratly Islands between April and September 2024.

On 31 May 2024, at the annual Shangri-la Dialogue gathering of decision-makers from across the Asia-Pacific, North America, Europe and the Middle East to discuss the most pressing regional security issues and to share policy responses, President Marcos, Jr., responding to a hypothetical situation from a delegate in the audience, said that if by "a wilful act" a Filipino were killed, this would be "very, very close to what we define[d] as an act of war and therefore

[126] Interview with President Ferdinand R. Marcos, Jr., by the China Global Television Network prior to his State visit to China, https://www.youtube.com/watch?v=GLCoiOS8UOQ.

we [would] respond accordingly".[127] At the same event, China's minister of national defence, Admiral Dong Jun, reiterated Beijing's commitment to the Five Principles of Peaceful Co-existence and its vision of creating a Southeast Asia nuclear-free zone, a collective security arrangement that is sustainable and based on cooperation. However, Dong lamented that there were external forces seeking to undermine the region's status quo and asserted that false narratives were being spread about the "illegal arbitration ruling", clearly understood by all to be the *South China Sea Arbitration* award.

After seven servicemen of the Philippines were injured in a confrontation with the CCG on 17 June 2024 near the Second Thomas Shoal, the Philippine government treated the incident not as an armed attack but as a probable misunderstanding or accident, although it condemned these actions by the CCG against the Philippines' troops.

On 8 November 2024, the Philippines enacted the Act Declaring the Maritime Zones under the Jurisdiction of the Republic of the Philippines, defining the Philippines' internal waters, archipelagic waters, territorial sea, contiguous zone, exclusive economic zone and continental shelf; and the Act Authorizing the President of the Philippines to Establish the Archipelagic Sea Lanes in Philippine Archipelagic Waters. The former act clarifies the Philippines' claims in the South China Sea based on the 2016 *South China Sea Arbitration* award. The latter act establishes three designated passages for foreign vessels to navigate through the Philippine archipelago. The Chinese government immediately protested, urging the Philippines to earnestly respect China's territorial sovereignty and maritime rights and interests, immediately stop any unilateral moves that might escalate disputes or complicate the situation, and uphold peace and stability in South China Sea through concrete action. According to the Chinese government, many provisions contained in the Philippines' Archipelagic Sea Lanes Act are also incompatible with international law and resolutions of the International Maritime Organization. The Chinese side demanded that the Philippine side earnestly abide by international law and refrain from undermining the legitimate rights of all parties under international law, including UNCLOS. On 10 November 2024, the Chinese government issued a statement declaring the baselines of the territorial sea adjacent to Huangyan Dao (or Scarborough Shoal). In 1996, China indicated that it would eventually declare baselines around Nansha Qundao (Spratly Islands), Dongsha Qundao (Pratas Reef) and Zhongsha Qundao (Scarborough Shoal and underwater features including

[127] Tessa Wong, "Philippine President Warns China against 'Act of War'", BBC, 1 June 2024, https://www.bbc.com/news/articles/c7223knz3ezo.

Macclesfield Bank). Yet the new baselines are confined to Scarborough Shoal. Also, on 10 November 2024, China's Ministry of Natural Resources announced official geographic names for 64 features in the South China Sea as well as published an updated map for Sansha, China's southernmost city on the Hainan Island, featuring new designations for the districts of Paracel (Xisha in Chinese) and Spratly (Nansha in Chinese). Sansha's jurisdiction covers more than 280 islands, shoals, reefs and related maritime features, together with the waters surrounding them, comprising much of China's nine-dash line claims.

Malaysia has also lodged a formal protest against the Philippines' two new laws, which Malaysia considers to violate the maritime boundaries of Malaysia's Sabah State in northern Borneo.

In parallel, the Chinese and US governments have agreed to increase their military-to-military communications to avert a misunderstanding that leads to conflict arising from confrontations in the South China Sea.

In pursuing CBMs, the parties to the South China Sea disputes should understand how to make use of the international law on critical date, the value of peaceful protest as well as "without prejudice" clauses in their management of the conflict in the South China Sea, stressing that use of force of whatever scale or effect is totally prohibited without any excuse, legal or otherwise.[128]

Furthermore, there is still room for sovereignty disputes to be settled by third-party dispute settlement mechanisms even against the will of one of the disputing parties arguing that it has excluded the jurisdiction of international courts or tribunals over territorial disputes as well as disputes concerning "military activities". It is true that the Arbitral Tribunal in the *South China Sea Arbitration* held that a dispute that requires the determination of a question of territorial sovereignty is excluded from its jurisdiction.[129] However, that Arbitral Tribunal and other international courts and tribunals, including ITLOS, have exercised jurisdiction over "mixed" disputes, that is, disputes *partly* involving claims to territorial sovereignty, provided that the territorial dispute is necessary for the resolution of disputes concerning the interpretation or application of UNCLOS and is *merely ancillary* to the UNCLOS disputes, unless there is an agreement between the parties that expressly excludes such ancillary

---

[128] Cf. Youngmin Seo, "Power Shift, the South China Sea Dispute, and the Role of International Law", *Michigan Journal of International Law* 45 (2024): 93, where the author argues that any legal resolution to the South China Sea dispute must be scrutinised through the lens of balance-of-power considerations, and proposes practical recommendations to enhance the clarity and efficacy of some of the UNCLOS institutions.

[129] Award of 12 July 2016, 33 R.I.A.A. 153 (2016), at p. 184 [5].

territorial dispute. The Arbitral Tribunal in *Chagos Marine Protected Area Arbitration (Mauritius v. United Kingdom)* opined that, as a general matter, "where a dispute concerns the interpretation or application of UNCLOS, the jurisdiction of a court or tribunal pursuant to Article 288(1) extends to making such findings of fact or ancillary determinations of law as are necessary to resolve the dispute presented to it" but, where the "real issue in the case" and the "object of the claim" do not relate to the interpretation or application of UNCLOS, an incidental connection between the dispute and some matter regulated by UNCLOS is insufficient to bring the dispute, as a whole, within the ambit of Article 288(1).[130] This approach was followed in the judgment of the ITLOS Special Chamber in *Dispute concerning Delimitation of the Maritime Boundary between Mauritius and Maldives in the Indian Ocean (Mauritius/Maldives)* (Preliminary Objections).[131]

Also, activities by naval vessels/warships are not necessarily "military activities" that states parties to UNCLOS may exclude from the jurisdiction of dispute settlement mechanisms under UNCLOS—they can be law enforcement activities depending on the factual context at hand. This is because the distinction between military and law enforcement activities cannot be based solely on whether naval vessels or law enforcement vessels are employed in the activities in question. On the whole, the distinction between military and law enforcement activities must be based primarily on an objective evaluation of the nature of the activities in question, taking into account the relevant circumstances in each case.[132]

Self-Defence to Recover Territories?

One of the objectives of the Organisation of Islamic Cooperation as stipulated in Article 1(4) of its charter is "[t]o support the restoration of complete sovereignty and territorial integrity of any Member State under occupation, as a result

[130] *Arbitration regarding the Chagos Marine Protected Area between Mauritius and the United Kingdom of Great Britain and Northern Ireland*, Award of 18 Mar. 2015, 31 R.I.A.A. 359 (2015) at para. 220.
[131] ITLOS Judgment of 28 Jan. 2021 at paras. 110, 130–9, 246–51.
[132] *Case concerning the Detention of Three Ukrainian Naval Vessels (Ukraine v. Russian Federation,* Provisional Measures, ITLOS Order of 25 May 2019, paras. 64–6; *Dispute concerning the Detention of Ukrainian Naval Vessels and Servicemen*, Award on the Preliminary Objections of the Russian Federation, 27 June 2022, PCA Case No. 2019–28, paras. 104–25.

of aggression, on the basis of international law and cooperation with the relevant international and regional organizations".

A question then arises: when a state's territory or part thereof is occupied by another state for a prolonged duration, can the former state have lawful recourse to military force to recover it?

One school of thought answers this question in the negative, and for the following reasons.[133] First, an invocation of the right of self-defence in this context would appear prima facie difficult to reconcile with the *immediacy requirement*—a close proximity in time must exist between the start of an armed attack and a response in self-defence. The wording "if an armed attack *occurs*" in Article 51 of the UN Charter suggests a more or less instantaneous event, or a series of events, happening at a particular point in time—that is, the initial invasion or attack resulting in occupation, rather than a prolonged state of affairs characterised by an absence of active hostilities. Therefore, the state whose territory is invaded in violation of the law prohibiting the use of force will lose the ability to invoke the right of self-defence if it either (1) refrains from responding with counterforce for a prolonged period of time (taking into account the need for negotiation, military preparation, efforts to seek third-state support and so on) or (2) responds with counterforce, but ultimately fails to repel the invading forces from its territory before a prolonged cessation of active hostilities occurs. In both cases, the right of self-defence ceases to apply when a new territorial status quo is established, whereby the occupying state *peacefully* administers the territory concerned for a prolonged period. Those in favour of this view concede that state practice is mixed. For instance, Argentina's attempt to justify its military intervention in the Falklands/Malvinas in 1982 as an exercise of self-defence in response to the "illegal occupation" of those islands by the United Kingdom was overwhelmingly rejected by the UNSC, and even states supporting Argentine's territorial claims over the islands denounced the invasion as an unlawful use of force. Yet Egypt and Syria effectively argued that Israel's occupation of their respective territories in the aftermath of the 1967 Six Day War amounted to a continuing armed attack justifying their recourse to self-defence. Their unsuccessful efforts to recover the territories by use of force were not formally condemned by the UNGA or the UNSC but instead received support from several states. Some reservations are nonetheless in order. There could be many reasons why the UNGA and the UNSC acted in this way, such

---

[133] Tom Ruys and Felipe Rodríguez Silvestre, "Illegal: The Recourse to Force to Recover Occupied Territory and the Second Nagorno-Karabakh War", *European Journal of International Law* 32 (2021): 1287.

as the continued armed clashes between these states and Israel and the territories in question were hardly under the *peaceful* administration of Israel at the time. As regard the 2020 Nagorno-Karabakh war, where Azerbaijan tried to recover its territories that had been under Armenian occupation for more than two decades, Azerbaijan did not unequivocally rely on the notion of occupation as a continuing armed attack but instead claimed that it was conducting a "counter-offensive" following intensive shelling of its armed forces by Armenia. Türkiye asserted that Azerbaijan was exercising its inherent right of self-defence, since the hostilities were taking place exclusively on its own sovereign territory. Russia, France and the United States jointly condemned the escalation of violence during the war. The authors of this view contend that there have been remarkably few cases where states used armed force to challenge the existing territorial status quo and even fewer cases where they have done so by relying on the right of self-defence against a continuing armed attack.

Also, the threat or use of force as a means of solving international disputes, including territorial disputes and problems concerning frontiers of states, is prohibited under customary international law. Although it is frustrating to see the aggressor rewarded for its aggression through the consolidation of the unlawful territorial status quo, the maintenance of international peace and security and the peaceful resolution of disputes between states underpin the international legal order. Article 2(3) of the UN Charter stipulates that international disputes shall be settled only by peaceful means, which itself follows from the prohibition of the use of force in Article 2(4) of the Charter. Moreover, the human cost is at stake. To cite just one example, the 44-day war between Armenia and Azerbaijan in 2020 claimed the lives of 5,000 soldiers and no fewer than 140 civilians, with more than 130,000 civilians displaced by the fighting and hundreds of homes and vital infrastructure such as schools and hospitals destroyed. While Azerbaijan recovered part of the occupied area from Armenia, and the parties agreed to the deployment of Russian peacekeepers, the ceasefire agreement merely "refreezed" the new status quo.

Another school of thought disagrees with the above view, and for the following reasons.[134] Where occupation follows from an unlawful armed attack, the occupation is a continuing armed attack and the attacked state does not lose its right to self-defence simply because of the passage of time. Although territorial disputes cannot be resolved by recourse to force, there is an important distinction between a territorial dispute and a situation of armed attack

[134] Dapo Akande and Antonios Tzanakopoulos, "Legal: Use of Force in Self-Defence to Recover Occupied Territory", *European Journal of International Law* 32 (2021): 1299.

resulting in occupation of territory. Furthermore, the passage of time between the initial attack and the use of force in self-defence may signify that there is no other reasonable means of bringing the armed attack and occupation to an end except by the attacked and occupied state's use of force in self-defence. There are cases where a state is in occupation of territory that is claimed by another state but where the use of force occurred *before* the prohibition of the use of force in international relations came into effect and, as such, the occupation will not have resulted from an *unlawful* armed attack given the state of the law when the attack took place. For example, as regards the Falklands/Malvinas, the United Kingdom established control over the islands in 1833, more than a century before the entry into force of the UN Charter. Consequently, when the United Kingdom responded, in alleged self-defence against the Argentinian invasion, this was much better received than Argentina's stance to recover the islands by force.

According to this second school of thought, Article 3(a) of UNGA Resolution 3314 (XXIX) on the Definition of Aggression, adopted on 14 December 1974, provides that "military occupation *resulting from an invasion or attack*" constitutes aggression, and the ICJ has, in numerous instances, practically equated the notion of "aggression" with the notion of "armed attack" by relying on the Definition of Aggression in order to determine whether a particular use of force constitutes an armed attack.[135] Also, the wording "if an armed attack occurs" in Article 51 of the UN Charter does not linguistically confine the attack to a specific point in time. The Charter says "*if* an armed attack occurs", not "when", and fighting can go on for several years after the initial armed attack. There may be a situation where a lapse of time between an armed attack and an attempt to respond is merely an indication that the use of force is no longer necessary to repel the attack—where the armed attack has taken place, is complete or over, and there is nothing to repel anymore, absent any occupation. If an armed attack leads to occupation of territory, then it is continuing for as long as the territory is under occupation and it may actually mean that self-defence is necessary *precisely* because the state resorting to force in self-defence has no other means of bringing the armed attack and occupation to an end. Under Principle 1(5) of the 1970 Declaration on Friendly Relations, when an armistice or demarcation line is agreed, it is no longer necessary to use force. But when this armistice line is no longer "temporary" and it turns into status quo, then at some point it becomes necessary again to use

---

[135] For example, *Nicaragua*, ICJ Rep. 1986, pp. 103–4 [195]; *Armed Activities on the Territory of the Congo*, ICJ Rep. 2005, pp. 222–3 [146] (emphasis added).

force in self-defence, all other means to repel the armed attack having failed. Since prolonged occupation arising out of force is a continuing attack, the element of immediacy is (continuously) met, and the question then turns to the last resort element of necessity. Although such recaptures of occupied territory by force hardly ever happen since the vanquished also tends to be the weaker one, international law cannot fix such things as factual inequality, but at the very least it must be interpreted in such a way as to give its subjects an equal chance.

There was an interesting development in the aftermath of the 44-day Armenia–Azerbaijan war that might be cited to support the second school of thought. As part of the efforts to secure a lasting peace agreement between the two countries, in May 2024 Armenia returned to Azerbaijan four Azerbaijani villages, including several tiny enclaves entirely surrounded by Armenian territory, which Armenia had seized since the early 1990s. These lands, which had been uninhabited for over 30 years, are of strategic value to Armenia as they straddle the main road between Armenia's capital city of Yerevan and the Armenian–Georgian border. A 12.7-kilometre land boundary has been redrawn accordingly. It could be argued that the return of these lands to Azerbaijan would not have been possible if Azerbaijan had not engaged in a war to recover its territories from Armenia in the first place. On 8 August 2025, the two countries signed a peace agreement to end their 37-year-long Nagorno-Karabakh conflict.

Let's assume for the sake of argument that the second school of thought is technically correct. An overriding consideration for any national leader of sound mind is whether to order the use of force to recover a territory invaded and seized by another state in light of the potential human costs of war at stake,[136] as well as potential impact on the national economy. Even without waging a war to recover a territory now occupied by an aggressor state, the title to that territory remains with its rightful owner according to the peremptory norm of international law (jus cogens) proscribing aggression as a consequence of which no state shall recognise as lawful a situation created by the aggression, nor render aid or assistance in maintaining that acquisition of territories by means of the use of force.[137] Acquisition of a foreign territory by force also violates the right of

---

[136] Eliav Lieblich, "Wars of Recovery", *European Journal of International Law* 34 (2023): 349, 369–76.

[137] UN International Law Commission, "Identification and Legal Consequences of Peremptory Norms of General International Law (*Jus Cogens*)", *Yearbook of the International Law Commission*, 2022, vol. II, Part Two, Conclusions 19(2) and 23.

self-determination of the people occupying that territory, and self-determination is a jus cogens norm the violation of which entails non-recognition by other states of such forceful territorial acquisition. This will be examined in detail in Chapter 5.

While this chapter deals with interstate conflicts related to sovereignty, the next chapter examines intrastate conflict premised on "self-determination" that undermines state sovereignty.

CHAPTER 4

Insurgency and Self-Determination

Self-Determination as Recognised in International Instruments

The right to self-determination is consecrated in, inter alia, Articles 1(2) and 55 of the UN Charter, Article 1 of the 1966 International Covenant on Civil and Political Rights (ICCPR) and Article 1 of the 1966 International Covenant on Economic, Social and Cultural Rights (ICESCR), as well as in the jurisprudence of the International Court of Justice (ICJ).[1] This right has been recognised as a peremptory norm of international law (jus cogens).

The Ten Principles adopted by the Asian-African Conference in Bandung in 1955 include the principle of respect for the sovereignty and territorial integrity of all nations. The newly independent Asian and African states participating in the conference did not add the principle of self-determination as one of the Ten Principles, probably being wary of minorities and tribal groups within their respective states that might demand secession because they disagreed with or were adversely affected by the boundaries of these newly independent states, which were legacies of Western colonialism.

In 1960, the UN General Assembly (UNGA) adopted the Declaration on the Granting of Independence to Colonial Countries and Peoples.[2] The

[1] *Legal Consequences for States of the Continued Presence of South Africa in Namibia (South West Africa) notwithstanding Security Council Resolution 276 (1970)*, pp. 31–2 [52]–[3]; *Western Sahara*, Advisory Opinion, ICJ Rep. 1975, p. 12 at pp. 31–3 [54]–[9].
[2] A/RES/1514 (XV).

preamble of the declaration expresses, among other things, the UNGA's awareness of the increasing conflicts resulting from the denial of or impediments in the way of the freedom of "dependent peoples", which constitute a serious threat to world peace, as well as recognition that the peoples of the world ardently desire the end of colonialism in all its manifestations.

The declaration therefore declares, first of all, that the subjection of peoples to alien subjugation, domination and exploitation constitutes a denial of fundamental human rights, is contrary to the UN Charter and is an impediment to the promotion of world peace and cooperation. Second, all peoples have the right to self-determination; by virtue of that right they freely determine their political status and freely pursue their economic, social and cultural development. Third, inadequacy of political, economic, social or educational preparedness should never serve as a pretext for delaying independence. Fourth, all armed action or repressive measures of all kinds directed against dependent peoples shall cease in order to enable them to exercise peacefully and freely their right to complete independence, and the integrity of their national territory shall be respected. Fifth, immediate steps shall be taken, in trust and non-self-governing territories *or all other territories which have not yet attained independence*, to transfer all powers to the peoples of those territories, without any conditions or reservations, in accordance with their freely expressed will and desire, without any distinction as to race, creed or colour, in order to enable them to enjoy complete independence and freedom. Sixth, any attempt aimed at the partial or total disruption of the national unity and the territorial integrity of a country is incompatible with the purposes and principles of the UN Charter. Lastly, all states shall observe faithfully and strictly the provisions of the UN Charter, the 1948 Universal Declaration of Human Rights[3] and this declaration on the basis of equality, non-interference in the internal affairs of all states, and respect for the sovereign rights of all peoples and their territorial integrity.

Use of Force in Asia against Western Colonialism

The last use of force in Asia in the name of self-determination against Western colonialism was that of India's, when in 1961 it "liberated" Goa from "Portuguese colonialism".

On 18 December 1961, Indian troops crossed the border into Goa and, after launching land, sea and air strikes for more than 36 hours, the Portuguese forces

[3] A/RES/217(III).

unconditionally surrendered on 19 December 1961. For India, Goa was historically, culturally and demographically Indian territory. According to India, the Portuguese government had refused repeated requests of the Indian government since February 1950 to negotiate the transfer of the Portuguese possessions in India and invented a legal fiction that they were not colonies but part of metropolitan Portugal. India contended that the question before the UN Security Council (UNSC) as raised by Portugal was "a colonial question in the sense that part of Indian territory had been illegally occupied by conquest by Portugal"—Portugal had no sovereign right over that territory and there was no legal frontier between India and Goa since Goa was an integral part of India. Therefore, in India's view, a question of aggression could not arise. India asked the UNSC to tell Portugal to vacate Goa and the coastal enclaves of Daman and Diu on the Arabian Sea coast that were part of Portuguese India, and to give effect to the numerous resolutions of the UNGA with regard to the freedom of dependent peoples.[4]

Statements deploring India's use of force were made by governmental leaders and official spokespeople in many countries, including the United Kingdom, the United States, Canada, Australia, New Zealand, Pakistan, France, Netherlands, Spain and West Germany. On the other hand, full support for the Indian action was expressed by the Soviet Union and all Soviet bloc countries, along with Yugoslavia, the Arab states, Ghana, Ceylon and Indonesia. The delegates of Liberia, Ceylon and the UAE, which supported India against Portugal, presented a draft resolution to the UNSC that: (1) stated that "the enclaves claimed by Portugal in India constitute a threat to international peace and security and stand in the way of the unity of the Republic of India"; (2) asked the UNSC to reject the Portuguese charge of aggression against India; and (3) called upon Portugal "to terminate hostile action and cooperate with India in the liquidation of her colonial possessions in India". This draft resolution was not adopted, having been supported only by the Soviet Union. Thereafter, a draft resolution was presented by the United States, the United Kingdom, France and Turkey that: (1) called for the immediate cessation of hostilities; (2) called upon India to withdraw its forces immediately to the positions prevailing before 17 December 1961; (3) urged India and Portugal to work out a permanent solution of their differences by peaceful means in accordance with the principles embodied in the UN Charter; and (4) asked the

[4] UNGA, Complaint by Portugal (Goa), Decisions of 18 Dec. 1961, 987th and 998th mtgs. (S/5030). See further, Prabhakar Singh, "India before and after the *Right of Passage* Case", *Asian Journal of International Law* 5 (2015): 176.

UN secretary-general to provide such assistance as may be appropriate. The preamble of this draft resolution: (1) recalled that Article 2 of the UN Charter obligated all UN members to settle their disputes by peaceful means and refrain from the threat or use of force; (2) deplored "the use of force by India in Goa, Daman and Diu"; and (3) recalled that Article 1 of the UN Charter specifies as one of the purposes of the United Nations the development of friendly relations among nations based on respect for the principle of equal rights and self-determination of peoples. This latter draft resolution received seven votes in favour (the four sponsors plus Chile, Ecuador and Nationalist China) and four against (the Soviet Union, Ceylon, Liberia and the UAE). It was thus defeated by the Soviet Union's veto.[5]

When in 1970 the UNGA was considering adopting the Declaration on Friendly Relations, which the ICJ has considered to reflect customary international law,[6] UN members were careful not to allow a possibility of invoking the right to self-determination beyond the context of Western colonialism. The pertinent part of this declaration's principle of equal rights and self-determination reads (emphasis added):

> The establishment of a sovereign and independent State, the free association or integration with an independent State or the emergence into any other political status freely determined by a people constitute modes of implementing the *right of self-determination* by that people.
>
> Every State has the duty to refrain from any forcible action which deprives peoples referred to above in the elaboration of the present principle of their *right to self-determination* and freedom and independence . . .
>
> . . .
>
> *Nothing in the foregoing paragraphs shall be construed as authorizing or encouraging any action which would dismember or impair, totally or in part, the territorial integrity or political unity of sovereign and independent States conducting themselves in compliance with the principle of equal rights and self-determination of peoples as described above* and thus possessed of a government representing the whole people belonging to the territory without distinction as to race, creed or colour.

[5] *Keesing's Record of World Events*, 8 (Mar. 1962). 18659.

[6] *Nicaragua*, ICJ Rep. 1986, p. 94 [176].

Self-Determination and Insurgencies in Asia after Western Colonialism

The sanctity of this principle after Western colonialism was put to the test in the Indo-Pakistan War of 1971 that led to the independence of East Pakistan, renamed Bangladesh.[7]

The 1971 independence of Bangladesh, which seceded from Pakistan, was unique in many ways. Following independence from British rule in 1947, India was partitioned into two independent sovereign states—India and Pakistan, the latter comprising two regions lying on either side of India and separated geographically by thousands of kilometres of Indian territory. East Bengal, inhabited mostly by ethnic Bengalis, was renamed East Pakistan in 1955. It has never been linked in any way to West Pakistan, except they were both under British rule. The vast geographical separation between West Pakistan and East Pakistan was compounded by the former's political domination over the latter—which made the Bengali nationalist movement repeatedly claim that East Bengal/Pakistan was being treated as a colony of West Pakistan and that, therefore, it had a right to self-determination. Moreover, huge linguistic, cultural and ethnic differences existed, as well as regional disparity in economic growth that weighed heavily in favour of West Pakistan despite the fact that exports from East Pakistan such as jute made up a majority of Pakistan's export income. The December 1970 general elections in Pakistan gave the East Pakistan-based Awami League a mandate for the autonomy of East Pakistan, having won 167 out of the 313 National Assembly seats. However, the West Pakistani leadership prevented the League from forming a government, banned it and declared martial law. In March 1971, the West Pakistan Army launched Operation Searchlight to brutally suppress the separatist Bengali nationalist movement in East Pakistan, to the extent that it was allegedly tantamount to genocide, and that the creation of a new nation state was the only option to stop it and ensure the survival of the ethnic Bengalis.

The international community failed to intercede owing to West Pakistan's argument that the events leading up to the deployment of the West Pakistan Army to quell the separatist forces in East Pakistan were matters strictly within the internal jurisdiction of Pakistan. Citing the flow of refugees from East Pakistan into the Indian state of West Bengal, which placed unbearable financial strains on the already impoverished regional economy, India asserted the

---

[7] See also V.S. Mani, "An Indian Perspective on the Evolution of International Law on the Threshold of the Third Millennium", *Asian Yearbook of International Law* 9 (2004): 31, 73–4.

right to take action in defence of its territorial sovereignty. India's use of force to assist East Pakistan's struggle for independence was not condemned by the UNSC as the Soviet Union helped delay any UNSC resolution until India accomplished its military action.[8] Nonetheless, several states did not accept India's action and argument and urged India to cease hostilities and withdraw from East Pakistan.[9]

In hindsight, the impact of having an independent East Pakistan on Pakistan and the rest of the world was insignificant. After the Indian military victory over West Pakistan in 1971, East Pakistan met all the traditional requirements for recognition as a state—with a permanent population, a defined territory, a government and capacity to enter into relations with other states.[10] Most UN member states recognised Bangladesh as a new independent sovereign state within months of West Pakistan's military defeat by India. On 17 September 1974, Bangladesh became a new member of the United Nations.

Other claims of self-determination in Asia outside the context of Western colonialism included armed struggles in Aceh (1976–2005); West Papua after 1962, when it came under Indonesia's control; and East Timor after Indonesia's military invasion and occupation of Portugal's non-self-governing territory of East Timor.[11] Kurds in Iran, Iraq, Syria and Türkiye are the largest ethnic group in the world without an independent state and there has been a postcolo-

---

[8] Ved Nanda, "Self-Determination in International Law: The Tragic Tale of Two Cities—Islamabad (West Pakistan) and Dacca (East Pakistan)", *Asian Journal of International Law* 66 (1972): 321; Joshua Castellino, "The Secession of Bangladesh in International Law: Setting New Standards?", *Asian Yearbook of International Law* 7 (2000): 83.

[9] *United Nations Security Council Official Records*, 26th year, 1606th and 1608th mtgs, paras 185 and 262 The US representative emphasised that the action was contrary to the UN Charter (1606th mtg, paras 193–4). See also para. 237 (China); paras 201–13, 213 (Italy); paras 220–7 (France); and paras 279–92 (Belgium). Cited in Mohammad Taghi Karoubi, "Unilateral Use of Armed Forces and the Challenge of Humanitarian Intervention in International Law", *Asian Yearbook of International Law* 10 (2005): 95, 119–20.

[10] This is in accordance with the oft-cited definition of "the State as a person of international law" in Article 1 of the 1933 Montevideo Convention on the Rights and Duties of States (165 *League of Nations Treaty Series* 19, in force 26 Dec. 1934). See also Steven Wheatley, "The Emergence of New States in International Law: The Insights from Complexity Theory", *Chinese Journal of International Law* 15 (2016): 579, 598–606.

[11] Suzannah Linton, "International Humanitarian Law in Indonesia", in *Asia-Pacific Perspectives on International Humanitarian Law*, ed. Suzannah Linton, Tim McCormack and Sandesh Sivakumaran (Cambridge: Cambridge University Press, 2020), ch. 30, esp. at pp. 507, 527–37.

nial separatist war in Iraqi Kurdistan between Kurdish separatists and the central Iraqi government in Bagdad.[12]

In 2021 the Asia Foundation published a report on ongoing insurgents in Asia.[13] In Myanmar, there are more than 20 ethnic armed groups fighting the central government, the largest being the United Wa State Army, which runs a largely autonomous region along the Myanmar–China border. Over several decades of military rule in Myanmar, Burmese nationalism became increasingly associated with the ethnic and religious superiority of the Bamar Buddhist majority. In Pakistan, Balochistan, the largest but least populous province, continues to be affected by separatist conflict, driven by a number of grievances and inequities associated with the decolonisation process and partition, including lack of autonomy, lack of Baloch representation in the government and military, and economic oppression. Pakistani officials accuse India of involvement in perpetuating the conflict by providing Baloch militants with training and financial support through its 26 consulates established along the Balochistan border in Afghanistan and Iran. In the Philippines, since the 1960s, Moro (or indigenous Muslim) nationalist groups in Mindanao have engaged in rebellion against the Philippines, calling for greater rights and self-determination. Although two prominent groups, the Moro National Liberation Front and the Moro Islamic Liberation Front, signed peace deals with the Philippine government in 1996 and 2014, respectively, violence has continued, with extremist factions not involved in the peace deals being the main protagonists. There are also some armed organisations affiliated with the Islamic State in Iraq and the Levant (ISIL), including the Abu Sayyaf Group and the Maute Group, which remain active in the southern Philippines.[14] Thailand continues to be plagued by an "ethno-nationalist insurgency" in its southernmost provinces, rooted in the historical grievances

[12] See Yaniv Voller, *Second-Generation Liberation Wars: Rethinking Colonialism in Iraqi Kurdistan and Southern Sudan* (Cambridge: Cambridge University Press, 2022); Loqman Radpey, *Towards an Independent Kurdistan: Self-Determination in International Law* (Abingdon: Routledge, 2023).

[13] Asia Foundation, *The State of Conflict and Violence in Asia 2021: Identity-Based Conflict and Extremism* (San Francisco: Asia Foundation, 2022). See also Peter Chalk, "The History of Terrorism in Southeast Asia", in *Routledge Handbook of U.S. Counterterrorism and Irregular Warfare Operations*, ed. Michael A. Sheehan, Erich Marquardt and Liam Collins (Abingdon: Routledge, 2022), pp. 117–33.

[14] See also Soliman M. Santos, Jr., "*Jihad* and International Humanitarian Law: Three Moro Rebel Groups in the Philippines", in *Asia-Pacific Perspectives on International Humanitarian Law*, ch. 23.

of the area's Malay Muslim majority towards the Thai state. The total number of fatalities attributed to the violence in the southernmost provinces of Thailand between January 2004 and the end of 2020 was 7,201.

With respect to West Papua, which had the world's richest copper and gold deposits, it was set to gain independence from the Netherlands in 1970. According to certain narrative accounts, Indonesia allegedly wanted the territory for its mineral wealth, to resettle its surplus population, provide jobs for its oversized army and bureaucracy, and satisfy its ambition for territorial expansion. In 1962, the United States reportedly put pressure on the Netherlands to hand over West Papua to Indonesia in return for Indonesia's strategic concessions to the United States and mining concessions to a major US company. Indonesia and the Netherlands signed the Agreement concerning West New Guinea in August 1962[15] to transfer authority over the territory from the Netherlands to Indonesia, with a guarantee that the Papuan people would be allowed an "Act of Free Choice" (referendum) to determine their political status. The agreement provides for a UN Transitional Administration in West New Guinea (West Irian) for the aforesaid transfer of authority and for organising the conduct of the Act of Free Choice. In 1963, Indonesia, then run by the military-dominated government under General Suharto, who ruled Indonesia with an iron fist from March 1966 to May 1998, invaded West Papua. In the Act of Free Choice referendum in 1969 only 1,022 Papuan tribal representatives were allowed to vote, and they were reportedly coerced into voting in favour of formal integration with Indonesia, and many international observers including journalists and diplomats criticised the referendum as being manipulated by Indonesia. In November 1969, 84 UN member states voted in favour for the United Nations "taking note" of the result of that referendum, with 30 others abstaining. The Free Papua Movement has waged a low-intensity guerrilla war against Indonesia since 1962. No country except Vanuatu supports the Free Papua Movement politically, and none does so materially, because West Papua is small fry compared to Indonesia. Certain West Papuans proclaimed West Papua's independence from Indonesia in 1971, and in 1984 they raised the West Papuan flag in provincial assembly buildings and throughout West Papua. Those supporting independence have been reportedly murdered in large numbers. Although the Indonesian National Commission on Human Rights declared in 2003 that the Indonesian military had committed gross

[15] 6311 *United Nations Treaty Series* 274.

abuses in West Papua, the perpetrators have not been punished to date.[16] In 2017 the United Nations' decolonisation committee reportedly refused to accept a petition signed by 1.8 million West Papuans, or 70 per cent of the West Papuan population, calling for independence, on the ground that West Papua's cause was outside the committee's mandate. The petition asked the United Nations to appoint a special representative to investigate human rights abuses in West Papua and to "put West Papua back on the decolonization committee's agenda and ensure their right to self-determination . . . is respected by holding an internationally supervised vote".[17]

As for Thailand's southernmost provinces, they are situated on the Malay Peninsula, which has been inhabited since time immemorial. In or about 1295, the Siamese Kingdom of Sukhothai under King Ram Khamheng extended its rule down to the southernmost part of the Malay Peninsula, including what is now Singapore and Aceh in Indonesia. In approximately 1455, during the Siamese Ayudhya Kingdom, which succeeded the Sukhothai Kingdom, Malacca became strong, rejected Ayudhya's rule and spread Islamic teachings in the Malay Peninsula. Around 1457, the Kingdom of Patani was built on the Malay Peninsula and its Buddhist ruler converted to Islam. Between 1500 and 1530, Patani became known as "the mirror and corridor of Mecca". In 1786, the Siamese Kingdom of Rattanakosin, which succeeded the Ayudhya and Thornburi Kingdoms, respectively, regained Siamese rule over Patani and, in 1816, divided it into seven vassal states or protectorates for the sake of checks and balances among the local rulers. In 1909, Siam had to cede four of the aforesaid vassal states (namely, Kedah, Kelantan, Perlis and Terengganu) to Britain, while still retaining as part of Siam the other three (Pattani, Yala and Narathiwat), which had been incorporated into Siam in 1902. Siam was subsequently renamed Thailand in 1939. In 1947, there was a Muslim movement demanding the Thai government to reconsider how to govern the Muslim-majority southernmost provinces as a special case. In or around 1977,

---

[16] These narrative accounts are from Ron Crocombe, *Asia in the Pacific Islands: Replacing the West* (Suva: IPS Publications, University of South Pacific, 2007), pp. 12, 284–8; Thomas D. Musgrave, "An Analysis of the 1969 Act of Free Choice in West Papua", in *Sovereignty, Statehood and State Responsibility*, ed. Christine Chinkin and Freya Baetens (Cambridge: Cambridge University Press, 2015), pp. 209–28; Emma Kluge, "A New Agenda for the Global South: West Papua, the United Nations, and the Politics of Decolonization", *Humanity* 13 (June 2022): 66.

[17] Ben Doherty and Kate Lamb, "West Papuan Independence Petition Is Rebuffed at UN", *The Guardian,* 30 Sept. 2017, https://www.theguardian.com/world/2017/sep/30/west-papua-independence-petition-is-rebuffed-at-un.

a movement for the separation of the provinces from the rest of Thailand emerged. The current armed clashes between the separatists and the government have been on and off since 2004.[18] At present, Thailand's southernmost provinces of Pattani, Yala and Narathiwat and the Malay-speaking districts of Songkhla have a combined population of between 1.8 and 2 million people, of whom more than 1.5 million are ethnic Malays who profess the Islamic faith.[19]

An empirical study published in 2010 by an American professor of political science with in-depth knowledge of Thailand came to the following conclusions.[20] The study considered the four predominantly Muslim provinces (Satun, Narathiwat, Pattani and Yala) in Thailand and a largely Muslim contiguous province (Songkhla) to determine characteristics of the populations in these provinces. Based on the data from a survey taken in 2006, sympathy for the insurgency lay not in religion but in defending practices associated with loyalty to specific forms of Malay culture that characterise Thailand's southernmost region. Discourses surrounding the causes of the insurgency in the south vary dramatically. Scholars often rely on historical explanations linking the current violence to the separatist movements of militant rebel organisations—the Pattani United Liberation Organization (PULO), the smaller but more radical Berisan Revolusi Nasional (BRN, more specifically the BRN-Coordinate) and a larger coordinating group known as BERSATU (United Front for the Independence of Pattani). Yet new organisations without linkages to the historic conflict have appeared on the scene—Geragan Mujahideen Islam Pattani; the Runda Kampulan Kecil, an armed wing of the BRN; and the

---

[18] See also Wan Kadir bin Che Man, *Muslim Separatism: The Moros in Southern Philippines and the Malays in Southern Thailand* (PhD thesis, Australian National University, 1987), pp. 50–6; Ibrahim Syukri, *History of the Malay Kingdom of Patani*, trans. Conner Bailey and John N. Miksic (Athens, OH: Ohio University Press, 1985); Srisompop Jitpiromsri, Paul Chambers and Napisa Waitoolkiat, "Special Issue: Quagmire of Violence in Thailand's Southern Borderlands Chapter 1: Introduction", *Asian Affairs: An American Review* 45(2) (2018): 43; Onanong Thippimol, *Review Histories of Pat(t)ani: Different Point of Views* (Bangkok: Thailand Science Research and Innovation, 2020).

For an analysis of the situation on the ground from an international humanitarian law perspective, see Benjamin Zawacki, "Politically Inconvenient, Legally Correct: A Non-international Armed Conflict in Southern Thailand", *Journal of Conflict & Security Law* 18 (2013): 151.

[19] See further Joseph Chinyong Liow, *Religion and Nationalism in Southeast Asia* (Cambridge: Cambridge University Press, 2016), pp. 99–134.

[20] Robert B. Albritton, "The Muslim South in the Context of the Thai Nation", *Journal of East Asian Studies* 10 (2010): 61.

South Warriors of Valaya, with origins in Indonesia via Malaysia. In contrast, the International Crisis Group and the US Department of State find the insurgency driven by local grievances.

The evidence gathered by that author of the study indicated that whatever cleavages existed were not related specifically to Islam and Buddhism as much as they were related to a cultural identity and assimilation to the Thai state that served as a wedge between the two cultures. Thus, it is inaccurate to describe insurgencies as representative of "Muslim" opposition to Thai governance of the southern region. For example, Satun Province, which is heavily Muslim but Thai-speaking, exhibits little of the unrest that characterises the other predominantly Muslim-majority provinces. A majority of Muslims in Thailand are loyal to the Thai nation, in the sense of being proud to be Thai citizens (99.4 per cent) and in being willing to fight for Thailand should there be a war (83.6 per cent). In all categories, over three-quarters of all Thai Muslims are proud to be citizens of Thailand, roughly two-thirds are willing to fight for Thailand should the necessity arise, over three-quarters would choose to be Thai citizens and, perhaps more significantly, a substantial majority support the view that Thailand should remain one nation without part of the country allowed to become fully separate. Thai-speaking Muslims are more assimilated than Muslims who identify primarily as "Malay", but overall levels of patriotism and identification as "Thais" include large majorities of both cultural traditions. Over one-third of religious Muslims identify above all as "Thais". Over two-thirds of all Muslims would fight for Thailand and even more are proud to be Thais. Of Muslims who identify primarily as "Malay", however, only half would be willing to fight for Thailand, but these are not citizens for whom "Muslim" is a primary identification and they constitute only about 2.6 per cent of the population in the five southern provinces. It can be inferred from the analysis of data obtained from respondents in southern Thailand that the insurgency represents such a small minority of the Muslim community that characterisations of the crisis as "Muslim" are distortions of the true picture. Besides, southern Thai Buddhists are equally, if not more, at variance with the rest of Thailand in fundamental attitudes and values. The data provides support for hypotheses that Buddhists and Muslims are not very distinguishable in terms of basic orientations to government and society, and that there are numerous congruencies that offer optimism for the ability of Buddhists and Muslims to live together. More ominous is the perception by Muslims of government as more corrupt, especially at the national level rather than at the local level. The data indicates that these views are based upon Muslims experiencing more contact with corrupt officials than their

Buddhist counterparts. The sharp differences between perceptions of local and national government pose a somewhat strained environment under circumstances where government emanates from the national level, which includes efforts to resolve conflicts by forces that are not indigenous to the area, the policy to govern from Bangkok without sufficient sensitivity to attitudes and opinions at the local level, and a long-standing policy in the past of sending to the south government officials who have not performed well in other areas of the country as a kind of punishment for their past failures. The author therefore suggested there must be sensitivity to the life and culture of the peoples of Narathiwat, Pattani, Yala and even Satun and Songkhla, and any serious effort at unification and resolution of the conflicts in southern Thailand required an acknowledgement that Thais who live in the region, both Buddhist and Muslim, including Malay-speaking and Thai-speaking Muslims, are overwhelmingly loyal fellow citizens and must be recognised as holding equal citizenship with Buddhists in the nation of Thailand. Besides respect for the local culture, there should be a greater commitment to decentralisation of government and administration.

None of those claiming the right to self-determination in Asia, except for the East Timorese, have successfully emulated the people of East Pakistan to secede. The case of East Timor deserves to be separately analysed in Chapter 5 since it involves another Asian state using force to annex it.

There are two main reasons why Bangladesh is still the "unique precedent" of all the movements for secession studied in this chapter. First, the other insurgencies have not been able to seriously challenge the respective governments. Second, and even more importantly, as a matter of principle the empathy extended by Asian states to peoples under Western colonialism does not extend to peoples of states that have been liberated from Western colonialism and attained independence.

For Asian states, national integrity and territorial sovereignty are of utmost significance. This was made clear by them during the diplomatic conferences held from 1974 to 8 June 1977 to conclude Additional Protocol I and Additional Protocol II to the four Geneva Conventions of 12 August 1949 that establish international standards for humanitarian treatment in war/armed conflict.[21]

---

[21] See their positions during the drafting of these two instruments in Kriangsak Kittichaisaree, "International Humanitarian Law and the Asia-Pacific Struggles for National Liberation", in *Asia-Pacific Perspectives on International Humanitarian Law*, ch. 10.

Furthermore, the Helsinki Final Act adopted in 1975 by the Conference on Security and Cooperation in Europe refers in Principle VIII (Equal Rights and Self-Determination of Peoples) to the importance of realising self-determination in conformity with the principle of territorial integrity of states.

In the same vein, paragraph 2 of the Vienna Declaration and Programme of Action, adopted by the World Conference on Human Rights on 25 June 1993, reads (emphasis added):

> All peoples have the right of self-determination. By virtue of that right they freely determine their political status, and freely pursue their economic, social and cultural development.
>
> Taking into account the particular situation of peoples under colonial or other forms of alien domination or foreign occupation, the World Conference on Human Rights recognizes the right of peoples to take any legitimate action, in accordance with the Charter of the United Nations, to realize their inalienable right of self-determination. The World Conference on Human Rights considers the denial of the right of self-determination as a violation of human rights and underlines the importance of the effective realization of this right.
>
> In accordance with the [1970 Declaration on Friendly Relations], *this shall not be construed as authorizing or encouraging any action which would dismember or impair, totally or in part, the territorial integrity or political unity of sovereign and independent States conducting themselves in compliance with the principle of equal rights and self-determination of peoples and thus possessed of a Government representing the whole people belonging to the territory without distinction of any kind.*

In the declaration on becoming party to the ICCPR and the ICESCR in 1979, India states that the right to self-determination referred to in Article 1 of these covenants shall apply only to "the peoples under foreign domination" and not to "sovereign independent states or to a section of a people or nation—which is the essence of national integrity".

Indonesia has declared that, consistent with the UNGA's Declaration on the Granting of Independence to Colonial Countries and Peoples of 14 December 1960 and the 1970 Declaration on Friendly Relations and the relevant paragraph of the Vienna Declaration and Programme of Action of 1993, the words "the right of self-determination" in Common Article 1 of the ICCPR and the ICESCR do not apply to a section of people within a sovereign independent state and cannot be construed as authorising or encouraging any action that would dismember or impair, totally or in part, the territorial integrity or political unity of sovereign and independent states.

Laos has declared that Article 1 of the ICCPR concerning the right to self-determination shall be interpreted as being compatible with the 1970 Declaration on Friendly Relations and the 1993 Vienna Declaration and Programme of Action. Surprisingly, Laos has not made a similar declaration regarding Article 1 of the ICESCR, to which Laos is also a party.

For Thailand, the term "self-determination" in Common Article 1 of the ICCPR and the ICESCR shall be interpreted as being compatible with that expressed in the 1993 Vienna Declaration and Programme of Action.

Myanmar, which has been confronting separatist rebellions for decades, declares that term "the right of self-determination" in Article 1 of the ICESCR to which Myanmar is a party does not apply to any section of people within a sovereign independent state and cannot be construed as authorising or encouraging any action that would dismember or impair, totally or in part, the territorial integrity or political unity of a sovereign and independent state. In addition, the term shall not be applied to undermine section 10 of the 2008 Constitution of Myanmar, which stipulates that no part of Myanmar's territory shall secede from the country. Myanmar's declaration has been objected to by many states, such as Austria, Finland, Germany, Ireland, Latvia, the Netherlands, Portugal and Sweden, insofar as it is tantamount to a reservation of a general and indeterminate scope as it aims at applying a provision of the ICESCR only in conformity with the Constitution of Myanmar. Myanmar is not party to the ICCPR.

China's written statement to the ICJ, which was being asked by the UNGA to render an advisory opinion on Kosovo's unilateral declaration of independence, emphasised that, although the principle of self-determination has become a basic principle of international law, cases where such a right was exercised and endorsed by the United Nations were all related to territories under colonial rule or foreign occupation, such as Southern Rhodesia, Namibia, Western Sahara, East Timor, African territories under Portuguese administration, Palestine and Pacific islands (trust territories). Even after colonial rule ended in the world, the scope of application of the principle of self-determination has not changed. In China's view, self-determination in international law is different in nature from secession from a sovereign state—the latter is not recognised by international law and has always been opposed by the international community of states.

Bangladesh itself became party to the ICESCR in 1998 and the ICCPR in 2000. It has declared its understanding that the words "the right of self-determination of peoples" in Article 1 of the ICESCR apply "in the historical context of colonial rule, administration, foreign domination, occupation and similar situations". In December 1999, Germany objected to this declaration, considering it to be a reservation that places conditions on the exercise of the right of all peoples to self-determination that are not provided for in international law, and that such conditions could undermine the concept of self-determination and seriously weaken its universally acceptable character. Also, in December 1999, the Netherlands objected to this reservation by Bangladesh, since the right of self-determination as embodied in the ICESCR is "conferred upon all peoples"—this follows not only from the very language of Article 1 of the ICESCR but also from the most authoritative statement of the law concerned, that is, the 1970 Declaration on Friendly Relations. Like Germany, the Netherlands is of the view that any attempt to limit the scope of this right or to attach conditions not provided for in the relevant instruments would undermine the concept of self-determination itself and would thereby seriously weaken its universally acceptable character. Bangladesh has not made any declaration on the right of self-determination in Article 1 of the ICCPR probably because of these objections it has encountered in relation to its declaration concerning Article 1 of the ICESCR. After the successful secession of Bangladesh from Pakistan in 1971, can any insurgency in Asia ever invoke the right of self-determination for the purpose of secession these days?

A frequently cited judicial pronouncement on the right to self-determination is that of the Supreme Court of Canada in *Reference re Secession of Quebec*.[22] According to the Canadian Supreme Court, the international law right to self-determination only generates, at best, a right to *external* self-determination in situations of former colonies; where a people is oppressed, as for example under foreign military occupation; or where a definable group is denied meaningful access to government to pursue their political, economic, social and cultural development. In all three situations, the people in question are entitled to a right to external self-determination because they have been denied the ability to exert internally their right to self-determination. A state whose government represents the whole of the people or peoples resident within its territory, on a basis of equality and without discrimination, and respects the principles of self-determination in its internal arrangements, is entitled to maintain its territorial

---

[22] [1998] 2 Canada Supreme Court Rep. 217 at paras 138 and 154. For discussion of judicial or quasi-judicial decisions on self-determination, see Tom Sparks, *Self-Determination in the International Legal System: Whose Claim, to What Right?* (Oxford: Hart, 2023), pp. 129–85, 194–226.

integrity under international law and to have that territorial integrity recognised by other states.[23]

On 17 February 2008, Kosovo unilaterally declared its independence from Serbia. Kosovo had been under the rule of the Ottomans for more than four centuries, until Serbia acquired the territory during the First Balkan War in 1912–13. Kosovo was incorporated into the Kingdom of the Serbs, Croats and Slovenes (later named Yugoslavia) after the First World War. During the Second World War, parts of Kosovo were absorbed into Italian-occupied Albania and, afterwards, Kosovo became an autonomous province of Serbia in the Socialist Federal Republic of Yugoslavia, which comprised six constituent republics: Bosnia and Herzegovina, Croatia, Macedonia, Montenegro, Serbia and Slovenia. Serbia itself comprised the Yugoslav capital city of Belgrade plus two autonomous Yugoslav provinces: Kosovo and Vojvodina. In 1981, riots erupted and were violently suppressed after Kosovo Albanians demonstrated to demand that Kosovo be granted a full republic status. In 1989, Serbian president Slobodan Milosevic eliminated Kosovo's autonomy and imposed direct rule from Belgrade and ordered the dismissal of most ethnic Albanian state employees, whose jobs were then taken up by Serbs. In response, Kosovo Albanian leaders began a peaceful resistance movement in the early 1990s. They established a parallel government funded mainly by the Albanian diaspora. When this movement failed to yield results, an armed resistance emerged in 1997 in the form of the Kosovo Liberation Army (KLA) to secure Kosovo's outright independence. By then the Socialist Federal Republic of Yugoslavia had disintegrated, with Croatia and Slovenia having seceded and gained some international recognition in 1991. The Socialist Federal Republic of Yugoslavia dissolved along the borders of federated republics, expedited by the start of the Yugoslav Wars, and the federation formally broke up on 27 April 1992. Two republics, Serbia and Montenegro, remained within a reconstituted state known as the Federal Republic of Yugoslavia. In late 1998, Milosevic ordered a brutal police and military campaign against the KLA, which included widespread ethnic cleansing against Kosovo's ethnic Albanian population, leading to NATO's aerial bombing from 24 March to 10 June 1999 to halt the violence in Kosovo. After 78 days of bombing, Milosevic capitulated. On 10 June 1999, the UNSC acting under Chapter VII of the UN Charter

[23] Quoted with approval by the UK Supreme Court in *Reference by the Lord Advocate of Devolution Issues under paragraph 34 of Schedule 6 to the Scotland Act 1998*, Judgment of 23 Nov. 2022, paras 88–9.

adopted Resolution 1244 (1999)[24] by 14 votes to none against, with China abstaining.[25]

The preamble of UNSC Resolution 1244 (1999) expresses the UNSC's determination "to resolve the grave humanitarian situation in Kosovo, Federal Republic of Yugoslavia, and to provide for the safe and free return of all refugees and displaced persons to their homes", as well as condemns "all acts of violence against the Kosovo population as well as all terrorist acts by any party". While reaffirming "the commitment of all UN Member States to the sovereignty and territorial integrity of the Federal Republic of Yugoslavia and the other States of the region, as set out in the Helsinki Final Act", the preamble also reaffirms the call in previous UNSC resolutions for substantial autonomy and meaningful self-administration for Kosovo, as well as determines that the situation in the region continues to constitute a threat to international peace and security. The resolution authorises the UN secretary-general to establish an international civil presence in Kosovo in order to provide "an interim administration for Kosovo . . . which will provide transitional administration while establishing and overseeing the development of provisional democratic self-governing institutions". Paragraph 3 demands "in particular that the Federal Republic of Yugoslavia put an immediate and verifiable end to violence and repression in Kosovo, and begin and complete verifiable phased withdrawal from Kosovo of all military, police and paramilitary forces according to a rapid timetable". Pursuant to paragraph 5, the UNSC decided on the deployment in Kosovo, under the auspices of the United Nations, of international civil and security presences and welcomed the agreement of the Federal Republic of Yugoslavia to such presences. The powers and responsibilities of the security presence were further clarified in paragraphs 7 and 9. Paragraph 15 demanded that the KLA and other armed Kosovo Albanian groups immediately end all offensive actions and comply with the requirements for demilitarisation.

In June 2005, the UN secretary-general appointed Norwegian diplomat Kai Eide as his special envoy to carry out a comprehensive review of Kosovo. In the wake of the comprehensive review report he submitted to the UN secretary-general, there was consensus within the UNSC that, notwithstanding

---

[24] S/RES/1244 (1999).

[25] Office of the Historian, US Department of State, "A Guide to the United States' History of Recognition, Diplomatic, and Consular Relations, by Country, since 1776: Kosovo". See also Tim Judah, *Kosovo: What Everyone Needs to Know* (New York: Oxford University Press, 2008).

the challenges still facing Kosovo and the wider region, "the time has come to move to the next phase of the political process" to determine Kosovo's future status, as foreseen in UNSC Resolution 1244 (1999). In November 2005, the UN secretary-general appointed Martti Ahtisaari, former president of Finland, as his special envoy for the future status process for Kosovo. Between 20 February and 8 September 2006, several rounds of negotiations were held, at which the Serbian and Kosovan delegations addressed, in particular, the decentralisation of Kosovo's governmental and administrative functions, cultural heritage and religious sites, economic issues and community rights.

On 26 March 2007, the UN secretary-general submitted the report of his special envoy to the UNSC; in the report the special envoy concluded that the negotiations' potential to produce any mutually agreeable outcome on Kosovo's status had been exhausted, and that "the only viable option for Kosovo [was] independence, to be supervised for an initial period by the international community". Between 9 August and 3 December 2007, further negotiations on the future status of Kosovo were held under the auspices of a troika comprising representatives of the European Union, Russia and the United States. On 4 December 2007, the troika submitted its report to the UN secretary-general, which came to the conclusion that, despite intensive negotiations, the parties were unable to reach an agreement on Kosovo's status and neither side was willing to yield on the basic question of sovereignty.

On 17 November 2007, elections were held for the Assembly of Kosovo, 30 municipal assemblies and their respective mayors. The Assembly of Kosovo held its inaugural session on 4 and 9 January 2008. The declaration of independence was adopted at a meeting held on 17 February 2008 by 109 out of the 120 members of the Assembly of Kosovo, including the prime minister of Kosovo, and by the president of Kosovo (who was not a member of the Assembly). The ten members of the Assembly representing the Kosovo Serb community and one member representing the Kosovo Gorani community decided not to attend this meeting. The declaration was written down on two sheets of papyrus and read out, voted upon and then signed by all representatives present. It was not transmitted to the special representative of the UN secretary-general and was not published in the Official Gazette of the Provisional Institutions of Self-Government of Kosovo. After the declaration of independence was issued, Serbia informed the UN secretary-general that Serbia considered the declaration to be a forceful and unilateral secession of a part of Serbia's territory, and did not produce legal effects either in Serbia or in the international legal order. At the emergency public meeting of the UNSC on 18 February 2008, Serbia's president denounced the declaration of independence as an unlawful act that had been declared null and void by the National Assembly of Serbia. The UNGA then requested an advisory opinion from the ICJ: "Is the unilateral declaration of independence by the Provisional Institutions of Self-Government of Kosovo in accordance with international law?"[26]

The ICJ is not required by this question to take a position on whether international law confers a positive entitlement on Kosovo unilaterally to declare its independence or, a fortiori, on whether international law generally confers an entitlement on entities situated within a state unilaterally to break away from it. While the UNSC has condemned particular declarations of independence, in all of those instances it was making a determination as regards the concrete situation existing at the time when those declarations of independence were made. The ICJ noted that:

> [T]he illegality attached to the declarations of independence thus stemmed not from the unilateral character of these declarations as such, but from the fact that they were, or would have been, connected with the unlawful use of force or other egregious violations of norms of general international law, in particular those of a peremptory character (*jus cogens*).

In the context of Kosovo, the UNSC has never taken this position. The ICJ found it unnecessary in the case to resolve the questions of whether, outside the context of non-self-governing territories and peoples subject to alien subjugation, domination and exploitation, the international law of self-determination confers upon part of the population of an existing state a right to separate from that state and whether and, if so, in what circumstances international law provides for a right of "remedial secession"—the right to separate from a state. The ICJ concluded that general international law contains no applicable prohibition of declarations of independence, and that Kosovo's declaration of independence of 17 February 2008 did not violate international law.[27]

At the time of writing, 108 states had formally recognised Kosovo as an independent sovereign state, of which the following are from Asia: Afghanistan, Bahrain, Bangladesh, Brunei, Fiji, Israel, Japan, Jordan, Kiribati, Kuwait, Malaysia, the Maldives, the Marshall Islands, Micronesia, Oman, Pakistan, Palau, Qatar, Samoa, Saudi Arabia, Singapore, South Korea, Thailand, Timor-Leste, Tonga, Tuvalu, UAE, Vanuatu and Yemen. India has consistently opposed

---

[26] *Accordance with International Law of the Unilateral Declaration of Independence in Respect of Kosovo*, Advisory Opinion, ICJ Rep. 2010, p. 403, at pp. 426–35 [57]–[77].
[27] Ibid., pp. 436–9 [78]–[84] and pp. 452–3 [123(3)].

Kosovo's independence, fearing, among other things, that Kosovo's independence would set a precedent for Kashmir's independence.[28] Kosovo is not yet a member of the United Nations owing to the opposition from China and Russia, which consider its unilateral declaration of independence to be illegal. China sees Kosovo's independence as setting a bad example for Taiwan, which China considers to be part of its territory.

Of direct relevance to the legal principles raised in this chapter are the views of Judges Koroma, Cançado Trindade and Yusuf in the ICJ's Advisory Opinion on Kosovo.

In his dissenting opinion, Judge Koroma from Sierra Leone found that Kosovo's declaration of independence violated the principle of respect for the sovereignty and territorial integrity of states, which entails an obligation to respect the definition, delineation and territorial integrity of an existing state. He cited Article 2(4) of the UN Charter and the 1970 Declaration on Friendly Relations in support of his conclusion. Judge Koroma also referred to the finding made by the Supreme Court of Canada in *Reference re Secession of Quebec* that "international law does not specifically grant component parts of sovereign States the legal right to secede unilaterally from their 'parent' State". While Judge Koroma took the view that the Supreme Court of Canada correctly answered the question posed to it, he emphasised that the question before the ICJ was different and provided an opportunity to complete the picture partially drawn by the Supreme Court of Canada. In particular, the ICJ should have made clear that the applicable law in this case contains explicit and implicit rules against the unilateral declaration of independence.[29]

The separate opinions of Judge Yusuf from Somalia and Judge Cançado Trindade from Brazil addressed the postcolonial conception of the right of self-determination and its scope of application. According to these two ICJ judges, postcolonial self-determination has two dimensions: *internal* and *external* self-determination. The former is in the context of the relationship between peoples and their own state, especially (1) a right of the entire population of the state to determine its own political, economic and social destiny and the equal right to choose a representative government; and (2) a right of a defined part of the population, which has distinctive characteristics on the basis of race or ethnicity, to participate in the political life of the state, to be represented in its government,

[28] Arvind Sivaramakrisnan, "Kashmir Issue Clouds Indian View of Kosovo", *The Hindu*, 4 Apr. 2011, https://www.thehindu.com/news/the-india-cables/Kashmir-issue-clouds-Indian-view-of-Kosovo/article14670496.ece.

[29] ICJ Rep. 2010, p. 467, at pp. 475–7.

and not to be discriminated against. External self-determination serves as "remedial secession" and the exception to the cardinal rule of territorial integrity of states. This is permissible if the state (1) denies such groups an exercise of their right of internal self-determination and (2) subjects them to systematic discrimination, persecution due to racial or ethnic characteristics, and egregious violations of human rights (such as torture, mass killing, ethnic cleansing, mass forced displacement of the population, and inhuman treatment) or humanitarian law. Denial of autonomous political structures or a decision by the UNSC to intervene could allow an additional criterion to be considered. All possible remedies for the realisation of internal self-determination must be exhausted before external self-determination can be invoked.[30]

Applying this reasoning, Judge Cançado Trindade considered that Kosovo's declaration of independence could only be appropriately considered in light of the complex and tragic factual background of the grave humanitarian crisis of Kosovo, which culminated in UNSC Resolution 1244 (1999). In his view, contemporary international law is no longer indifferent to the fate of the population, the most precious constitutive element of statehood—states exist for human beings and not vice-versa. States transformed into machines of oppression and destruction cease to be states in the eyes of their victimised population, who may therefore seek refuge and survival in international law to attain "emancipation from tyranny and systematic oppression".[31]

Judge Yusuf found it regrettable that the ICJ decided not to touch upon the important aspect of the question posed by the UNGA, namely the scope and normative content of the postcolonial right of self-determination. Addressing the question of self-determination and clarifying its applicability to this specific case would have allowed the ICJ to contribute, inter alia, to the prevention of the misuse of this important right by groups promoting ethnic and tribal divisions within existing states. He rightly noted that claims to separate statehood by ethnic groups or other entities within a state can create situations of armed conflict and may pose a threat not only to regional stability but also to international peace and security.[32]

---

[30] Separate Opinion of Judge Yusuf, ICJ Rep. 2010, p. 618 at pp. 621–4 [9]–[16] and Separate Opinion of Judge Cançado Trindade, ICJ Rep. 2010, p. 523 at pp. 592–609, [174]–[217]. See also Milena Sterio, *The Right to Self-Determination under International Law: "Selfistants", Secession, and the Rule of the Great Powers* (Abingdon: Routledge, 2013).

[31] ICJ Rep. 2010, p. 617 [239]–[240].

[32] Ibid., pp. 619–20 [4]–[6]. For an in-depth and critical analysis of internal self-determination, external self-determination and remedial secession, see Przemysaw Tacik,

There are other instances of external self-determination after Western colonialism and subsequent to insurgencies, armed conflicts or civil wars.

Self-determination because of dissolution of a sovereign state took place when the Soviet Union dissolved in 1991 and Czechoslovakia was split into the Czech Republic and Slovakia in 1993.

Eritrea became an independent sovereign state in 1993 after winning the war of resistance to Ethiopia's annexation of Eritrea lasting from 1 September 1961 to 24 May 1991. Adhering to its commitment to hold an internationally supervised referendum, the victorious Eritrean People's Liberation Front, a coalition of Eritrean resistance groups opposed to Ethiopian rule, decided against an outright declaration of independence but decided to seek a legal, democratic conclusion to the conflict so as to promote stability and gain the full support of the international community. In the referendum supervised by the United Nations in April 1993, 99.83 per cent of the turnout of 98.5 per cent of eligible Eritrean voters cast their vote in favour of Eritrea's independence.[33]

South Sudan became an independent state on 9 July 2011. There were civil wars in Sudan from 1955 to 1972 and 1983 to 2005, the latter resulting in a peace agreement that gave the south autonomy for six years, followed by a referendum on independence. The referendum in January 2011 overwhelmingly approved the south's independence from Sudan. On 9 July 2011, the UNSC, determining that the situation faced by South Sudan continued to constitute a threat to international peace and security in the region, set up the United Nations Mission in the Republic of South Sudan for an initial period of one year and has renewed it for further periods ever since.

Another attempted secession in Africa has failed, however. The Tigray War was fought primarily in Ethiopia's Tigray region between the Tigray People's Liberation Front (TPLF), a left-wing ethnic paramilitary group, on the one side, and the Ethiopia federal government and Eritrea, on the other side, from 3 November 2020 to the ceasefire on 3 November 2022 that cost thousands of lives and widespread destruction. Ethiopia adopted a federal system of government in 1994 in which different ethnic groups control the affairs of ten Ethiopian regions. The 1995 Constitution of Ethiopia[34] is unique in that it explicitly recognises, in Article 5, "an unconditional right to self-determination, including

Deconstructing Self-Determination in International Law: Sovereignty, Exception, and Biopolitics (Leiden: Brill/Nijhoff, 2023), pp. 293–339.

[33] Boutros Boutros-Ghali, *The United Nations and the Independence of Eritrea* (New York: United Nations, 1996).

[34] https://www.wipo.int/edocs/lexdocs/laws/en/et/et007en.pdf.

the right to secession" by every "Nation, Nationality or People", defined as "a group of people who have or share large measure of a common culture or similar customs, mutual intelligibility of language, belief in a common or related identities, a common psychological make-up, and who inhabit an identifiable, predominantly contiguous territory". Every nation, nationality or people has the right to a full measure of self-government, which includes the right to establish institutions of government in the territory that it inhabits and to equitable representation in state and federal governments. The right to self-determination, including secession, of every nation, nationality or people shall come into effect: (1) when a demand for secession has been approved by a two-thirds majority of the members of the legislative council of the nation, nationality or people concerned; (2) when the federal government has organised a referendum, which must take place within three years from the time it received the concerned council's decision for secession; (3) when the demand for secession is supported by a majority vote in the referendum; (4) when the federal government has transferred its powers to the council of the nation, nationality or people who have voted to secede; and (5) when the division of assets is effected in a manner prescribed by law. The Tigray War has proved how precarious the self-determination envisaged in Article 5 of the 1995 constitution Ethiopia can be if it is literally construed.

The main cause of the Tigray War seemed to be the denial to the 5.443 million people of the Tigray National Regional State, the northernmost regional state in Ethiopia, their internal self-determination. In 2019, the TPLF opposed the central government's reforms, which it considered to be an attempt to centralise power and destroy Ethiopia's federal system of government. After the national elections were postponed because of the COVID-19 pandemic, Tigray defied the central government to hold its own regional election, which the central government denounced as illegal. The Tigray War broke out after Tigrayan forces were accused by the central government of attacking army bases to steal weapons and the central government sent troops to fight them and the fighting quickly escalated into a full-scale war. On 2 November 2022, the federal government of Ethiopia and the TPLF signed the Agreement for Lasting Peace through a Permanent Cessation of Hostilities, brokered by the African Union and mediated by former Nigerian president Olusegun Obasanjo. Of special relevance to our discussion in this chapter is that the agreement obliges the parties to recognise that Ethiopia has only one defence force, that Tigrayan rebel forces should demobilise and reintegrate, and that the TPLF must completely disarm within 30 days of signing the agreement. The agreement also stipulates that the Ethiopian federal government must be allowed to re-establish authority in the

Tigray Region, and, in return, the federal government guarantees that Tigray will be properly represented in government institutions, so as to not violate the Ethiopian constitution. Should the agreement collapse and Tigrayans are deprived of their right to internal self-determination, Tigrayans may demand external self-determination but the federal government is unlikely to take the necessary procedural steps stipulated in Article 5 of the 1995 Ethiopian Constitution. An important question is, if the TPLF can eventually exercise effective control over the Tigray National Regional State, will the international community recognise a new sovereign state of Tigray despite the lack of fulfilment of the procedural conditions under Article 5 of the 1995 Ethiopian Constitution?

Recognition of New States

Under customary international law on the recognition of states, the recognition by another state is merely declaratory of the fact that an entity is already a state. According to the International Law Association's Committee on Recognition and Non-recognition in International Law, where competing regimes have sought recognition as a state's government, the various approaches taken have not reflected firmly established criteria for assessing governmental legitimacy.[35] International law is also silent as far as the lawfulness of secessions is concerned, subject to two exceptions: when a secession is the result of the unlawful use of force by another state (such as the Japanese intervention in China that led to Manchuria/Manchukuo's secession from China from 1932 to 1945) or is an attempt to suppress the majority population, as was the case when Rhodesia seceded from the United Kingdom in 1965. Otherwise, under international law, secession is an internal matter for the state concerned. However, once the secessionist movement has been so successful and can claim to fulfil all statehood criteria, international law does not prohibit its recognition as a new state, as in the cases of Bangladesh, Eritrea, Kosovo and South Sudan.[36]

On the whole, since the independence of Bangladesh in 1971, the other states that have gained independence as mentioned above have gone through

[35] Paras 1 and 6 of Resolution 3/2018 of the Committee on Recognition and Non-Recognition in International Law, 78th Conference of the International Law Association, Sydney, Australia, 19–24 Aug. 2018.

[36] Patrick C.R. Terry, "The Recognition of New States in Times of Secession: Is State Recognition Turning into Another Means of Intervention?", *Asian Yearbook of International Law* 20 (2014): 53, 64, 83, 85, 91, 98–9, 113. See also Pavle Kilibarda, *Recognition of States under International Law* (Oxford: Oxford University Press, 2024).

either civil wars or wars of liberation of such a massive scale attracting the involvement of the international community, especially the United Nations.

International Humanitarian Law and the Law Enforcement Paradigm

Where certain conditions are met, insurgencies and their suppression may be subject to the regime of international humanitarian law (IHL) regulating armed conflicts under Article 3 common to the four Geneva Conventions of 12 August 1949, to which all Asian states are parties, or under the 1977 Protocol Additional to the Geneva Conventions of 12 August 1949, and relating to the Protection of Victims of Non-international Armed Conflicts (AP II), which has 170 parties, where applicable.

Common Article 3 of the four Geneva Conventions of 1949 reads as follows:

> In the case of armed conflict not of an international character occurring in the territory of one of the High Contracting Parties, each Party to the conflict shall be bound to apply, as a minimum, the following provisions:
> 1) Persons taking no active part in the hostilities, including members of armed forces who have laid down their arms and those placed hors de combat by sickness, wounds, detention, or any other cause, shall in all circumstances be treated humanely, without any adverse distinction founded on race, colour, religion or faith, sex, birth or wealth, or any other similar criteria.
>
> To this end, the following acts are and shall remain prohibited at any time and in any place whatsoever with respect to the above-mentioned persons:
> a) violence to life and person, in particular murder of all kinds, mutilation, cruel treatment and torture;
> b) taking of hostages;
> c) outrages upon personal dignity, in particular humiliating and degrading treatment;
> d) the passing of sentences and the carrying out of executions without previous judgment pronounced by a regularly constituted court, affording all the judicial guarantees which are recognized as indispensable by civilized peoples.
> 2) The wounded and sick shall be collected and cared for.
>
> An impartial humanitarian body, such as the International Committee of the Red Cross, may offer its services to the Parties to the conflict. The Parties to the conflict should further endeavour to bring into force, by means of special agreements, all or part of the other provisions of the present Convention.

> The application of the preceding provisions shall not affect the legal status of the Parties to the conflict.

For this Common Article 3 to be applicable, there must be protracted armed confrontations occurring between governmental armed forces and the forces of one or more armed groups, or between such groups arising on the territory of a state party to the Geneva Conventions, provided that the armed confrontation reaches the requisite threshold of intensity and the parties involved in the conflict must have a certain level of organisation as objectively assessed based on the facts of each case. These two criteria serve to distinguish an armed conflict under IHL from banditry; unorganised and short-lived insurrections or terrorist activities; isolated and sporadic acts of violence; and situations of internal disturbances and tensions, such as riots, or other acts of a similar nature, which are not subject to IHL.[37]

Various indicative factors have been taken into account by international criminal tribunals and domestic courts to assess the "intensity" of the conflict. These include the seriousness of attacks and whether there has been an increase in armed clashes, the spread of clashes over territory and over a period of time, any increase in the number of government forces and mobilisation and the distribution of weapons among both parties to the conflict, as well as whether the conflict has attracted the attention of the UNSC and whether any UNSC resolutions on the matter have been passed. Also taken into account are the number of civilians forced to flee from the combat zones; the type of weapons used, in particular the use of heavy weapons, and other military equipment, such as tanks and other heavy vehicles; the blocking or besieging of towns and the heavy shelling of these towns; the extent of destruction and the number of casualties caused by shelling or fighting; the quantity of troops and units deployed; existence and change of front lines between the parties; the occupation of territory, and towns and villages; the deployment of government forces to the crisis area; the closure of roads; ceasefire orders and agreements, and the attempt of representatives from international organisations to broker and enforce ceasefire agreements.[38] While isolated acts of terrorism may not reach the threshold of armed conflict for this purpose, when there is protracted

[37] *Prosecutor v. Ljube Boškoski and Johan Tarčulovski*, Case No. IT-04-82-T, ICTY Trial Chamber II, Judgment, 10 July 2008, paras 175, 176 and 185; Article 8(2)(d) of the 1998 Rome Statute of the International Criminal Court.

[38] *Boškoski and Tarčulovski*, paras 177, 180–3.

violence of this type, especially where they require the engagement of the armed forces in hostilities, such acts are relevant to assessing the requisite level of intensity.[39]

The following indicative factors have been taken into account by international criminal courts to ascertain the "organisation" of an armed group for the purpose of Common Article 3, none of which is, in itself, essential to establish whether the "organisation" criterion is fulfilled. These fall into the following five broad sets of indicators: (1) factors signalling the presence of a command structure; (2) factors indicating the armed group's ability to carry out operations in an organised manner, such as the group's ability to determine a unified military strategy and to conduct large-scale military operations and its capacity to control territory; (3) factors indicating a level of logistics, such as the ability to recruit new members, the providing of military training, and the organised supply of military weapons; (4) factors relevant to determining whether an armed group possessed a level of discipline and the ability to implement the basic obligations of Common Article 3; and (5) factors indicating that the armed group is able to speak with one voice, such as its capacity to act on behalf of its members in political negotiations with representatives of international organisations and foreign countries; and its ability to negotiate and conclude agreements such as ceasefire or peace accords.[40]

Additional Protocol II develops and supplements Common Article 3 and applies in non-international armed conflicts between the armed forces of a state and "dissident armed forces or other organized armed groups which, under responsible command, exercise such control over a part of its territory as to enable them to carry out sustained and concerted military operations and to implement this Protocol". AP II strengthens protection beyond the minimum standards contained in Common Article 3 by including prohibitions against direct attacks on civilians, collective punishment, acts of terrorism, rape, forced prostitution and indecent assault, slavery and pillage. It also provides rules on the treatment of persons deprived of their liberty. The parties to AP II from the Asian region covered by this book are Afghanistan, Bahrain, Bangladesh, Brunei, Cambodia,

---

[39] Ibid., paras 187–90.

[40] Ibid., paras 198–202. This was upheld by the ICTY Appeals Chamber (*Prosecutor v. Ljube Boškoski and Johan Tarčulovski*, Case No. IT-04-82-A, Judgment of 19 May 2010). See also Jann K. Kleffner, "The Legal Fog of an Illusion: Three Reflections on 'Organization' and 'Intensity' as Criteria for the Temporal Scope of the Law of Non-International Armed Conflict", *International Law Studies* 95 (2019): 161.

China, Japan, Jordan, Kuwait, Laos, Lebanon, the Maldives, Mongolia, Oman, the Philippines, Qatar, the Republic of Korea, Saudi Arabia, the State of Palestine, Timor-Leste, the UAE and Yemen. Several Asian states are not willing to become parties to AP II for fear that this would, among other things, mean conceding that they have lost control over a part of their territory to dissident armed forces or other organised armed groups.

There is also the 1977 Protocol Additional to the Geneva Conventions of 12 August 1949, and relating to the Protection of Victims of International Armed Conflicts (AP I). Pursuant to its Article 1(4), AP I regulates "armed conflicts in which peoples are fighting against colonial domination and alien occupation and against racist régimes in the exercise of their right of self-determination, as enshrined in the [UN Charter] and the [1970 Declaration on Friendly Relations]". Asian states that support the distinction between self-determination against Western colonialism and the paramount principle of territorial integrity of post-colonial, independent states find Article 1(4) of AP I obsolete.[41] Furthermore, most commentators agree that this provision binds only parties to AP I and does not reflect customary international law.[42]

A group of experts convened by the International Committee of the Red Cross in January 2012 reached the following conclusions of relevance to this chapter. In a situation of armed conflict, the use of lethal or potentially lethal force by armed forces and law enforcement officials is governed by two different paradigms: the conduct of hostilities paradigm, derived from IHL and the law enforcement paradigm, mainly derived from international human rights law. The principles (necessity, proportionality and precaution) governing the conduct of hostilities and law enforcement paradigms operate differently.

As for *necessity*, the presumption under IHL is that combatants/fighters can be attacked with lawful means while civilians are protected against direct attack, unless and for such time as they take a direct part in hostilities. In contrast, under the law enforcement paradigm, the principle of "absolute necessity" implies that the use of force must be the last resort and can be undertaken only in order to

---

[41] AP I has 175 parties, including the following Asian states in the region covered by this book: Afghanistan, Bangladesh, Bahrain, Brunei, Cambodia, China, the Democratic Republic of Korea, Iraq, Japan, Jordan, Kuwait, Laos, Lebanon, Maldives, Mongolia, the Philippines, Qatar, the Republic of Korea, Saudi Arabia, the State of Palestine, Syria, Timor-Leste, the UAE, Vietnam and Yemen.

[42] Michael N. Schmitt, "Ukrainian Symposium: Classification of the Conflict(s)", *Lieber Institute-West Point,* 14 Dec. 2022, https://lieber.westpoint.edu/classification-of-the-conflicts/.

pursue a legitimate aim, such as self-defence, effecting a lawful arrest, preventing the escape of a person lawfully detained, or quelling a riot.

With respect to the principle of *proportionality*, IHL prohibits an attack against a legitimate target if this attack "may be expected to cause incidental loss of civilian life, injury to civilians, damage to civilian objects, or a combination thereof, which would be excessive in relation to the concrete and direct military advantage anticipated". The legitimate target of an attack (combatant, fighter or civilian directly participating in hostilities) is not covered by the principle of proportionality under IHL. By contrast, when a state agent is using force against an individual under human rights law, the proportionality principle requires a balancing between the risks posed by the individual versus the potential harm to this individual as well as to bystanders. Thus, the life of the individual posing an imminent threat himself is to be taken into account, in contradistinction to IHL. If the individual is not posing an imminent threat of death or serious injury, the use of lethal (or potentially lethal) force would not be considered proportionate (even if the necessity requirement were to be fulfilled). In addition, whenever the lawful use of force and firearms is unavoidable, the human rights proportionality test leads to a need to use the smallest amount of force necessary (including possibly through the use of less-than-lethal weapons) and to apply an escalation of force procedure unless this appears impossible. Finally, in human rights law, the use of force must avoid as far as possible deaths or injuries of bystanders, while the IHL principle of proportionality prohibits only *excessive* incidental civilian losses.

Regarding the principle of *precaution*, under IHL this principle requires belligerents to take constant care to spare the civilian population, civilians and civilian objects. By contrast, under the law enforcement paradigm, all precautions must be taken to avoid, as far as possible, the use of force as such, and not merely incidental civilian death or injury or damage to civilian objects. State agents shall thus endeavour, to the greatest extent possible, to minimise injury and respect and preserve human life.[43]

In practice, most Asian states facing insurgencies prefer not to admit that the situations qualify as an armed conflict under Common Article 3 of the four Geneva Conventions and/or, where applicable, AP II, for fear of the "internationalisation" of the conflicts within their respective territories and any "international legitimacy" the insurgencies may achieve, by preventing "outsiders" from intervening, monitoring and restricting how the states concerned may

---

[43] Gloria Gaggioli, ed., *The Use of Force in Armed Conflicts: Interplay between the Conduct of Hostilities and Law Enforcement Paradigms* (Geneva: ICRC, 2013), pp. 8–9, 30–2.

quell the insurgencies, and subject insurgents to punishment under the criminal law of the states concerned; that is, strictly under the law enforcement paradigm.

Freedom Fighters or Terrorists?

This issue is complicated by efforts by some states to exclude "terrorists" from the reach of criminal law insofar as they exercise the right to self-determination, hence the cliché "one man's terrorist is another man's freedom fighter".[44]

International efforts to conclude a draft comprehensive convention on international terrorism have not been successful after decades of negotiation. This failure has been caused mainly by the disagreement on the proposed differentiation between "terrorism" and acts of violence in armed conflicts involving so-called "freedom fighters". It should also be noted that Pakistan maintains its reservation to the 1997 International Convention for the Suppression of Terrorist Bombings[45] to exclude self-determination struggles. This reservation has been objected to by several states, including India, Israel and Japan.

Significantly, the 1999 Organisation of Islamic Cooperation (OIC) Convention on Combatting International Terrorism, in force on 7 November 2002, provides in Article 1(2) that "terrorism" means any act of violence or threat thereof notwithstanding its motives or intentions perpetrated to carry out an individual or collective criminal plan with the aim of terrorising people or threatening to harm them or imperilling their lives, honour, freedoms, security or rights or exposing the environment or any facility or public or private property to hazards or occupying or seizing them, or endangering a national resource, or international facilities, or threatening the stability, territorial integrity, political unity or sovereignty of independent states. Article 2(a) of this convention stipulates, however, that "[p]eoples' struggle including armed struggle against foreign occupation, aggression, colonialism, and hegemony, aimed at liberation and self-determination in accordance with the principles of international law shall not be considered a terrorist crime". The OIC's practice to date seems to affirm that this exception focuses on the struggle by Palestinians to "obtain their inalienable rights guaranteed by the resolutions of international legitimacy, to get rid

---

44 Ben Ganor, "Defining Terrorism: Is One Man's Terrorist Anther Man's Freedom Fighter?", *Media Asia* 29 (2002): 123.

45 2149 *United Nations Treaty Series* 256, in force 23 May 2001.

of occupation and to establish the Palestinian State with Al Quds Sharif as its capital".[46]

Insurgents or separatists in Southeast Asia are not interested in deviating from political goals linked to a specific territory, language, culture and/or shared history to join movements led by Middle Easterners such as Al Qaeda or ISIL, except for certain groups in the Muslim south of the Philippines.[47] These insurgents or separatists may be labelled "terrorists" if their conduct falls within the definition of acts of terrorism under the relevant international conventions on terrorism.

Where an insurgent/separatist movement is designated terrorist by the international community and competent international organisations, the government of the state against whom the insurgency is waged can easily resort to quelling it without much outcry from other states, provided that the government agencies of that state do not themselves commit atrocities or serious violations of human rights when taking law enforcement measures against the insurgents.[48] This is especially the case for insurgent groups that have committed atrocities amounting to serious crimes of international concern, including acts of terrorism.

International Human Rights Oversights and Internal Self-Determination

Instead of focusing solely on dealing with insurgencies from an IHL and/or law enforcement paradigm(s), the Asian state concerned should dedicate its resources to addressing the grievances arising from its disregard of legitimate *internal* self-determination. If and when these grievances are duly taken care of, there will be no justification for any entity or group of persons to demand *external* self-determination to secede from the state.

International organisations do have roles within their respective mandates to put states' human rights record under scrutiny.

---

[46] OIC Press Release announcing the death of Palestinian president Yassir Arafat, 11 Nov. 2004.

[47] Sidney Jones, "Identity Conflicts in Southeast Asia: An Overview", in *The State of Conflict and Violence in Asia 2021: Identity-Based Conflict and Extremism*, ed. Asia Foundation (San Francisco: Asia Foundation, 2022), p. 31 at pp. 32–3.

[48] See also Sascha Nanlohy, "R2P, Terrorism, and the Protection of Civilians—Are All Humans Human? Or Are Some More Human than Others?", *Global Responsibility to Protect* 14 (2022): 178.

Each state's human rights record is scrutinised by the UN Human Rights Council (HRC), a subsidiary organ of the UNGA. The HRC is mandated to contribute, through dialogue and cooperation, towards the prevention of human rights violations and respond promptly to human rights emergencies. Apart from the 47 members of the HRC, every four and a half years, on a rotational basis, all UN member states undergo a universal periodic review (UPR), an interactive review of the human rights situation in their respective states. UPR sessions are held for two weeks, three times a year. Fourteen states are reviewed in each session, totalling 42 each year. The human rights issues under review are those arising from the UN Charter, the 1948 Universal Declaration of Human Rights, the human rights treaties to which the reviewed state is party and IHL. Any UN member state may participate in the discussions held during a UPR led by groups of three randomly selected states ("troikas"). During each state review, lasting three and a half hours, special independent experts ("special rapporteurs") present information and evidence as well as pose questions. Any UN member state and NGO can also submit questions and evidence. The state under review then explains the actions already taken or that it plans to take to address the issues raised. The troika subsequently prepares a report with the involvement of the reviewed state and technical assistance from the Office of the UN High Commissioner for Human Rights, providing a summary of the discussion, questions and comments. It also sets out recommendations officially made and any necessary technical assistance suggested, as well as the reviewed state's responses. The HRC, meeting in a plenary a few days after the review, discusses and adopts the report. The reviewed state has the primary responsibility of implementing the recommendations in the final report and keeping the HRC updated on developments in this regard. If the reviewed state fails to implement the recommendations in the final report, the HRC may pursue a series of measures, such as specific investigations and the setting up of committees to put pressure on the non-cooperating states and shaming them by drawing the world's attention to their non-implementation of the recommendations. A confidential complaint procedure has been set up by the HRC since 19 June 2007 to deal with allegations of consistent patterns of gross and reliably attested violations of all human rights and fundamental freedoms anywhere in the world and under whatever circumstances. To be admissible, the alleged violation must not be already subject to a special procedure (that is, under the mandate of an independent human rights expert who reports and advises on human rights from a thematic or country-specific perspective) or a treaty body, or other UN or similar regional human rights complaints procedure. Two working groups are set up to examine the communications and to bring to the attention of the HRC such human rights violations.

The bodies entrusted with monitoring the implementation of the major international human rights treaties violation of which may give rise to demands for self-determination are the Human Rights Committee in the case of the ICCPR; the Committee on Economic, Social and Cultural Rights in the case of the ICESCR; the Committee on the Elimination of Racial Discrimination in the case of the 1965 International Convention on the Elimination of All Forms of Racial Discrimination; the Committee on the Elimination of Discrimination against Women in the case of the 1979 Convention on the Elimination of All Forms of Discrimination Against Women; the Committee Against Torture in the case of the 1984 Convention against Torture and Other Cruel, Inhuman or Degrading Treatment or Punishment; the Committee on the Rights of the Child in the case of the 1989 Convention on the Rights of the Child; and the Committee on Enforced Disappearance in the case of 2006 International Convention for the Protection of All Persons from Enforced Disappearance. These treaty bodies are competent to receive and consider petitions from individuals, issue general comments and recommendations addressed to all states parties, issue concluding observations and concluding comments addressed to a particular state party, and issue views/decisions, suggestions and recommendations in response to individual communications or petitions, where applicable. General comments of treaty bodies inform states parties how each treaty body interprets the conventions under its competence. The other mechanisms require the cooperation of the states parties concerned and therefore resemble dialogues between the treaty body and the states in question, with the former providing constructive feedback at the end of the process. The substance of the findings, concluding observations or comments, views or decisions, suggestions or recommendations, as well as general comments of these human rights treaty-monitoring bodies, has been duly taken into consideration by domestic courts dispensing internal justice in the context of repression of freedoms and rights. The Subcommittee on Prevention of Torture, unlike the other treaty bodies just mentioned, discharges its preventive mandate pursuant to the 2002 Optional Protocol to the Convention against Torture by visiting places of detention and advising National Preventive Mechanisms of States Parties to the Convention against Torture.

The OIC has asserted its role in protecting Muslims even outside OIC member states. According to Article 1(16) of the 1969 OIC Charter, in force in

1972, as amended in 2008, the OIC shall "safeguard the rights, dignity and religious and cultural identity of Muslim communities and minorities in non-Member States". The OIC secretary-general and delegations of permanent representatives to the OIC visit Thailand, which has had observer status in the OIC since 1 October 1997, from time to time to witness first-hand the situation of the Muslim communities in the southern border provinces of Thailand as part of the OIC mission to preserve Islamic values and solidarity among OIC member and observer states. The Thai government, for its part, welcomes such visits to show that Muslims in these provinces, like anywhere else in Thailand, do not have a legitimate claim to external self-determination. OIC delegations focus on key issues related to the situation on the ground, such as economic, social, education and security issues and interact with competent Thai authorities as well as academic institutions such as the Islamic College at Prince of Songkla University and the Fatoni University. The delegations also have opportunities to meet and interact with local communities and civil society organisations in the areas.

National human rights commissions that are truly independent of government control or influence can identify human rights violations in their respective states and demand redress. They thus serve as yardsticks to measure how legitimate a claim for external self-determination asserted by a separatist movement is.

In extreme cases of gross violations of human rights, the Asian state concerned can be subject to international sanctions. For example, the HRC, in Resolution 39/2, adopted in September 2018, established:

> an ongoing independent mechanism to collect, consolidate, preserve and analyze evidence of the most serious international crimes and violations of international law committed in Myanmar since 2011, and to prepare files in order to facilitate and expedite fair and independent criminal proceedings, in accordance with international law standards, in national, regional or international courts or tribunals that have or may in the future have jurisdiction over these crimes, in accordance with international law.[49]

In November 2019, the Gambia initiated proceedings against Myanmar in the ICJ for the latter's alleged breaches of the 1948 Convention on the Prevention

[49] See further, Kriangsak Kittichaisaree, *The Rohingya, Justice and International Law* (Abingdon: Routledge, 2021).

and Punishment of the Crime of Genocide[50] against the Rohingya, an ethnic and religious minority group normally residing in Myanmar's Rakhine State. The ICJ has ruled that it has jurisdiction over the case.[51] Also in 2019, the prosecutor of the International Criminal Court (ICC) officially started investigating possible crimes against humanity perpetrated against the Rohingya. The ICC has ruled that, although Myanmar is not party to the 1998 Rome Statute of the International Criminal Court,[52] the ICC may exercise jurisdiction over crimes when part of the criminal conduct takes place on the territory of a state party to the Rome Statute. More specifically, the alleged deportation of Rohingya across the Myanmar–Bangladesh border, which involved victims crossing that border, clearly establishes a territorial link on the basis of the proscribed conduct of this crime (that is, the crossing by the victims into Bangladesh, a state party to the Rome Statute). Besides, the ICC prosecutor is authorised to investigate in relation to *any crimes* within the ICC's jurisdiction, including any future crimes, committed at least in part on Bangladesh's territory, or on the territory of any other state party or state that would accept the ICC's jurisdiction on an ad hoc basis, insofar as such crimes are sufficiently linked to the Rohingya situation and allegedly committed after the date of entry in force of the Rome Statute for those states parties. Regarding alleged crimes that have a continuous nature, the ICC prosecutor may extend their investigation even when such crimes commenced before the date of entry into force of the statute for any relevant state party insofar as the crimes continued after this date.[53]

After the 1 February 2021 military takeover of the government in Myanmar and the resultant widespread human rights abuses in that country,[54] ASEAN has been excluding Myanmar from ASEAN meetings, in a departure from the long-entrenched ASEAN tradition of non-interference in the internal affairs of its member states. The Myanmar military regime installed after the military coup has met with sustained internal armed resistance as well as

[50] 78 *United Nations Treaty Series* 277, in force 12 Jan. 1951.

[51] *Application of the Convention on the Prevention and Punishment of the Crime of Genocide (The Gambia v. Myanmar)*, Preliminary Objections, ICJ Judgment of 22 July 2022.

[52] 2187 *United Nations Treaty Series* 3, in force 1 July 2002.

[53] *Decision on the "Prosecution's Request for a Ruling on Jurisdiction under Article 19(3) of the Statute"*, Case ICC-RoC46(3)-01/18, 6 Sept. 2018; *Decision Pursuant to Article 15 of the Rome Statute on the Authorization of an Investigation into the Situation in the People's Republic of Bangladesh/Republic of the Union of Myanmar*, No ICC-0-1/19, 14 Nov. 2019.

[54] See, for example, Office of the UN High Commissioner for Human Rights, "Situation of Human Rights in Myanmar since 1 February 2021", A/HRC/49/72 (15 Mar. 2022).

widespread civil disobedience and the junta has been using lethal force against those opposed to it. In March 2021, those opposed to the coup set up a National Unity Government (NUG) aiming at weakening the governance mechanisms of the military government, supporting the civil disobedience movement and making arrangements for national defence. Armed groups that call themselves "People's Defence Forces" have sprung up across the country to fight the military government and have drawn the troops into a bloody stalemate of clashes and reprisals.

On 24 April 2021, a special ASEAN Summit adopted a "Five-Point Consensus". First, there shall be immediate cessation of violence in Myanmar and all parties shall exercise utmost restraint. Second, constructive dialogue among all parties concerned shall commence to seek a peaceful solution in the interests of the Myanmar people. Third, a special envoy of the ASEAN chair shall facilitate mediation of the dialogue process, with the assistance of the secretary-general of ASEAN. Fourth, ASEAN shall provide humanitarian assistance through the ASEAN Coordinating Centre for Humanitarian Assistance on Disaster Management. Fifth, the special envoy and delegation shall visit Myanmar to meet with all parties concerned. Since 2021 the United Nations credentials committee has decided to defer its decision on whether to accept the credential of the representative/ambassador to the United Nations appointed by the Myanmar military regime while there is a rival claim to Myanmar's seat at the United Nations from the NUG, opposed to the junta, as the rightful government of Myanmar.

For its part, on 23 December 2022 the president of the United States, one of the Western nations playing a leading role regarding Myanmar, signed into law the Burma Unified through Rigorous Military Accountability Act of 2022 (BURMA Act) as part of the 2023 National Defence Authorization Act. The BURMA Act, among other things, affirms the policy of the United States to support the efforts of the NUG in Burma and support the restoration of the civilian government with constitutional reforms. The act enables the US government to provide technical and non-lethal assistance to the People's Defence Forces set up under the NUG and Myanmar's ethnic armed organisations opposed to the Myanmar military regime. The act also authorises funding during the fiscal years 2023 to 2027 to support the pro-democracy movement, civil society organisations, and the political entities and affiliates of ethnic armed organisations in Myanmar.

China, the only P5 member of the UNSC that shares a border with Myanmar, wants stability and the end of the internal armed conflict in Myanmar.

China has been in direct contact with ethnic armed groups in Myanmar to convince them to this end.[55]

The Rohingya Solidarity Organization's armed rebellion in the 1980s lost its military potency in the late 1990s. The Arakan Rohingya Salvation Army attacked Myanmar government security forces on 9 October 2016, in one of the largest armed attacks by Muslim non-state actors on Myanmar government forces in living memory. The United Wa State Army is the largest ethnic armed group in Myanmar, with a standing force of approximately 25,000 and de facto control over its autonomous enclave on Myanmar's northern border with China, which it names Wa State Government Special Administrative Region. The United Wa State Army wants autonomy and control of the lucrative illicit drugs trade and natural resources in the territory under its control, rather than outright independence from Myanmar. On 27 October 2023, the combined forces of approximately 15,000 ethnic armed personnel from the Ta'ang National Liberation Army, the Arakan Army and the Myanmar National Democratic Alliance Army launched "Operation 1027" to seize the Myanmar junta's army camps, command centres, military bases and strategic towns in Myanmar. They and several other ethnic armed groups that have followed their lead have been able to carry out sustained and concerted military operations in the regions inside Myanmar and inflicted heavy casualties and strategic losses on the junta's armed forces.[56]

Nevertheless, the armed conflicts between the military government in Myanmar and those non-state armed groups opposed to it are not related in any way whatsoever for the latter's struggle for secession from Myanmar—they want to topple the military government and rule the country without jeopardising Myanmar's territorial integrity. An increasingly common goal among ethnic armed groups is a nation comprising federal states, like the United States of America.

---

[55] "China's New Special Envoy to Myanmar Meets Ethnic Armed Organizations", *Irrawaddy*, 29 Dec. 2022, https://www.irrawaddy.com/news/burma/chinas-new-special-envoy-to-myanmar-meets-ethnic-armed-organizations.html; "Chinese Envoy's Visits Signal Growing Tensions with US over Myanmar", *Irrawaddy*, 22 Feb. 2023, https://www.irrawaddy.com/opinion/analysis/chinese-envoys-visits-signal-growing-tensions-with-us-over-myanmar.html.

[56] See, for example, Aye Shan Hsu, "Myanmar Ethnic Armed Groups' Advances against Junta: State-by-State Breakdown", *Irrawaddy*, 14 May 2024, https://www.irrawaddy.com/opinion/analysis/myanmar-ethnic-armed-groups-advances-against-junta-state-by-state-breakdown.html.

In conclusion, none of the non-state armed groups currently fighting the government in Asia has any realistic chance of successfully invoking the right to external self-determination for the purpose of secession. Yet the Asian states facing insurgencies within their respective borders should diligently ensure that there be no credible justifications for external self-determination by addressing grievances and upholding human rights of those living in the areas where the insurgencies are fomented.

CHAPTER 5

Annexation

The UN General Assembly's 1970 Declaration on Friendly Relations declares categorically that the territory of a state shall not be the object of acquisition by another state resulting from the threat or use of force, and that no territorial acquisition resulting from the threat or use of force shall be recognised as legal. The International Court of Justice (ICJ) has reaffirmed the "illegality of territorial acquisition resulting from the threat or use of force" as a "corollary" to the principles of the use of force incorporated in the UN Charter, which reflect customary international law.[1] In the case of non-self-governing territories, the ICJ has confirmed the customary law character of their right to territorial integrity as a corollary of the right to self-determination.[2]

It may be recalled that the Ten Principles of the Asian-African Conference held in Bandung in 1955 include the principle of refraining from acts or threats of aggression or the use of force against the territorial integrity or political independence of any country.

Indonesia's Annexation of East Timor

Apart from the annexation of Kuwait by Iraq under Saddam Hussein in 1990–91 (which has already been subject to extensive analyses in the literature), the

[1] *Legal Consequences of the Construction of a Wall in the Occupied Palestinian Territory*, Advisory Opinion, ICJ Rep. 2004, p. 136 at p. 171 [87].

[2] *Legal Consequences of the Separation of the Chagos Archipelago from Mauritius in 1965*, Advisory Opinion, ICJ Rep. 2019, p. 95 at p. 134 [160]. For an exhaustive analysis of international law applicable to annexation of territories, see Ingrid Brunk and Monica Hakimi, "The Prohibition of Annexations and the Foundations of Modern International Law", *American Journal of International Law* 118 (2024): 417.

other incident of annexation in Asia is Indonesia's annexation of East Timor (1975–99).

Facts concerning the latter may be summarised as follows.[3]

In the 16th century, East Timor was colonised by Portugal, and remained so until 1975. The western part of the island came under Dutch rule and later became part of independent Indonesia. Portugal accepted East Timor as its non-self-governing territory in 1974. Following internal disturbances in East Timor, on 27 August 1975 the Portuguese civil and military authorities withdrew from the mainland of East Timor to the island of Atauro. On 7 December 1975, the Indonesian armed forces intervened in East Timor, ostensibly due to fears of a communist government in East Timor. On 8 December 1975 the Portuguese authorities departed from the island of Atauro and thus left East Timor altogether.

Indonesia at that time was ruled by President Suharto, who had come to power by a military coup in 1965. Indonesia was then a nation so much different from the democratic Indonesia of today.[4]

Asserting that on 31 May 1976 the people of East Timor had asked Indonesia "to accept East Timor as an integral part of the Republic of Indonesia", on 17 July 1976 Indonesia enacted a law incorporating East Timor as part of its national territory. The Indonesian government conducted forced resettlement and imposed the Indonesian language and what were considered "Indonesian values" on the East Timorese. Many migrants arrived from Indonesia, and Indonesians (including local military leaders) established business interests.

Resistance to Indonesian authority, led by the Revolutionary Front for an Independent East Timor (FRETILIN), persisted for 24 years. FRETILIN's armed wing carried out guerrilla warfare against Indonesian security forces during this period.

International Response

Following the intervention of the Indonesian armed forces in East Timor and the withdrawal of the Portuguese authorities, the question of East Timor became

---

[3] Sources: *East Timor (Portugal v. Australia)*, ICJ Rep. 1995, p. 90 at pp. 95–7 [11]–[16]; Asia Foundation, *The State of Conflict and Violence in Asia 2021: Identity-Based Conflict and Extremism* (San Francisco: Asia Foundation, 2022), p. 164.

[4] See Marcus Mietzner, "Indonesia: The Military's Transformation from Praetorian Ruler to Presidential Coalition Partner", in *The Oxford Encyclopedia of the Military in Politics*, ed. William R. Thompson and Hicham Bou Nassif, n.p. (New York: Oxford University Press, 2020).

the subject of two resolutions of the UN Security Council (UNSC) and of eight resolutions of the UN General Assembly (UNGA).

The UNSC's Resolution 384 (1975) of 22 December 1975 called upon "all States to respect the territorial integrity of East Timor as well as the inalienable right of its people to self-determination", called upon "the Government of Indonesia to withdraw without delay all its forces from the Territory" and further called upon "the Government of Portugal as administering Power to cooperate fully with the United Nations so as to enable the people of East Timor to exercise freely their right to self-determination". UNSC Resolution 389 (1976) of 22 April 1976 adopted the same terms with regard to the right of the people of East Timor to self-determination, called upon "the Government of Indonesia to withdraw without further delay all its forces from the Territory" and further called upon "all States and other parties concerned to cooperate fully with the United Nations to achieve a peaceful solution to the existing situation".

UNGA Resolution 3485 (XXX) of 12 December 1975 referred to Portugal as "the administering Power", called upon it "to continue to make every effort to find a solution by peaceful means" and "strongly deplore[d] the military intervention of the armed forces of Indonesia in Portuguese Timor". In Resolution 31/53 of 1 December 1976, and again in Resolution 32134 of 28 November 1977, the UNGA rejected "the claim that East Timor has been incorporated into Indonesia, inasmuch as the people of the Territory have not been able to exercise freely their right to self-determination and independence".

UNSC Resolution 389 (1976) of 22 April 1976 and UNGA Resolutions 31/53 of 1 December 1976, 32/34 of 28 November 1977 and 33/39 of 13 December 1978 made no reference to Portugal as the administering power. Portugal was so described, however, in UNSC Resolution 384 (1975) of 22 December 1975 and in the other resolutions of the UNGA. Also, those resolutions that did not specifically refer to Portugal as the administering power recalled another resolution or other resolutions which did so. No further resolution on the question of East Timor has been passed by the UNSC since 1976 or by the UNGA since 1982, although the UNGA kept the situation in Timor on its agenda. East Timor continued to be included in the list of non-self-governing territories within the meaning of Chapter XI of the UN Charter, and the Special Committee on the Situation with Regard to the Implementation of the Declaration on the Granting of Independence to Colonial Countries and Peoples remains seized of the question of East Timor. The UN secretary-general was also engaged in a continuing effort, in consultation with all parties directly concerned, to achieve a comprehensive settlement of the East Timor problem.

Support for East Timor at the United Nations was generally limited to a relatively small group of countries such as Angola, Cape Verde, Guinea-Bissau, Mozambique, São Tomé and Príncipe, Portugal, Brazil, Vanuatu, Benin and Algeria. In the meantime, Australia, the United States, Japan and the United Kingdom actively increased their commercial and economic engagements with Indonesia over the years 1975–99.[5] Japan, the United States and Benin were the only three UNSC members that abstained when the UNSC adopted Resolution 389 (1976), which had the support of all the other 12 UNSC members.

One author credits Indonesia's continued annexation of East Timor to the skills of Indonesian diplomats and its friends in the international community, and especially the Cold War freeze in the UNSC, as a result of which the UNSC did not initiate or approve Chapter VII enforcement measures against Indonesia. Likewise, except for strongly deploring Indonesia's "military intervention" in East Timor, none of the resolutions by the UNGA or the UNSC condemned Indonesia's aggression, nor was there any reference to an invasion or to Indonesia's continued presence as being belligerent occupation. The United States, the United Kingdom and France sold arms to Indonesia, allegedly for use against the resistance and civilians in East Timor who were hostile to Indonesia's annexation, thereby directly supporting an illegal occupation and suppression of the right of Timorese to self-determination.[6]

This widespread international disregard of the right of East Timorese to self-determination and opposition to blatant annexation is extremely depressing when compared to Iraq's invasion and annexation of Kuwait on 2 August 1990. The UNSC, acting under Chapter VII of the UN Charter, immediately adopted Resolution 660 (1990) of 2 August 1990 to condemn the Iraqi invasion of Kuwait; demand that Iraq withdraw immediately and unconditionally all its forces to the positions in which they had been located on 1 August 1990; call upon Iraq and Kuwait to immediately begin intensive negotiations for the resolution of their differences and support all efforts in this regard, and especially those of the League of Arab States; and decide to meet again as necessary to consider further steps to ensure compliance with the resolution. It was adopted by 14 votes to none, with Yemen not participating in the voting. UNSC Resolution 678 (1990) of 29 November 1990, also adopted by the UNSC acting under

[5] Suzannah Linton, "International Humanitarian Law in Occupied East Timor: Displacement, Relocation and Famine", in *Asia-Pacific Perspectives on International Humanitarian Law*, ch. 24 at pp. 418–19.

[6] Ibid., pp. 417–19. See also Peter Britton, "Indonesia's Neo-Colonial Armed Forces", *Critical Asian Studies* 7 (1975): 14, 19–20.

Chapter VII of the UN Charter, demanded that Iraq comply fully with Resolution 660 (1990) and all subsequent relevant resolutions, and decided, while maintaining all its decisions, to allow Iraq one final opportunity, as a pause of goodwill, to do so. Paragraph 2 of the resolution authorised UN members co-operating with the government of Kuwait, unless Iraq fully implemented these resolutions on or before 15 January 1991, "to use all necessary means to uphold and implement Resolution 660 (1990) and all subsequent relevant resolutions and to restore international peace and security in the area". It asked "all States to provide appropriate support for the actions undertaken in pursuance of paragraph 2 above". The latter resolution was adopted by 12 votes to two (Cuba and Yemen), with one abstention (China). The subsequent military campaign of a 35-nation military coalition led by the United States pursuant to these UNSC resolutions eventually liberated Kuwait from Iraq on 25 February 1991. Does the different treatment by the international community given to Indonesia's annexation of East Timor and Iraq's annexation of Kuwait lie in the fact that Kuwait is an oil-rich nation?

ASEAN showed a double standard. ASEAN condemned and imposed severe sanctions against Vietnam, then not yet an ASEAN member state, for its invasion in December 1978 and its subsequent military occupation of Cambodia (then under the Khmer Rouge) for over a decade but it turned a blind eye to Indonesia's invasion and annexation of East Timor.

According to one study,[7] the international and regional reaction to the Indonesian annexation of East Timor was based on the perceived political and diplomatic imperative of maintaining friendly relations with the anti-communist regime in Indonesia. Several Asian states, including Japan, Malaysia and the Philippines, supported the Indonesian annexation of East Timor against the communist-inclined FRETILIN. For its part, China urged respect for non-intervention in the internal matters of East Timor and kept voting in favour of Indonesia's withdrawal from East Timor in the UNGA from 1975 to 1982. The shift in international public opinion, particularly in Australia and the United States, came after the massacre of no fewer than 250 pro-independence demonstrators in Dili, East Timor's capital city, by Indonesian troops on 12 November 1991, putting international pressure on Indonesia to resolve the East Timor problem. However, Asian states continued to support Indonesia's occupation of East Timor, particularly after the 1998 regime change in

[7] Hitoshi Nasu, "Revisiting the Principle of Non-Intervention: A Structural Principle of International Law or a Political Obstacle to Regional Security in Asia?", *Asian Journal of International Law* 3 (2013): 25, 39–41.

Indonesia with the collapse of President Suharto's more than three decades of military-dominated government and Indonesia's transition to a democratic society, for fear that external pressure might weaken the precarious legitimacy of the new Habibie government in Indonesia and eventually destabilise Indonesia. East Timor's independence movement gained domestic and international momentum following the end of Suharto's rule in Indonesia. In January 1999, after talks mediated by the United Nations regarding East Timor's status and in response to international pressure and in an effort to secure his political position, Habibie announced his plan to hold a referendum for East Timorese to choose between broad autonomy within Indonesia or transition to self-rule.

Meanwhile, Portugal instituted proceedings against Australia before the ICJ in February 1991, contending that Australia, in negotiating and concluding the 1989 "Timor Gap" Treaty, which created a zone of cooperation in a maritime area between "the Indonesian Province of East Timor and Northern Australia", acted unlawfully, in that Australia infringed the rights of the people of East Timor to self-determination and to permanent sovereignty over its natural resources, infringed the rights of Portugal as the administering power, and contravened UNSC Resolutions 384 and 389. Australia raised objections to the ICJ's jurisdiction.

In its judgment in *East Timor (Portugal v. Australia)* in 1995, the ICJ found that it had no jurisdiction over this case since one of the fundamental principles of its statute was that it could not decide a dispute between states without the consent of those states to its jurisdiction—and Indonesia did not consent to the ICJ's jurisdiction in this particular case. In the view of the ICJ, Australia's behaviour could not be assessed without first entering into the question of why it was that Indonesia could not lawfully have concluded the 1989 treaty, while Portugal allegedly could have done so. Regarding Portugal's argument based on the principle of self-determination, this norm and the rule of consent to the ICJ's jurisdiction are two different things. Whatever the nature of the obligations invoked, the ICJ could not rule on the lawfulness of the conduct of a state when its judgment would imply an evaluation of the lawfulness of the conduct of another state not a party to the case before the ICJ. Portugal's third argument rested on the premise that the UN resolutions, and in particular those of the UNSC, could be read as imposing an obligation on states not to recognise any authority on the part of Indonesia over East Timor and, where the latter was concerned, to deal only with Portugal. The ICJ was not persuaded, however, that the relevant resolutions went so far. The ICJ could not infer from the sole fact that the aforesaid UNGA and UNSC resolutions, by referring to Portugal as the administering power of East Timor, intended to establish an obligation on third states to deal exclusively with Portugal regarding the maritime area of East Timor. The ICJ noted, furthermore, that several states had concluded with Indonesia treaties capable of being applied to East Timor without any reservation in regard to it. Finally, observed the ICJ, by a letter of 15 December 1989, the permanent representative of Portugal to the UN transmitted to the UN secretary-general the text of a note of protest addressed by the Portuguese embassy in Canberra to the Australian Department of Foreign Affairs and Trade on the occasion of the conclusion of the 1989 treaty; that the letter of the permanent representative was circulated, at his request, as an official document of the UNGA, under the item entitled "Question of East Timor", and of the UNSC; and that no responsive action was taken either by the UNGA or the UNSC. In this case, the effects of the ICJ's judgment requested by Portugal would amount to a determination that Indonesia's entry into and continued presence in East Timor were unlawful and that, as a consequence, it did not have the treaty-making power in matters relating to the maritime resources of East Timor. Indonesia's rights and obligations would thus constitute the very subject matter of such a judgment made in the absence of Indonesia's consent.

Timor-Leste after the Referendum for Independence

On 30 August 1999, nearly 80 per cent of the population voted for independence from Indonesia. In the lead-up to and during the referendum, pro-Indonesia militias attacked civilians across Timor, killing hundreds and destroying property. More than 75 per cent of the population was displaced. Approximately 200,000 fled to Indonesian West Timor and other areas.[8] In late 1999, as a multinational military force mandated by the United Nations arrived, the last Indonesian soldiers left the territory. While anti-independence militias were active throughout 1999 and early 2000, the transition from a UN-led administration occurred on schedule. Asian states maintained, more or less, the same position even when the militia violence increased drastically in the aftermath of the popular referendum. Cambodia, India, Laos, the Philippines, the Republic of Korea and Singapore even continued to call upon the Indonesian government to take necessary measures in a decisive and vigorous manner to restore law and order, while Vietnam stated that the deployment of any multinational forces in East Timor had to have the consent of the Indonesian government. Asian states also refused to participate in the special ministerial

[8] See further, Angel Rabasa and John Haseman, *The Military and Democracy in Indonesia* (Santa Monica, CA: Rand, 2002), pp. 39–41.

meeting on East Timor convened by the Asia-Pacific Economic Cooperation (APEC) at the APEC Summit in Brunei in November 2000.[9]

In May 2002, East Timor officially became the independent Democratic Republic of Timor-Leste.

The Commission for Reception, Truth, and Reconciliation in East Timor estimates that no fewer than 102,800 Timorese civilians died between 1974 and 1999. Approximately 18,600 of these were killed or forcibly disappeared, and 84,200 died of famine and disease, while Indonesian security forces committed widespread human rights violations.

The UN Transitional Authority for East Timor (UNTAET), established by UNSC Resolution 1271 (1999) on 25 October 1999, set up the UN Special Panels within the District Court of Dili, East Timor's capital, and created the Serious Crimes Investigation Unit to investigate and prosecute the crimes committed in East Timor. The Dili District Court was given exclusive jurisdiction over genocide, war crimes, crimes against humanity, murder, sexual offences and torture committed between 1 January and 25 October 1999. Special panels set up to exercise this exclusive jurisdiction were composed of both East Timorese and international judges.

By June 2000, more than 50 militia members were being held in UN custody accused of these crimes. The hybrid Serious Crimes Panel, composed of two international judges and one East Timorese judge, began hearing these cases in early 2001. In the first such case to be completed, a panel of three judges—from Burundi, Italy and East Timor—sentenced a 22-year-old militia member to 12 years in prison on a single count of murder. The so-called "East Timor Tribunal" had a budget of US$6.3 million for the year 2002, of which US$6 million went to the prosecution, which nevertheless had failed to take any high-level perpetrators into custody. The balance was almost all for the salaries of international judges, who sorely lacked adequate administrative and clerical support.

The tribunal has been criticised for failing to respect the rights of the defendants and incorrect application of international law. Above all, the objective of bringing to justice those most responsible for the bloodshed was doomed to failure since Indonesia refused to cooperate by extraditing the key high-level suspects in the Indonesian militia and government or compelling witnesses to appear. Indonesia explained that Indonesia was also conducting its own trials before the Ad Hoc Human Rights Court for Timor-Leste in Jakarta, estab-

[9] Nasu, "Revisiting the Principle of Non-Intervention", 40–1.

lished under an Indonesian law of 2000.[10] UNTAET's mandate in prosecuting serious crimes in East Timor ended in May 2005, after 55 trials that led to 84 people being convicted and three people acquitted.

In his report to the UNSC in July 2006, the UN secretary-general explained that the Commission of Inquiry into Human Rights Violations in East Timor (KPP-HAM), established by the Indonesian authorities, had conducted its inquiry in a comprehensive, credible and objective manner, in compliance with international standards. However, the KPP-HAM also found that the prosecutions before the Ad Hoc Human Rights Court for Timor-Leste were manifestly deficient and the judicial process before the Ad Hoc Court had not been effective in delivering justice for the victims of serious violations of human rights and the people of Timor-Leste. While some of the 18 individuals indicted under the process were convicted and sentenced, all but one were acquitted on appeal. On 13 March 2006, however, the Supreme Court of Indonesia rejected a final appeal by a former militia leader, Eurico Guterres, and overturned the decision of an appellate court to halve the ten-year jail sentence handed down in 2002 by the Ad Hoc Human Rights Court, thereby restoring the full sentence.[11]

The impunity enjoyed by Indonesian military officers is understandable in light of the fact that the Indonesian military still wielded considerable influence in Indonesia after the country's transition to full democracy in May 1998 following 32 years of authoritarian rule by President Suharto.[12]

In 2011, Timor-Leste applied to join ASEAN. Timor-Leste needs Indonesia's full support for it to become a member state of ASEAN. For more than a decade, Timor-Leste's application for ASEAN membership was dogged by two

---

[10] David Cohen, "Seeking Justice on the Cheap: Is the East Timor Tribunal Really a Model for the Future?", *Analysis from the East-West Center* 61 (Aug. 2002): 1; Suzanne Katzenstein, "Hybrid Tribunals: Searching for Justice in East Timor", *Harvard Human Rights Journal* 16 (2003): 245, 251–77; Lia Kent, "Interrogating the 'Gap' between Law and Justice: East Timor's Serious Crime Process", *Human Rights Quarterly* 34 (2012): 1021.

[11] Report of the Secretary-General on Justice and Reconciliation for Timor-Leste, S/2006/580 (26 July 2006), paras 14–15.

[12] Joint Report by KontraS and the International Center for Transitional Justice, *Derailed: Transitional Justice in Indonesia since the Fall of Soeharto* (2011); Patrick Burgess, "De Facto Amnesty? The Example of Post-Soeharto Indonesia" in *Amnesty in the Age of Human Rights Accountability*, ed. Francesca Lessa and Leigh Payne (Cambridge: Cambridge University Press, 2012), pp. 263–90; Sri Lestari Wahyuningroem, *Transitional Justice from State to Civil Society: Democratization in Indonesia* (Abingdon: Routledge, 2021); Jiwon Suh, *The Politics of Post-Suharto Transitional Justice in Indonesia* (PhD thesis, Ohio State University, 2012), pp. 64–270.

concerns. There was some doubt as to whether Timor-Leste could afford the costs associated with ASEAN membership, and Timor-Leste's close relationship with China caused uneasiness among those ASEAN member states worried about China's geopolitical ambition in the region. ASEAN membership would give Timor-Leste's 1.37 million people access to the ASEAN Economic Community and would open its market to the 683 million people in ASEAN. With ASEAN membership, Timor-Leste's economy would become more resilient, allowing it to diversify from oil and gas, into areas of agriculture and tourism, among others. On 26 October 2025, Timor-Leste officially became the eleventh member state of ASEAN.

The 1989 Timor Gap Treaty between Australia and Indonesia, which was the focus of the *East Timor* case in the ICJ, provided for a joint development in the Timor Sea that separates Australia and East Timor, with Australia and Indonesia having a 50/50 share of the oil and gas revenue in the central area and a 90/10 revenue split in favour of Indonesia to the north and Australia to the south of the central area.

On 20 May 2002, the day of Timor-Leste's independence, Timor-Leste signed the Timor Sea Treaty with Australia, implementing a joint development scheme between Australia and Timor-Leste that replaced the 1989 Timor Gap Treaty, with a split of 90/10 in favour of Timor-Leste. Annex E of the 2002 Timor Sea Treaty provided for the unitisation of two of the oil and gas deposits, Sunrise and Troubadour, which became known as the "Greater Sunrise" field. Unable to reach an agreement to permanently delimit their maritime boundaries, Australia and Timor-Leste concluded the Treaty on Certain Maritime Arrangements in the Timor Sea in January 2006, which came into force in February 2007, to divide the proceeds from the Greater Sunrise field and to accept a 50-year moratorium on their maritime boundary delimitation. Still unsatisfied with these arrangements with Australia, in April 2016 Timor-Leste commenced compulsory conciliation proceedings against Australia under the 1982 UN Convention of the Law of the Sea, eventually leading to the signing in March 2018 of the Treaty between Australia and Timor-Leste Establishing their Maritime Boundaries in the Timor Sea. The 2018 treaty replaces the previous agreements and establishes permanent maritime boundaries between Australia and Timor-Leste in the Timor Sea, as well as establishing the Greater Sunrise Special Regime for the joint development, exploitation and management of the Greater Sunrise petroleum deposits.[13] It entered into force on

[13] Hao Duy Phan, Tara Davenport and Robert Beckman, eds. *The Timor-Leste/Australia Conciliation: A Victory for UNCLOS and Peaceful Settlement of Disputes* (Singapore: World

30 August 2019. Timor-Leste has, therefore, regained what would have been lost in relation to the Timor Sea and its natural resources had Indonesia still been occupying East Timor.

One crucial question is: what are the future implications of the outcome of Indonesia's annexation of East Timor, in which those involved in the armed annexation have never been brought to face justice for this blatant act in violation of international law? The answer would be that the international community will have to use mechanisms to force the annexing state to bear state responsibility for its illegal invasion, annexation and consequential violations of human rights and international humanitarian law as well as to bring to justice the individuals involved in these illegal acts. Since state responsibility and individual criminal responsibility arise from illegal war/armed conflict of all types, and not just illegal annexation, they will be analysed as part of the suggestion for the future in Chapter 9.

Scientific, 2019); Stuart Kaye, "Conciliation in International Dispute Resolution: An Evaluation of the Timor Sea Dispute", in *Peaceful Management of Maritime Disputes*, ch. 7; Katrina Cooper, "Law and Diplomacy in the Compulsory Conciliation between Australia and Timor-Leste", in *Research Handbook on Law and Diplomacy*, ed. Margaret E. McGuiness and David P. Stewart (Cheltenham: Edward Elgar Publishing, 2022), pp. 41–60.

CHAPTER 6

Humanitarian Intervention and the Responsibility to Protect (R2P) Doctrine

Humanitarian intervention and the doctrine of the responsibility to protect have been cited to support the legitimacy of the use of force against or in another nation.

Humanitarian Intervention

The evolution of the doctrine of humanitarian intervention can be traced back to Aristotle (384–322 BCE), St Augustine (fifth century), Thomas Aquinas (late 13th century), Vitoria (16th century), Grotius (1625), John Stuart Mill (1859), France–Great Britain–Russia's joint armed intervention to protect Christians from the Ottoman Empire's human rights abuses in 1829 followed by massacres in 1840, during the Crimean War (1853–56) and so on.[1]

[1] Mohammad Taghi Karoubi, "Unilateral Use of Armed Forces and the Challenge of Humanitarian Intervention in International Law", *Asian Yearbook of International Law* 10 (2005): 95, 98–111; A. Sharan, "From Non-intervention to R2P", *Indian Journal of International Law* 56 (2021): 81, 83–5; Simon Chesterman, *Just War or Just Peace? Humanitarian Intervention and International Law* (Oxford: Oxford University Press, 2001), ch. 1. For a debate on theoretical underpinnings for humanitarian intervention, see Colin Seow, "Chasing the Frontier in Humanitarian Intervention Law: The Case for *Aequitas ad Bellum*", *Asian Journal of International Law* 6 (2016): 294.

It has been pointed out that, although India's backing of Bangladesh's secession from Pakistan in 1971, Vietnam's invasion and occupation of Cambodia starting from December 1978 and Tanzania's invasion of Uganda then under Idi Amin in October 1978–June 1979 were grounded in the right to self-defence, the use of force by these states alleviated human sufferings in the targeted states. Armed intervention by the North Atlantic Treaty Organization (NATO) in Kosovo in 1999 was considered by some to be based on the right of humanitarian intervention.[2] It has also been argued that humanitarian intervention may be carried out by any state as long as the UN Security Council (UNSC) authorises it, and that, ideally, a very large majority of states may override the exercise of the veto power in the UNSC over a specific humanitarian intervention.[3]

As regards NATO's armed intervention in Kosovo in 1999, putatively to avert an impending humanitarian disaster in Kosovo, Belgium justified it on the ground that NATO's action was "not an intervention against the territorial integrity or independence of the former Republic of Yugoslavia" but one "to rescue a people in peril, in deep distress", being "an armed humanitarian intervention, compatible with Article 2, paragraph 4, of the UN Charter, which covers only intervention against the territorial integrity or political independence of a State".[4]

The other state justifying NATO's action in Kosovo on the basis of humanitarian intervention was the UK. The UK has an entrenched position in support of humanitarian intervention, born out of a legacy of global engagement from the time of the British Empire, a sense of moral righteousness and a show of military prowess, including as regards NATO's armed intervention in Kosovo and Syria, even without authorisation from the UNSC.[5]

Writing in 2018, Judge Shi Jiuyong, former president of the International Court of Justice (ICJ) from China, expressed his view on humanitarian intervention as follows. The legal justification for humanitarian intervention has much in common with the narrow approach to the interpretation of Article 2(4) of the UN

---

[2] Peter Hilpold, "Intervening in the Name of Humanity: R2P and the Power of Ideas", *Journal of Conflict & Security Law* 17 (2012): 49.

[3] Miguel Lemos, "*Jus Cogens* Versus the Chapter VII Powers of the Security Council: With Particular References to Humanitarian Intervention and Terrorism", *Chinese Journal of International Law* 19 (2020): 1.

[4] *Legality of the Use of Force (Yugoslavia v. Belgium)*, Request for the Indication of Provisional Measures, CR 99/15 (Oral Pleadings), 10 May 1999, quoted in Sharan, "From Non-intervention to R2P", 88.

[5] Edward Newman, "Exploring the UK's Doctrine of Humanitarian Intervention", *International Peacekeeping* 28 (2021): 632, 633, 640–50.

Charter, using the phrase "or in any other manner inconsistent with the purposes of the United Nations" to lever human rights considerations into the prohibition on the use of force. This is a difficult position to sustain, and garners little support for it to become an established rule of international law. Early examples of what might now be characterised as humanitarian interventions were not framed in those terms, perhaps in part because the legal justification was inchoate at the time. These included India's invasion of East Pakistan to facilitate the secession of what is now Bangladesh, Tanzania's invasion and occupation of Uganda that ended the ruthless rule of Idi Amin, the Vietnamese invasion of Cambodia, France's intervention in the Central African Republic several times since the latter's independence from France in 1960, and the military intervention by several Western nations to enforce a northern protection zone to protect the ethnic Kurdish minority in Iraq in 1991. These actions never resulted in affirmative statements of support for an exception to the prohibition on the use of force for humanitarian reasons. This conclusion is reinforced by other evidence from the period. In the first instance, the idea of humanitarian intervention gains no support from the UN General Assembly's (UNGA) 1970 Declaration on Friendly Relations or the 1974 Definition of Aggression. As for NATO's intervention in Kosovo, a draft UNSC resolution condemning the NATO use of force garnered only three votes in favour, to 12 against. Later, UNSC Resolution 1244 (1999) endorsed the agreement between the parties to end the conflict, although it remains controversial as to whether this constituted an ex post facto acceptance of the legality of the NATO action. This practice is not wholly unambiguous since there may be many reasons why a state chooses not to condemn another—but it is indicative that the opinion of the international community had softened. When Serbia and Montenegro instituted proceedings in the ICJ against the ten NATO member states involved in the military intervention in Kosovo for their alleged violations of their obligation not to use force against another state, the ICJ held it had no jurisdiction and therefore was not called upon to decide the issue of humanitarian intervention. Nonetheless, the ICJ made some general observations by expressing its profound concern with the use of force in Yugoslavia, which under the circumstances raised very serious issues of international law.[6] Therefore, concluded Judge Shi, the mainstream position in the scholarship is that humanitarian intervention remains illegal.[7]

[6] *Legality of Use of Force (Yugoslavia v. Belgium)*, Provisional Measures, Order of 2 June 1999, ICJ Rep. 1999, p. 124 at p. 132 [17].

[7] Shi Jiuyong, "Prohibition of Use of Force in International Law", *Chinese Journal of International Law* 17 (2018): 8–11.

Judge Shi is correct in many respects. Even the UK, which is always supportive of the doctrine of humanitarian intervention, condemned the Vietnamese invasion of Cambodia in 1978, stating that: "Whatever is said about human rights in [Cambodia], it cannot excuse Vietnam, whose human rights record is deplorable, for violating the territorial integrity of [Cambodia], an independent State Member of the United Nations."[8] In the case of the military intervention in northern Iraq in 1991, it came subsequent to UNSC Resolution 688 (1991) on 5 April 1991, which expressed grave concern with respect to "the repression of the Iraqi civilian population in many parts of Iraq, including most recently in Kurdish-populated areas, which led to a massive flow of refugees towards and across international frontiers and to cross-border incursions which threaten international peace and security in the region". Although the resolution did not expressly authorise the use of force or refer to Chapter VII of the UN Charter, French, UK, US, Dutch, Italian, Spanish and Australian forces launched a military intervention, "Operation Provide Comfort", to protect Iraqi Kurds and Shiites fleeing persecution. Approximately a year later, the UK began to openly claim the doctrine of humanitarian intervention as the basis for Operation Provide Comfort, but this justification was not espoused by the US or other coalition countries. Instead, the US relied on implied authorisation by the UNSC pursuant to Resolution 688 (1991). When the US carried out Tomahawk missile strikes against Syria on 6 April 2017, following a chemical weapons attack allegedly carried out two days earlier by Syria's Assad regime in Khan Sheikhoun, which killed approximately 80 civilians, the strikes were arguably punitive or retaliatory in nature, rather than for humanitarian purposes, and the US had yet to formally adopt the doctrine of humanitarian intervention as such.[9]

For its part, the International Law Association concludes in its Final Report on Aggression and the Use of Force (2018) that:

> A minority of writers hold to the view that the use of force to avert a humanitarian catastrophe is lawful, whereas others emphasize that a use of force to avert a humanitarian catastrophe will, if stringent conditions are met, fall into a legal grey area. The existence of such minority positions means, at least,

---

[8] *United Nations Security Council Official Records*, 34th year, 2110th mtg, para. 65, quoted in Karoubi, "Unilateral Use of Armed Forces", 121.

[9] Elinor Buys and Andrew Garwood-Gowers, "The (Ir)relevance of Human Suffering: Humanitarian Intervention and Saudi Arabia's Operation Decisive Storm in Yemen", *Journal of Conflicts & Security Law* 25 (2019): 1, 17–18, 21–2.

> that it is difficult to conclude that a right of humanitarian intervention is unquestionably unlawful.[10]

The potential for fallacy that lies behind the doctrine of humanitarian intervention is that it is inherently subjective. Consider, for instance, Russia's "special military operation" against Ukraine starting in February 2022. The Russian government has claimed, inter alia, that the operation aims at "denazifying" Ukraine and at preventing the Ukrainian government from committing genocide in the Donbas in eastern Ukraine. This justification has not been accepted by the West, including those in favour of the doctrine of humanitarian intervention.[11]

Any possible existence of the right to humanitarian intervention has been rejected by the Group of 77, representing 134 developing countries, convinced it has no legal basis in the UN Charter or in the general principles of international law.[12]

Responsibility to Protect (R2P)

The doctrine of humanitarian intervention is often perceived to have been reincarnated as part of the concept of "responsibility to protect", or R2P.

The World Summit, organised by the United Nations in September 2005 to take bold decisions in the areas of development, security, human rights and reform of the United Nations, adopted the Outcome Document, which reads in its pertinent part as follows (emphasis added):

> Each individual State has the *responsibility to protect* its populations from genocide, war crimes, ethnic cleansing and crimes against humanity. This responsibility entails the *prevention* of such crimes, including their incitement, through appropriate and necessary means. We accept that responsibility and will act in accordance with it. The international community should, as ap-

---

[10] ILA, *Final Report*, p. 24

[11] See, for example, Anastasiya Kotova and Ntina Tzouvala, "In Defense of Comparisons: Russia and the Transmutations of Imperialism in International Law", *American Journal of International Law* 116 (2022): 710, 714–19; Olivier Corten and Vaios Koutroulis, "The 2022 Russian Intervention in Ukraine: What Is the Impact on the Interpretation of *Jus contra Bellum*", *Leiden Journal of International Law* 36 (2023): 1101–7.

[12] Declaration of the Group of 77, South Summit, Havana, 10–14 Apr. 2000, para. 54, quoted in S. Pandiaraj, "Sovereignty as Responsibility: Reflections on the Legal Status of the Doctrine of Responsibility to Protect", *Chinese Journal of International Law* 15 (2016): 795, 805 (n. 25).

> propriate, encourage and help States to exercise this responsibility and support the United Nations in establishing an early warning capability.
>
> The international community, *through the United Nations*, also has the responsibility to use appropriate diplomatic, humanitarian and other peaceful means, in accordance with Chapters VI [Peaceful Settlement of Disputes] and VIII of the Charter, to help protect populations from genocide, war crimes, ethnic cleansing and crimes against humanity. In this context, we are *prepared to take collective action, in a timely and decisive manner, through the Security Council, in accordance with the Charter, including Chapter VII, on a case-by-case basis and in cooperation with relevant regional organisations as appropriate*, should peaceful means be inadequate and national authority *manifestly fail* to protect the populations from genocide, war crimes, ethnic cleansing and crimes against humanity. . . . We *also* intend to commit ourselves, as necessary and appropriate, to *helping States build capacity to protect* their population from war crimes, ethnic cleansing and crimes against humanity and to assisting those which are under stress *before crises and conflicts break out*.[13]

R2P, therefore, has three pillars. Under Pillar I, states have the responsibility to protect their own populations. Pursuant to Pillar II, states have the responsibility to offer assistance to other states to fulfil their Pillar I responsibilities, whereas Pillar III elaborates the international community's responsibility to respond in a timely and decisive manner when a state manifestly fails to provide such protection, including with the use of force if necessary. However, the UNSC should be the principal authority to decide on a military intervention and in accordance with the UN Charter.

The Non-Aligned Movement (NAM), comprising 115 member states, has expressed concerns about the possible abuse of R2P "by expanding its application to situations that fall beyond the four areas defined in the 2005 World Summit Document and by misusing it to legitimize unilateral coercive measures or intervention in the internal affairs of States". There are also pertinent questions about the role to be played by each of the principal organs of the United Nations within their respective institutional mandates and responsibilities in that regard.[14]

---

[13] Paras 138–9 of the 2005 World Summit Outcome Document.

[14] UN GAOR, 63rd Sess., 97th plenary mtg at 5–6, UN Doc. A/63/PV.97 (23 July 2009) (statement of Egypt on behalf of NAM), quoted in Pandiaraj, "Sovereignty as Responsibility", 810.

According to ICJ Judge Hisashi Owada from Japan, if the intention behind R2P was to call these emerging guiding principles and evolving customary international law, then it would be nothing else than simply to replace the old denomination of the "right to intervene" by the new denomination of "responsibility to protect". It would be tantamount to an attempt to invest the same action to intervene through a group of states acting in the form of a "coalition of the willing" or through a regional organisation, with a cloak of legality or legitimacy in the absence of an authorisation by the UNSC. This type of approach would be meaningless unless one can precisely define this R2P concept in relation to such questions as: what was meant by "the international community"; who could claim to represent it and on what basis; and, most importantly, who could have the power to decide on these questions as well as on the question of determining whether the situation amounted to a level where R2P was to be set in motion. As long as these questions are not clarified and left to the individual judgement of each actor, such an approach, well-meant as it might be, would be little more than an attempt to cloak something that in its essential character was neither legal nor legitimate in a new garb that would give the semblance of something else endowed with legality and legitimacy and thereby jeopardising the very system of collective security under the UN Charter, constructed to create a viable structure of international governance based on the rule of law.[15]

R2P was reportedly invoked by France in 2008 after Cyclone Nargis caused the worst-ever natural disaster in Myanmar, implying that humanitarian aid might have to be brought in by force if the government of Myanmar kept on resisting large-scale international aid.[16] Myanmar, nonetheless, did not agree to having foreign personnel accompany the assistance, perhaps for fear that they might intervene in its domestic affairs or even harbour an ulterior motive of orchestrating a regime change in Myanmar. That was why Myanmar had serious concerns regarding France's wish to use Myanmar's air and naval bases in Pathein on the bank of a tributary of the Ayeyarwady delta, which was the worst affected area, to support its relief operations and regarding the US's offer to send an aircraft carrier to provide disaster relief. The official explanation by the

---

[15] Hisashi Owada, "The United Nations and the Maintenance of International Peace and Security—The Current Debate in the Light of Reform Proposals", *Japanese Annual of International Law* 48 (2005): 9–10. For a similar view, see Hanqin Xue, "Chinese Observations on International Law", *Chinese Journal of International Law* 6 (2007): 89–91.

[16] "Responsibility to Protect: The Lessons of Libya", *Economist*, 19 May 2011, https://www.economist.com/international/2011/05/19/the-lessons-of-libya.

Myanmar government was that it had enough human resources to handle the disaster relief efforts. In fact, contrary to mainstream Western media reports, according to several colleagues of the present author who were involved in arranging foreign humanitarian assistance for Myanmar, the Myanmar government agreed to accept foreign humanitarian assistance two or three days after Nargis had wreaked devastation upon Myanmar. Thailand and China were the first and second foreign states whose assistance Myanmar accepted. Nargis made landfall in Myanmar on the evening of Friday, 2 May 2008, and the Myanmar government accepted Thailand's offer to provide disaster relief assistance on Monday, 5 May 2008, at 10 A.M. A tripartite committee was subsequently set up comprising Myanmar, ASEAN and the United Nations to coordinate disaster relief efforts.

When the UN International Law Commission (ILC) was working on its Draft Articles on the Protection of Persons in the Event of Disasters, the issue of R2P came up several times during the debate within the ILC and the incident relating to Cyclone Nargis was often referred to by the present author, who was then an ILC member. "Disaster" for the purpose of the ILC's work on this topic means "a calamitous event or series of events resulting in widespread loss of life, great human suffering and distress, mass displacement, or large-scale material or environmental damage, thereby seriously disrupting the functioning of society". No limitation is included concerning the origin of the event, that is, whether it is natural or human-made. The ILC's decision to exclude the R2P concept from the scope of application of the draft articles was endorsed by China, Colombia, Cuba, the Czech Republic, Ghana, Ireland, Iran, Israel, Japan, Myanmar, Russia, Spain, Sri Lanka, Thailand and Venezuela. Conversely, Poland was of the view that the R2P concept should apply to disaster situations. Hungary, Finland (on behalf of the Nordic states) and Portugal suggested that R2P be kept in mind in the situations covered in the draft articles. Austria, while acknowledging that the ILC had excluded the relevance of R2P from the draft articles, observed that it was conceivable that international law could evolve.[17]

The final version of the Articles on the Protection of Persons in the Event of Disasters adopted by the ILC in 2016[18] proceeds on the basis that R2P has no place in this kind of situation. Article 10 of the articles provides that the affected state has the duty to ensure the protection of persons and provision of

---

[17] Special Rapporteur's eighth report on the protection of persons in the event of disasters, A/CN.4/697 (17 Mar. 2016), p. 11 [10].

[18] Report of the ILC on the work of its sixty-eighth session (2 May–10 June and 4 July–12 Aug. 2016), A/71/10, ch. IV.

disaster relief assistance in its territory or in territory under its jurisdiction or control, and that the affected state has the primary role in the direction, control, coordination and supervision of such relief assistance. To the extent a disaster manifestly exceeds the national response capacity of the affected state, Article 11 imposes a duty on the affected state to seek external assistance from, as appropriate, other states, the United Nations and other potential assisting actors. Paragraph 8 of the commentary to Article 11 explains that the phrase "as appropriate" is adopted by the ILC to emphasise the discretionary power of the affected state to choose from among states, the United Nations and other potential assisting actors the assistance that is most appropriate to its specific needs and this duty does not imply that the affected state is obliged to seek assistance from every source listed in Article 11. According to Article 13, the provision of external assistance requires the consent of the affected state, which shall not be withheld arbitrarily, and when an offer of external assistance is made in accordance with the articles the affected state shall, whenever possible, make known its decision regarding the offer in a timely manner. As clarified by paragraph 8 of the commentary to Article 13, the determination of whether the withholding of consent is arbitrary must be determined on a case-by-case basis, although as a general rule several principles can be adduced. For example, withholding consent to assistance from one external source is not arbitrary if an affected state has accepted appropriate and sufficient assistance from elsewhere. Conversely, where an offer of assistance is made in accordance with the articles and no alternate sources of assistance are available, there would be a strong inference that a decision to withhold consent is arbitrary. Article 14 gives the affected state the right to condition assistance so as to deny unwanted or unneeded assistance and to determine what assistance is appropriate and when.[19]

In the context of Pillar II of R2P, the protection assistance action led by the US in response to the Iraqi government's request to assist it in protecting approximately 40,000 Yazidis trapped on Mount Sinjar in northern Iraq who were being targeted for massacre by the Islamic State in Iraq and the Levant (ISIL) in August 2014 was widely praised. This military and humanitarian assistance provided at Iraq's request helped reduce casualties and allowed local forces to evacuate the trapped members of the Yazidi ethno-religious minority group into

[19] This conclusion is reproduced from Kriangsak Kittichaisaree, *International Human Rights Law and Diplomacy* (Cheltenham: Edward Elgar Publishing, 2020), pp. 233–5.

Syria and away from the imminent risk posed.[20] Pillar II of R2P has also prompted states to intercede in internal affairs of another state short of armed intervention in response to atrocities happening in the latter. Such non-use of force intervention encompasses diplomatic measures, economic sanctions, restrictions of access to weapons to commit atrocities, and provision of non-lethal assistance to opposition groups.[21]

Libya and Syria

It was the expansive interpretation of UNSC Resolution 1973 (2011) of 15 March 2011 regarding Libya that has thrown Pillar III under R2P into disrepute.

The Arab Spring protest against the Gaddafi regime in Libya in February 2011 was met with ruthless suppression by government forces and a civil war broke out. The worsening humanitarian situation led the UNSC to adopt Resolution 1970 (2011) on 26 February 2011. The resolution expressed the UNSC's grave concern at the situation in Libya and condemnation of the violence and use of force against civilians. It also deplored the gross and systematic violation of human rights, including the repression of peaceful demonstrators, expressed deep concern at the deaths of civilians, and rejected unequivocally the incitement to hostility and violence against the civilian population made from the highest level of the Libyan government. The UNSC considered that the widespread and systematic attacks taking place in Libya may have amounted to crimes against humanity, The resolution welcomed the condemnation by the Arab League, the African Union and the Organisation of Islamic Cooperation (OIC) secretary-general of the serious violations of human rights and international humanitarian law (IHL) being committed in Libya. Recalling "the Libyan authorities' responsibility to protect its population", the UNSC, acting under Chapter VII of the UN Charter, demanded an immediate end to the violence and called for steps to fulfil the legitimate demands of the population of Libya; urged the Libyan authorities to, among other things, act with the utmost restraint, respect human rights and IHL, and allow immediate access for international human rights monitors; and referred the situation in Libya

---

[20] Josie Hornung, "Terrorism and Pillar Two Protection Assistance: The Yazidis on Mount Sinjar", *Global Responsibility to Protect* 14 (2022): 232.

[21] See, for example, Stacey Henderson, *Atrocity Crimes and International Law: Responsibility to Protect, Intercession, and Non-Forceful Responses* (Abingdon: Routledge, 2022), pp. 38–151.

since 15 February 2011 to the prosecutor of the International Criminal Court (ICC) to bring those responsible for atrocities in Libya to face justice in the ICC, which on 27 June 2011, issued arrest warrants against Gaddafi and several other persons in the Libyan leadership.

Subsequently, UNSC Resolution 1973 (2011) was adopted on 15 March 2011, with ten affirmative votes and abstentions from China, Russia, Brazil, India and Germany. In its preamble, the resolution reiterates "the responsibility of the Libyan authorities to protect the Libyan population and reaffirming that parties to armed conflicts bear the primary responsibility to take all feasible steps to ensure the protection of civilians". Paragraph 4 of the resolution authorised UN member states that have notified the UN secretary-general, acting nationally or through regional organisations or arrangements, and acting in cooperation with the UN secretary-general, "to take all necessary measures . . . to protect civilians and civilian populated areas under threat of attack in [Libya], while excluding a foreign occupation force of any form on any part of Libyan territory", and asked the member states concerned to inform the UN secretary-general immediately of the measures they take pursuant to the authorisation conferred by this paragraph, which shall be immediately reported to the UNSC. The resolution also set up a no-fly zone, with paragraph 8 authorising "all necessary means" to enforce compliance. NATO launched airstrikes against Libyan government forces on 21 March 2011, ostensibly to protect civilians, invoking UNSC Resolution 1973 (2011) as authorising the airstrikes in Libya.

Instead of casting its veto, China abstained from adopting UNSC Resolution 1973 (2011), apparently because the Arab world was united in international intervention in Libya and the three African states in the UNSC at that time (Gabon, Nigeria and South Africa) supported the resolution. Explaining their decision to abstain, China and Russia declared they were always against the use of force, and they had serious difficulty with parts of the resolution since both of them preferred the crisis in Libya to be settled through peaceful means. Russia also questioned by whom the measures referred to in the resolution would be enforced and what the limits of the engagement would be. India, Germany and Brazil, having also abstained, equally stressed the need for peaceful resolution of the conflict and warned against unintended consequences of armed intervention. Almost immediately after NATO's military action in Libya started, China expressed concerns over civilian casualties caused by NATO bombing and called for an immediate ceasefire. China, Brazil, Russia and India subsequently accused Western powers of exceeding the mandate provided by Resolution 1973 (2011), which limited the use of force to the protection of civilians. NATO's targeting of the Gaddafi government in Libya and the provision of arms to rebel forces was perceived as an attempt at regime change, which eventually happened.[22]

After several months of intense fighting, Tripoli, Libya's capital city, fell to the rebels and the Qaddafi government collapsed in August 2011. Since the overthrow of Qaddafi's government, transitional governing bodies have failed to restore stability to the country and multiple UN-facilitated peace processes have stalled. Throughout Libya's conflicts, armed militias have committed extrajudicial killings, torture and abductions and have indiscriminately attacked civilian areas. Nearly a decade of fighting left more than 270,000 people internally displaced and 900,000 in need of humanitarian assistance.[23]

Lessons from the Libyan intervention made it impossible to adopt a similar UNSC resolution concerning Syria on 4 October 2011. In the aftermath of the Arab Spring uprising in March 2011 against Syria's Assad regime and the consequent ongoing civil war, the regime has been accused of crimes against humanity and war crimes committed against those opposed to it. It was estimated that 306,887 civilians were killed between 1 March 2011 and 31 March 2021 in Syria as a result of the conflict.[24] As of November 2022, 14.6 million people were in need of humanitarian assistance and protection in Syria and there were 6.7 million displaced persons in Syria and 6.6 million Syrian refugees worldwide, of whom 5.5 million were hosted in countries near Syria.[25]

The draft UNSC resolution voiced deep concern over the recent violence in Syria and strongly condemned "the continued grave and systematic human rights violations and the use of force against civilians by the Syrian authorities". Urging "all sides to reject violence and extremism", the draft resolution called

---

[22] Andrew Garwood-Gowers, "China and the Responsibility to Protect: The Implications of the Libyan Intervention", *Asian Journal of International Law* 2 (2012): 375, 385–9. See also Xue, "Chinese Contemporary Perspectives on International Law": 104–5, 112–13, 115; Mauro Barelli, "Preventing and Responding to Atrocity Crimes: China, Sovereignty and the Responsibility to Protect", *Journal of Conflict & Security Law* 23 (2018): 173, 188–97; Simon Chesterman, "Responsibility to Protect and Humanitarian Intervention: From Apology to Utopia and Back Again", in *The Oxford Handbook of the International Law of Global Security*, ed. Robin Geiß and Nils Melzer (Oxford: Oxford University Press, 2021), ch. 44.

[23] Global Centre for Responsibility to Protect, Libya, 2 Apr. 2022, https://www.globalr2p.org/countries/libya/.

[24] Report of the Office of the UN High Commissioner for Human Rights, A/HRC/50/68 (28 June 2022).

[25] Office of the UN High Commissioner for Refugees, https://www.unhcr.org/syria-emergency.html.

for "an inclusive Syrian-led political process conducted in an environment free from violence, fear, intimidation and extremism, and aimed at effectively addressing the legitimate aspirations and concerns of Syria's population". By the time the draft resolution was tabled in the UNSC, an estimated 2,700 people had been killed in Syria since the beginning of the Arab Spring uprising. China and Russia vetoed the draft resolution. The countries voting in favour of the draft resolution were Bosnia and Herzegovina, Colombia, France, Gabon, Germany, Nigeria, Portugal, the UK and the US. The four abstaining UNSC members were Brazil, India, Lebanon and South Africa.[26]

Explaining its veto, Russia said it did not support the Assad regime but the draft resolution would not promote a peaceful resolution of the crisis. In Russia's opinion, the majority of Syrians wanted gradual political change, rather than quick regime change, and the draft resolution also did not adequately take into account the behaviour of extremist groups in opposition to Syrian authorities. For China, while it was highly concerned about the violence in Syria, the draft resolution would only complicate existing tensions since it was overly focused on exerting pressure on Syria, and included the threat of sanctions, which would not resolve the situation.

In May 2014, Russia and China vetoed a draft resolution for the UNSC, acting under Chapter VII of the UN Charter, to refer to the ICC prosecutor the situation in Syria in which one or more crimes within the jurisdiction of the ICC appeared to have been committed, so that the ICC prosecutor might investigate the situation for the purpose of determining whether one or more specific persons should be charged with the commission of such crimes. For Russia, the draft resolution was an attempt to use the ICC to further inflame political passions and lay the groundwork in the end for eventual outside military intervention. Russia was convinced justice in Syria would eventually prevail, but before those guilty of perpetrating grave crimes were to be punished peace was needed. In China's opinion, the UNSC submitting the Syrian situation to the ICC would only make the situation even more complex and the problem even more difficult to solve, and, ultimately, those suffering would be the people of Syria and other countries in the region. Neither China nor Russia is a party to the Rome Statute of the ICC.

---

[26] See further, Sienho Yee, "The Dynamic Interplay between the Interpreters of Security Council Resolutions", *Chinese Journal of International Law* 11 (2012): 613, 618–22. See also Michael Byers, "Still Agreeing to Disagree: International Security and Constructive Ambiguity", *Journal on the Use of Force & International Law* 8 (2021): 91, 98–9, 110.

On 22 August 2011, the UN Human Rights Council set up the Independent International Commission of Inquiry on the Syrian Arab Republic to investigate human rights violations during the Syrian Civil War and to establish the facts and circumstances that may amount to violations and crimes and, where possible, to identify those responsible to be prosecuted in the future. The report of the Commission of Inquiry issued in August 2022, based on investigations conducted between 1 January and 30 June 2022, documents grave violations of fundamental human rights and humanitarian law across the country, with increased threats of further military operations and terrorist activity. In Syrian government-controlled areas, arbitrary detention, including torture and ill-treatment in incommunicado detention, also leading to death, remained systematic. Appalling conditions in displacement camps in the north-west of the country have left many with little choice but to return to their homes in frontline areas where active hostilities and indiscriminate attacks against civilians have claimed countless lives and targeted food and water resources. The worsening conditions for some 37,000 children in the Hawl and Rawj camps for internally displaced persons were exacerbated by an increase in the number of murders and recurring armed clashes. Insecurity continued in Syrian government-controlled areas, particularly in the south of the country. The dire situation for Syrian civilians was compounded by the worst economic and humanitarian crisis the country has faced since the start of the armed conflict. The commission calls upon UN member states supporting or otherwise influencing parties to the conflict to take action to ensure rights-respecting and law-compliant action by the parties they support, deterring their commission of violations, in line with their obligations under customary IHL; Common Article 1 of the four Geneva Conventions of 12 August 1949, whereby the High Contracting Parties undertake to respect and to ensure respect for the Geneva Conventions of 1949 in all circumstances; and other relevant treaties. Such action should include: (1) conditioning any support to the parties upon their public announcement and respect of rules of conduct that are in line with international human rights law and IHL standards; (2) refraining from providing arms, military support, funding or other forms of support to parties to the conflict when there are reasonable grounds to believe that such parties have committed violations of IHL, including war crimes, or where there is an expectation that such support may be used to commit or enable further violations of IHL; and (3) ensuring that any support to parties is conditioned on verifiable internal measures of compliance with IHL, such as regular individual reviews for internment for continued "imperative reasons of security", and ensuring that individuals are not unlawfully deprived of their liberty.[27]

In December 2016, the UNGA set up the International, Impartial and Independent Mechanism to Assist in the Investigation and Prosecution of Persons Responsible for the Most Serious Crimes under International Law Committed in the Syrian Arab Republic since March 2011. The mechanism is neither a court nor a tribunal. Instead, it is specifically mandated to assist competent jurisdictions in their pursuit of justice, in particular national courts with jurisdiction for such crimes, and will assist national, regional and international courts or tribunals that may become seized of the Syrian situation in the future. By 24 April 2024, the mechanism had received 367 requests for assistance from 16 jurisdictions, relating to 271 distinct investigations into core international crimes committed in Syria, and it had already supported some 254 of these requests, relating to 185 distinct investigations.[28] Evidence of atrocities committed by the Assad regime includes the 53,000 images smuggled out of Syria by a military police photographer known as "Caesar", who defected in 2013, showing 6,786 people who starved or were tortured to death inside Syrian government detention centres.

An important question is whether the use of force to protect human rights can never be legally permissible even in extreme circumstances such as the prevention of mass extermination of Jews by Nazi Germany. The Nazi regime used poisonous gas to put Jews to death in concentration camps.

The Assad regime in Syria used chemical weapons in Ghouta, eastern Damascus, on 21 August 2013, leaving more than 800 people dead. Soon thereafter, it pledged to ensure the destruction of its chemical weapons capability. Still haunted by the wariness and widespread negative global impacts of the Iraq War against Saddam Hussein—a war fought under false assumptions of Iraq having weapons of mass destruction, with hundreds of thousands killed and the US's standing and credibility in the world severely undermined—and due to popular resistance against another military intervention in the Middle East, the UK Parliament, the German chancellor and the US Congress rejected military action against Syria in response to the chemical attacks, and US presi-

[27] Office of the UN High Commissioner for Human Rights, "Report of the Independent International Commission of Inquiry on the Syrian Arab Republic," A/HRC/51/45 (17 Aug. 2022).

[28] Remarks by the Head of the Mechanism before the UNGA on 24 Apr. 2024, https://iiim.un.org/wp-content/uploads/2024/05/240424-IIIM-remarks-GA_ENG.pdf. See also Syrian British Consortium, *A Decade after the Daraya: Documenting a Massacre* (London: Syrian British Consortium, 2022).

dent Obama hesitantly pulled back from ordering US military attacks against the Assad regime.

The UNSC itself even adopted Resolution 2254 (2015) in December 2015 to reaffirm the UNSC's "strong commitment to the sovereignty, independence, unity and territorial integrity" of Syria, and to the purposes and principles of the UN Charter. It reiterated that the only sustainable solution to the current crisis in Syria is through an inclusive and Syrian-led political process that meets the legitimate aspirations of the Syrian people, including through the establishment of an inclusive transitional governing body with full executive powers, which shall be formed on the basis of mutual consent while ensuring continuity of governmental institutions. The resolution therefore encouraged the diplomatic efforts of the International Syria Support Group (ISSG) to help bring an end to the conflict in Syria.[29] The ISSG comprises the five permanent members of the UNSC, along with Egypt, Germany, Iran, Iraq, Italy, Jordan, Lebanon, Oman, Qatar, Saudi Arabia, Türkiye, the UAE, the Arab League, the European Union and the United Nations, with Russia and the US as co-chairs. In November 2015, the ISSG issued a statement demanding ceasefires by all the parties to the conflict in Syria, but this was not achieved since no side in the conflict was prepared to yield and the states supporting the Assad regime did not want to see Assad removed from power without knowing that his replacement would be willing to ally with them.

In March 2017, China and Russia vetoed a draft UNSC resolution to establish a sanctions regime, a committee and an expert panel to hold accountable those using and producing chemical weapons in Syria following the use of chemical weapons by both the Assad regime and ISIL in Syrian territory, with the majority of the attacks using chemical weapons being carried out by the Assad regime itself. The draft resolution would also impose sanctions on a number of individuals and entities linked to the use of chemical weapons.

Subsequently, the Assad regime was accused of using chemical weapons in Khan Sheikhoun in April 2017, killing around 80 Syrian civilians and injuring hundreds.

On 6 April 2017, the US launched an attack employing 59 US Navy Tomahawk Land Attack Missiles against the Shayrat airfield in response to Syria's use of chemical weapons against civilians two days earlier. The US actions received broad support from the UK, France, Australia, Canada, Israel, Japan, Spain, Italy, Saudi Arabia, Jordan, Germany, Türkiye, Poland and the UAE, among others. There was no UNSC authorisation or mandate for the use of force

[29] S/RES/2254 (18 Dec. 2015).

in response to the chemical weapons attack. Syria did not consent to the attack on its facilities and there was no evidence to suggest that Syria intended to launch chemical weapons, or any other weapons for that matter, against either its neighbours or the US (including US forces in the Middle East) in the future. The US's missile strikes were partly a response to Syria's failure to abide by its international legal obligations regarding chemical weapons. Although Syria violated UNSC Resolution 2118 (2013), unanimously adopted by the UNSC after Syria's first use of chemical weapons on 21 August 2013, that resolution did not envisage the use of force by individual states in response to a Syrian breach thereof. It merely endorsed the expeditious destruction of Syria's chemical weapons programme, with inspections to begin by 1 October 2013, and stipulated that in the event of non-compliance the UNSC would impose "Chapter VII" measures. Furthermore, on 28 February 2017, Russia and China vetoed the UNSC's draft resolution, which would have authorised a resort to force in response to the use of chemical weapons. It has been pointed out that the suffering caused by the Syrian chemical weapons attack in April 2017 was significantly less than the then ongoing humanitarian catastrophe in Syria. Additionally, the US's missile strikes cannot reasonably have been believed to deter any abuses other than the use of the outlawed chemical weapons.[30]

On 7 April 2018, another chemical attack was carried out, this time in Douma, by forces of the Assad regime, causing up to 75 civilian deaths and more than 500 injuries. A week later, the US, the UK and France carried out a series of military strikes involving aircraft and ship-based missiles against multiple government sites in Syria. US president Donald Trump announced the strikes in a televised address, arguing they were part of the effort to stop Assad from using chemical weapons, and he added that the US was prepared to sustain this response until this was achieved.[31] The French president said France's "red line" had been crossed. The British prime minister informed Parliament it was legally and morally right for the UK to join air strikes against the Syrian regime to prevent further human suffering after exploring every diplomatic channel in response but failed to find any alternative to the limited, carefully targeted action eventually taken.

[30] Michael N. Schmitt and Christopher M. Ford, "Assessing U.S. Justifications for Using Force in Response to Syria's Chemical Attacks: An International Law Perspective", *Journal of National Security Law & Policy* 9 (2017): 283.

[31] See also Mary B. DeRosa, "Lawyering and the Use of Force in Libya and Syria Operations", in *Research Handbook on Law and Diplomacy*, ed. Margaret E. McGuiness and David P. Stewart (Cheltenham: Edward Elgar Publishing, 2022), ch. 4 at pp. 74–81.

The UK government also disseminated its official legal position on the legality of UK military action to alleviate the extreme humanitarian suffering of the Syrian people by degrading the Syrian regime's chemical weapons capability and deterring their further use, following the chemical weapons attack in Douma.

In the UK's view, the use of chemical weapons by the Syrian regime, which had been killing its own people for seven years, had exacerbated human suffering and was, therefore, a serious crime of international concern, as a breach of the customary international law prohibition on the use of chemical weapons, and amounted to a war crime and a crime against humanity. The UK was permitted under international law, on an exceptional basis, to take measures in order to alleviate overwhelming humanitarian suffering. The legal basis for the use of force was "humanitarian intervention", requiring three conditions to be met: (1) that there was convincing evidence, generally accepted by the international community as a whole, of extreme humanitarian distress on a large scale, requiring immediate and urgent relief; (2) that it was objectively clear that there was no practicable alternative to the use of force if lives were to be saved; and (3) that the proposed use of force was necessary and proportionate to the aim of relief of humanitarian suffering and strictly limited in time and in scope to this aim (that is, the minimum necessary to achieve that end and for no other purpose). The UK government considered that the military action met the requirements of humanitarian intervention in the circumstances of the present case for the following reasons. The Syrian regime had been using chemical weapons since 2013. Over 400,000 people had died over the course of the conflict in Syria, the vast majority civilians. Over half of the Syrian population had been displaced, with over 13 million people in need of humanitarian assistance. The repeated, lethal use of chemical weapons by the Syrian regime constituted a war crime and a crime against humanity, and it was highly likely that the regime would seek to use chemical weapons again, leading to further suffering and loss of civilian life as well as the continued displacement of the civilian population. Actions by the UK and its international partners to alleviate the humanitarian suffering caused by the use of chemical weapons by the Syrian regime at the UNSC had been repeatedly blocked by the regime and its allies in disregard of international norms, including the international law prohibition on the use of chemical weapons. Since 2013, neither diplomatic action nor tough sanctions, nor the US strikes against the Shayrat airbase in April 2017 had sufficiently degraded Syrian chemical weapons capability or deterred the Syrian regime from causing extreme humanitarian distress on a large scale through its persistent use of chemical weapons. There was no practicable alternative to the truly exceptional use of force to degrade the Syrian regime's chemical weapons capability and deter their further use by the Syrian regime in order to alleviate humanitarian suffering. In these circumstances, and as an exceptional measure on grounds of overwhelming humanitarian necessity, military intervention to strike carefully considered, specifically identified targets in order effectively to alleviate humanitarian distress by degrading the Syrian regime's chemical weapons capability and deterring further chemical weapons attacks was necessary and proportionate and therefore legally justifiable. Such an intervention was directed exclusively to averting a humanitarian catastrophe caused by the Syrian regime's use of chemical weapons, and the action was the minimum judged necessary for that purpose.[32]

In November 2018, the UK government reiterated and developed its position on humanitarian intervention without UNSC authorisation, which it claimed to be "consistent with international law". In addition to the three conditions listed above, humanitarian intervention would only be considered by the UK government "where there is no other legal basis for the use of force, such as self-defence, a Chapter VII UN Security Council resolution authorizing force or host-State consent".[33]

Those considering the military action against Syria in April 2018 to be legally justified were Albania, Bulgaria, Canada, the Czech Republic, Denmark, Estonia, Germany, Greece, Italy, the Netherlands, Poland, Romania, Spain, Türkiye, the EU and NATO. However, it was condemned by Iran since there was no proof the Assad regime was responsible for the chemical attack on Douma. The Collective Security Treaty Organization, whose membership comprises Armenia, Belarus, Kazakhstan, Kyrgyzstan, Russia and Tajikistan, denounced the action as contrary to international law. Russia called for an emergency meeting of the UNSC on 14 April 2018 but its draft resolution to condemn the attacks failed to be adopted, with only Bolivia and China supporting it.

There were other parallel developments.

In June 2018, the Conference of the States Parties to the 1993 Convention on the Prohibition of the Development, Production, Stockpiling and Use of

---

[32] Prime Minister's Office, "Syria Action: UK Government Legal Position" (14 Apr. 2018), https://www.gov.uk/government/publications/syria-action-uk-government-legal-position/syria-action-uk-government-legal-position.

[33] UK Government, "Global Britain: The Responsibility to Protect and Humanitarian Intervention: Government Response to the Committee's Twelfth Report", cited in Newman, "Exploring the UK's Doctrine of Humanitarian Intervention", 641. See also Michael Wood, "International Law and the Use of Force: What Happens in Practice?", *Indian Journal of International Law* 53 (2013): 345, 360–1.

Chemical Weapons and on Their Destruction, to which Syria is a party, decided to establish the Investigation and Identification Team to identify the perpetrators of specific instances of chemical weapons use in Syria.[34] The team began its work in June 2019 and has submitted four reports at the time of writing. It found reasonable grounds to believe that the Syrian air force perpetrated the use of sarin as a chemical weapon on 24 and 30 March 2017, and the use of chlorine as a chemical weapon on 25 March 2017 in Ltamenah, affecting no fewer than 106 civilians; released chlorine over a large area in Saraqib on 4 February 2018, affecting 12 named individuals; and dropped two yellow cylinders that hit two residential buildings in a central area of Douma on 7 April 2018, during a major military offensive aimed at regaining control of the city. The fourth report, dated 22 February 2024, concluded that there were reasonable grounds to believe that, on 1 September 2015, during sustained attacks aimed at capturing the Syrian town of Marea, units of ISIL deployed sulphur mustard, using one or more artillery guns.

In April 2021, the Organisation for the Prohibition of Chemical Weapons suspended Syria from its membership owing to the Assad regime's failure to disclose its chemical weapon stockpiles and its violation of the 1993 Convention.

Syria was suspended from the League of Arab States on 12 November 2011, with Syria, Yemen and Lebanon being the only three voting against Syria's suspension, while Iraq abstained. Syria was suspended from the OIC in August 2012. During the Assad regime's suspension from the OIC and the League of Arab States, several Arab states reconsidered their positions regarding Syria and recognised the Assad regime as the only viable regime in Syria. The UAE reopened its embassy in Damascus, Syria, in December 2018, followed by exchanges of high-level official visits between the two states. In April 2023, Syria and Tunisia agreed to reopen their embassies in each other's countries, after more than a decade of strained diplomatic ties. In February 2023, Assad paid an official visit to Oman, the first official engagement between Syria and Oman since the start of the Syrian Civil War in 2011. In April 2023, Syria's foreign minister paid an official visit to Saudi Arabia, which severed its diplomatic relations with Syria in 2012, at the invitation of his Saudi counterpart, being the first such visit since 2011. In a joint statement issued at the end of the visit, both sides agreed on the need for a comprehensive political settlement of the Syrian crisis that would achieve national reconciliation, and contribute to the return of Syria to its Arab fold. This visit came after Saudi Arabia had agreed to a rapprochement with Iran, a key ally of the Syrian government, in March 2023. On 7 May 2023, the Arab

[34] Decision C-SS-4/DEC.3, dated 27 June 2018.

League ended its suspension of Syria's membership, although it also emphasised the need to end Syria's civil war as well as the resulting refugee crisis and smuggling into Middle East states of Captagon, an addictive, amphetamine-type stimulant mass-produced in Syria. A committee comprising Egypt, Saudi Arabia, Lebanon, Jordan and Iraq was set up to help Syria achieve those goals. Despite the end of the Arab League's membership suspension, it is up to each Arab state whether to resume its bilateral diplomatic relationship with Syria. On 10 May 2023, the Syrian embassy in Riyadh and the Saudi Arabian embassy in Damascus resumed their functions for the first time after the severance of the Saudi–Syrian diplomatic relations in 2012. For these states, humanitarian intervention or R2P no longer applies in the case of Syria, if it ever did. Nonetheless, on 8 December 2024 the Assad regime collapsed after surprise military attacks by rebel forces that have taken over ruling the country ever since.

China's Responsible Protection (RP) Concept

In June 2012, the China Institute of International Studies came up with China's responsible protection (RP) concept, which has six elements. First, the object of RP must be the innocent people of the target country and peace and stability of the relevant region, not specific political parties or armed forces; impartiality of those intervening; and reference to regional peace and security. Second, the legitimacy of the "protection" executors must be established. The government of a given state bears the primary responsibility for protecting its citizens. Besides that, the UNSC is the only legitimate actor to perform this duty, while no countries have such a right, let alone the legal status to do so. Third, the means of "protection" must be strictly limited. The prerequisite for invoking protection should be exhaustion of diplomatic and political means of solution. Non-military means like diplomatic efforts, though time-consuming, produce long-lasting results with lesser side effects. Fourth, the purpose of "protection" must be to mitigate humanitarian catastrophe. It is absolutely forbidden to create greater humanitarian disasters because of protection, let alone to use protection as a means to overthrow the government of a given state. Fifth, the "protectors" should be responsible for the "post-intervention" and "post-protection" reconstruction of the state concerned. Sixth, the United Nations should establish mechanisms of supervision, outcome evaluation and *post factum* accountability to ensure the means, process, scope and results of "protection". The idea of RP is believed to better embody the purposes and principles of the UN Charter as well as the basic norms governing international relations, better conform to the trends of peace and development of the present-day world, and to be more conducive to building a just and reasonable new international order. Moreover, this idea is broadly based internationally.[35] Although RP has not yet been formally adopted by the Chinese government, it was the subject of an international conference organised by the Institute in Beijing in October 2013, which involved delegates from a number of states.

Reassessment of R2P

The Group of Friends of R2P[36] has underlined that R2P needs to be at the heart of a shared mission to advance peace and security, human rights and development and that effective prevention of atrocities can only be achieved if the UN system responds holistically by using all the tools and mechanisms at its disposal, including by greater cross-departmental collaboration. Many states have emphasised that translating early warning into early action remains a challenge, and highlighted ongoing crises in Myanmar, Ethiopia, Syria, Sudan (Darfur), Ukraine and elsewhere. While the discussion on R2P at the UNGA in June 2023 broadly reflected widespread support for R2P, the Group of Friends in Defence of the Charter of the United Nations, then representing 19 states and one observer mission,[37] as well as some of the group's members—China, Cuba, North Korea, Iran, Nicaragua, Russia, Syria and Venezuela—challenged the application of R2P. In expressing concern about the unequal implementation of R2P, this group underlined that, "instead of pushing for controversial and divisive approaches that have the potential of further increasing tensions and mistrust around the globe, the international community should make greater use of the tools provided by multilateralism and diplomacy for the peaceful settlement of disputes". Seventy-four states and the EU

---

[35] Ruan Zongze, "Responsible Protection: Building a Safer World", *China Institute of International Studies* 34 (2012): 19–41, discussed in Garwood-Gowers, "China and the Responsibility to Protect".

[36] An informal intergovernmental platform for Permanent Missions to the United Nations in both New York and Geneva, established in 2008 in New York and 2015 in Geneva and currently consists of 56 members from across all regions as well as the European Union. France, the UK and the US are the three permanent members of the UNSC that are also members of the Group. Bangladesh, Japan, Qatar, Marshall Islands, South Korea and Singapore are the members from Asia.

[37] Algeria, Angola, Belarus, Bolivia, Cambodia, China, Cuba, Equatorial Guinea, North Korea, Eritrea, Iran, Laos, Mali, Nicaragua, Russia, St Vincent and the Grenadines, Syria, Venezuela, Zimbabwe and the State of Palestine (observer). Angola and Cambodia withdrew from the group in Apr. 2024.

highlighted the important role the UNSC has as the primary organ responsible for maintaining international peace and security and in ensuring timely and decisive action in the case of mass atrocities. Various initiatives aimed at guiding the voting behaviour of UNSC members were mentioned by 70 states and the EU owing to their concern regarding ongoing UNSC inaction in situations where states have manifestly failed to uphold their responsibility to protect vulnerable populations. Many states emphasised the need for UNSC reform and the restraint of veto powers in situations of mass atrocities.[38]

In his report in May 2025 on the 20th anniversary of the adoption of R2P at the 2005 World Summit, the UN secretary-general highlighted a troubling trend: despite the unanimous commitment to end atrocity crimes, such crimes have increased around the world, exposing a persistent gap between promises and meaningful action, particularly in the world's gravest cases. He warned that continued failures to protect populations—despite our improved understanding of risk factors and enhanced capacity for response—denote a deeper, alarming challenge to mobilising response. To address these challenges, the secretary-general emphasised the urgent need for renewed strategic investment and consistent, collective international action, offering concrete recommendations to more effectively implement R2P's three pillars moving forward.[39]

Myanmar and Syria were the two flashpoints in Asia whose ongoing crises were highlighted by the UNGA's aforesaid plenary meeting in June 2023. The situation in Syria has been discussed above and will be further analysed from a different angle in Chapter 7.

Applying Pillar III of R2P to, or use of force as humanitarian intervention in, Myanmar is not politically feasible. Myanmar is situated in China's southern backyard, sharing a 2,227-kilometre-long land border with China, which has strong geopolitical and economic interests in Myanmar. As of the end of 2020, China was Myanmar's second-biggest investor, behind Singapore, with US$21.5 billion in approved foreign capital, or a quarter of foreign direct investment in Myanmar. The Chinese telecommunications giant Huawei has been building Myanmar's 5G telecommunications networks. China also accounts for approximately one-third of all Myanmar's trade, making it Myanmar's most important trading partner, with their bilateral trade accounting for approximately US$11 billion in 2018. China is interested in pursuing with Myanmar

[38] Global Centre for Responsibility to Protect, *Summary of the 2023 UN General Assembly Plenary Meeting on the Responsibility to Protect* (14 July 2023).

[39] https://www.globalr2p.org/publications/summary-2025-report/.

its Belt and Road Initiative,[40] the China–Myanmar Economic Corridor, including the Kyaukpyu Special Economic Zone to serve as China's strategic route to the Indian Ocean, and Chinese investment projects such as the 6,000-megawatt Myitsone Dam project. Myanmar is strategically situated to give China's landlocked western provinces potential port access to the Indian Ocean and the Bay of Bengal and on to the Middle East and Africa. This access will also help China bypass the need to navigate through the Straits of Malacca and Singapore. China is also reported to have set up a maritime reconnaissance and electronic intelligence station on Myanmar's Great Coco Island in the Bay of Bengal, approximately 300 kilometres south of Myanmar's mainland, and another one on Little Coco Island in the Alexandra Channel between the Indian Ocean and the Andaman Islands. During Chinese president Xi's visit to Myanmar in January 2020, China and Myanmar signed 33 agreements to expedite infrastructure projects in Myanmar that are part of China's Belt and Road Initiative, including the development of the China–Myanmar Economic Corridor, worth billions of US dollars, with agreements on railways linking south-western China to the Indian Ocean; a US$1.3 billion deep sea-port in Kyaukpyu in Rakhine State; a special economic zone on the border between the two countries; and a letter of intent for new urban development in Yangon, Myanmar's biggest city.

In February 2022, China's foreign minister reportedly told the foreign minister of the Myanmar military government that, "[n]o matter how the situation changes, China will support Myanmar in safeguarding its sovereignty, independence, and territorial integrity, and in exploring a development path suited to its national conditions".[41] Obviously China would not stand idle if any state ever tried to use force either singularly or in collaboration with some other like-minded states to strive for regime change in Myanmar in the name of R2P or humanitarian intervention. And China has a veto in the UNSC.

The UK has been a leading voice in the United Nations against Myanmar for its alleged genocide and crimes against humanity, particularly ethnic

---

[40] A global infrastructure development strategy adopted by the Chinese government in Oct. 2013 to connect China with 150 countries across Asia, Europe and Africa via a "New Silk Road" of railways, highways and ports.

[41] Sebastian Stranglio, "China Pledges Support for Myanmar's Junta 'No Matter How the Situation Changes'", *The Diplomat*, 4 Apr. 2022, https://thediplomat.com/2022/04/china-pledges-support-for-myanmars-junta-no-matter-how-the-situation-changes/. See also Thompson Chau and John Liu, "China Rolls Dice with Myanmar's Military, Sidelines Democratic NUG", *Nikkei Asia*, 16 Feb. 2022, https://asia.nikkei.com/Spotlight/Myanmar-Crisis/China-rolls-dice-with-Myanmar-s-military-sidelines-democratic-NUG.

cleansing, against the Rohingya ethnic and religious group normally residing in Myanmar's Rakhine State.[42] The UK has also imposed sanctions on certain Myanmar individuals for their roles in human rights suppression following the 1 February 2021 military takeover of the Myanmar government. Britain fought three wars in order to occupy the entirety of Myanmar, then officially named Burma, and establish colonial rule. In the Burmese-language book *The Problems at Myanmar's Western Gate*, published in 2016, General Khin Nyunt, the former head of Burmese military intelligence and prime minister of Myanmar from 25 August 2003 to 18 October 2004, who is now alleged to have masterminded the policy of ethnic cleansing leading to the persecution of the Rohingya, states that the problems with the Rohingya, who are Muslims, have existed since British rule, because they brought these "Bengali" labour from Bangladesh as migrants whom the Burmese people could not accept. Therefore, in the eyes of successive Myanmar governments and military as well as Myanmar nationalists, Britain has been a major troublemaker, not a saviour, and any British initiative via-à-vis Myanmar, including by invoking the British conviction in the right to humanitarian intervention, will never be historically, morally or logically credible to these people.

Libya's President Gaddafi was a pariah whom the African Union and the League of Arab States wanted to see the last of, making it possible for the UNSC to adopt Resolution 1973 (2011). ASEAN, of which Myanmar is a member state, has not gone that far. ASEAN's Five-Point Consensus demands, inter alia, that there shall be immediate cessation of violence in Myanmar and "all parties" shall exercise utmost restraint, and that "constructive dialogue among all parties concerned shall commence to seek a peaceful solution in the interests of the people". Also, ASEAN shall provide "humanitarian assistance through the ASEAN Coordinating Centre for Humanitarian Assistance on Disaster Management". ASEAN member states strongly subscribe to the principle of territorial sovereignty and integrity.

On 21 December 2022, the UNSC adopted a resolution[43] by a vote of 12 in favour to none against, with three abstentions (China, India and Russia). The resolution calls for the immediate end to all forms of violence in Myanmar and urges restraint, the de-escalation of tensions and the immediate release of all arbitrarily detained prisoners, including President Win Myint and State Counsellor Aung San Suu Kyi, ousted by the 1 February 2021 military coup. The

[42] Kriangsak Kittichaisaree, *The Rohingya, Justice and International Law* (Abingdon: Routledge, 2021), pp. 51–5.
[43] S/RES/2669 (2022).

resolution reiterates the UNSC's call to uphold democratic institutions and processes and pursue constructive dialogue and reconciliation in accordance with the will and interests of Myanmar's people. All parties must respect human rights, fundamental freedoms and the rule of law. It acknowledges the central role of ASEAN in finding a peaceful solution to the crisis and encourages the international community to support the ASEAN-led mechanism and process in this regard. It calls for concrete and immediate actions to effectively and fully implement ASEAN's Five-Point Consensus. Reiterating the necessity for full, safe and unhindered humanitarian access, the UNSC underlines the need for scaled-up humanitarian assistance to all people in need in Myanmar and to ensure the full protection, safety and security of humanitarian and medical personnel. It also stresses the need to address the root causes of the crisis in Rakhine State and create the conditions necessary for the voluntary, safe, dignified and sustainable return of Rohingya refugees and internally displaced persons. It encourages diplomatic efforts between the parties concerned to help address the issues facing the Rohingya, further emphasises the importance of providing continued protection and assistance to refugees and displaced persons, and decides to remain seized of the matter.

This is the first ever UNSC resolution on Myanmar. Explaining its abstention in adopting the resolution, China considered it more appropriate for the UNSC to adopt a presidential statement rather than a resolution, noting that the tone of the text lacks balance. China emphasised there is no quick fix for the Myanmar issue and the solution to the conflict depends on Myanmar itself. The large-scale prisoner release in November 2022 by the Myanmar authorities should be recognised and encouraged. China also emphasised that ASEAN has a unique advantage in dealing with Myanmar-related issues, and the international community should listen to ASEAN's views, support its leadership and allow ASEAN time and space to build consensus. China joined the consensus in the UNSC to issue ten outcome documents on Myanmar in 2021. China reiterated its policy of friendship towards Myanmar, full support for ASEAN and the implementation of the Five-Point Consensus. Russia considers the situation in Myanmar not to represent a threat to international peace and security. In Russia's opinion, as the text mainly focuses on the human rights situation, the Third Committee (Social, Humanitarian and Cultural) would be a better discussion forum. Russia also abstained because the wording of the resolution was not balanced. While recognising that states can have different opinions about the policies of the military government in Myanmar, Russia thinks that UNSC members should not destabilise the situation on the ground and undermine ASEAN's mediation efforts. Noting that the resolution was not consensus-based, Russia decided not to block it, recalling that the only topic on the UNSC's agenda on Myanmar should be the Rohingya situation in Rakhine State. India abstained because the complex situation in Myanmar calls for quiet, patient diplomacy, and any other course will not help resolve outstanding issues and may even entrench the parties in inflexible positions. India urged the UNSC to carefully weigh its action and consider the interests of neighbouring countries, such as India, most affected by instability in Myanmar.

Tom Andrews, UN special rapporteur on the situation of human rights in Myanmar, criticises that the UNSC resolution does not go far enough since the UNSC is merely "expressing deep concern" and demanding that certain actions be taken, but without any use of the UNSC's Chapter VII enforcement authority to compel the Myanmar junta not to attack and destroy the lives of the 54 million people being held hostage in Myanmar. Essentially, the resolution does not stipulate the consequences for the failure to meet the UNSC's demands and it does not impose sanctions and accountability for crimes the Myanmar military has committed to date. He refers to UN secretary-general Guterres' declaration in November 2022 that, with respect to Myanmar, the international community has failed. In Andrews' view, this failure cannot be rectified by resolutions that have no consequences—it can only be responsibly addressed with targeted, coordinated action by UN member states who have the political will to address this failure, including coordinating sanctions, cutting off the flow of revenue that is financing the junta's military assaults, an embargo on weapons and dual-use technology and robust humanitarian aid that can reach those most in need, among other measures.[44]

Therefore, it is clear that invoking Pillar III of R2P or the concept of humanitarian intervention to use force to uphold human rights in Myanmar is not accepted by the UNSC, especially China, India, Russia and ASEAN.

In conclusion, Pillar III of R2P and the doctrine of humanitarian intervention cannot be realistically applied in present-day Asia.

---

[44] "Statement by Thomas H. Andrews, UN Special Rapporteur on the Situation of Human Rights in Myanmar," 22 Dec. 2022, https://www.ohchr.org/en/press-releases/2022/12/myanmar-action-needed-stop-carnage-says-un-expert-after-adoption-security.

CHAPTER 7

Terrorism and Self-Defence against Non-state Actors

International Regime after 11 September 2001

A state may ask other states to help it suppress terrorists within its border. To cite just one example, since 2021 the South African Development Community and several African states have assisted Mozambique in its military operations against the militants known as Ansar al-Sunna that has pledged allegiance to Islamic State in Iraq and the Levant (ISIL).[1]

After the terrorist attacks of 11 September 2001 on US soil, the UN Security Council (UNSC) adopted Resolutions 1368 and 1373, both of which categorised the terrorist acts as threats to international peace and security and reaffirmed "the inherent right of individual or collective self-defence in accordance with the [UN] Charter". This has given rise to the situation where a state uses force in the territory of another state allegedly in the exercise of the right to self-defence against terrorists or other armed non-state actors located in the territory of the latter state. For example, Kenya launched military Operation Linda Nchi in Somalia from 16 October 2011 to 31 May 2012 in response to a series of kidnappings that had taken place on Kenyan territory allegedly carried out by the militant group Al-Shabaab, a non-state actor affiliated with Al Qaeda. In its letter of 17 October 2011, Kenya informed the UNSC of the operation in response to "serious challenges emanating from the collapse of the State of Somalia over the past two decades", where the situation had recently

[1] Patrick M. Butchard and Jasmin Johurun Nessa, "Digest of State Practice: 1 July–31 December 2021", *Journal on the Use of Force & International Law* 9 (2022): 171, 180–3.

worsened, with dozens of incursions from Somalia that had been repulsed by Kenyan military and police forces. Kenya added that scores of Kenyans had lost their lives over the preceding 36 months in border towns and communities owing to terrorist actions and incursions from Al-Shabaab militants. Kenya's armed invasion into Somalia for this purpose gained the support of the African Union, Israel, the US and France. It could be considered "extra-territorial law enforcement" against terrorists in a state that is unable to effectively police its own territory.[2] After terminating Operation Linda Nchi, Kenya joined the African Union Mission in Somalia, a regional peacekeeping mission operated by the African Union with the approval of the UNSC. Another foreign state using forces in Somalia is the US, which has carried out several airstrikes against Al-Shabaab in Somalia in support of, in coordination with, or at the request of the Somali government.

Since all states have an international legal obligation not to allow their territory to be used by non-state actors to carry out armed attacks against another state, there is growing international support for the right of self-defence against non-state actors in the territory of a state that is "unable or unwilling" to prevent their armed attack on another state. If a state is willing but unable (for example because it does not control a part of its territory that is being used for armed attacks against another state), self-defensive measures without the consent of the territorial state amount to violation of its sovereignty and unlawful interference in its internal affairs. The willing state will have to request external assistance for it to prevent armed attack by non-state actors against another state. If a state is unwilling to take effective measures to prevent its territory from being used by non-state actors that attack another state, it becomes a harbouring or accomplice state and self-defensive measures, either individual or collective, can arguably be carried out on the territory of such a state even without its consent.[3]

Members of a non-state armed group or terrorists who launched an armed attack against a state may be moving between the territories of two or more states. However, the exercise of the right of self-defence by the attacked state must be

---

[2] Daley J. Birkett, "The Legality of the 2011 Kenyan Invasion of Somalia and Its Implications for the *Jus ad Bellum*", *Journal of Conflict & Security Law* 18 (2013): 427.

[3] Rein Müllerson, "Self-Defence against Armed Attacks by Non-State Actors", *Chinese Journal of International Law* 18 (2019): 751, 765–71. See also Chloe Goldthorpe, "The Armed Attack Requirement and Customary International Law: Whose Views Count?", *Journal on the Use of Force & International Law* 10 (2023): 49. *Contra*: Oona A. Hathaway, "How the Erosion of U.S. War Powers Constraints Has Undermined International Law Constraints on the Use of Force", *Harvard National Security Journal* 14 (2023): 336, 349–55.

specifically justified vis-à-vis *each and every* state on whose territory self-defence action is taken.[4]

These legal arguments concerning the use of force against terrorists and other non-state actors are largely endorsed by the group of experts writing the *Oslo Manual on Select Topics of the Law of Armed Conflict: Rules and Commentary*,[5] published in 2020, which came up with the following rules applicable in response to armed attack by non-state actors.

Under Rule 153, the right of self-defence applies in response to an armed attack by non-state armed groups. Pursuant to Rule 154, a state may exercise its right of self-defence against non-state armed groups in a foreign state in response to an armed attack mounted by them from outside the victim state's territory, subject to the UN Charter. According to the accompanying commentary to Rule 154, the inherent right of self-defence, enshrined in Article 51 of the UN Charter, is not contingent on the armed attack being attributable to another state. If the foreign state knowingly provides shelter to the armed group, or otherwise connives with it, it may bear responsibility for an armed attack carried out by the armed group. An armed attack by non-state armed groups may be launched from foreign territory, where there is no connivance by the territorial state notwithstanding the fact that the armed group has its base of operations within that territory. If the victim state exercises its right of self-defence, it will likely do so within the territory of the state in which that base of operations is situated. Nevertheless, the exercise of self-defence will be directed against the non-state armed groups and not against the foreign state itself. According to Rule 155, self-defence may be exercised in the circumstances referred to in Rule 154 without the consent of the incumbent territorial government if the latter is *unable or unwilling* to take the action necessary to suppress armed attacks by a non-state armed group against the victim state. The commentary accompanying Rule 155 clarifies that this mode of non-consensual self-defence is in conformity with the general practice of states and the UN Charter and is sometimes called "extra-territorial law enforcement", which is permissible when a local government is unable or unwilling to suppress armed attacks carried out by non-state armed groups against foreign states. The commentary observes, however, that the scale of the use of force in self-defence against ISIL within Syria—by the US-led coalition, operating without the consent or invitation of the Syrian government—is

[4] Claus Kress, "Some Reflections on the International Legal Framework Governing Transnational Armed Conflicts", *Journal of Conflict & Security Law* 15 (2010): 245, 251–2, 267.
[5] Yoram Dinstein and Arne Willy Dahl, *Oslo Manual on Select Topics of the Law of Armed Conflict: Rules and Commentary* (Cham: Springer, 2020), pp. 145–7.

extraordinary. As in all other instances of self-defence, the exercise of the right has to be carried out in accordance with the customary conditions of necessity, proportionality and immediacy. Under Rule 156, the right of self-defence against non-state armed groups in the circumstances referred to in Rule 154 may be exercised either individually or collectively. The accompanying commentary to Rule 156 notes that the United States and other members of the international coalition have justified their military operations in Syria against ISIL on the basis of collective self-defence in response to an armed attack against Iraq. Yet some other members of the coalition fighting ISIL may have different rationales for their operations in Syria. Rule 157 stipulates that the extra territorial exercise of the right of self-defence against non-state armed groups does not in and of itself bring into existence an international armed conflict. For example, in the case of the armed conflict in Syria (beginning in 2011) the states conducting operations are engaged in fighting there either by invitation of the Syrian government or—if operating without such invitation—they are confronting non-state armed groups in the exercise of the right of individual or collective self-defence against an armed attack. The crux of the matter is that, broadly speaking, the states belonging to the anti-ISIL coalition and the Syrian government have largely chosen not to engage one another with military force.

One controversial international legal issue is how to distinguish between an "imminent" armed attack by terrorists from a mere "threat" of armed attack. While imminent armed attack may give rise to the right to self-defence pursuant to the *Caroline* test, as explained in Chapter 2, there is no right to self-defence to prevent the threat, however persistent, from actually materialising. There are four cumulative conditions under the *Caroline* test: (1) the existence of a grave and pressing danger against the security of a state or its citizens necessitating such action, (2) the absence of means of protection other than the measures taken or to be taken, (3) the illegal nature of this danger and (4) proportionality.[6] This depends on the factual circumstances in each case.[7]

Targeted killings of terrorists located in another state have been legally controversial. The killing of Osama bin Laden in Pakistan by a US special operations force, for example, raises the legal issues of whether the United States violated Pakistan's sovereignty, violated bin Laden's right to life under international human rights law by killing him although he might have been captured

---

[6] Bin Cheng, "Pre-Emptive or Similar Type of Self-Defense in the Territory of Foreign States", *Chinese Journal of International Law* 12 (2013): 1, 4.

[7] See Chris O'Meara, "Reconceptualising the Right of Self-Defence against 'Imminent' Armed Attacks", *Journal on the Use of Force & International Law* 9 (2022): 278.

alive, and violated international humanitarian law by targeting a person who was not a combatant or a person who participated directly in hostilities against the United States.[8] On 31 July 2022, Al Qaeda leader Ayman al-Zawahiri was killed in a CIA drone strike in Afghanistan. US president Joe Biden justified the US action on the ground that Zawahiri was deeply involved in the planning of the 11 September 2001 terrorist attacks on US soil, killing 2,977 people, and that, for decades, Zawahiri was the mastermind of attacks against Americans. Biden added that this drone strike demonstrated the United States' resolve and capacity to defend the American people against those who seek to do harm to Americans, no matter how long it takes, no matter where they hide—if they are a threat to Americans, the United States will find them and take them out. This US presidential statement reveals that the target killing served as a reprisal and a deterrence for terrorists—not a lawful exercise of the right to self-defence against an ongoing or imminent attack.[9]

India v. Pakistan

India has often invoked the right to self-defence against non-state actors based in Pakistan. For instance, on 29 September 2016 India carried out eight synchronised raids across Kashmir's Line of Control, inside Pakistan, along a 250-kilometre arc, to demolish terrorist launchpads used by "terrorists who were planning to infiltrate into [Indian] territory". India accused Pakistan of being *unable* to control terrorist activities in Pakistan's territory as well as being *unwilling* to prevent these terrorists from destabilising India's Jammu and

[8] Sikander Ahmed Shah, *International Law and Drone Strikes in Pakistan: The Legal and Socio-political Aspects* (London: Routledge, 2015), pp. 32–193, 230; Meagan S. Wong, "Targeted Killings and the International Legal Framework: With Particular Reference to the US Operation against Osama Bin Laden", *Chinese Journal of International Law* 11 (2012): 127, 147, 149, 155, 163; Christian Schaller, "Using Force against Terrorists 'Outside' Areas of Active Hostilities–The Obama Approach and the Bin Laden Raid Revisited", *Journal of Conflict & Security Law* 20 (2015): 195; Mary Ellen O'Connell, "Twenty Years of Drone Attacks", *EJIL Talk!*, 15 Nov. 2022, https://www.ejiltalk.org/twenty-years-of-drone-attacks/.

[9] Craig Martin, "What Was the International Legal Basis for the Strike on al-Zawahiri?", *Just Security*, 9 Aug. 2022, https://www.justsecurity.org/82605/what-was-the-international-legal-basis-for-the-strike-on-al-zawahiri/. See also Phani Dascalopoulou-Livada, *Contemporary Issues in International Law* (The Hague: Eleven International Publishing, 2019), pp. 163–86; Zainub R. Ali, "Assessing the Effectiveness of Leadership Decapitation as a U.S. Counterterrorism Strategy: The Case of Iranian General Qassem Soleimani's Death by Drone Strike", *West Point Journal of Politics & Security* 1 (2021): 10.

Kashmir. The Indian surgical strike was said to be in response specifically to an earlier incident, on 18 September 2016, in which some 19 Indian army soldiers had been killed. This surgical strike passed without causing any significant concern in the international community.[10] There have been frequent allegations and counter-allegations between India and Pakistan on cross-border terrorism.[11] Yet India did not report the aforesaid incident in 2016 to the UNSC, and Pakistan insisted the surgical strikes did not take place at all, probably to de-escalate the tension. On 4 February 2019, more than 40 Indian Central Reserve Police Force personnel were killed by a suicide bomb in the state of Jammu and Kashmir. The Pakistani-based Jaish-e-Mohammed (JeM) reportedly claimed responsibility. As a response, on 26 February 2019 the Indian Air Force carried out airstrikes against an alleged JeM training camp in Pakistan.

Pakistan condemned the Indian airstrikes as an aggression in violation of Pakistan's sovereignty and territorial integrity. On 27 February 2019, Pakistan declared that its air force had undertaken airstrikes against a non-military target across the Line of Control from within Pakistan's airspace, not in retaliation to Indian belligerence but to demonstrate Pakistan's right, will and capability for self-defence while avoiding human loss and collateral damage. On the same day, India's Ministry of External Affairs confirmed Pakistan's airstrikes and that India had foiled Pakistan's attempts to target military installations and even shot down one Pakistani fighter aircraft, while India lost one MiG 21 and an Indian pilot was missing in action, whose his release by Pakistan India demanded. Pakistan did release the pilot and handed over him to India on 1 March 2019. Neither India nor Pakistan reported its military action to the UNSC. While most governments called both India and Pakistan to show restraint, France also defended India's legitimate right to guarantee its security against transboundary terrorism and called on Pakistan to end the activities of terrorist groups on Pakistan's territory.[12]

At the time of writing, there is still insufficient information to objectively analyse the four-day armed conflict between India and Pakistan in May 2025 in the wake of the killing of 26 Indian civilians in Indian-administered Jammu and

---

[10] P.S. Rao, "Non-state Actors and Self-Defence: A Relook at the UN Charter Article 51", *Indian Journal of International Law* 56 (2016): 127, 128.

[11] Srinivas Burra, "Use of Force and Self-Defence against Non-State Actors and TWAIL Considerations: A Critical Analysis of India's State Practice", *Asian Yearbook of International Law* 24 (2018): 106, 114–19.

[12] Müllerson, "Self-Defence against Armed Attacks by Non-state Actors", 762–3.

Kashmir on 22 April 2025, which India attributed to a certain terrorist organisation allegedly supported by Pakistan.

Syria

It is Syria that has been subjected to the most frequent cross-border attacks by other states against ISIL which proclaimed a caliphate across Syria and Iraq in 2011 amid the chaos of the Syrian civil war.[13] Even Iran, a close ally of the Assad regime in Syria, has done so.

For example, in October 2018 Iran reported to the UNSC that a brutal terrorist attack had taken place in the city of Ahvaz, the capital of Iran's Khouzestan Province, on 22 September 2018, killing 24 Iranian citizens, including a four-year-old child, and wounding 60 others. The Iranian armed forces, "acting in legitimate self-defence recognized by Article 51 of the UN Charter", took limited and measured military action on 1 October 2018 in Syria, targeting terrorist elements that are also linked to the terrorist act in Ahvaz.[14]

Israel has carried out hundreds of airstrikes against Syria since the war broke out in Syria in 2011, targeting Syrian government troops as well as allied Iran-backed forces and fighters from Lebanon's Shia group Hezbollah, which has carried out attacks against Israel and which has sent thousands of fighters to support Syria's Assad regime.

Since 2011, Türkiye has carried out no fewer than four military offensive in northern Syria against the Kurdish People's Protection Units (YPG), which it considers a terrorist organisation and an extension of the outlawed Kurdistan Workers' Party (PKK), which has waged a decades-long armed campaign for an independent Kurdish state in the mountainous Kurdish-majority regions in south-east Türkiye and northern Iraq. For example, at night on 19 November 2022 and early morning of the 20th, Türkiye's air force carried out "precision bombings" against targets in northern Syria and Iraq allegedly used by the PKK and affiliated Syrian Kurdish groups accused of being behind an explosion in central Istanbul in Türkiye on 13 November 2022 that killed six and injured more than 80 people. Türkiye's Ministry of Defence invoked the right of self-defence under Article 51 of the UN Charter to justify the aerial

---

[13] See, generally, Michael P. Scharf, Milena Sterio and Paul Williams, *The Syrian Conflict's Impact on International Law* (Cambridge: Cambridge University Press, 2020), pp. 29–58; Alex J. Bellamy, *Syria Betrayed: Atrocities, War, and the Failure of International Diplomacy* (New York: Columbia University Press. 2022), pp. 176–98.

[14] S/2018/891 (3 Oct. 2018).

bombings that reportedly killed no fewer than 31 persons. In response, rockets were fired from Syria on 20 November 2022, killing three people in the Turkish district of Karkamis, near the Syrian border. The YPG is allied with the West in fighting ISIL. In May 2025, the PKK declared that it would heed the call by its leader, Abdullah Ocalan, who has been imprisoned in solitary confinement in Türkiye since 1999, for the PKK to lay down its weapons and dissolve.

One study divides foreign states' use of force against terrorists in Syria into three phases.[15] The first phase commenced in autumn 2014, when a coalition comprising the United States, Bahrain, Jordan, Saudi Arabia and the UAE began airstrikes on ISIL positions, as well as those of the Al Qaeda offshoot Khorasan and the al-Nusra Front in Iraq and Syria. Strikes continued on a regular basis throughout 2015. By 23 November 2015, 64 states considered themselves to be members of this coalition. As of 11 January 2017, the United States and its partners had conducted a total of 17,370 strikes, 6,520 of which had taken place in Syria. Only 5 per cent of the coalition's strikes affecting Syria were conducted by states other than the United States. On 23 September 2014, the UN secretary-general received a letter from the US ambassador justifying military actions in Syria and Iraq on the ground of the inherent right of individual and collective self-defence, as reflected in Article 51 of the UN Charter, when the government of the state where the threat is located is unwilling or unable to prevent the use of its territory for such attacks. The other coalition partners directly engaging in strikes in Syria refrained from making explicit legal claims and they did not notify the UNSC either. UN secretary-general Ban Ki-moon confirmed the airstrikes were not authorised by Syria but he observed that they had taken place at areas not under Syria's effective control. The operations were criticised by Argentina, Iran and Russia. Russia was unwilling to support any such operations without prior authorisation by the UNSC, in which Russia has a veto. The Ecuadorian foreign minister emphasised that the operations lacked Syrian consent, whereas China, Cuba, Venezuela and Chad underscored the need to respect Syrian sovereignty. The Assad government in Syria initially approved the US-led strikes against ISIL in Syria, provided there was "coordination" between the US and the Syrian governments. However, in September 2015 the Syrian government sent a letter to the UNSC explicitly objecting to the US-led strikes in Syria and contended that in their decision to intervene militarily in Syria the United States, the United Kingdom, France,

[15] Paulina Starski, "Silence within the Process of Normative Change and Evolution of the Prohibition on the Use of Force: Normative Volatility and Legislative Responsibility", *Journal on the Use of Force & International Law* 4 (2017): 14, 45–65.

Canada and Australia had not consulted with the Syrian government, and hence the strikes were illegal.

The second phase of foreign states' use of force against terrorists in Syria ran from 2015 until the Paris terrorist attacks on 13 November 2015. Canada informed the UNSC on 31 March 2015 of its collective and individual self-defence operations, referring to Syria's unwillingness and inability to prevent ISIL's attacks. Besides collective self-defence, Canada also invoked individual self-defence. In August 2015, Australia invoked collective self-defence to do the same. France began launching airstrikes in Syria in September 2015. Syria protested these actions while continuing to express its willingness to coordinate with other States to combat the threat posed by ISIL from Syrian soil.

The third phase came after the Paris terrorist attacks in November 2015, with France and the United Kingdom joining the United States in taking the lead against terrorists in Syria, citing UNSC Resolution 2249 (2015).[16] Preambular paragraph 7 of the resolution expressed the UNSC's determination "to combat by all means this unprecedented threat to international peace and security". Operative paragraph 1 of the resolution unequivocally condemned in the strongest terms the horrifying terrorist attacks perpetrated by ISIL on 26 June 2015 in Sousse, on 10 October 2015 in Ankara, on 31 October 2015 over Sinai, on 12 November 2015 in Beirut and on 13 November 2015 in Paris, and all other attacks perpetrated by ISIL, including hostage-taking and killing, and noted ISIL's capability and intention to carry out further attacks and regards all such acts of terrorism as a threat to peace and security. Operative paragraph 5 of the resolution therefore called upon UN member states that have the capacity to do so to:

> [T]ake all necessary measures, in compliance with international law, in particular with the United Nations Charter, as well as international human rights, refugee and humanitarian law, on the territory under the control of ISIL also known as Da'esh, in Syria and Iraq, to redouble and coordinate their efforts to prevent and suppress terrorist acts committed specifically by ISIL . . . and all other individuals, groups, undertakings and entities associated with Al Qaeda, and other terrorist groups, as designated by the [UNSC] . . . and

[16] S/RES/2249 (20 Nov. 2015). One author points out that until then the UNSC was not in a position to decide on action and adopt measures against ISIL in Iraq and Syria owing to the use of the veto by China and Russia, and only after the Paris terrorist attacks did all UNSC members clearly realise the danger posed by ISIL outside Iraq and Syria (Dascalopoulou-Livada, *Contemporary Issues in International Law*, p. 14).

> to eradicate the safe haven they have established over significant parts of Iraq and Syria.

They were joined by Germany, which emphasised the partial collapse of state authority, without "effective control" by the Syrian government over the part of the territory used by ISIL. Denmark, the Netherlands, Belgium and Norway followed suit, although they did not give the same legal justifications.

The author of that study concluded that there are so many ambiguities surrounding legal claims by the parties that carried out military actions against terrorists in Syria as well as UNSC members that adopted Resolution 2249 (2015) that the legal justifications given by the states using force against terrorists in Syria cannot be considered as having been widely endorsed by the international community.[17]

More recently, in November 2023, Russia carried out air strikes in Syria's Idlib province, the last stronghold of the rebels fighting the Assad regime, reportedly killing 34 rebels and injuring 60. For its part, the US carried out two air strikes against Iran-linked groups in Syria and two series of strikes in Iraq against Iran-backed militias, in response to the more than 40 attacks on US and coalition troops in Iraq and Syria by Iran-backed forces in the preceding weeks. The US continued its military strikes in Iraq in the following months in response to the militias' attacks on US troops.

In cataloguing communications to the UNSC of measures taken by UN member states in purported exercise of the right defence against non-state actors from the establishment of the United Nations on 24 October 1945 through 31 December 2018, Harvard Law School found that, although various UN member states had made "Article 51 communications" in relation to purported exercises of the right of self-defence directed against non-state actors, UNSC reactions have been inconsistent. In this context, it is not always clear whether the UNSC is or is not reacting to a claim (or multiple claims) of self-defence directed against a non-state actor in foreign territory without the consent of the territorial/host state—and, if so, what the legal effects of that (non-)reaction may be. Further complicating the legal situation, in "Article 51 communications" to the UNSC reporting military action taken against ISIL in Syria, the United Kingdom, Germany, Denmark, the Netherlands, Norway and Belgium expressly referred to UNSC Resolution 2249 (2015), thereby raising the question of whether those states meant to claim not only self-defence but perhaps also (at least some measure of) purported UNSC authorisation in relation to

[17] Starski, "Silence within the Process of Normative Change", 64–5.

their respective actions. Despite these limited examples, the UNSC, by and large, does not respond formally—in the sense of the adoption of an act of the UNSC or the issuance of a UNSC presidential statement—to "Article 51 communications", irrespective of whether the purported self-defence measures are directed against state actors, non-state actors or a combination of both. Nor do other states respond with regularity to those communications. This might be because other states are not aware of them or, if they are aware of them, those states may not think that it is advisable to respond to a particular "Article 51 communication".[18]

Syria itself has written to the UNSC several times in response to the "Article 51 communications" sent to the UNSC by states using force against non-state actors in Syrian territory. Syria condemns the attacks and accuses these states of attempting to invoke the provisions of the UN Charter to justify its aggression and illegal occupation of parts of Syrian territory, which must be stopped.

In addition, Syria accuses the United States and Türkiye of instructing terrorist militias to implement policies to obstruct security and stability within Syrian territory, and Syria demands the immediate withdrawal of US and Turkish forces from Syria.[19] Syria also accuses Türkiye of attempting to create a buffer zone, or a "safe zone", between Türkiye and Syria on Syrian territory, which Syria considers to be an act of aggression against it. Syria reserves its right to take all measures allowed under the UN Charter and international law in order to end to foreign states' aggression, occupation and ethnic cleansing in Syria.[20]

Indeed, even after ISIL's last Syrian outpost was overrun by Kurdish-led forces in March 2019, approximately 2,000 US troops have remained at al-Tanf, a Syrian desert on the strategically important Baghdad–Damascus highway near the border with Iraq and Jordan, and other bases in the Kurdish-controlled

---

[18] Dustin A. Lewis, Naz K. Modirzadeh and Gabriella Blum, "Quantum of Silence: Inaction and *Jus ad Bellum*", in *Annex HLS PILAC Catalogue of Communications to the Security Council of Measures Taken by United Nations Member States in Purported Exercise of the Right of Self-Defense: October 24, 1945 through December 31, 2018* (Cambridge, MA: Harvard Law School, 2019), pp. 59–70.

[19] Identical letters dated 24 Jan. 2022 from the Permanent Representative of Syria to the United Nations addressed to the Secretary-General and the President of the UNSC, S/2022/47 (25 Jan. 2022).

[20] Identical letters dated 25 May 2022 from the Permanent Representative of Syria to the United Nations addressed to the Secretary-General and the President of the UNSC, A/76/845-S/2022/424 (25 May 2022).

north-east such as Tell Beydar, as part of the US-led coalition's continuing campaign against ISIL remnants or sleeper cells as well as training Syrian fighters, ostensibly for the war against ISIL. Nine hundred of the aforesaid US soldiers were on long-term deployment, while the rest were temporary rotational forces. The US-led coalition battling ISIL also provides support for the Kurdish-led Syrian Democratic Forces, spearheaded by the YPG, arguably based on the novel theory that collective self-defence could be undertaken on behalf of non-state actor partners, with the US government trying to connect the use of force to the ongoing self-defence mission by the US-led coalition in Syria.[21] In March 2023, the United States military carried out multiple air strikes in eastern Syria against allegedly Iran-aligned groups that it blamed for a deadly drone attack that killed a contractor, injured another and wounded five US soldiers in Syria. The US air strikes reportedly killed 19 persons. Syria has strongly condemned the US-led coalition's presence and military operations as flagrant violation of the sovereignty and integrity of Syrian territory and support for separatist armed groups.

On 2 July 2021, the Russian foreign minister explained that Russia was in Syria on an invitation from Syria's legitimate government and that Russia was helping the Syrian security forces and army to eradicate the remaining hotbeds of terrorism from Syrian territory. Furthermore, the Russian foreign minister accused the United States of occupying "significant portions of Syria" and illegally exploiting Syria's natural resources. On 9 September 2021, the Russian foreign minister repeated the claim that a significant part of Syrian territory was under the illegal occupation of the United States.[22] For its part, Iran claims that it only has military advisers on the ground in Syria at the request of the Syrian government, rejecting US and Israeli claims that Iran's elite Islamic Revolutionary Guard Corps has a sizeable military presence in Syria.

Even the European Parliament passed a resolution on the Syrian conflict on 11 March 2021 stating, among other things, that Türkiye's illegal invasion and occupation and activities in Syria were jeopardising peace in the country. During a meeting of the UNSC on 20 January 2021, China declared that the current security threats to Syria are mainly from foreign occupation and, "faced with foreign military and terrorist forces, the Syrian government has the right

[21] Hathaway, "How the Erosion of U.S. War Powers Constraints Has Undermined International Law Constraints", 355–9.

[22] Butchard and Nessa, "Digest of State Practice: 1 July–31 December 2021", 191.

to defend the country's sovereignty and territorial integrity and to conduct counter-terrorism operations to defend its national security".[23]

The report of the UN Human Rights Council's Independent International Commission of Inquiry on the Syrian Arab Republic, issued in August 2022 and based on investigations conducted between 1 January and 30 June 2022, states that in the north-east the announcement on 23 May 2022 by President Erdogan of Türkiye of another planned incursion was followed by episodes of military escalation, mutual bombardment and mobilisation by all parties. An attack launched by ISIL on Al-Sina'a prison, in the north-east, on 20 January 2022, revealed the capacity of the terrorist group to launch complex attacks and the threat it continues to pose. The attack on Al-Sina'a prison, the biggest military operation by ISIL since its territorial defeat in 2019, caused hundreds of deaths.[24]

ICJ judge Hisashi Owada from Japan, writing in 2005, recognised that a terrorist attack carried out by non-state actors can pose a direct serious challenge to the public order of the international community, going beyond a mere infringement of the national interest of a particular state that falls victim to the attack. Under such circumstances, he suggested that the situation falls more appropriately within the framework of the UN Charter regime on collective security, rather than on the basis of the right of self-defence to be exercised by the victim state.[25]

A convincing argument has also been made that terrorist groups, especially groups that emerged in the last few decades, are often highly decentralised and it may well be difficult to conclusively prove the link between a group and an individual terrorist in such circumstances. Nevertheless, some political actors may well play on the inevitable uncertainty that is involved in such assessments to argue that a tight connection need not be proven in order for a counterterrorist intervention to be warranted. Building states' capacity to prevent and combat terrorism on their respective territories—that is, in accordance with Pillar II of the responsibility to protect—is less susceptible to manipulation by states that are intent on using force in the territory of a state where the terrorists are allegedly based.[26] This is, of course, provided that the territorial state is willing to

---

23 Patrick M. Butchard and Jasmin Johurun Nessa, "Digest of State Practice: 1 January–30 June 2021", *Journal on the Use of Force & International Law* 8 (2021): 343, 356–8.

24 Office of the UN High Commissioner for Human Rights, "Report of the Independent International Commission of Inquiry on the Syrian Arab Republic," A/HRC/51/45 (17 Aug. 2022).

25 Hisashi Owada, "The United Nations and the Maintenance of International Peace and Security—The Current Debate in the Light of Reform Proposals", *Japanese Annual of International Law* 48 (2005): 12–13.

26 Isaac Taylor, "The Responsibility to Protect from Terror: The Ethics of Foreign Counterterrorist Interventions", *Global Responsibility to Protect* 14 (2022): 155, 175–7.

cooperate in suppressing or preventing attacks by the terrorists. What if the territorial state is unwilling? It has been pointed out that the manipulation of the boundaries of the unwilling or unable doctrine is fundamentally premised on political will rather than legal theory, which has, in turn, resulted in theoretical incoherence, and that the unwilling or unable doctrine is, in fact, a policy rather than a legal doctrine.[27] Therefore, Judge Owada's wise opinion should be duly heeded.

Until the unexpected collapse of Assad regime on 8 December 2024, Syria was caught in endless armed conflicts for more than a decade, mainly because most states other than Russia and Iran were loath to support the Assad regime. A draft UNSC resolution in October 2011 to authorise international actions in Syria was vetoed by China and Russia, after the expansive interpretation of UNSC Resolution 1973 (2011) of March 2011 that had led to the regime change in Libya.

It is likely that diplomacy, and not international law, is the solution. It is foreseeable that, if Syria under the new, post-Assad regime cooperates with Türkiye to effectively address the latter's security concerns as regards terrorist armed groups using Syria as its base to attack Türkiye, Türkiye will cease its military operations in Syrian territory against the groups.

Iran and Russia grounded their military involvement in Syria on the invitation from the Assad government. Armed intervention by invitation can lead to endless wars, as the next chapter will show.

[27] Sarah McGibbon, "The 'Unwilling or Unable' Doctrine Unmasked: A Case Study of ISIL in Syria", *Hague Yearbook of International Law* 32 (2021): 69. See also Jeremy Julian Sarkin and Ross Callum Capazorio, "The Syrian Conflict as a Test Case for the Limits of the International Community and International Law: Global Politics and State Sovereignty Versus Human Rights Protection", *Human Rights Quarterly* 44 (2022): 476.

CHAPTER 8

Intervention by Invitation

International Law

The use of force may be lawful if it is at the invitation of the state in whose territory the force is used. The International Court of Justice (ICJ) has stated that "it is difficult to see what would remain of the principle of non-intervention in international law if *intervention*, which *is already allowable at the request of the government of a State*, were also to be allowed at the request of the opposition".[1] In practice, this is not a simple and clear-cut matter, as manifested in the ongoing fiasco in Yemen. The complexity of intervention by invitation is always reduced solely to the issue of recognition: who can speak for a state? This is a highly political question insofar as actions are explained by the intervening government's political preferences and its rhetorical appeal to so-called international community values.[2]

The International Law Association's (ILA) *Final Report on Aggression and the Use of Force* in 2018[3] alluded to the fact that the government of a state is able to provide consent to the use of force upon its territory opens up questions with regard to identifying the government. The entity consenting to the use of force may be the de jure governmental authority even if it no longer controls some or all of the state's territory although it does represent the constitutional government and/or democratically elected power. An entity may also have governmental power through exercising effective control over the territory and

[1] *Military and Paramilitary Activities in and against Nicaragua (Nicaragua v. USA)*, ICJ Rep. 1986, p. 14 at p. 126 [246] (emphasis added).
[2] Quoc Tan Trung Nguyen, "Rethinking the Legality of Intervention by Invitation: Toward Neutrality", *Journal of Conflict & Security Law* 24 (2019): 201.
[3] ILA, *Final Report on Aggression and the Use of Force*, pp. 19–20.

population of a particular state. External recognition by other states may affect the international legitimacy of a governmental regime. Requests or approval coming from members of a previous government no longer in office, or from the military/intelligence services not authorised to speak on behalf of the state, will not suffice. For consent to be recognised as emanating from the state, it must be freely given by the authorised representatives of the government and given expressly prior to the entry of the foreign armed forces into the state. Any contradiction between a public denial of consent occurring alongside secret approval by the same government is a question of evidentiary fact. Generally speaking, consent can allow for the sending of armed forces into a state following the request by its government for assistance in quelling an insurrection. It has been argued that if such internal unrest is to reach the level of a civil war then assistance to either side is prohibited, unless one side is being given assistance, in which case it might be possible for states to counter-intervene on the side of the other. However, state practice such as that by France in Mali in 2013 to help its former colony to quell a revolt in the north of the country, and the United States and its allies in Afghanistan and Iraq, might suggest otherwise. What *is* clear is that the giving of consent, while possibly ruling out a violation of Article 2(4) of the UN Charter, will not authorise an otherwise unlawful act such as quelling a legitimate struggle for self-determination or engaging in massive human rights violations amounting to crimes under international law. Although there were differing views about providing support to groups fighting to achieve an internationally recognised right to external self-determination, or in cases of popular mass uprisings against abusive regimes, it is generally prohibited to forcibly intervene on behalf of a rebel movement.

Intervention by invitation differs from collective self-defence, although they are often simultaneously invoked by the states concerned. First, collective self-defence requires an armed attack reaching the requisite threshold to trigger the right of self-defence. Second, the force used as part of an intervention by invitation is used within the requesting state's territory, usually to assist the requesting state in its struggle against a non-state actor,[4] or, in the case of a military alliance, against a third state.

[4] Laura Visser, "Intervention by Invitation and Collective Self-Defence: Two Sides of the Same Coin?", *Journal on the Use of Force & International Law* 7 (2020): 292, 308, 314–15.

The Problems with Yemen

The ongoing civil war in Yemen is a situation in which several states have been intervening, arguably at the invitation of Yemen's legitimate government.

The following is a concise narrative of Yemen's civil war.[5] In 2011, there was a popular uprising against the 33-year rule of Yemen's President Ali Abdullah Saleh as part of the Arab Spring movement in the Middle East and Arab countries in North Africa. The Initiative and Implementation Mechanism Agreement of 23 November 2011 brokered by the Gulf Cooperation Council (GCC) granted Saleh complete immunity from prosecution and transferred power to Vice-President Abd Rabbo Mansour Hadi. A National Dialogue Conference was held, accompanied by a constitution-making process. The Houthi movement, the political arm of which is officially called "Ansar Allah",[6] comprising mostly Zaidi Shia Muslims from northern Yemen, opposes the Sunni Muslim-dominated Yemeni government under President Saleh and President Hadi. The Houthis are believed to be supported by Iran, the world's largest Shia Muslim-majority nation. Unrest began after the Yemeni government increased the price of fuel in August 2014, with the Houthis taking a leading role in the protests against the government. Finally, on 21 September 2014 the Houthis captured the Yemeni capital, Sana'a, which was characterised as a coup by the Yemeni government and led to President Hadi's resignation and house arrest.

Since the situation in Yemen was worsening, the UN Security Council (UNSC) adopted Resolution 2201 (2015) on 15 February 2015. This resolution was not adopted by the UNSC acting under Chapter VII of the UN Charter, however.

---

[5] Sources: Masoud Zamani and Majid Nikouei, "Intervention by Invitation, Collective Self-Defence and the Enigma of Effective Control", *Chinese Journal of International Law* 16 (2017): 663, 684–5; Helen Lackner, *Yemen in Crisis: Autocracy, Neo-Liberalism and the Disintegration of a State* (London: Saqi Books, 2017); Elizabeth Kendall, "Jihadi Militancy and Houthi Insurgency in Yemen", in *Routledge Handbook of U.S. Counterterrorism and Irregular Warfare Operations*, ed. Michael A. Sheehan, Erich Marquardt and Liam Collins (Abingdon: Routledge, 2022), pp. 83–94; "Timeline for Yemen's Seven Year Conflict", *Arab News*, 7 Apr. 2022, https://www.arabnews.com/node/2058946/middle-east; Mohammed Haddah, "Infographic: Yemen's War Explained in Maps and Charts", *Al Jazeera*, 9 Feb. 2022, https://www.aljazeera.com/news/2022/2/9/yemens-war-explained-in-maps-and-charts-interactive.

[6] "Houthi" is the family name of its late founder of Ansar Allah, Husayn al-Houthi, and his brother, Abdul-Malik Houthi, its current leader.

The resolution strongly deplored actions taken by the Houthis to dissolve parliament and take over Yemen's government institutions, including acts of violence. It reiterated the UNSC's call for all parties in Yemen to adhere to resolving their differences through dialogue and consultation, reject acts of violence to achieve political goals, and refrain from provocation and all unilateral actions to undermine the political transition. The resolution expressed the UNSC's grave concern over the takeover by the Houthis of state media outlets and rejected the use of the media to incite violence. It strongly called upon all parties, in particular the Houthis, to abide by the GCC's Initiative and its Implementation Mechanism, the outcomes of the comprehensive National Dialogue Conference, and the Peace and National Partnership Agreement and its security annex,[7] which provide for a Yemeni-led democratic transition. It urged all parties, in particular Houthis, to accelerate inclusive United Nations-brokered negotiations, to continue the political transition in order to reach a consensus solution in accordance with the GCC's Initiative and its Implementation Mechanism, the outcomes of the comprehensive National Dialogue Conference, and the Peace and National Partnership Agreement and its security annex, and to implement it. It urged all parties to agree upon and announce publicly dates for completing the constitutional consultation process, to hold a referendum on the constitution, and to conduct elections under the new electoral law pursuant to the new constitution. In this connection, the resolution demanded that the Houthis immediately and unconditionally: (1) engage in good faith in the United Nations-brokered negotiations; (2) withdraw their forces from government institutions, including in the capital, Sana'a, normalise the security situation in the capital and other provinces, and relinquish government and security institutions; (3) safely release President Hadi, Prime Minister Bahah, members of the cabinet and all individuals under house arrest or arbitrarily detained; and (4) refrain from further unilateral actions that could undermine the political transition and the security of Yemen. In addition, the resolution demanded that all parties in Yemen cease all armed hostilities against the people and the legitimate authorities of Yemen and relinquish the arms seized from Yemen's military and security institutions. It also called on all UN member states to refrain from external interference that seeks to foment conflict and instability and instead to support the political transition. The resolution stressed the importance of the United Nations' close coordination with

[7] The Agreement of 21 Sept. 2014 is a roadmap for the creation of a new, federal democratic Yemeni state, with an annex on the cessation of hostilities and disarmament in specified regions. It has not been signed by any party.

international partners, including the GCC, the Group of Ambassadors in Sana'a, and other actors, in order to contribute to the successful transition, and asked the UN secretary-general to continue to coordinate assistance from the international community in support of the transition.

The resolution also reiterated the need for comprehensive, independent and impartial investigations consistent with international standards into alleged human rights violations and abuses in line with the outcomes of the comprehensive National Dialogue Conference, the GCC's Initiative and its Implementation Mechanism, to ensure full accountability. The UNSC reaffirmed its full support for, and commitment to, the efforts of the special adviser of the UN secretary-general on Yemen. Expressing concern at the ability of Al Qaeda in the Arabian Peninsula (AQAP) to benefit from the deterioration of the political and security situation in Yemen, the resolution condemned the growing number of attacks carried out or sponsored by AQAP, and expressed the UNSC's determination to address this threat in accordance with the UN Charter and international law including applicable human rights, refugee and humanitarian law, and through the Al Qaeda sanctions regime administered by the committee set up by the UNSC for this purpose.

Six days after the UNSC's adoption of Resolution 2201 (2015), the ousted Hadi escaped to the port city of Aden in the south of Yemen and retracted his resignation. As the Houthis were advancing to Aden, Hadi fled to Saudi Arabia, the world's largest Sunni Muslim-majority nation, which shares 1,300 kilometres of land border with northern Yemen and is an arch-enemy of Iran. In March 2015, Saudi Arabia formed a coalition with Bahrain, Egypt, Jordan, Kuwait, Morocco, Senegal, Sudan and the UAE to carry out military action at the request of President Hadi. On 20 March 2015, a Saudi-led "Coalition to Restore Legitimacy in Yemen" intervened militarily in Yemen by carrying out airstrikes against the Houthis so as to restore President Hadi's government, secure Saudi Arabia's southern border with Yemen from raids and attacks by drones and missiles by the Houthis, and reverse growing Iranian influence on the Arabian Peninsula. Saudi Arabia, the UAE, Bahrain, Qatar and Kuwait submitted a joint statement to the UNSC justifying their military operation on the grounds of a letter from the ousted President Hadi based on the principle of self-defence under Article 51 of the UN Charter, and on the basis of the Charter of the League of Arab States and the Treaty of Joint Arab Defence[8] to provide in-

[8] Articles 2 and 3 of the Treaty of Joint Arab Defence authorise its parties to take defensive measures in cases where it is determined that "the territorial integrity, independence, or security of any one of the parties is threatened".

stant support by all necessary means, including military intervention, to protect Yemen and its people from continuous Houthi aggression. The US government said it had assisted the coalition by providing logistics and intelligence.

On 14 April 2015, the UNSC, this time acting under Chapter VII of the UN Charter, adopted Resolution 2216 (2015) by 14 votes in favour and one abstention (Russia).

Resolution 2216 (2015) takes note of the letter dated 24 March 2015 from the permanent representative of Yemen to the United Nations, transmitting a letter from President Hadi of Yemen, in which he informed the UNSC president that "he has requested from the Cooperation Council for the Arab States of the Gulf and the League of Arab States to immediately provide support, by all necessary means and measures, including military intervention, to protect Yemen and its people from the continuing aggression by the Houthis". The resolution, inter alia, reaffirmed the UNSC's support for the legitimacy of President Hadi, and reiterated its call for all parties and UN member states to refrain from taking any actions that undermine the unity, sovereignty, independence and territorial integrity of Yemen, and the legitimacy of the president of Yemen, while also condemning in the strongest terms the ongoing unilateral actions taken by the Houthis, and their failure to implement the demands in Resolution 2201 (2015).[9]

The UNSC, acting under Chapter VII of the UN Charter through Resolution 2216 (2015), demanded that all Yemeni parties, in particular the Houthis, fully implement Resolution 2201 (2015) and refrain from further unilateral actions that could undermine the political transition in Yemen. It further demanded that the Houthis immediately and unconditionally: (1) end the use of violence; (2) withdraw their forces from all areas they had seized, including the capital, Sana'a; (3) relinquish all additional arms seized from military and security institutions, including missile systems; (4) cease all actions that are exclusively within the authority of the legitimate government of Yemen; (5) refrain from any provocation or threats to neighbouring states, including through acquiring surface-to-surface missiles, and stockpiling weapons in any bordering

---

[9] The resolution also noted with concern the destabilising actions taken by the former president of Yemen, Ali Abdullah Saleh, including Saleh's support for the Houthis' actions. Saleh was eventually killed by the Houthis while he was trying to escape from Sana'a in Dec. 2017, two days after Saleh had announced the end of his three-year alliance with the Houthis in order to mend his ties with Saudi Arabia and the other Arab states in the Coalition to Restore Legitimacy in Yemen.

territory of a neighbouring state; (6) safely release Major-General Mahmoud al-Subaihi, the minister of defence of Yemen, all political prisoners and all individuals under house arrest or arbitrarily detained; and (7) end the recruitment and use of children and release all children from their ranks. The resolution also imposed sanctions on certain individuals. Once again, the UNSC called on all parties to comply with their obligations under international law, including applicable international humanitarian law (IHL) and human rights law. With respect to the arms embargo, the UNSC decided that all UN member states shall immediately take the necessary measures to prevent the direct or indirect supply, sale or transfer arms and related materiel of all types to, or for the benefit of, those playing leading roles to destabilise Yemen under President Hadi, and all designated individuals and entities and those acting on their behalf or at their direction in Yemen, from or through their territories or by their nationals, or using their flag vessels or aircraft. They are also prohibited from providing technical assistance, training, financial or other assistance, related to military activities or the provision, maintenance or use of any arms and related materiel, including the provision of armed mercenary personnel whether or not originating in their territories. UN member states, in particular states neighbouring Yemen, are to inspect, seize and dispose of (such as through destruction, rendering inoperable, storage or transferring to a state other than the originating or destination states for disposal), in accordance with their national authorities and legislation and consistent with international law, in particular the law of the sea and relevant international civil aviation agreements, all cargo to Yemen, in their territory, including seaports and airports, if the state concerned has information that provides reasonable grounds to believe the cargo contains items the supply, sale or transfer of which is prohibited by the resolution.

Although Resolution 2216 (2015) noted President Hadi's request for military support and the joint statement by the coalition, it did not mention the military operation in Yemen by the Saudi-led coalition.

Amid the instability in Yemen, several other armed groups emerged, including AQAP and the separatist Southern Transitional Council (STC). The bulk of Yemen's northern highlands, as well as Sana'a, remain under the control of the Houthis. The coalition forces were able to help pro-government forces secure Aden, which has since become the temporary home of Yemen's internationally recognised government. Saudi Arabia mainly carries out airstrikes, while forces loyal to Yemen's internationally recognised government and militia such as the Southern Giants Brigade, which receives extensive military and financial support from the UAE, fight the Houthis on the battleground. Over the years, the Houthis have targeted strategic infrastructure across Saudi Arabia and, since

17 January 2022, the UAE, including airports, gas fields and oil tankers in the Red Sea, using drones and missiles. The Houthis have been classified by Saudi Arabia and the UAE as a terrorist organisation.

Iran has been accused of supporting the Houthis. Yemen and Saudi Arabia have complained to the UNSC detailing concerns of alleged attacks in Yemen and Saudi Arabia by "Iran-backed terrorist Houthi militias". For its part, the League of Arab States has denounced Iran several times. For example, it adopted a resolution on 3 March 2021 to condemn the continued deployment of drones and firing of "Iranian-made ballistic and other missiles by Iranian-affiliated Houthi terrorist militias" from Yemeni territory towards Saudi Arabia, which was a "blatant act of aggression" against Saudi Arabia, which had the right to defend its territory pursuant to Article 51 of the UN Charter. The League of Arab States added that it would support any measures Saudi Arabia decided to take, within the framework of international law, in response to Iranian violations.[10] On 9 September 2021, the League of Arab States adopted Resolution 8685, entitled "Iranian Interference in the Internal Affairs of Arab States", to condemn the "continued use of drones and the firing of Iranian-made ballistic and other missiles by the Iranian-affiliated Houthi militias from Yemeni territory towards Saudi Arabia", which the League considered to be a blatant act of aggression. It reaffirmed the legitimate right of Saudi Arabia to defend its territory pursuant to Article 51 of the UN Charter. In a letter dated 14 September 2021 to the UNSC, Kuwait, on behalf of the League, expressed support for any measures Saudi Arabia might decide to take, within the framework of international law, in response to Iranian violations. At the UNSC meeting on 14 December 2021, the United States condemned "the intensification of the Houthi cross-border attacks on Saudi Arabia" and argued that these attacks "underscore the need for Iran to end its lethal support to the Houthis". During the same UNSC meeting, the representative of Yemen accused Iran of continuing to provide the Houthi militias with arms and military expertise.[11] British, French and United States navies have seized anti-tank missiles, fins for ballistic missile assemblies and other armaments from ships allegedly from Iran bound to supply the Houthis in Yemen.

Indeed, the coalition's military operation in Yemen was launched without prior authorisation from the UNSC. It was in response to a "direct request" for

[10] Patrick M. Butchard and Jasmin Johurun Nessa, "Digest of State Practice: 1 January–30 June 2021", *Journal on the Use of Force & International Law* 8 (2021): 343, 373.

[11] Patrick M. Butchard and Jasmin Johurun Nessa, "Digest of State Practice: 1 July–31 December 2021", *Journal on the Use of Force & International Law* 9 (2022): 171, 201–2, 210.

"immediate support" in a letter dated 24 March 2015 from Yemen's President Hadi, who had already fled Yemen for Saudi Arabia. Those supporting this justification by the coalition include the United States, Canada, Jordan, Türkiye and the United Kingdom, whereas those opposed to it include Russia, Iran and, to a lesser extent, China. Setting aside the self-defence justifications, several legal questions arise as regards this armed intervention in Yemen by President Hadi's invitation.[12] First, although the then President Hadi was widely recognised by the international community and the UNSC as the legitimate president of Yemen, he lost effective control over substantial regions and state infrastructure, including the capital and several sections of the military. Second, in times of civil war, can a government legally give consent to other states to use force on its territory without violating the principle of non-intervention and the right to self-determination? Third, is the objective of protecting Yemen and its people from "the continuing aggression by the Houthis" mentioned in Hadi's invitation letter not far outweighed by the ongoing humanitarian crises besetting the Yemeni?

On the first legal question, an oft-cited authority on recognition of government is *Tinoco Claims Arbitration (Great Britain v. Costa Rica)*.[13] In 1917 the Costa Rican government was overthrown by Frederico Tinoco, who assumed undisputed power, called an election and established a new constitution. The Tinoco regime was not recognised by Great Britain and the United States. When the Tinoco regime was removed in 1919, the new Costa Rican government nullified all contracts concluded by that regime, including an oil concession to a British company. Great Britain claimed that the oil concession could not be repudiated because the Tinoco government was the only government in existence at the time of the granting of the concession. For its part, Costa Rica argued, inter alia, that the Tinoco regime was not a recognised government capable of entering into contracts on behalf of Costa Rica. The sole arbitrator, US Chief Justice William H. Taft, ruled that a government need not conform to a previous constitution if the government had established itself and maintained a peaceful de facto administration, and that non-recognition of the government by other governments did not destroy the de facto status of the government.

[12] Elinor Buys and Andrew Garwood-Gowers, "The (Ir)relevance of Human Suffering: Humanitarian Intervention and Saudi Arabia's Operation Decisive Storm in Yemen", *Journal of Conflicts & Security Law* 25 (2019): 1ff.
[13] 1 R.I.A.A. 369 (1923).

On the second legal question—intervention in civil wars—some international legal scholars contend that, although certain government opposition fighters, or insurgents, have invited foreign militaries to assist them, this practice has not crystallised into an accepted rule of international law owing to the jus cogens prohibition on the use of force as well as the principles of non-intervention and self-determination. According this view, under current law, only the UNSC and a government still in effective control can provide the requisite consent to military intervention, irrespective of the legitimacy of the rebels' cause.[14] Above all, the ICJ in *Nicaragua* declared unequivocally that the principle of non-intervention under customary international law "would certainly lose its effectiveness as a principle of law if intervention were to be justified by a mere request for assistance made by an opposition group in another State".[15]

Other scholars of international law argue that the absence of any explicit reliance on the right to self-determination in UNSC debates or the reactions of states to military assistance on request of the recognised government or a transitional government, including the invitation by the Assad government in Syria for Russia to assist it to suppress the rebels whom the government regards as terrorists, suggests that there is no rule in general international law prohibiting such assistance during a civil war—as long as the government retains its recognised, de jure status.[16] It has also been contended that, where armed groups in a state's territory have received prior, external military assistance during a civil war, this undermines the ability of the people of the state to determine their political future without external interference, and that the recognised government may therefore request military assistance by third states so as to uphold or restore the right to self-determination. It may be recalled that the ILA in its Final Report of 2018 considers the view that if an internal unrest against the government reaches the level of a civil war then assistance to either side is prohibited, unless one side is being given assistance, in which case it might be possible for states to counter-intervene on the side of the other. But the ILA found that some state practice exists contrary to this view. This argument in support of counter-intervention may be rebutted since, first of all, it is very difficult to verify whether claims of prior intervention on the side of armed groups

[14] Chiara Redaelli. *Intervention in Civil Wars: Effectiveness, Legitimacy, and Human Rights* (Oxford: Hart, 2021), pp. 251–62 and *passim*.

[15] ICJ Rep. 1986, p. 126 [246].

[16] Erika de Wet, "The (Im)permissibility of Military Assistance on Request during a Civil War", *Journal on the Use of Force & International Law* 7 (2020): 26.

is accurate or fabricated by governments in order to justify requests for military assistance. Second, if the purpose of the counter-intervention is to restore the rights of the people within a state to determine their political future without external interference, the extent of the military support provided to the recognised government should not go beyond neutralising the impact of the prior external intervention on the side of the armed opposition groups—but this is impractical.[17]

Let us apply these arguments to the actual situations on the ground in Yemen. The Houthis have been exercising de facto authority and effective control over most of Yemen's territory for years. The test of effective control arguably prevents abuses by states that intervene to assist their puppet governments or governments toppled by popular uprisings, in violation of the self-determination of the peoples. Nevertheless, as the ILA conceded in its Final Report of 2018, there have been instances where foreign states have intervened to assist governments that had lost effective control over most of the territory in question. For example, France intervened in January 2013 in Mali to save the newly elected Malian government that had just been toppled by a military coup from military defeat by the Malian military junta, although the government had lost effective control over large swaths of Malian territory to jihadist groups and the northern Tuareg ethnic group opposed to the government. France justified its action on the grounds of the appeal and request from Mali's "legitimate", albeit interim, government, Article 51 of the UN Charter, the request by the Economic Community of West African States, of which Mali is a member, and the African Union's position, among others. On 30 September 2015, Russia commenced its first wave of air strikes in Syria, relying exclusively on the consent of the Syrian regime, which had lost effective control over a large portion of the Syrian territory.[18] However, another view posits that the government's lack of effective control over remote tribal areas, the so-called "ungoverned space", does not deprive the government of its right to invite external armed intervention, provided that it maintains control over the rest of the state, unless the conflict has reached the level of a civil war, in which case consent is unavailable. This is because the doctrine of consent to external intervention is subject to "great conceptual and normative vagueness, allowing for a broad spectrum of interpretation, which manifests in its ability to provide a wide range of lawful justifications for uses of force, with the potential to

[17] Ibid., 33–4. See also Erika de Wet, *Military Assistance on Request and the Use of Force* (Oxford: Oxford University Press, 2020).

[18] Zamani and Nikouei, "Intervention by Invitation", 675–84.

be used not just for security but to assert the geopolitical dominance of powerful States".[19]

Since there are conflicting views on international legal regime regulating the answers to the first two questions, the correct answer to the third question on the delicate balance between the resultant costs and benefits can be decisive to the legitimacy and lawfulness or otherwise of such an intervention by invitation of a government that has lost effective control over the state's territory.

According to one commentator, Yemen may be considered a state of fragmented authority because the de jure government has been unable, for an extensive period of time, to sustain a claim either that it represents the whole of Yemenis, or that it exercises complete and unifying control over Yemen. On the other hand, the Houthis have been ostracised by those supporting the coalition, contrary to the peace plans and the transition procedure from which the then President Hadi derives his lawfulness. It is, therefore, arguable that the coalition's armed intervention, which is causing considerable harm to Yemen and Yemenis, nullifies the legitimacy of the consent given by Hadi. According to this view, the Houthis have the right to exercise self-defence against the Saudi-led intervention and against Yemen's recognised government, in order to protect the welfare of Yemenis, meet international obligations and respect international law.[20]

Since March 2017, the Office for the Coordination of Humanitarian Affairs of the United Nations has designated Yemen as the world's largest humanitarian crisis. In April 2018, out of a population of 29.3 million, 22.2 million people were in need of humanitarian assistance, including 11.3 million in acute need. Needs extend across all sectors, including health, food, sanitation and water, housing and protection.[21] Yemen, beset by internationalised intra-state conflict with foreign governments participating with troops supporting either the recognised government or the rebels, is the least peaceful country in

---

[19] Max Byrne, "Consent and the Use of Force: An Examination of 'Intervention by Invitation' as a Basis for US Drone Strikes in Pakistan, Somalia and Yemen", *Journal on the Use of Force & International Law* 3 (2016): 97, 108–25.

[20] Themis Tzimas, "Self-Defence by Non-state Actors in States of Fragmented Authority", *Journal of Conflict & Security Law* 24 (2019): 175, 185–99.

[21] Report of the UN High Commissioner for Human Rights containing the findings of the Group of Eminent International and Regional Experts and a summary of technical assistance provided by the Office of the High Commissioner to the National Commission of Inquiry, A/HRC/39/43 (17 Aug. 2018), para. 26.

the world in the 2024 Global Peace Index, followed by Sudan, South Sudan, Afghanistan and Ukraine.[22]

In 2017, the UN Human Rights Council (HRC) set up the Group of Eminent International and Regional Experts on Yemen to carry out a comprehensive examination of all alleged violations and abuses of international human rights and other appropriate and applicable fields of international law committed by all parties to the conflict in Yemen since September 2014, as well as to establish the facts and circumstances surrounding the alleged violations and abuses and, where possible, to identify those responsible. The group's mandate was renewed annually in 2018, 2019 and 2020. The group submitted its fourth report to the HRC in September 2021, covering the period from July 2020 to June 2021. The report detailed violations of international law, which include airstrikes[23] and shelling that fail to abide by IHL principles; humanitarian restrictions as well as obstacles to access to food and healthcare; arbitrary detention; enforced disappearances; gender-based violence, including sexual violence; torture and other forms of cruel, inhuman or degrading treatment; denial of fair trial rights; violations of fundamental freedoms; persecution and violations against journalists, human rights defenders, minorities, migrants and internally displaced persons; and violation of children's rights. Responsibility for the violations rests with all parties to the conflict, with violations committed by the government of Yemen, the STC, members of the Saudi-led coalition and the de facto authorities. Some of the violations identified may amount to war crimes and crimes against humanity under international criminal law.

The fourth report expressed the concern of the Group of Eminent Experts on Yemen that impunity continues largely unabated for those who perpetrate serious violations, which only adds to the insecurity in Yemen since violations of human rights are threats to peace, security and development, and a key driver of conflict. The group regretted that, to a large extent, recommendations made over the past three mandates had not been acted upon. It reiterated the urgency for parties to the conflict to agree to a full cessation of hostilities and to achieve a sustainable and inclusive peace. The group also stressed that all measures should be taken, by the parties as well as by the international community, to realise victims' rights to truth, justice and reparation. It reiterated its call for states to

---

[22] Institute for Economics & Peace, *Global Peace Index 2024: Measuring Peace in a Complex World* (Sydney: IEP, 2024).

[23] For international law regulating air bombardment, see Mateusz Piatkowski, "War in the Air from Spain to Yemen: The Challenges in Examining the Conduct of Air Bombardment", *Journal of Conflict & Security Law* 26 (2021): 493.

stop providing arms and military support to the parties to the civil war in Yemen given the role of such transfers in perpetuating the conflict and potentially contributing to violations. The group recommended that the UNSC integrate the human rights dimensions of the conflict in Yemen more fully into its agenda and ensure there is no impunity for the most serious crimes by, inter alia, referring the situation in Yemen to the International Criminal Court and expanding the list of persons subject to UNSC sanctions. The list comprises individuals or entities designated by the Sanction Committee set up by UNSC Resolution 2140 (2014) as engaging in or providing support for acts that threaten the peace, security or stability of Yemen, including by: (1) obstructing or undermining the successful completion of the political transition, as outlined in the GCC's Initiative and Implementation Mechanism Agreement of 2011 that brought Hadi to power; (2) impeding the implementation of the outcomes of the final report of the comprehensive National Dialogue Conference through violence, or attacks on essential infrastructure; or (3) planning, directing or committing acts that violate applicable international human rights law or IHL, or acts that constitute human rights abuses, in Yemen.

On 7 October 2021, despite efforts by several states, the HRC rejected a resolution to renew the mandate of the Group of Eminent Experts on Yemen. Twenty-one of the HRC's 47 member states voted against the Dutch resolution to renew the group's mandate. Those opposed to the resolution were Bahrain, Bangladesh, Bolivia, Burkina Faso, China, Cuba, Eritrea, Gabon, India, Indonesia, Libya, Mauritania, Pakistan, the Philippines, Russia, Senegal, Somalia, Sudan, Togo, Uzbekistan and Venezuela. The 18 members voting in favour of the mandate renewal included the United Kingdom, France, the Republic of Korea and Germany. There were seven abstentions (including Japan and Nepal from Asia) and Ukraine's delegation was absent. The United States had observer status, without the right to vote. This termination of the group's mandate further underscores the group's assessment that there is a lack of political will to address the situation in Yemen.

In February 2021, the United States terminated its support for the coalition's military operations and removed the Houthis from a "terrorist" blacklist, in order to allow more humanitarian aid for Yemen. Shortly thereafter, the Houthis resumed an offensive to seize Yemen's oil-rich Marib province, the Yemeni government's last northern stronghold. On 26 March 2022, the Houthis called a unilateral three-day truce. On 29 March 2022, the Saudi-led coalition announced its own ceasefire, which coincided with the opening of talks in Riyadh that the Houthis refused to attend. The truce mediated by the UN special envoy for Yemen, the first nationwide truce since 2016, started on the first day of Ramadan on 2 April 2022. The Saudi-led coalition also agreed to allow fuel shipments into Hodeidah and commercial flights to resume from Houthi-held Sana'a, as demanded by the Houthis. On 5 April 2022, President Hadi announced from Riyadh, Saudi Arabia, that he was handing his powers to a new leadership council. Saudi Arabia welcomed the announcement and pledged US$3 billion in aid and support, some of it to be paid by the UAE.

By a Yemeni presidential decree of 7 April 2022, the Presidential Leadership Council was set up in Riyadh as the executive organ of Yemen's internationally recognised government, with all the powers of the president and vice president of Yemen transferred to the Council. It is entrusted with seeking a comprehensive political solution to the war in Yemen. The Council is composed of eight members under the chairmanship of Rashad Muhammad Al-Alimi, a former adviser to Hadi. The other members are a Yemeni military commander and the nephew of the late President Saleh who leads the National Resistance, an elite unit of around 3,000 to 10,000 previous members of Yemen's Republican Guard and Central Security Organization; one of the most prominent tribal and military figures, who is also governor of Marib Governorate and a member of the Al-Islah Party, founded with Saleh's blessing; a Salafist who is the leader of the UAE-backed Southern Movement's pro-Yemeni government militia called the Giants Brigade; a prominent member of the Ai-Islah Party who is considered one of Hadi's inner circle; a tribal leader in the governorate of Sa'dah, the main stronghold of the Houthis; the current president and commander of the STC and de facto leader of the Southern Movement in Yemen; and a former governor of Hadramaut, Yemen's largest of the 21 governorates, and former commander of the second military region that operates in Hadramaut. It should be noted that the Southern Movement, backed by the UAE, has been active in the south of Yemen since 2007, demanding secession of southern Yemen from the rest of Yemen and the revival of the former independent nation called the People's Democratic Republic of Yemen, or South Yemen, before its unification with the Yemen Arab Republic, or North Yemen, in 1990. The STC, while officially part of the Saudi-led coalition, has fought Yemeni government forces in the past and is in de facto control of the port city of Aden.[24] The Al-Islah Party is an Islamist party and a part of the Muslim Brotherhood, which is designated as a terrorist organisation by the UAE, Saudi Arabia, Bahrain, Egypt, Russia and Syria, al-

[24] See further, Public International Law & Policy Group and Resonate! Yemen, *Policy Planning White Paper: The Southern Question* (Washington, DC: Public International Law & Policy Group, Apr. 2022).

though Saudi Arabia has softened its stance somewhat since it needs Al-Islah's help in fighting the Houthis.

The Presidential Leadership Council is more representative than Yemeni institutions in the past, reflecting dynamics on the ground by including Yemen's new generation of leaders who are northerners and southerners, from groups with a military genealogy as well as from the local and governorate-level. The biggest obstacle for the Council is its lack of cohesion for the purpose of effective decision-making owing to inherent power rivalries and competing agendas. With so many internal contradictions, the Council risks not having a sufficiently strong bargaining power to reach an agreement with the Houthis. Furthermore, there are likely to be political disagreements among Council members regarding territorial control and chains of command.[25]

Yet the foreign ministers of the Group of 7 (comprising Canada, France, Germany, Italy, Japan, the United Kingdom and the United States), who met in Germany in May 2022, issued a joint press release expressing, inter alia, their appreciation of the government reform in Yemen, including the formation of the Presidential Leadership Council, as an important step towards peace and stability in Yemen. They called on the parties to the conflict to engage in constructive talks under the leadership of the United Nations, to convert the ongoing truce into a lasting ceasefire and to ultimately reach a durable peace. They called for accountability for human rights violations and abuses and violations of IHL. They demanded that all parties to the conflict allow and facilitate rapid and unimpeded passage of humanitarian access and the unimpeded flow of humanitarian aid and commodities, especially fuel, into and throughout the country. They also called on the international community, especially countries from the region, to provide substantial financial support for the humanitarian response, then US$3 billion in deficit.

Regrettably, on 2 October 2022 parties to the conflict in Yemen failed to renew the UN-mediated truce that had been in effect since 2 April 2022. The Presidential Leadership Council could not agree to accept the Houthis' demand for the full and unrestricted opening of the Sana'a airport and the lifting of the entire blockade on Hodeidah. According to the Global Centre for Responsibility to Protect, an NGO, although civilian casualties and armed hostilities did not completely halt during the truce, they were significantly decreased. Between April and October 2022 there were no recorded airstrikes by the Saudi-led co-

[25] Eleonora Ardemagni, "Yemen's Post-Hybrid Balance: The New Presidential Council", *Carnegie Endowment for International Peace*, 9 June 2022, https://carnegieendowment.org/sada/87301.

alition but some attacks on civilians and civilian objects, including ground shelling, drone attacks and the use of landmines, continued, including 14 indiscriminate ground attacks, eight attacks on medical facilities and 21 attacks that targeted or affected schools. Other human rights violations and abuses also continued during the truce, including child recruitment, arbitrary detentions, enforced disappearances and torture. Since the end of the truce, there have been reports of civilians being in grave danger, as human rights violations and abuses, as well as attacks, have increased in frequency, including by sniper attacks and shelling, as well as a drone attack on a port facility. The Centre submitted that a sustainable end to the conflict in Yemen would only be reached if peace were pursued alongside justice efforts, and that, therefore, the international community should take steps to establish a new mechanism to advance accountability and reparations for perpetrators of war crimes and crimes against humanity in Yemen.[26]

What has gone wrong with the civil war in Yemen is that the parties invited by the de jure government under Hadi to intervene by the use of force in Yemen are not neutral and have their own vested interests in the conflict in Yemen.

The conflict between the Houthis and Saudi Arabia can be traced back to 2004, when the Houthis accused Saudi Arabia of pressuring the Yemeni government then under President Saleh to crack down on the Houthis and of funding him with a large sum of money. According to an analyst, Saudi Arabia has had a single, overarching goal in the war in Yemen: push the Houthis out of Sana'a, restore President Hadi to power (that is, before the setting up of the Presidential Leadership Council) and prevent the rise of a Hezbollah-like group with strong ties to Iran on Saudi Arabia's southern border. The UAE, for its part, has three distinct goals in Yemen, each of which has fed into its broader regional strategy. First, it wants to be a good ally and partner with Saudi Arabia, which has asked for its military help in fighting the Houthis, and with the United States in fighting Al Qaeda and ISIL. Second, the UAE wants to weaken the Muslim Brotherhood throughout the Middle East, including the Al-Islah Party in Yemen. Third, as a commercial and logistics hub in the Middle East region, the UAE wants to safeguard its strategic coastlines and shipping lanes. Unlike Saudi Arabia, the UAE can probably live with a Houthi-controlled Yemeni government

---

[26] Global Centre for Responsibility to Protect, "Atrocity Alert Number 325" (9 Nov. 2022).

in the north, but not in southern Yemen and this why the UAE has been supporting the Southern Movement and its STC.[27]

According to another analyst, ending civil wars depends on finding the right answers to the questions of *when* civil wars are ripe for resolution, *who* are to be included in the attempts to resolve conflicts in order for them to be successful, *what* type of arrangements and peace agreements can resolve civil wars, and *how* third parties can best contribute to the resolution of these types of intrastate armed conflicts.[28]

What the then President Hadi should have invited to intervene in Yemen from the beginning is not the GCC but a United Nations peacekeeping force. UN peacekeeping operations can only be deployed with the consent of the "main parties to the conflict". This requires a commitment by the parties to a political process and allows the United Nations the necessary freedom of action, both political and physical, to carry out its mandated tasks. The emphasis is on the consent from the main parties to the deployment of a United Nations peacekeeping operation, and this does not necessarily imply or guarantee that there will also be consent at the local level, particularly if the main parties are internally divided or have weak command and control systems. It is conceded that universality of consent becomes even less probable in volatile settings, characterised by the presence of armed groups not under the control of any of the parties, or by the presence of other spoilers. UN peacekeeping operations have to observe impartiality in their dealing with the parties to the conflict. They may use force at the tactical level, with the authorisation of the UNSC, if acting in self-defence and defence of the mandate. Significantly, in certain volatile situations, the UNSC may authorise UN peacekeeping operations to "use all necessary means" to deter forceful attempts to disrupt the political process, protect civilians under imminent threat of physical attack, and/or assist the national authorities in maintaining law and order.[29]

At this juncture, the Houthis are still in control of most of Yemen's territory. Sunni Muslim-majority Saudi Arabia, the Houthis' arch-enemy, and Shia Muslim-majority Iran have been arch-rivals in the Middle East since the 1979 Islamic Revolution in Iran, which toppled the Iranian monarchy, and Iran's then Supreme Leader Ayatollah Ruhollah Khomeini called for other Muslim-majority

[27] Gregory D. Johnsen, "The UAE's Three Strategic Interests in Yemen" (Arab Gulf States Institute in Washington, 24 Feb. 2022).
[28] Isak Svensson, "Conflict Resolution in Civil Wars", in *Routledge Handbook of Civil Wars*, ed. Edward Newman and Karl DeRouen, Jr. (Abingdon: Routledge, 2014), pp. 363–75.
[29] https://peacekeeping.un.org/en/principles-of-peacekeeping.

countries to emulate the Iranian Islamic Revolution, whereas most Saudis are Sunnis who consider some Shiite practices to be violations of Islam.[30] Saudi Arabia severed diplomatic relations with Iran, accused of supporting the Houthis, in January 2016 after an Iranian mob stormed the Saudi embassy in Tehran and set it on fire following Saudi Arabia's execution of prominent Saudi Shia leader Nimr al-Nimr.

Some analysts opine that Saudi Arabia and its coalition partner countries want an exit after more than eight years of military engagement, provided that their security interests are safeguarded. In 2023, Saudi Arabia has begun mending bilateral relations and negotiating directly with Iran, Syria and Yemen's Houthis as it redirects its focus on economic growth at home, which requires regional stability. For their part, all the Yemenis involved in Yemen's civil war will need to agree among themselves how to share power. Without intervention from other states in support of any side to the civil war, Yemenis may find it much easier to reach consensus on the future of Yemen, preferably under the auspices of the United Nations.

To sum up, the civil war in Yemen is ripe for resolution now, before many more Yemenis perish.

This suggestion is line with in the Statement of the Riyadh Summit for Cooperation and Development between the GCC and the People's Republic of China, issued on 9 December 2022 after the summit between the two sides. The leaders of the participating nations affirmed their support for the Presidential Leadership Council in Yemen, expressing their hope to reach a political solution in accordance with the GCC initiative and its Executive Mechanism, the outcomes of the Yemeni National Dialogue Conference and UNSC Resolution 2216 (2015). They called on all Yemeni parties to immediately initiate direct negotiations under the auspices of the United Nations, and to adhere to the continuation of the armistice, and to support the humanitarian, relief and development needs of the Yemeni people, and the leaders condemned all terrorist attacks launched by the Houthi militia on civilian targets in Saudi Arabia, the UAE, the Yemeni interior and in the waterways and international shipping routes, and called on all countries to cooperate in combating these acts and to abide by the arms embargo stipulated in UNSC Resolutions 2216 and 2624.

There is hope for the end of the proxy war in Yemen. On 10 March 2023, Iran and Saudi Arabia agreed, after several days of their meetings mediated by

---

[30] See further, Ibrahim Fraihat, *Iran and Saudi Arabia: Taming a Chaotic Conflict* (Edinburgh: Edinburgh University Press, 2020); Talal Mohammad, *Iranian-Saudi Rivalry since 1979: In the Words of Kings and Clerics* (London: I.B. Tauris, 2023).

China in Beijing, to restore their diplomatic relations, while affirming the respect for the sovereignty and the non-interference in internal affairs of other states. Iran has reportedly agreed to stop encouraging cross-border attacks on Saudi Arabia from Yemen by the Houthis. Less than a month later, Saudi and Omani delegations held talks with Houthi officials in the Yemeni capital, Sana'a, as part of international efforts to find a settlement to Yemen's nine-year conflict, including a timeline for foreign forces to leave Yemen. In an exclusive interview with *CNN*, Mohamed Ali al-Houthi, member of the Supreme Political Council and former head of Yemen's Houthi Supreme Revolutionary Committee, said the Houthis were willing to share power and resources with the Yemeni people and expect Saudi Arabia to ensure the departure of all foreign forces, including the UAE, from Yemen and meet the Houthis' demands such as removing the blockade on ports, opening Yemen's airspace and paying the salaries of public sector employees. Internal matters, including demands by the STC for the south of Yemen to secede, will be dealt with at a later stage, with the STC given what was rightful to them, but not more, he said, without ruling out a secession of the south but emphasising that any solutions to the "southern issue" must be taken without foreign influence.[31]

After the Israel/Hamas war broke out on 7 October 2023, the Houthis, long opposed to Israel, stepped up their campaign in support of Palestinians in Gaza, using their control of Yemen's western seaboard in the Red Sea to launch attacks on ships with owners linked to Israel and ships going to and from Israeli ports. Up to October 2024, the Houthis had attacked 193 ships linked to Israel, the USA and the UK,[32] putting on hold the peace plan for Yemen that was negotiated with Saudi Arabia and handed to the UN envoy for Yemen. On 10 January 2024, the UNSC adopted Resolution 2722 (2024) by a vote of 11 in favour to none against, with four abstentions (Algeria, China, Mozambique and Russia). According to operative paragraph 3 of the resolution, the UNSC:

> *Affirms* the exercise of navigational rights and freedoms by merchant and commercial vessels, in accordance with international law, must be respected, and takes note of *the right of Member States, in accordance with international*

[31] Nadeem Ebrahim, "Houthis Try to Assure Skeptics They Won't Seek Full Control of Yemen, as Saudis Eye Exit", CNN, 14 Apr. 2023, https://edition.cnn.com/2023/04/14/middleeast/yemen-saudi-houthi-interview-mime-intl/index.html.

[32] "Houthis Targeted 193 Ships Linked to Tel Aviv, US, UK in the Past Year", *Middle East Monitor*, 7 Oct. 2024, https://www.middleeastmonitor.com/20241007-houthis-targeted-193-ships-linked-to-tel-aviv-us-uk-in-the-past-year/.

> *law, to defend their vessels from attacks*, including those that undermine navigational rights and freedoms. (Emphasis added)

On 11 January 2024, the US together with the UK, with support from Australia, Bahrain, Canada and the Netherlands, launched more than 100 precision-guided munitions against no fewer than 60 command and control nodes, munitions depots, production facilities and air defence radar systems in Yemen used by the Houthis to endanger ships in the Red Sea. The attacking states considered these necessary and proportionate responses to the unprovoked and unacceptable Houthi attacks on commercial shipping in the Red Sea.[33] Subsequently, they continued to respond in this manner whenever the Houthis launched attacks against ships in the Red Sea. In March 2024, the EU Naval Force launched Operation Aspides, an EU defensive maritime security operation under the EU Common Security and Defence Policy, to repel the attacks on ships by the Houthis in the Red Sea.

On 4 March 2025, the US government redesignated the Houthis as "specially designated global terrorists" considered to threaten the security of the US, thereby triggering sanctions for anyone or any state or entity trying to provide material support for the Houthis and blocking the money due to be put into banks for the payment of civil servant salaries, a key Houthi demand for the first phase of the peace plan, as well as freezing the planned opening of any seaports or airports in Yemen, thereby keeping Yemen's economy in ruins. This was followed, on 16 March 2025, by US president Trump's order for the US military to launch decisive and powerful military action against the Houthi terrorists in Yemen who had waged an unrelenting campaign of piracy, violence and terrorism against American, and other, ships, aircraft and drones. The US military action against the Houthis continued up to the first week of May 2025, when the two sides reached a ceasefire agreement mediated by Oman whereby the Houthis would stop targeting shipping in the Red Sea except for Israeli-flagged vessels, in return for the US cessation of military action against the Houthis. However, in July 2025 the Houthis announced that they would attack any ships

[33] For debates on the legality or otherwise of their military actions, see Leonie Brassat, "The Lawfulness of Military Strikes against the Houthis in Yemen and the Red Sea", *EJIL Talk!*, 19 Mar. 2024, https://www.ejiltalk.org/the-lawfulness-of-military-strikes-against-the-houthis-in-yemen-and-the-red-sea/; Christian Henderson, "A Reply to Brassat: The Lawfulness of Military Strikes against the Houthis in Yemen and the 'Fourth Problem' of Necessity and Proportionality", *EJIL Talk!*, 1 Apr. 2024, https://www.ejiltalk.org/a-reply-to-brassat-the-military-strikes-against-the-houthis-in-yemen-and-the-fourth-problem-of-necessity-and-proportionality/.

belonging to companies that do business with Israeli ports, regardless of their nationalities, as part of their military operations against Israel in order to pressure Israel to halt its aggression and lift the blockade on the Gaza Strip.

International law and diplomacy have thus far failed to put an end to the immeasurable sufferings of Yemenis despite strenuous efforts by several of those entities directly involved. The next chapter will endeavour to explore whether the international order may somehow find long-lasting solutions to wars ravaging Yemen and elsewhere in Asia and attain eternal peace.

CHAPTER 9

Present and Future Directions of War and Peace in Asia

Stocktaking

International law regulating the force of force is well established. Nonetheless, states have raised points of contention, or "grey areas", that, owing to power asymmetry especially in terms of military strength, have been manipulated to serve relatively more powerful nation states at the disadvantage of their less powerful Asian counterparts.

Chapter 1 informed readers how Asian states cherish the Five Principles, the Ten Principles and so forth that are different in some respects from those adhered to in the West. In spite of these lofty aspirations among Asian states, their actual implementation has much to desire.

Chapter 2 elaborated the international law applicable to the use of force *(jus ad bellum)*. The Vietnamese invasion of Cambodia was used as a case study to show how the pretext of the exercise of the right to self-defence was never accepted and was brought to an end after the change in the geopolitical landscape, not legal arguments, with the demise of the Soviet Union, which had been Vietnam's major ally, and the solidified opposition by ASEAN against Vietnam and its puppet regime in Cambodia.

The sovereignty disputes covered in Chapter 3 are the most sensitive issues for all states concerned. Even Cambodia and Thailand, which are both ASEAN member states, fought one another and ASEAN could hardly intercede to end the armed conflict. Several confidence-building measures have been resorted to in order to contain or manage sovereignty disputes, such as by maintaining the status quo and agreeing to a ceasefire or a truce. During an armed confrontation between parties to a territorial or border dispute, both sides need to have a "cooling-off" period to consider carefully how to prevent the situation from escalating into an armed conflict or a full-scale war. They must not use sabre-rattling rhetoric to arouse patriotism, nationalism or irredentism. Prior personal interaction and connections among those responsible for management or containment of the dispute in question help to ensure that actors on both sides see one another as human beings and not as mere pawns in a chess game of territorial conquest and resistance. Regional organisations to which they belong or any state or person that or who may use good offices to mediate their dispute should be approached. Demilitarisation of the areas under dispute has been used in some armed conflicts.[1]

Chapter 4 elaborated how external self-determination for the purpose of secession is not realistic in present-day Asia. In order to lay to rest any potential justification for secession, national governments faced with insurgencies must protect and enhance the human rights of ethnic, racial, religious and other minorities to alleviate any grievance they may have and ensure that all peoples live in harmony and without discrimination within the same shared border.

Chapter 5, on the Indonesian armed annexation of East Timor, explored how and why the international community virtually neglected the people of East Timor, initially for the selfish interests of those states with sufficient clout to prod Indonesia to leave East Timor and subsequently for fear of the collapse of the Indonesian government after Indonesia's transition to democracy. Justice still has not been done to and seen to be done by most of the people of Timor-Leste who suffered during the annexation. There is a silver lining. The Treaty between Australia and Timor-Leste Establishing their Maritime Boundaries in the Timor Sea, which came into force in August 2019, has given Timor-Leste the maritime entitlement and its natural resources that Timor-Leste would have lost had it remained under Indonesia's annexation.

Chapter 6 explained why the doctrine of humanitarian intervention and Pillar III of the concept of responsibility to protect have no place among Asian nations.

Chapter 7, using Syria as the case study, explained how and why the alleged right of self-defence against non-state armed groups hardly works in a proxy war among different states belonging to different geopolitical blocs.

---

[1] See also Marco Roscini and Marco Longobardo, "Demilitarised Zones", in *Research Handbook on International Arms Control Law*, ed. Eric Myjer and Thilo Marauhn (Cheltenham: Edward Elgar Publishing, 2022), pp. 467–80.

The proxy war in Yemen covered by Chapter 8 arose mainly from the invocation of the invitation by the internationally recognised government that has lost effective control over most of Yemen's territory, plus the claim of self-defence against the Houthis, the non-state armed group effectively controlling most of the territory in Yemen. The invitation to intervene by the use of force in Yemen was given to the Gulf Cooperation Council (GCC), the member states of which are enemies of Iran, which they accuse of supporting the Houthis, hence the ongoing proxy war in hapless Yemen.

Many Southeast Asian states used to be mired in their fear of the spread of communism, and this led to several armed conflicts in this subregion. Spheres of geopolitical influence are still at play in Asia and the proxy wars in Yemen and Syria have caused unfathomable devastation, in disregard of the lives and sufferings of fellow human beings. Dividing countries and persons into either "friends" or "foes" is tragically erroneous, as history has clearly shown. It is best to eliminate any misunderstanding, miscalculations, differences and disputes by peaceful means.

Armed conflict can start with a misunderstanding between the states concerned about factual circumstances. Such misunderstanding often develops into a miscalculation and a dispute that, if left unsettled, generates distrust and, worse still, hatred between the disputing parties. Reconciliation is best done at the phase of misunderstanding. Compromises may be reached to end the dispute, provided that they are not seen as unacceptable "appeasements" by the populace of either of the states concerned.

Inherent Paradox in Intergroup Conflict and Peace

An empirical study about intergroup conflict and peace[2] has reached the following conclusions. The pursuit of peace entails an inherent paradox. The urgent need to save lives and alleviate human suffering necessitates swift solutions to the problem of intergroup conflict. However, because the human mind associates peace with longer "time horizons", people anticipate peace more when considering the distant rather than the near future. Increasing people's distance from entities and events makes people think about them abstractly. When considered against a backdrop of hostility and struggle between groups, peace is often viewed as an aspirational state. Peace contrasts sharply

[2] Nir Halevy and Yair Berson, "Thinking about the Distant Future Promotes the Prospects of Peace: A Construal-Level Perspective on Intergroup Conflict Resolution", *Journal of Conflict Resolution* 66 (2022): 1119.

with the adverse everyday experiences that intergroup conflict often bears. Asking participants to plan several months into the future resulted in broader and more inclusive categories. Thus, temporal distance from the execution of a negotiated agreement helps people focus on the bigger picture and promotes integrative agreements. Transitioning from warfare to peace, or from conflict to reconciliation, requires time, effort and additional resources (for example, by investing money in educational enterprises and public opinion campaigns). Negotiators who expected the negotiated agreement to be implemented in the distant rather than in the near future engaged in more integrative bargaining behaviours by bundling issues and exchanging offers that involved trade-offs between higher-value and lower-value issues, thereby increasing joint outcomes for both parties in the negotiation. And interpersonal interactions tend to be more cooperative than intergroup interactions.

That people see peace as coming in the long run rather than in the near future is hardly surprising. Those living and suffering on the frontline of armed conflicts simply lose all realistic hope for an immediate end of hostilities. Peace is thus a far-distant dream. Hardened positions of parties to the armed conflict necessitate compromises and reconciliation of their differences, and these normally come after protracted negotiations. Instead of using threat-based strategies of conflict management, the conclusion from the aforesaid empirical study affirms that the use of reassurance and diplomacy by parties to an armed conflict in their negotiation to narrow or end their differences is the better alternative.[3]

There are other factors that could impact war and peace in Asia in the future.

New Agenda for Peace

On 10 September 2021, UN secretary-general António Guterres proposed a "new agenda for peace". This agenda for promoting peace and preventing conflicts aims to reduce strategic risks (nuclear weapons, cyberwarfare and autonomous weapons); strengthen international foresight; reshape responses to all forms of violence; invest in prevention and peacebuilding, including the UN Secretary-General's Peacebuilding Fund and the Peacebuilding Commission; support regional prevention; and put women and girls at the centre of security policy. It will also strive for peaceful, secure and sustainable use of outer space, including

[3] See also Richard Ned Lebow, *Avoiding War, Making Peace* (Cham: Palgrave Macmillan, 2018).

through a multi-stakeholder dialogue on outer space.[4] This new agenda for peace apparently takes some of the time horizon findings on peace-making into account.

The UN Secretary-General's Peacebuilding Fund is the United Nations' financial instrument of first resort to sustain peace in countries or situations at risk or affected by violent conflict. It may invest with UN entities, governments, regional organisations, multilateral banks, national multi-donor trust funds or civil society organisations. From 2006 to 2021, the fund allocated nearly US$1.67 billion to 65 recipient countries. The fund received US$771,371,991 between 2020 and 1 June 2024 from voluntary contributions from governments, with Germany being the largest donor (US$185.8 million), followed by the Netherlands (US$123.68 million) and Sweden (US$101 million). From Asia, South Korea was the ninth largest donor (US$18 million), followed by Japan (US$16 million).[5] The fund supports integrated UN responses to fill critical gaps, respond quickly and with the flexibility to peacebuilding opportunities and catalyse processes as well as resources in a risk-tolerant fashion.

As for the Peacebuilding Commission, this was set up in 2005 by the UN General Assembly (UNGA) and the UN Security Council (UNSC) to provide political accompaniment and advocacy to conflict-affected countries, with their consent. In 2016, the commission's mandate was expanded for it to advise the UNGA and the UNSC on peacebuilding and sustaining peace; to promote an integrated, strategic and coherent approach to peacebuilding; to act as a bridge among the principal organs and relevant UN entities by sharing advice on peacebuilding needs and priorities; and to convene all relevant actors within and outside the United Nations. In 2020, both the UNGA and the UNSC called upon the commission to continue strengthening its advisory, bridging and convening roles in support of nationally owned priorities and efforts in the countries and regions under its consideration. Recent engagements highlighted by the commission in May 2022, however, were mostly in Africa and Colombia and not in Asia.

As pointed out in Chapter 1, the Chinese government's Global Security Initiative (GSI) lists among the 20 priorities for cooperation the government's active participation in formulating the new agenda for peace, in particular by supporting UN efforts to enhance conflict prevention and fully harnessing the peacebuilding architecture to assist post-conflict states in peacebuilding.

---

[4] *Report of the UN Secretary-General, Our Common Agenda* (New York: United Nations, 2021).

[5] https://www.un.org/peacebuilding/content/contributions.

United Nations Security Council Reform

International peace and security under the UN Charter system are still entrusted to the five permanent members of the UNSC (P5), each of which has a veto.[6] China is the only Asian state among the P5, and it is a party to some of the disputes covered by this book.

Article 108 of the UN Charter requires that amendments to this Charter shall "come into force for all Members of the United Nations when they have been adopted by a vote of two-thirds of the members of the General Assembly and ratified in accordance with their respective constitutional processes by two-thirds of the Members of the United Nations, including all the permanent members of the Security Council". The UNSC's structure has been changed only once, by UNGA Resolution 1991-XVIII (1963) of 17 December 1963. Considering that the composition of the UNSC was at that time "inequitable and unbalanced" in terms of geographical representation, the resolution amended the UN Charter to expand the UNSC's non-permanent members from six to ten. The amendment came into effect on 31 August 1965, having been ratified by 93 members, that is, in excess of two-thirds of the UN members, including all of the P5.[7]

In addition to failures to find consensus among UN member states as to which other countries besides the P5 should be permanent members as well as on the entitlement of any new permanent member to a veto, not all the current permanent members of the UNSC welcome other states to join their rank.

The current ongoing movement for the reform of the UNSC therefore encompasses proposals to prevent any of the P5 from abusing the veto power in the face of threats or occurrence of gross atrocities of international concern such as genocide, crimes against humanity and war crimes. The Accountability, Coherence and Transparency Group (ACT), set up in 2013 and comprising 27 small and mid-sized countries,[8] has been working to improve the working methods of the UNSC. The ACT proposed, in July 2015, a one-page "Code of

[6] For a drafting history of the UN Charter provisions on the UNSC, see Brian Cox, "United Nations Security Council Reform: Collected Proposals and Possible Consequences", *South Carolina Journal of International Law & Business* 6 (2009): 89, 91–9.

[7] Egon Schwelb, "Amendments to Articles 23, 27 and 61 of the Charter of the United Nations", *American Journal of International Law* 59 (1965): 834, 835–44.

[8] Austria, Chile, Costa Rica, Denmark, Ecuador, Estonia, Finland, Gabon, Ghana, Hungary, Ireland, Jordan, Latvia, Liechtenstein, Luxembourg, the Maldives, New Zealand, Norway, Papua New Guinea, Peru, Portugal, Rwanda, Saudi Arabia, Slovenia, Sweden, Switzerland (coordinator) and Uruguay.

Conduct Regarding UNSC Action against Genocide, Crimes against Humanity and War Crimes". The code is not only for the P5 but also for the UNSC non-permanent members, as well as for any UN member state that may, at some point in time, become a non-permanent member of the UNSC. The code comprises a general and positive pledge to support the UNSC's action to prevent or end the crimes covered by the code that the UN secretary-general has brought to the UNSC's attention. This general and positive pledge is complemented by a more specific pledge to be made by all 15 members of the UNSC not to vote against any credible draft resolution aiming at preventing or halting these crimes. More than 100 UN members have supported the code.

Also in 2015, France and Mexico presented a one-page "Political Statement on the Suppression of the Veto in Case of Mass Atrocities", open to signature by UN member states, which proposes a collective and voluntary agreement among the P5 to refrain from using the veto to prevent the UNSC from taking action with the aim of preventing or bringing an end to situations involving the commission of mass atrocities, the veto being considered not a privilege but "an international responsibility". As of March 2025, 107 UN member states and two UN observers have signed the statement. Of the P5, France and the United Kingdom have supported both the code of conduct and the political statement. Silence by the other three UNSC permanent members does not bode well for the future realisation of either the code or the political statement.

In October 2013, in an unprecedented move, Saudi Arabia, which a day earlier had just been elected for the first time to be a non-permanent member of the UNSC, gave official notification that it would not take up the seat. Saudi Arabia's Foreign Ministry denounced the "work mechanisms and double-standards" at the UNSC that prevented the UNSC from carrying out its duties and assuming its responsibilities in keeping world peace, leaving Saudi Arabia with no other option but to turn down the UNSC membership until it was reformed and given the means to accomplish its duties and assume its responsibilities in preserving the world's peace and security. The ministry criticised the UNSC's failure for 65 years to find a solution to the Palestinian cause, which had led to numerous wars that have threatened world peace, as well as the UN's failure to rid the Middle East region of weapons of mass destruction, including nuclear weapons. The ministry also accused the UN of allowing the Syrian government to kill its own people with chemical weapons without confronting it or imposing any deterrent sanctions. In early December 2013, the UNGA elected Jordan to fill the seat vacated by Saudi Arabia.

India and Japan have joined Brazil and Germany (collectively called "the G4") in their campaign to become permanent members of the UNSC. Japan and Germany are among the largest contributors to the UN's annual budgets.

A former deputy permanent representative of Japan to the UN in New York cogently summarised the prevailing situations as regards the enlargement of UNSC membership as follows.

More than 100 states support the addition of permanent seats in the UNSC to reflect today's geopolitical realities. This issue has been debated in the UNGA ever since 1993 under the agenda item "Question of Equitable Representation on and Increase in the Membership of the Security Council and Other Matters related to the Security Council". In the Inter-Governmental Negotiations (IGNs) on Security Council Reform conducted within the UNGA under this agenda item since 2009, UN member states have made repeated statements, with little progress. Five key issues have been identified over the 14 years of the IGN process: (1) the membership categories; (2) the veto question; (3) regional representation; (4) the size of an enlarged UNSC and its working methods; and (5) the relationship between the UNSC and UNGA. There are groups of states that take unified positions on these issues: the G4, the UfC (the 12-state Uniting for Consensus group led by Italy, Pakistan and Mexico), the 54-state African Union, the L.69 group (a group named after draft resolution A/61/L.69 of 2007 and currently comprising 42 developing states led by India) and the 14-state Caribbean Community. The 2005 G4 proposal was to add six new permanent seats but the G4 was unable at the time to specify the two additional African states. During the campaign, it was clear that India and Japan had the strongest support in seeking permanent seats. The appropriate number of additional non-permanent seats is a tricky matter. All five regional groups of the UN (the African Group, the Asia-Pacific Group, the Group of Latin American and Caribbean States, the Eastern European Group and the Western Europe and Others Group) want additional non-permanent seats but the P5 states want to limit the total number of seats to 25 or fewer. Among the G4, both Japan and Germany were willing to renounce the veto power, but not so India and Brazil. The compromise reached in the 2005 G4 proposed draft resolution (A/59/L.64) was that the new permanent members shall not exercise the right of veto until a new decision is made based on the review mandated to be conducted 15 years after the UNSC reform. The African Union takes the position that the veto should be abolished but, so long as it exists, it should be extended to all members, including the new permanent members. The African Union demands two African permanent seats with veto rights "as a matter of common justice" and asserts that the African Union, not the UNGA, should be responsible for the selection of African representatives on the UNSC.[9]

India's quest for a permanent seat at the UNSC traces back to the early 1990s, coinciding with India's rise in global economic and political prominence. India's start of atomic tests in 1998 demonstrated its capabilities as a nuclear power. India contends that, as the world's largest democracy and a significant global player, its inclusion as a permanent member of the UNSC would better represent the interests of developing nations and align with the contemporary geopolitical landscape. India also emphasises its substantial contributions to UN peacekeeping missions to uphold international peace and security. However, China has opposed India's inclusion as a permanent member. Furthermore, there are reservations among member states regarding India's insistence on having a veto power.[10]

In the meantime, there are suggestions to cope with situations where one or more of the P5 cast a veto.[11] The UNGA's Uniting for Peace Resolution adopted in 1950 and the "Veto Initiative" it adopted in April 2022 are frequently mentioned. It is also suggested that a closer look be taken at Article 27(3) of the UN Charter, which stipulates that decisions of the UNSC on all non-procedural matters shall be made by an affirmative vote of seven members including the concurring votes of the P5, provided that, in decisions under Chapter VI (Pacific Settlement of Disputes), and under Article 52(3),[12] a party to a dispute shall abstain from voting. Creatively interpreted, this voting abstention rule can be utilised to exclude any P5 member from UNSC resolutions on peaceful settlement of disputes to which that P5 member is a disputing party, including, for example, the South China Sea dispute and the land boundary dispute with India covered by this

---

[9] Toshiro Osawa, "On Pursuing UN Security Council Reform", Association of Japanese Institutes of Strategic Studies (AJISS) Commentary, 11 Dec. 2023.

[10] Ashok Sharma, "India's Quest for UN Security Council Permanent Membership: A Holy Grail of Its Foreign Policy", *Times of India*, 1 Apr. 2024, https://timesofindia.indiatimes.com/blogs/ashoks-statecraft/indias-quest-for-un-security-council-permanent-membership-a-holy-grail-of-its-foreign-policy/.

[11] Shamala Kandiah Thompson, Karin Landgren and Paul Romita, "The United Nations in Hindsight: The Long and Winding Road to Security Council Reform", *Just Security*, 30 Sept. 2022, https://www.justsecurity.org/83310/the-united-nations-in-hindsight-long-winding-road-to-security-council-reform/.

[12] Article 52(3), coming under Chapter VIII (Regional Arrangements), stipulates: "The Security Council shall encourage the development of pacific settlement of local disputes through such regional arrangements or by such regional agencies either on the initiative of the States concerned or by reference from the Security Council."

book. According to one view, the P5 were never granted, nor could they be granted, the power to violate the UN's Purposes and Principles, or obligations of international law, such as respect for jus cogens, which includes the prohibition of aggression.[13] A view has also been expressed that UNSC decisions should be subject to judicial review by the International Court of Justice (ICJ).[14]

Since the Russian's "special military operation" in Ukraine starting on 24 February 2022, the split between the West led by the United States on the one side and Russia and its allies on the other has grown even wider. In terms of global geopolitical rivalry, the PRC has been leaning closer to Russia than to the West. The PRC has also forged a closer relationship with Saudi Arabia and Iran, as well as other members of the GCC. China welcomes the participation of GCC countries in China's GSI in a joint effort to uphold regional peace and stability.

Each of the P5 possesses a large number of nuclear warheads. So do India, Israel, Pakistan and North Korea.[15] As explained in Chapter 1, the ICJ's Advisory Opinion on *Legality of the Threat or Use of Nuclear Weapons* concluded that, in view of the state of international law in 1996, and of the elements of fact at its disposal, the ICJ "cannot conclude definitively whether the threat or use of nuclear weapons would be lawful or unlawful in an extreme circumstance of self-defence, in which the very survival of a State would be at stake".[16] This has given rise to serious concerns that one day one or more P5 members, entrusted by the UN Charter to be the guarantor of collective security under the UN Charter, or a non-P5 state in possession of nuclear weapons, might find it necessary to use nuclear weapons to ensure its very "survival" that is "at stake".

Nuclear Weapon Threats

On 24 April 2014, the Marshall Islands instituted proceedings in the ICJ against nine states: China, North Korea, France, India, Israel, Pakistan,

---

[13] Jennifer Trahan, "Legal Issues Surrounding Veto Use and Aggression", *Case Western Reserve Journal of International Law* 55 (2023): 93.

[14] Ibid., 140–6; Sreenivasa Rao Pemmaraju, "Optimum World Order beyond War: A Long View on Current Challenges", *Cambridge International Law Journal* 11 (2022): 154.

[15] Arms Control Association, "Nuclear Weapons: Who Has What at a Glance", https://www.armscontrol.org/factsheets/nuclear-weapons-who-has-what-glance.

[16] ICJ Rep. 1966, pp. 266–7 [105(2)]. See also Brian Drummond, "UK Nuclear Deterrence Policy: An Unlawful Threat of Force", *Journal on the Use of Force & International Law* 6 (2019): 193.

Russia, the United Kingdom and the United States, accusing them of not fulfilling their obligations with respect to the cessation of the nuclear arms race at an early date and to nuclear disarmament. India, Pakistan and the United Kingdom had recognised the ICJ's compulsory jurisdiction pursuant to Article 36(2) of the ICJ Statute, whereas the other six states did not give any consent to the ICJ's jurisdiction in the applications brought by the Marshall Islands against them. On 5 October 2016, the ICJ delivered its judgments, finding that the Marshall Islands had failed to prove before the ICJ the existence of its disputes with the United Kingdom, India and Pakistan on their respective obligations to negotiate cessation of the nuclear arms race and to nuclear disarmament.[17]

Nevertheless, in 2017 the United Nations was able to conclude the Treaty on the Prohibition of Nuclear Weapons,[18] which was opened to signature on 20 September 2017 and entered into force on 22 January 2021. Pursuant to Article 1 of the Treaty, each state party undertakes never under any circumstances to: (1) develop, test, produce, manufacture, otherwise acquire, possess or stockpile nuclear weapons or other nuclear explosive devices; (2) transfer to any recipient whatsoever nuclear weapons or other nuclear explosive devices or control over such weapons or explosive devices directly or indirectly; (3) receive the transfer of or control over nuclear weapons or other nuclear explosive devices directly or indirectly; (4) use or threaten to use nuclear weapons or other nuclear explosive devices; (5) assist, encourage or induce, in any way, anyone to engage in any activity prohibited to a state party under this Treaty; (6) seek or receive any assistance, in any way, from anyone to engage in any activity prohibited to a state party under the treaty; or (7) allow any stationing, installation or deployment of any nuclear weapons or other nuclear explosive devices in its territory or at any place under its jurisdiction or control.

At the time of writing, the 2017 treaty has 73 parties. The parties from Asia-Pacific are Bangladesh, Cambodia, the Cook Islands, Fiji, Kazakhstan, Kiribati, Laos, Malaysia, Maldives, Mongolia, Nauru, Niue, Palau, the Philippines, Samoa, the Solomon Islands, Sri Lanka, the State of Palestine, Thailand,

---

[17] *Obligations Concerning Negotiations relating to Cessation of the Nuclear Arms Race and to Nuclear Disarmament (Marshall Islands v. United Kingdom),* Preliminary Objections, ICJ Rep. 2016, p. 833; *Obligations concerning Negotiations relating to Cessation of the Nuclear Arms Race and to Nuclear Disarmament (Marshall Islands v. India),* Jurisdiction and Admissibility, ICJ Rep. 2016, p. 255; *Obligations concerning Negotiations relating to Cessation of the Nuclear Arms Race and to Nuclear Disarmament (Marshall Islands v. Pakistan),* Jurisdiction and Admissibility, ICJ Rep. 2016, p. 552.

[18] A/CONF.229/2017/8, CN.476.2017.TREATIES-XXVI-9.

Timor-Leste, Tuvalu, Vanuatu and Vietnam. None of the states in possession, or suspected to be in possession, of nuclear weapons is party to the 2017 treaty, however.

In their armed conflicts, India and Pakistan never threaten one another with the use of nuclear weapons.[19] As a confidence-building measure, on 1 January of each year since 1992, India and Pakistan exchange the latest lists of their respective nuclear installations and facilities. India and China, which have had armed conflicts along the McMahon Line for decades, never threaten one another with nuclear weapons.

Israel's possession of nuclear weapons is avowedly for its survival. Invoking the right to anticipatory self-defence, Israel has carried out airstrikes to destroy what it suspects to be sites for nuclear research reactors in Iraq and Syria, as it did against Iraq's Osiraq nuclear reactor in June 1981 and Syria's Al Kibar site in September 2007. Israel has also been accused of assassinating a number of nuclear scientists in Iran suspected by Israel of working on developing Iran's nuclear weapons. Four Iranian scientists associated with the nuclear programme were assassinated between 2010 and 2012 and the prominent Iranian military scientist Mohsen Fakhrizadeh was killed in November 2020. The head of Iran's Atomic Energy Organization from 2011 to 2013 survived an assassination attempt in 2010 but was seriously wounded. After Israel's airstrike against the Iranian embassy complex in Damascus on 1 April 2024, Iran responded on 13 April 2024 by launching missiles and drone attacks against military targets in Israel and the Israeli-occupied Golan Heights. These mutual attacks by Israel and Iran did not escalate into a full-scale war, arguably because Israel has nuclear weapons. On 19 April 2024, Israel carried out an air strike deep inside Iranian territory, in close proximity to the Isfahan Nuclear Technology Centre, which hosts nuclear research reactors, a uranium conversion plant and a fuel production plant, among other facilities. This could be both Israel's retaliation against the Iranian attack a

---

[19] In his book *Never Give an Inch: Fighting for the America I Love* (Northampton, MA: Broadside Books, 2023), former US secretary of state Mike Pompeo claims that in late Feb. 2019 the United States narrowly averted a nuclear war between India and Pakistan after his then Indian counterpart, the late Sushma Swaraj, told him on the telephone Pakistan was planning a nuclear offensive against India in the wake of India's airstrike against an alleged Jaish-e-Mohammed training camp in Pakistan on 26 Feb. 2019 after more than 40 Indian Central Reserve Police Force personnel had been killed by a suicide bomb in the State of Jammu and Kashmir on 4 Feb. 2019, and that India was preparing its own nuclear escalation response. Pompeo's account has never been confirmed by either India or Pakistan.

few days earlier and a warning to Iran not to develop nuclear weapons. For the Iranian government, this could serve as a strong incentive for Iran to develop nuclear weapons.[20] On 13 June 2025 Israel launched surprise attacks on nuclear and military facilities in Iran, killing several prominent Iranian military leaders and nuclear scientists as well as slightly injuring the Iranian president. Iran retaliated by launching military attacks inside Israel, while the Houthis, Iran's putative ally, also fired many missiles from Yemen at Israel. The United States assisted Israel by bombing three Iranian nuclear sites and Iran responded by firing missiles at a US military base in Qatar. Although the warring parties eventually agreed to a ceasefire on 24 June 2025, this incident shows how much of a threat to world peace the Iranian–Israel military confrontation is.

The West, Israel and Iran's Arab neighbouring states are worried about Iran's nuclear weapon ambition. Iran has publicly denounced Israel's existence. Iran is the only non-Arab nation in the midst of Arab countries in the Middle East and Iran is not on good terms with many Western nations, especially the United States, the UK, France and Canada. Iran has been alleged to have built up the "axis of resistance", a network of armies, militias and other non-state armed groups opposed to the West and the West's allies.[21] In 2015, the UNSC P5 plus Germany and the EU reached the Joint Comprehensive Plan of Action, a nuclear deal framework, with Iran to ensure Iran would never develop nuclear weapons and, in return, the West would end their sanctions imposed on Iran. The United States withdrew from this undertaking after accusing Iran of reneging on its commitment thereunder. The secretary-general of the League of Arab States claimed, during the UNSC's meeting on 23 March 2022, that Iran was responsible for interfering in the internal affairs of Arab states, and that Iran's missile programme was a source of legitimate concern for many members of the League of Arab States.[22] In response, Iran rejected these comments as misinformation and baseless claims levelled against Iran's missile programme which was solely for defensive purposes within Iran's inalienable right to develop conventional weapons, including

[20] Darya Dolzikova and Matthew Savill, "Why Iran May Accelerate Its Nuclear Program and Israel May Be Tempted to Attack It", *Bulletin of the Atomic Scientists*, 26 Apr. 2024, https://thebulletin.org/2024/04/why-iran-may-accelerate-its-nuclear-program-and-israel-may-be-tempted-to-attack-it/.

[21] See, for example, Guido Steinberg, *The "Axis of Resistance": Iran's Expansion in the Middle East Is Hitting a Wall* (Berlin: German Institute for International and Security Affairs, 2021).

[22] UNSC Verbatim Record (23 Mar. 2022) UN Doc. S/PV.9001, pp. 4–5.

ballistic missiles, to maintain its national security.[23] In this atmosphere of distrust and enmity, Yemen has become a major battleground for a proxy war between these geopolitical players in the Middle East, with Iran being accused of supporting the Houthis and the Saudi-led coalition supporting the Yemeni government.

On 9 December 2022, in the Statement of the Riyadh Summit for Cooperation and Development between the GCC and China, issued after the summit between the two sides, the leaders of the participating countries stressed the need to support the Treaty on the Non-proliferation of Nuclear Weapons, prevent the proliferation of weapons of mass destruction in the GCC region, and ensure the peaceful nature of the Iranian nuclear programme, in order to preserve regional and international security and stability. They reaffirmed the call on Iran to fully cooperate with the International Atomic Energy Agency. The leaders also stressed the need for relations between the GCC states and Iran to be based on following the principle of good neighbourliness and non-interference in internal affairs, respect for the independence, sovereignty and territorial integrity of states, and resolving disputes by peaceful means, in accordance with the UN Charter and international law, and not resorting to the use of force or threatening to use it, and maintaining regional and international security and stability. The leaders likewise stressed the importance of a comprehensive dialogue with the participation of the countries of the region to address the Iranian nuclear file and destabilising regional activities, address support for terrorist and sectarian groups and illegal armed organisations, prevent the proliferation of ballistic missiles and drones, ensure the safety of international navigation and oil installations, and adhere to UN resolutions and international legitimacy.[24]

Also to be worried about is North Korea's unpredictable behaviour that poses serious international concerns about its possible use of nuclear weapons. In November 2010, North Korean forces fired approximately 170 artillery shells and rockets at South Korea's Yeonpyeong Island, causing widespread damage to both military and civilian targets. North Korea claimed that it acted in response to a South Korean artillery exercise at sea near the island, which North Korea considered its territorial sea. South Korea fought back by shelling North Korean military positions. The armed conflicts resulted in four persons

[23] Letter dated 28 Mar. 2022 from the Permanent Representative of the Islamic Republic of Iran to the United Nations addressed to the Secretary-General and the President of the UNSC, S/2022/270 (29 Mar. 2022).

[24] https://www.spa.gov.sa/en/20a265ac44u.

killed and 22 injured on both sides. The incident was the most serious crisis in the Korean Peninsula since the armistice on 27 July 1953 that terminated the fighting in the Korean War. The United States leaders had to persuade their South Korean counterparts not to further militarily escalate the tension beyond control.[25]

North Korea has been test-launching ballistic missiles. On 8 September 2022, North Korea's Supreme People's Assembly promulgated the law on the state policy on nuclear forces, amending the 2013 version of the law that permitted the use of nuclear weapons to repel invasion or attack from a hostile nuclear state. The new law allows pre-emptive nuclear strikes if an imminent attack by weapons of mass destruction or against North Korea's "strategic targets", including its leadership, is detected.[26]

On 19 June 2024, the North Korean and Russian leaders signed a comprehensive partnership agreement which includes, among other things, the provision of mutual assistance in the event of aggression against one of the parties to this agreement. Optimistically, this may make North Korea less paranoid about its own vulnerability to armed attacks by other states and become more rational in its relations with the rest of the world.

State Responsibility

An aggressor state can be held liable for its illegal use of force. Unilateral sanctions as well as sanctions by the competent international organisations have been imposed on aggressor states, as shown in the preceding chapters. States that engage in illegal uses of force must compensate injured states for the harm caused.[27] A competent international court or claims commission can ensure that the state concerned compensate for its illegal use of force. The following are just two examples.

In *Armed Activities in the Territory of the Congo (DR Congo v. Uganda)*, the ICJ had jurisdiction over the dispute because the two disputing parties had accepted the ICJ's compulsory jurisdiction under Article 36(2) of the ICJ Statute.

---

[25] Robert M. Gates, *Duty: Memoirs of a Secretary at War* (New York: Vintage Books, 2014), pp. 416–18, 497.

[26] Josh Smith, "New North Korea Law Outlines Nuclear Weapons Use, Including Preemptive Strikes", *Japan Times*, 9 Sept. 2022, https://www.japantimes.co.jp/news/2022/09/09/asia-pacific/north-korea-nuclear-weapons-policy/.

[27] Hannes Jöbstl and Dean Rosenberg, "The Humanization of War Reparations: Combatant Deaths and Compensation in Unlawful Wars", *Michigan Journal of International Law* 45 (2024): 39–91.

After holding Uganda responsible for armed activities in DR Congo in violation of international law, the ICJ fixed the following amounts for the compensation due from Uganda to DR Congo for the damage caused by the violations: US$225 million for damage to persons, US$40 million for damage to property and US$60 million for damage related to natural resources. The total amount due was required to be paid in five annual instalments of US$65 million starting on 1 September 2022. Should payment be delayed, post-judgment interest of 6 per cent would accrue on any overdue amount as from the day which follows the day on which the instalment was due.[28]

If the state that violates international law has not accepted the ICJ's compulsory jurisdiction, it should be ordered by the UNSC or the victorious state to accept the ICJ's jurisdiction on an ad hoc basis, so that the ICJ can decide the extent of compensation due by that state to the injured state.

In addition to the ICJ, the states concerned may set up a claims commission, as in the case of the Eritrea–Ethiopia armed conflict from May 1998 to December 2000 in which thousands were killed, thousands more injured and tens of thousands of people displaced from their homes.

The Eritrea–Ethiopia Claims Commission was established pursuant to Article 5 of the Agreement signed in Algiers on 12 December 2000 between the governments of Eritrea and Ethiopia, facilitated by the Organisation of African Unity (OAU), the predecessor to the African Union, of which they were members. The Algiers Agreement aimed to end the armed conflict between the parties, set up an inquiry by an independent body appointed by the OAU secretary-general into the causes of the conflict, set up a five-member boundary commission to delimit and demarcate the border, and set up a five-member Claims Commission to "decide through binding arbitration all claims for loss, damage or injury by one Government against the other" related to the 1998–2000 conflict between them that "result from violations of international humanitarian law, including the 1949 Geneva Conventions, or other violations of international law". Excluded from the jurisdiction of the Claims Commission were "claims arising from the costs of military operations, preparing for military operations or the use of force, except to the extent that such claims involve violations of international humanitarian law". Claims could be brought by the two states parties in their own right or on behalf of their nationals. The independent body to investigate the causes of the conflict was never established because issuing a report

---

[28] *Armed Activities in the Territory of the Congo (DR Congo v. Uganda) Reparations,* ICJ Rep. 2022, p. 13 at pp. 137–9 [409].

thereof would not be conducive to the maintenance of peace between the two states.[29]

The Ethiopia–Eritrea Claims Commission awarded Ethiopia US$174,036,520 in total, while Eritrea received US$161,455,000 plus an additional US$2,065,865 for individual Eritrean claimants.[30]

Some commentators have proposed institutionalising "collective countermeasures" to freeze sovereign assets of a state that has violated the international law on the use of force. They argue that frozen assets need not be returned to that state after the close of the war if it has failed to pay reparations to the victimised state. That is because the failure to pay reparations is itself an unlawful act for which countermeasures (continued freezing of assets) may be kept in place even if the unlawful war has ceased. Moreover, other states may join the victimised state, putting in place collective countermeasures, sometimes called "third-party" countermeasures. However, they argue against using countermeasures to simply seize the aggressor state's assets; such seizures would not properly qualify as countermeasures and thus would violate international law.[31]

A state launching a war against another state normally needs allies to sustain its offensive military campaign. A state aiding or assisting another state to violate the law regulating the use of force and other bodies of law (such as international human rights law, international humanitarian law (IHL) and/or international criminal law) must be brought to account to bear state responsibility therefor. An authoritative statement of the law in this matter is the UN International Law Commission's Articles on Responsibility of States for Internationally Wrongful Acts (ARSIWA).[32]

Article 16 ("Aid or Assistance in the Commission of an Internationally Wrongful Act") of ARSIWA reads: "A State which aids or assists another State in the commission of an internationally wrongful act by the latter is internationally responsible for doing so if: (a) that State does so with knowledge of the circumstances of the internationally wrongful act; and (b) the act would be internationally wrongful if committed by that State."

---

[29] Sean D. Murphy, Won Kidane and Thomas R. Snider, *Litigating War: Arbitration of Civil Injury by the Eritrea–Ethiopia Claims Commission* (New York: Oxford University Press, 2013), p. 23.

[30] Eritrea–Ethiopia Claims Commission—Final Award—Eritrea's Damages Claims 17 Aug. 2009 R.I.A.A., vol. xxvi, pp. 505–630.

[31] Oona A. Hathaway, Maggie M. Mills and Thomas M. Poston, "War Reparations: The Case for Countermeasures", *Stanford Law Review* 76 (2024): 971.

[32] *Yearbook of the International Law Commission*, 2001, vol. II, Part Two.

The accompanying commentary to Article 16 of ARSIWA explains as follows. This is the situation where a state voluntarily assists or aids another state in carrying out conduct that violates the international obligations of the latter, for example by knowingly providing an essential facility or financing the activity in question; providing means for the closing of an international waterway; facilitating the abduction of persons on foreign soil; or assisting in the destruction of property belonging to nationals of a third country. The state primarily responsible in each case is the acting state, and the assisting state has only a supporting role. The assisting state will only be responsible to the extent its own conduct has caused or contributed to the internationally wrongful act. Thus, in cases where that internationally wrongful act would clearly have occurred in any event, the responsibility of the assisting state will not extend to compensating for the act itself. Various specific substantive rules exist, prohibiting one state from providing assistance in the commission of certain wrongful acts by other states or even requiring third states to prevent or repress such acts, as in the case of Article 2(5) of the UN Charter, which obligates all UN members to refrain from giving assistance to any state against which the United Nations is taking preventive or enforcement action.

Article 16 of ARSIWA limits the scope of responsibility for aid or assistance in three ways. First, the relevant state organ or agency providing aid or assistance must be aware of the circumstances making the conduct of the assisted state internationally wrongful; second, the aid or assistance must be given with a view to facilitating the commission of that act, and must actually do so; and, third, the completed act must be such that it would have been wrongful had it been committed by the assisting state itself. State practice supports assigning international responsibility to a state that deliberately participates in the internationally wrongful conduct of another through the provision of aid or assistance, in circumstances where the obligation breached is equally opposable to the assisting state. For example, in 1984 Iran protested against the supply of financial and military aid to Iraq by the United Kingdom, which allegedly included chemical weapons used in attacks against Iranian troops, on the ground that the assistance was facilitating acts of aggression by Iraq. The UK government denied both the allegation that it had chemical weapons and that it had supplied them to Iraq. The obligation not to use force may also be breached by an assisting state through permitting the use of its territory by another state to carry out an armed attack against a third state. An example arose from the Tripoli bombing incident in April 1986. Libya accused the United Kingdom of responsibility for the event, based on the fact that the United Kingdom had allowed several of its air bases to be used for the launching of United States fighter planes to attack Libyan targets. The United Kingdom denied responsibility on the basis that the raid by the United States was lawful as an act of self-defence against Libyan terrorist attacks on United States targets. A proposed UNSC resolution concerning the attack was vetoed, but the UNGA adopted a resolution condemning the "military attack" as a violation of the UN Charter and of international law and calling upon all States "to refrain from extending any assistance or facilities for perpetrating acts of aggression against [Libya]".

The commentary to Article 16 of ARSIWA further clarifies that a state may incur responsibility if it assists another state to circumvent sanctions imposed by the UNSC or provides material aid to a state that uses the aid to commit human rights violations. In this respect, the UNGA has called on UN member states in a number of cases to refrain from supplying arms and other military assistance to countries found to be committing serious human rights violations. Where the allegation is that the assistance of a state has facilitated human rights abuses by another state, the particular circumstances of each case must be carefully examined to determine whether the aiding state was aware of and intended to facilitate the commission of the internationally wrongful conduct. By assisting another state to commit an internationally wrongful act, however, a state should not necessarily be held to indemnify the victim for all the consequences of the act but only for those that flow from its own conduct.

In the context of armed conflicts, state responsibility can arise from the giving of assistance by one state to another for purposes such as the sharing of intelligence, the lending of military bases and the provision of weapons. Assisting states are also bound by other rules of international law applicable to them, such as IHL and international human rights law, not to encourage, aid or assist in violations of these laws.[33]

Therefore, a state that facilitated a wrongful act of another state will incur state responsibility as an assisting state if, through its organs or agents, it provided assistance in any of the following three circumstances. First, if it had the purpose/direct intent of facilitating the wrongful act. This is a situation in which the facilitation of the wrongful act was the conscious object of the assisting state's conduct, regardless of any deficits in the assisting state's knowledge. Second, if it had the oblique/indirect intent of facilitating the wrongful act. This is a situation where the assisting state, while being practically certain that the assisted

[33] Harriet Moynihan, *Aiding and Assisting: Challenges in Armed Conflict and Counterterrorism* (London: Chatham House, 2022), pp. 24–36. See also Benjamin K. Nußberger, *Interstate Assistance to the Use of Force* (Baden-Baden: Nomos, 2023).

state will commit the wrongful act and practically certain that it will use the assistance provided to do so, consciously opts to provide the assistance despite this practical certainty. Third, if it acted with wilful blindness, with the purpose of avoiding acquiring information but for which the assisting state would have acted with indirect intent.[34]

Arms flew into Syria to virtually all sides in the Syrian civil war. For example, in May 2013 the EU conditionally approved the transfer of arms to the Syrian Opposition Council, whereas many states, including Russia, the United States, Qatar and Saudi Arabia, provided arms, funding and/or "non-lethal assistance" either to the Assad regime in Syria or to rebel forces combating the regime despite the fact that both sides were known to have committed serious violations of the law regulating armed conflicts, IHL and international human rights law. These arms transfers are unlawful unless the states have taken steps to ensure that the weapons supplied are not used for the commission of human rights violations and/or crimes of international concern such as genocide, crimes against humanity and war crimes[35] and/or serious violations of the law regulating armed conflicts.

The 2013 Arms Trade Treaty (ATT)[36] is relevant in the context of use of force with foreign intervention.[37]

Article 1 of the ATT stipulates that the object and purpose of the ATT are to establish the highest possible common international standards for regulating or improving the regulation of the international trade in conventional arms as well as prevent and eradicate the illicit trade in conventional arms and prevent their diversion, for the purpose of contributing to international and regional peace, security and stability; reducing human suffering; and promoting cooperation, transparency and responsible action by states parties in the international

---

[34] Marko Milanovic, "Intelligence Sharing in Multinational Military Operations and Complicity under International Law", *International Law* 97 (2021): 1269, 1387.

[35] Tom Ruys, "Of Arms, Funding and 'Non-lethal Assistance'—Issues Surrounding Third-State Intervention in the Syrian Civil War", *Chinese Journal of International Law* 13 (2014): 13, 20–53; ICRC, *Arms Transfer to Parties to Armed Conflict: What the Law Says* (Geneva: ICRC, 3 June 2024). See also Hannah Kiel, *Arms Transfer to Non-State Actors: The Erosion of Norms in International Law* (Cheltenham: Edward Elgar Publishing, 2024).

[36] 3013 *United Nations Treaty Series* 269, in force 24 Dec. 2014.

[37] Marco Roscini and Riccardo Labianco, "The Intersections between the Arms Trade Treaty and the International Law of Foreign Intervention in Situations of Internal Unrest", *Israel Yearbook of Human Rights* 52 (2022): 365. See also Tomas Hamilton, *The Arms Trade and International Criminal Law: Reframing Accountability for Complicit Weapon Suppliers* (Oxford: Oxford University Press, 2025).

trade in conventional arms, thereby building confidence among states parties. Pursuant to Article 2, the ATT shall apply to all conventional arms within the following categories: (1) battle tanks, (2) armoured combat vehicles, (3) large-calibre artillery systems, (4) combat aircraft, (5) attack helicopters, (6) warships, (7) missiles and missile launchers, and (8) small arms and light weapons. The activities of the international trade comprise arms transfer by means of export, import, transit, trans-shipment and brokering.

Article 6 of the ATT prohibits any transfer of conventional arms or items covered under the ATT, if the transfer would violate its obligations under measures adopted by the UNSC acting under Chapter VII of the UN Charter, in particular arms embargoes, or if the transfer would violate its relevant international obligations under international agreements to which it is a party. A state party to the ATT shall not authorise any transfer of these conventional arms or items covered under Article 2 (1) or of items covered under Article 3 (ammunitions/munitions) or Article 4 (parts and components), if it has knowledge at the time of authorisation that the arms or items would be used in the commission of genocide, crimes against humanity, grave breaches of the four Geneva Conventions of 1949,[38] attacks directed against civilian objects or civilians protected as such, or other war crimes as defined by international agreements to which it is a party.[39]

As of August 2025, the ATT has 116 parties, including most of the Western nations except the United States. The ATT's parties from Asia are Afghanistan, China, Japan, Kazakhstan, Lebanon, Maldives, the Philippines, the Republic of Korea and the State of Palestine. However, the United States, Russia, Ukraine, Belarus, Syria, India, Indonesia, Israel, Bangladesh, Cambodia, Myanmar, Pakistan, Türkiye, Iran, Iraq, North Korea, Qatar, Saudi Arabia, Singapore, Thailand, Timor-Leste, the UAE and Yemen are among those states that are not parties to the ATT.

Even states that are not parties to the ATT may participate in the United Nations Register of Conventional Arms (UNROCA), set up in 1991, which has

---

[38] That is, wilful killing, torture, or inhuman treatment of persons protected by these Geneva Conventions, including biological experiments and wilfully causing great suffering or serious injury to their body or health.

[39] On the question of whether arms transfers by neutral states to Ukraine after the Russia–Ukraine war started in Feb. 2022 may be justified as collective countermeasures in response to Russia's use of force, see Pearce Clancy, "Neutral Arms Transfer and the Russian Invasion of Ukraine", *International & Comparative Law Quarterly* 72 (2023): 527. See also Alexander Wentker, "The Armed Attack Exception to Neutrality in International Peace and Security Law", *International & Comparative Law Quarterly* 73 (2024): 963.

received reports from more than 170 states on official transfers of conventional arms. Its purpose is preventive diplomacy, by ensuring transparency in armaments and building confidence among countries against excessive or destabilising accumulations of arms as well as encouraging restraint in the transfer or production of arms. UNROCA covers the seven categories of arms that are deemed the most offensive, namely battle tanks, armoured combat vehicles, large-calibre artillery systems, combat aircraft and unmanned combat aerial vehicles, attack helicopters, warships, and missiles and missile launchers. Recently, countries decided that small arms and light weapons (such as machine guns, assault rifles and hand-held underbarrel and mounted grenade launchers) could be added to UNROCA. Most countries that report on their imports or exports now include small arms and light weapons in their yearly reports.

In March 2021, the EU set up the European Peace Facility (EPF) to enable the EU to provide all types of equipment and infrastructure to the armed forces of EU partners, in compliance with international human rights law and IHL. The EPF includes measures to ensure an adequate risk assessment and mitigating measures in compliance with international human rights law, IHL and EU arms export laws; monitor the respect of international laws and commitment by the beneficiary at country level and headquarters; and invite local civil society to report on violations of human rights and IHL. Assistance under the EPF can be suspended or terminated any time by the European Council in case of infringement and/or abuse by the beneficiary.

Apart from state responsibility arising from aiding and abetting wrongful acts in another state, states engaged in fighting civil wars in that other state through their "proxies" can incur state responsibility for this act.

According to Article 8 of ARSIWA, the conduct of a person or group of persons shall be considered an act of a state under international law if the person or group of persons is in fact acting on the instructions or under the direction or control of that state in carrying out the conduct. Article 8 derives from the ICJ's judgment in *Nicaragua*, where the ICJ had to determine whether the relationship between the Contras fighting the Nicaraguan government and the US government was such that it would be right to equate the Contras, for legal purposes, with an organ of the US government, or as acting on behalf of that government. The ICJ found the evidence at its disposal insufficient to demonstrate the total dependence of the Contras on United States aid. A partial dependency may be inferred from the fact that the Contra leaders were selected by the United States, and from other factors such as the organisation, training and equipping of the force, planning of operations, the choosing of targets and the operational support provided. There is no clear evidence that the United

States actually exercised such a degree of control as to justify treating the Contras as acting on its behalf. Therefore, concluded the ICJ, the Contras remained responsible for their acts, in particular the alleged violations by them of humanitarian law. For the United States to be legally responsible, it would have to be proved that the United States had "effective control" of the operations in the course of which the alleged violations were committed.[40]

In *Armed Activities on the Territory of the Congo (DR Congo v. Uganda)*, DR Congo accused Uganda of creating and controlling the Movement for the Liberation of the Congo (MLC), a rebel movement led by Jean-Pierre Bemba that operated in DR Congo and fought the country's government. Although Uganda acknowledged giving training and military support and there was evidence to that effect, the ICJ did not receive probative evidence that Uganda controlled, or could control, the manner in which Bemba put such assistance to use, or that the MLC's conduct was "on the instructions of, or under the direction or control of" Uganda in accordance with Article 8 of ARSIWA. The ICJ thus ruled that no issue arose in the case as to whether the requisite tests were met for sufficiency of control of paramilitaries as enunciated by the ICJ in *Nicaragua*. The ICJ added, however, that, even if the evidence did not suggest that the MLC's conduct was attributable to Uganda, the training and military support given by Uganda to the military wing of the MLC violated certain obligations of international law. The ICJ cited the 1970 Declaration on Friendly Relations, which provides, inter alia, that "[e]very State has the duty to refrain from organizing, instigating, assisting or participating in acts of civil strife or terrorist acts in another State or acquiescing in organized activities within its territory directed towards the commission of such acts, when the acts referred to in the present paragraph involve a threat or use of force" and that "no State shall organize, assist, foment, finance, incite or tolerate subversive, terrorist or armed activities directed towards the violent overthrow of the regime of another State, or interfere in civil strife in another State". The ICJ considered these provisions to be declaratory of customary international law[41] and ruled that the obligations arising under the principles of non-use of force and non-intervention had been violated by Uganda even if the objectives of Uganda had not been to overthrow DR Congo's President Kabila, and were directed at securing towns and airports for reason of its perceived security needs, and in support of the parallel activity of those engaged in civil war raging in DC Congo. The ICJ cited its judgment in *Nicaragua* to the effect that the principle of non-intervention

[40] *Nicaragua*, ICJ Rep. 1986, pp. 64–5 [115].
[41] ICJ Rep. 2005, p. 168, at pp. 226–7 [160].

prohibits a state from "interven[ing], directly or indirectly, with or without armed force, in support of an internal opposition in another State", and that acts that breach the principle of non-intervention "will also, if they directly or indirectly involve the use of force, constitute a breach of the principle of non-use of force in international relations". The unlawful military intervention by Uganda was of such a magnitude and duration that the ICJ considered it to be a grave violation of the prohibition on the use of force under Article 2(4) of the UN Charter.[42]

Recent developments have affirmed the "common interest" and consequential legal standing of any state party to the Convention against Torture and the Genocide Convention to sue another state party in the ICJ to stop a breach by the latter of these conventions. The obligations owed by each state party to every one of the other states parties are called "obligations *erga omnes partes*" in the sense that each state party has an interest in compliance with them in any given case.[43] It is to be seen whether obligations *erga omnes partes* also exist in other human rights treaties, the Geneva Conventions of 1949 and its AP I and AP II, the UN Charter (in particular Article 2(4)) and the ATT, such that any state party to any one of these international agreements may sue another state party thereto to stop an armed conflict and/or serious violations of IHL and/or international human rights law as well as hold the wrongful states responsible for their conduct.

Individual Criminal Responsibility

Individuals involved in launching a war of aggression, serious violations of international human rights law, IHL and/or international criminal law may be brought to face justice in an internationally constituted court or a domestic criminal court that has jurisdiction over the crime in question.

International criminal courts may be those set up on an ad hoc basis, or "hybrid" in nature with international elements added to local criminal justice or permanent ones.

Individual criminal responsibility for violations of these laws in the modern era can be traced back to the precedents right after the Second World

[42] Ibid., p. 227 [163]–[5].

[43] *Questions relating to the Obligation to Prosecute or Extradite (Belgium v. Senegal)*, ICJ Rep. 2012 (II), p. 422 at p. 449 [68]; *Application of the Convention on the Prevention and Punishment of the Crime of Genocide (The Gambia v. Myanmar)*, Preliminary Objections, ICJ Rep. 2022, p. 477 at pp. 515–16 [107]–[9].

War, in which German and Japanese leaders involved in invading and annexing other countries were prosecuted before and duly punished by the International Military Tribunal at Nuremberg and the International Military Tribunal for the Far East, respectively.

Article 6(a) of the Nuremberg Charter of 8 August 1945[44] stipulates that the tribunal shall have jurisdiction over crimes against peace, namely "planning, preparation, initiation or waging a war of aggression, or a war in violation of international treaties, agreements or assurances, or participation in a common plan or conspiracy for the accomplishment of any of the foregoing".[45] This was duplicated in Article 5(a) of the Charter of the International Military Tribunal for the Far East of 19 January 1946.[46]

After Iraq's President Saddam Hussein was captured by American forces on 13 December 2003, the Iraqi Special Tribunal was set up by the Coalition Provisional Authority, a transitional government of Iraq set up by the US-led multinational force after the collapse of Saddam Hussein's regime. The Iraqi Special Tribunal had jurisdiction over any Iraqi national or resident of Iraq accused of the crime of genocide, crimes against humanity and war crimes committed since 17 July 1968 and up until and including 1 May 2003, in Iraq's territory or elsewhere, "including crimes committed in connection with Iraq's wars against the Islamic Republic of Iran and the State of Kuwait". It also had jurisdiction over crimes committed against the people of Iraq (including its Arabs, Kurds, Turcomans, Assyrians and other ethnic groups, and its Shiites and Sunnis), whether or not committed in armed conflict.

On 1 July 2004, Hussein made his first appearance in court at his arraignment and was charged with, inter alia, the invasion of Kuwait and the gassing of the Kurds, to which he pleaded not guilty. On 5 November 2006, Hussein was sentenced to death by hanging for crimes against humanity with regard to events that took place after a failed assassination attempt against him in Dujail in 1982 by members of the Islamic Dawa Party, in retaliation of which 150 residents of Dujail were summarily executed. His sentence was upheld on

---

[44] 251 *United Nations Treaty Series* 280.

[45] See also Roger S. Clark, "Nuremberg and the Crime against Peace", *Washington University Global Studies Law Review* 6 (2007): 527. The results of the Nuremberg Tribunal's judgment are summarised in Page Wilson, *Aggression, Crime and International Security* (Abingdon: Routledge, 2009), p. 120.

[46] Neil Boister and Robert Cryer, eds. *Documents on the Tokyo International Military Tribunal: Charter, Indictments, and Judgments* (Oxford: Oxford University Press, 2008). The results of the Tokyo Tribunal's judgment are summarised in Wilson, *Aggression, Crime and International Security*, pp. 121–3.

26 December 2006 by an appellate chamber of the Iraqi High Tribunal. Hussein was executed by hanging on 30 December of that year before his trial for the invasion of Kuwait even started. The Dujail case was tried first because it was the most straightforward and easiest to prove case.[47]

Trials before ad hoc criminal tribunals have been accused of dispensing "victors' justice". This is why the establishment of a permanent international criminal court is preferred.

The International Criminal Court (ICC) set up by the 1998 Rome Statute of the ICC has jurisdiction over genocide, crimes against humanity and war crimes committed by state actors as well as non-state actors, such as insurgents and members of liberation movements provided that the state where the crime is committed or the state of nationality of the defendant is party to the Rome Statute or has accepted the ICC's jurisdiction on an ad hoc basis, or the UNSC has referred the situation to the ICC prosecutor for prosecution.

The Review Conference of the 1998 Rome Statute of the ICC adopted, on 11 June 2010, the amendments to include the crime of aggression within the ICC's jurisdiction for states parties to the Rome Statute that have accepted these amendments.

By virtue of Article 8 *bis*, for the purpose of the statute, "crime of aggression" means "the planning, preparation, initiation or execution, by a person in a position effectively to exercise control over or to direct the political or military action of a State, of an act of aggression which, by its character, gravity and scale, constitutes a manifest violation of the Charter of the United Nations". "Act of aggression" means the use of armed force by a state against the sovereignty, territorial integrity or political independence of another state, or in any other manner inconsistent with the UN Charter. Any of the following acts, regardless of a declaration of war, shall, in accordance with UNGA Resolution 3314 (XXIX) of 14 December 1974 on the Definition of Aggression, qualify as an act of aggression:

(a) The invasion or attack by the armed forces of a State of the territory of another State, or any military occupation, however temporary, resulting

[47] For criticisms of the Iraqi Special Tribunal and its trials, see M. Cherif Bassiouni and Michael Wahid Hanna, "Ceding the High Ground: The Iraqi High Criminal Court Statute and the Trial of Saddam Hussein", *Case Western Reserve Journal of International Law* 39 (2007): 21.

from such invasion or attack, or any annexation by the use of force of the territory of another State or part thereof;

(b) Bombardment by the armed forces of a State against the territory of another State or the use of any weapons by a State against the territory of another State;

(c) The blockade of the ports or coasts of a State by the armed forces of another State;

(d) An attack by the armed forces of a State on the land, sea or air forces, or marine and air fleets of another State;

(e) The use of armed forces of one State which are within the territory of another State with the agreement of the receiving State, in contravention of the conditions provided for in the agreement or any extension of their presence in such territory beyond the termination of the agreement;

(f) The action of a State in allowing its territory, which it has placed at the disposal of another State, to be used by that other State for perpetrating an act of aggression against a third State;

(g) The sending by or on behalf of a State of armed bands, groups, irregulars or mercenaries, which carry out acts of armed force against another State of such gravity as to amount to the acts listed above, or its substantial involvement therein.

Pursuant to Article 15 *bis* and Article 15 *ter*, the ICC shall have automatic jurisdiction over the crime of aggression committed within the territory of a state party *and* by a national of a state party, unless any of the states involved have previously declared that it does not accept the ICC's jurisdiction by lodging a declaration with the ICC registrar. The ICC shall also have jurisdiction over the crime of aggression when a situation is referred to the ICC prosecutor by the UNSC, irrespective of the location or the criminal conduct and nationality of the alleged perpetrator.[48] At the time of writing, there are 49 parties to these amendments. Mongolia, Samoa, the State of Palestine and Timor-Leste are the only ones from Asia.

There are also "hybrid" tribunals, with international involvement in the domestic criminal justice system as in the case of the East Timor Tribunal

[48] See further, Dapo Akande and Antonios Tzanakopoulos, "Treaty Law and ICC Jurisdiction over the Crime of Aggression", *European Journal of International Law* 29 (2018): 939.

discussed in Chapter 5. A variation of the "hybrid" model is the one concerning Kosovo.[49]

As an alternative to the ICC and to ensure that there be no impunity for the violent armed liberation movement for Kosovo's independence, Kosovo, which is not party to the Rome Statute, set up the Kosovo Specialist Chambers (KSC) in 2015 after pressure from the EU and Western nations led by the United States with the main goals of bringing the Kosovo Liberation Army (KLA) to justice for the KLA's campaign of armed violence against Serbs, Serb sympathisers and others deemed political opponents; strengthening the rule of law; and promoting reconciliation within Kosovo. The KSC has jurisdiction over crimes under both international and domestic Kosovar law, including crimes against humanity and war crimes recognised under international law, as well as select crimes recognised under Kosovar law either commenced or committed in Kosovo between 1 January 1998 and 31 December 2000. Both the KSC and its prosecutorial unit, the Specialist Prosecutor's Office, are based in The Hague, the Netherlands, staffed exclusively with international judges, counsel and staff, and financed primarily by the EU, with no financial implications for Kosovo. The KSC operates completely independently from Kosovo's domestic courts. This is to minimise local Kosovar involvement so that there will be no threat of political interference and witness tampering.

On 16 December 2022, the KSC rendered its first judgment, convicting and sentencing Salih Mustafa, a former KLA commander, to 26 years in prison for committing murder, torture, and arbitrary detention of at least six fellow ethnic Albanians accused of spying for Serb forces. In April 2023, the KSC commenced its trial of Hashim Thaçi, a Kosovar Albanian politician who was the president of Kosovo from April 2016 until his resignation on 5 November 2020 to be prosecuted by the KSC. During the period covered by the indictment, Thaçi was the KLA's head of the Political and Information Directorates and subsequently prime minister of the Provisional Government of Kosovo and KLA commander-in-chief. He is accused of committing the war crimes, in the context of a non-international armed conflict in Kosovo, of illegal or arbitrary arrest and detention, cruel treatment, torture and murder, and crimes against humanity, as part of a widespread and systematic attack against persons suspected of being opposed to the KLA, of imprisonment, other inhumane acts, torture, murder, enforced disappearance of persons, and persecution from at least March 1998 through September 1999 in several locations across

---

[49] Sara L. Ochs and Kirbi Walters, "Forced Justice: The Kosovo Specialist Chambers", *Duke Journal of Comparative & International Law* 32 (2022): 239.

Kosovo, as well as in Kukës and Cahan in Northern Albania, against hundreds of civilians and persons not taking part in hostilities. The victims included persons suspected of being opposed to the KLA and later the Provisional Government of Kosovo, namely: (1) the Serbian, Roma and Ashkali populations; (2) Catholics; (3) civilians allegedly collaborating with Serb authorities or allegedly interacting with Serbs; (4) Albanians affiliated with or supporting the Democratic League of Kosovo or other parties perceived as anti-KLA; (5) Albanians who did not join or support the KLA; and (6) individuals with current or former employment perceived as anti-KLA.

These various international criminal tribunal models have been subjected to ongoing debates by those supporting Ukraine against Russia's "special military operation" against Ukraine staring from 24 February 2022.[50] On 24 June 2025, the Council of Europe's Committee of Ministers decided to work on the establishment of the Special Tribunal for the Crime of Aggression against Ukraine, to be financed by a group of supportive states, with jurisdiction complementary to the ICC and focusing on senior political and military leaders responsible for planning, preparing, initiating, or executing "the crime of aggression against Ukraine". However, at the time of writing, some European states that support the idea of the Special Tribunal are still engaged in sensitive diplomatic discussions and weighing how to balance their legal commitments, political alliances and broader foreign policy goals.

---

[50] Ingrid (Wuerth) Brunk and Monika Hakimi, "Russia, Ukraine, and the Future World Order", *American Journal of International Law* 116 (2022): 687; Committee of Ministers' Deputies of the Council of Europe's Decision DD(2022)330-rev2 of 15 Sept. 2022; Parliamentary Assembly of the Council of Europe's Resolution 2482 (2023) of 26 Jan. 2023; Oona A. Hathaway, "The Case for Creating an International Tribunal to Prosecute the Crime of Aggression against Ukraine (Part I)", *Just Security*, 20 Sept. 2022, https://www.justsecurity.org/83117/the-case-for-creating-an-international-tribunal-to-prosecute-the-crime-of-aggression-against-ukraine/; Ukraine Task Force of The Global Accountability Network, Proposal for a Resolution by the United Nations General Assembly and Accompanying Proposal for a Statute of a Special Chamber for Ukraine on the Crime of Aggression, 7 Sept. 2022, https://2022.uba.ua/wp-content/uploads/2022/09/uktf_unproposal_specialtribunal_resolutionandstatute_7sep2022.pdf. See also Patryk I. Labuda, "Countering Imperialism in International Law: Examining the Special Tribunal for Aggression against Ukraine through a Post-Colonial Eastern European Lens", 49 *Yale Journal of International Law* (2024): 271; Kevin Jon Holler, "Creating a Special Tribunal for Aggression against Ukraine Is a Bad Idea", *Opinio Juris*, 3 July 2022, https://opiniojuris.org/2022/03/07/creating-a-special-tribunal-for-aggression-against-ukraine-is-a-bad-idea/; Carrie McDougall, "The Imperative of Prosecuting Crimes of Aggression Committed against Ukraine", 28 *Journal of Conflict & Security Law* (2023): 203.

Besides international criminal courts or tribunals, domestic criminal courts of some states can exercise "universal jurisdiction" over serious crimes of international concern (such as genocide, crimes against humanity, war crimes and torture), even though the crimes were not committed in the territory of the forum state where the prosecution is undertaken, even though neither the offender nor the victim is a national of that state, and even though the crime does not adversely affect the state's national interests.[51]

For example, in November 2018, Human Rights Watch, a human rights NGO, filed a complaint before an Argentine federal court to seek prosecution of Saudi Arabia's Crown Prince Mohammed bin Salman, who was scheduled to come to Buenos Aires to attend a two-day G20 summit. He was accused of, inter alia, war crimes of causing mass civilian casualties as a result of the Saudi-led coalition's military campaign in Yemen since March 2015. The Argentine government's position was that the crown prince would be protected by diplomatic immunity, that he was also travelling in his official status as representative of a foreign head of state, and that cases involving diplomatic immunity could only be decided by the Argentine Supreme Court and his visit would be too brief for the complaint to reach the Supreme Court. Indeed, although the federal court had accepted Human Rights Watch's complaint, and a prosecutor had asked a judge to determine if either Saudi Arabia or Yemen was investigating the crown prince for the alleged crimes before an Argentine court might exercise universal jurisdiction, the Saudi crown prince left Argentina after the G20 summit before the proceedings could reach the Argentine Supreme Court for a ruling on whether he was covered by diplomatic immunity.

In November 2018, six Yemeni victims and the International Alliance for Defending Rights and Freedom lodged a complaint in France against Mohammed Ben Zayed, president of the UAE, former crown prince and senior army official, for his alleged complicity in crimes of torture and war crimes perpetrated in Yemen. The complaint has been dismissed due to his head of state immunity.

Syrians accused of perpetrating atrocities in the Syrian civil war since 2011 have been prosecuted in several countries that exercise universal jurisdiction over crimes of international concern. Here are some examples.

In August 2016 a Swedish Court of Appeal sentenced Mohannad Droubi, a member of the Free Syrian Army fighting the forces loyal to the Assad regime, to eight years' imprisonment for crimes against international law (war crimes) in Syria. Haisam Omar Sakhanh, a former member of a Syrian armed group

---

[51] See further, Kriangsak Kittichaisaree, *The Obligation to Extradite or Prosecute* (Oxford: Oxford University Press, 2018), ch. 5.

fighting the Syrian government, has been sentenced by a Swedish court to life imprisonment for his participation in the summary execution "under particularly cruel circumstances" of seven injured Syrian soldiers in Syria in 2012, one year before he was granted a refugee status in Sweden. Mohamad Abdullah, a Syrian soldier who posed with dead and severely injured bodies and posted photographs thereof on social media, has been convicted of war crimes by Sweden's Södertörn District Court.

On 24 February 2021, the High Regional Court in Koblenz, Germany, sentenced Eyad al-Gharib, a former sergeant major in Syria's General Intelligence Directorate (GID), to four and a half years' imprisonment for aiding and abetting crimes against humanity of serious deprivation of physical liberty in violation of a general rule of international law, by accompanying the transportation of 30 detained demonstrators to the notorious Al-Khatib prison in Damascus in 2011 despite his knowing about the systematic torture in that prison. Al-Gharib was given a relatively lenient sentence owing to his low rank in the command hierarchy and for providing information that ultimately led to the indictment and conviction of Anwar Raslan, a former Syrian brigadier general who was in charge of the GID's Al-Khatib prison. Both al-Gharib and Raslan fled Syria's civil war and were granted asylum in Germany before their arrest in Berlin in February 2019 and were put on trial in April 2020. On 13 January 2022, Raslan was convicted by the High Regional Court in Koblenz of 4,000 cases of torture and severe deprivation of liberty, 27 murders and three cases of sexual violence as crimes against humanity. He was also found guilty of 27 murders, 25 cases of dangerous bodily harm, two sexual assaults and 14 cases of severe deprivation of liberty, two cases of hostage taking, and three cases of sexual abuse, one of which constitutes a particularly dangerous rape. Raslan was sentenced to life imprisonment. In February 2023, 55-year-old Moafak D., a Syrian Palestinian arrested after entering Germany as a refugee in 2021, was sentenced by a court in Berlin to life imprisonment for the murder of four persons as well as two counts of attempted murder and grievous bodily harm by firing a grenade into a crowd of people in Damascus in March 2014 to avenge the killing of his nephew two days earlier by the rebel Free Syrian Army.

On 2 March 2021, three NGOs—the Paris-based Syrian Centre for Media and Freedom of Expression, the Open Society Foundation's Justice Initiative and the Syrian Archive—filed a criminal complaint in France against certain Syrian officials on behalf of a group of survivors of the coordinated sarin gas attacks the Damascus suburb of Ghouta in August 2013 and in Douma in April 2018. On 15 November 2023, French magistrates issued international arrest warrants for Syria's then President Al-Assad, his brother Maher and military generals

Ghassan Abbas and Bassam al-Hassan for complicity in crimes against humanity and complicity in war crimes over the use of banned chemical weapons against civilians in Syria. Maher al-Assad headed an elite Syrian military unit, while the two military generals worked with a Syrian research agency accused of developing chemical weapons. In July 2025, the French highest court (the Court of Cassation) annulled the arrest warrant against President Al-Assad on the ground that he had personal immunity as head of state at the time of the issuance of the arrest warrant, but the court added that its decision did allow for a new arrest warrant to be issued now Al-Assad was no longer a head of state.

Officials in the Assad regime are not the only Syrians subject to the reach of universal jurisdiction in France. In February 2020, Majdi Mustafa Ne'ma (aka Islam Alloush), the spokesperson and a senior official of Jaysh al-Islam (or "Army of Islam"), with more than 20,000 fighters, which carried out a reign of terror in the rebel areas in Syria it controlled until April 2018, was arrested and indicted by the War Crimes Unit of the Paris Tribunal for war crimes, torture, enforced disappearance and complicity in these crimes. On 4 April 2022, the Paris Court of Appeal ruled that the defendant could be indicted for torture or inhumane acts, enforced disappearance, war crimes and participation in a criminal enterprise for these purposes, committed between mid-2013 and the end of 2016.

On 12 May 2023, in two cases concerning alleged atrocities in Syria, the full bench of the French Court of Cassation clarified the conditions under which the French justice system may exercise universal jurisdiction over a foreign national for crimes committed abroad against foreign victims, provided that they habitually reside on French territory. That person may be prosecuted and tried by the French courts if that person is suspected of having committed one of the following offences abroad: the crime of genocide defined in the French Criminal code; other crimes against humanity defined in the Criminal Code, if the facts are criminalised by the legislation of the state where they were committed or if that state or the state of nationality of the suspect is a party to the 1998 Rome Statute of the ICC; war crimes and offences defined in the Criminal Code, if the acts are punishable under the law of the state where they were committed or if that state or the state of nationality of the suspect is a party to the Rome Statute. In order for France to be considered the foreign national's habitual residence, there must be a sufficient connection between France and that person. The judge must assess this connection on the basis of a set of indicators: the duration of the individual's presence in the country, but also the reasons for their stay, the conditions under which it took place, the manifestations of an intention to reside for an extended period in France, and the existence of family, social, material or professional ties. Regarding the requirement of double criminality in France and the state where the crime is committed, it is not necessary that the acts covered in France by the offences of crimes against humanity or war crimes be qualified exactly in the same way by the laws of the foreign state—it suffices that the foreign legislation punishes these acts as common offences such as murder, rape or torture rather than specifically as crimes against humanity or war crimes. For the offence of torture, which requires the torturer to be a public official or a person acting in an official capacity, the concept of a person "acting in an official capacity" also includes a person acting for or on behalf of a non-governmental entity, in the situation where that entity occupies territory and exercises a quasi-governmental authority over the territory.[52]

In the Netherlands, on 16 July 2021, the Hague District Court found Ahmad Al-Khedr criminally involved in the execution of a captured Syrian military officer, a war crime, and sentenced him to 20 years' imprisonment.[53]

F. Hassan, a Syrian who had been a commander of a small Islamic State unit in Syria entrusted with terrorising and executing civilians and religious leaders who refused to side with the group and who was subsequently granted a refugee status in Greece, was arrested at Budapest airport in December 2018 after presenting forged travel documents for himself and a female travel partner. In December 2020, a Hungarian court sentenced him to life imprisonment for terrorism and crimes against humanity including personally taking part in the beheading of an imam in the town of al-Sukhnah and in the murder of another civilian in the area in May 2015. Authorities in Malta, Greece and Belgium as well as in Hungary participated in the investigation coordinated by Eurojust, the Hague-based EU agency dealing with judicial cooperation in criminal matters among agencies of the EU member states, and witnesses in Belgium, Malta and Hungary came to give testimony against him.

Non-Syrians involved somehow in the atrocities in Syria can also be brought to justice. In January 2024, the District Court of The Hague convicted Mustafa A., who had been living in the Netherlands since 2020 and had applied for asylum prior to his arrest in 2022, of war crimes and crimes against humanity for complicity in torture, inhumane treatment and illegal arrest and for membership of a criminal organisation. The court sentenced him to 12 years' imprisonment. As a leading member of the Liwa al-Quds or (the Jerusalem

[52] Appeal No. 22-80.057 and Appeal No. 22-82.468.

[53] See also Lachezar Yanev, "Syrian War Crimes Trials in the Netherlands: Claiming Universal Jurisdiction over Terrorist Offences and the War Crime of Outrages upon Personal Dignity of the Dead", *Netherlands Yearbook of International Law* 52 (2021): 301.

Brigade), an armed group comprising mostly Palestinian refugees living in Syria and founded during the early years of Syria's civil war, he was involved in the arrest of a man in 2012 in Syria whom he subsequently handed over to Syrian Air Force intelligence officials who ran a prison where the man was tortured. This is one way to bring anyone responsible for the mayhem in Syria to face justice and deter conduct contributing to the humanitarian catastrophe in Syria.[54]

Individual criminal responsibility may be incurred by any person providing arms with the knowledge that they will be used for the commission of violations of human rights and IHL in Syria and the person can be punished by a competent court with jurisdiction over the crimes and the person.[55]

[54] See also Beth van Schaack, *Imagining Justice for Syria* (New York: Oxford University Press, 2020).

[55] See also Sarah Lupi, "Is the Time Right to Make 'Provision of Weapons' an International Crime?", *Cambridge International Law Journal* 11 (2022): 75.

Epilogue

Peace is elusive because it requires resource-building and the possibility of seeing a future based on diplomatic efforts leading to concrete results. The exigencies of war prevent the fostering of these efforts. However, several challenges to peace are mounting. Peace is getting harder to obtain in the global context as individual conflicts have global ramifications. The specifics of the Asian perspectives on war and peace have to be accounted for to develop a deeper understanding of these issues. As the book demonstrates, while law regarding the use of force is well established, there are grey areas that are used by powerful nations at the expense of their Asian counterparts. This asymmetry hurts the peace process.

Nevertheless, there is an ever-greater need for efforts towards peace. Nuclear weapons present a threat that has the possibility of irreversible damage. The 2017 Treaty on the Prohibition of Nuclear Weapons endeavours to alleviate this heinous threat. However, states in possession of nuclear weapons are not parties to it and all of the P5 of the United Nations Security Council (UNSC) are nuclear powers. The grey area identified by the International Court of Justice (ICJ) in its Advisory Opinion on *Legality of the Threat or Use of Nuclear Weapons* in 1996 is also to blame. It may be recalled, once again, that the ICJ cannot conclude definitively whether the threat or use of nuclear weapons would be lawful or unlawful in an extreme circumstance of self-defence, in which the very survival of a state would be at stake. The world is thus left in a perilous state to balance international law and politics to ensure its own survival.

The inability of the UN to intervene meaningfully in conflicts because of the use of the veto by the P5 of the UNSC erodes trust in the United Nations. The alignment of China closer to Iran and Saudi Arabia and other initiatives like the membership expansion of BRICS, China's Global Security Initiative and the closer relationship between China and the Gulf Cooperation Council are considered by those opposed to China's predominant roles on the world stage to have further divided China and its geopolitical rivals.

In spite of this dark picture, reconciliation and post-conflict justice efforts have had many successes. History shows several models for this. This includes the Nuremberg Charter of 1945 setting up the International Military Tribunal in Nuremberg to try those Nazi leaders accused of crimes against peace and other international crimes; Saddam Hussein's conviction by a tribunal for his crimes; the case of Kosovo's tribunal as an alternative to the International Criminal Court; and the war reparations awarded by the ICJ in *Armed Activities in the Territory of the Congo (DR Congo v. Uganda)* and those awarded by the Eritrea–Ethiopia Claims Commission. In this light, the peace efforts by the UN secretary-general to build a new agenda for peace in 2021, including the Peace Building Fund and the Peacebuilding Commission, offer a new opening. Nonetheless, Asian states are still wary as regards international criminal justice insofar as such justice is "discriminatory"; for example, those nations and their leadership waging the Gulf War under false pretexts and fabricated evidence have not been brought to account before any international court or tribunal.

This book shows how international law interacts with international politics in the context of war and peace in Asia. International politics invokes international law to justify the former's goal. For its part, international law cannot fully regulate and end a conflict without the political will of the parties concerned to attain lasting peace.

Each nation has "doves" and "hawks" who are entrusted with national security issues. Doves prefer peace to war, whereas hawks, paradoxically, consider the use of force to be the surest guarantee to maintain national security and permanent peace. In general, diplomats are trained to be doves and soldiers are educated to be hawks. National leaders and policymakers need to mediate between the positions favoured by doves and hawks in light of the costs and benefits expected from the acts or omissions proposed by these two opposite camps.

Nations need to eliminate thinking of others as *either* friends *or* foes. Armed conflict can start over misunderstandings and/or attempts to appease the nationalist sentiment of citizens of the nations. While states must bear the consequences of breaking peace, from an international lawyer's perspective this has to be achieved through international law, although the international political context in which the law operates is also of significance. Ideally, also from an international lawyer's perspective, all nations and peoples must be subject to rules of international law, and without any discriminatory justice or double standards, if the world is to be free of wars and full of peace.

Bibliography

Akande, Dapo and Antonios Tzanakopoulos. "Treaty Law and ICC Jurisdiction over the Crime of Aggression." *European Journal of International Law* 29, no. 3 (2018): 939–59.

———. "Legal: Use of Force in Self-Defence to Recover Occupied Territory." *European Journal of International Law* 32, no. 4 (2021): 1299–1307.

Albritton, Robert B. "The Muslim South in the Context of the Thai Nation." *Journal of East Asian Studies (Seoul)* 10, no. 1 (2010): 61–90.

Ali, Zainub R. "Assessing the Effectiveness of Leadership Decapitation as a U.S. Counterterrorism Strategy: The Case of Iranian General Qassem Soleimani's Death by Drone Strike." *West Point Journal of Politics & Security* 1 (2021): 10–23.

Altamimi, Abdulmalik. "An Appraisal of the Gulf Cooperation Council's Mechanisms for Co-operation and the Settlement of Disputes." *Asian Journal of International Law* 10, no. 2 (2020): 321–45.

Amer, Ramses and Nguyen Hong Thao. "Vietnam's Border Disputes: Legal and Conflict Management Dimensions." *Asian Yearbook of International Law* 12 (2007): 111–27.

Ananthavinayagan, Thamil Venthan. "Breaking Bad Customs: Involving the Idea of *Opinio Juris Communis* in Asian State Practice." *Asian Yearbook of International Law* 24 (2018): 24–40.

Andrews, Thomas H. "Statement by Thomas H. Andrews, UN Special Rapporteur on the Situation of Human Rights in Myanmar." OHCHR, 22 Dec. 2022. https://www.ohchr.org/en/press-releases/2022/12/myanmar-action-needed-stop-carnage-says-un-expert-after-adoption-security.

Anghie, Antony. *Imperialism, Sovereignty and the Making of International Law.* Cambridge: Cambridge University Press, 2005.

———. "Rethinking International Law: A TWAIL Retrospective." *European Journal of International Law* 34 (2023): 7–112.

Anghie, Antony and B.S. Chimni. "Third World Approaches to International Law and Individual Responsibility in Internal Conflicts." *Chinese Journal of International Law* 2 (2003): 77–103.

Anich, Gabriel. "A New Life for Uniting for Peace?" *Revista Tribuna Internacional* 12, no. 23 (2023): 43–61.

Ardemagni, Eleonora. "Yemen's Post-Hybrid Balance: The New Presidential Council." Carnegie Endowment for International Peace, 9 June 2022. https://carnegieendowment.org/sada/87301.

Arms Control Association. "Nuclear Weapons: Who Has What at a Glance." https://www.armscontrol.org/factsheets/nuclear-weapons-who-has-what-glance.

Asia Foundation. *The State of Conflict and Violence in Asia 2021: Identity-Based Conflict and Extremism*. San Francisco: Asia Foundation, 2021.

Azaria, Danae. *State Silence as Acceptance: A Presumption and an Exception*. University College London Faculty of Laws: Research Paper Series No. 15/2023, 2023.

Balkaran, Raj and A. Walter Dorn. "Charting Hinduism's Rules of Armed Conflicts: Indian Sacred Texts and International Humanitarian Law." *International Review of the Red Cross* 104, no. 920–921 (Nov. 2022): 1762–97.

Barelli, Mauro. "Preventing and Responding to Atrocity Crimes: China, Sovereignty and the Responsibility to Protect." *Journal of Conflict & Security Law* 23 (2018): 173–201.

Bartels, Rogier. "The Classification of Armed Conflicts by International Criminal Courts and Tribunals." *International Criminal Law Review* 20, no. 4 (2020): 595–668.

Bassiouni, M. Cherif and Michael Wahid Hanna. "Ceding the High Ground: The Iraqi High Criminal Court Statute and the Trial of Saddam Hussein." *Case Western Reserve Journal of International Law* 39 (2007): 21–97.

Beckman, Robert and Tara Davenport. "South China Sea Dispute: Whitsun Reef—Awash in a Sea of (Legal) Uncertainty." *Straits Times*, 13 Apr. 2021.https://cil.nus.edu.sg/publication/whitsun-reef-awash-in-a-sea-of-legal-uncertainty-robert-beckman-and-tara-davenport-for-the-straits-times/.

Bellamy, Alex J. *Syria Betrayed: Atrocities, War, and the Failure of International Diplomacy*. New York: Columbia University Press, 2022.

Bergen, Peter and A.G. Sims. "America's Drone Wars Outside of Conventional War Zones." In *Routledge Handbook of U.S. Counterterrorism and Irregular Warfare Operations*, ed. Michael A. Sheehan, Erich Marquardt and Liam Collins, pp. 460–76. Abingdon: Routledge, 2022.

Bhat, P.I. "Peaceful Resolution of International Disputes: Drawing Lessons from the Indian Experiences." *Indian Journal of International Law* 59 (2021): 1–42.

Birkett, Daley J. "The Legality of the 2011 Kenyan Invasion of Somalia and Its Implications for the *Jus ad Bellum*." *Journal of Conflict and Security Law* 18, no. 3 (2013): 427–51.

Blank, Laurie. *International Conflict and Security Law*. Cheltenham: Edward Elgar Publishing, 2023.

Boisson de Charzournes, Laurence and Philippe Sands, eds. *International Law, the International Court of Justice and Nuclear Weapons*. Cambridge: Cambridge University Press, 1999.

Boister, Neil and Robert Cryer, eds. *Documents on the Tokyo International Military Tribunal: Charter, Indictments, and Judgments*. Oxford: Oxford University Press, 2008.

Boutin, Bérénice. "State Responsibility in Relation to Military Applications of Artificial Intelligence." *Leiden Journal of International Law* 36, no. 1 (2023): 133–50.

Boutros-Ghali, Boutros. *The United Nations and the Independence of Eritrea*. New York: United Nations, 1996.

———. "The Five Principles." *Chinese Journal of International Law* 3, no. 2 (2004): 373–8.

Brassat, Leonie. "The Lawfulness of Military Strikes against the Houthis in Yemen and the Red Sea." *EJIL Talk!*, 19 Mar. 2024. https://www.ejiltalk.org/the-lawfulness-of-military-strikes-against-the-houthis-in-yemen-and-the-red-sea/.

Britton, Peter. "Indonesia's Neo-Colonial Armed Forces." *Critical Asian Studies* 7 (1975): 14–21.

Brunk, Ingrid and Monica Hakimi. "The Prohibition of Annexations and the Foundations of Modern International Law." *American Journal of International Law* 118, no. 3 (2024): 417–67.

Brunk, Ingrid (Wuerth) and Monica Hakimi. "Russia, Ukraine, and the Future World Order." *American Journal of International Law* 116, no. 4 (2022): 687–97.

Burgess, Patrick. "De Facto Amnesty? The Example of Post-Soeharto Indonesia." In *Amnesty in the Age of Human Rights Accountability*, ed. Francesca Lessa and Leigh Payne, pp. 263–90. Cambridge: Cambridge University Press, 2012.

Burra, Srinivas. "Use of Force and Self-Defence against Non-state Actors and TWAIL Considerations: A Critical Analysis of India's State Practice." *Asian Yearbook of International Law* 24 (2018): 106–27.

Butchard, Patrick M. and Jasmin Johurun Nessa. "Digest of State Practice: 1 January–30 June 2021." *Journal on the Use of Force & International Law* 8 (2021): 343–98.

———. "Digest of State Practice: 1 July–31 Dec. 2021." *Journal on the Use of Force & International Law* 9 (2022): 171–228.

Buys, Elinor and Andrew Garwood-Gowers. "The (Ir)relevance of Human Suffering: Humanitarian Intervention and Saudi Arabia's Operation Decisive Storm in Yemen." *Journal of Conflicts & Security Law* 25 (2019): 1–33.

Byers, Michael. "Still Agreeing to Disagree: International Security and Constructive Ambiguity." *Journal on the Use of Force & International Law* 8 (2021): 91–114.

Byrne, Max. "Consent and the Use of Force: An Examination of 'Intervention by Invitation' as a Basis for US Drone Strikes in Pakistan, Somalia and Yemen." *Journal on the Use of Force & International Law* 3 (2016): 97–125.

Carswell, Andrew J. "Unblocking the UN Security Council: The Uniting for Peace Resolution." *Journal of Conflict & Security Law* 18 (2013): 453–80.

Castellino, Joshua. "The Secession of Bangladesh in International Law: Setting New Standards?" *Asian Yearbook of International Law* 7 (2000): 83–104.

Chalk, Peter. "The History of Terrorism in Southeast Asia." In *Routledge Handbook of U.S. Counterterrorism and Irregular Warfare Operations*, ed. Michael A. Sheehan, Erich Marquardt and Liam Collins, pp. 117–33. Abingdon: Routledge, 2022.

Chang, Yen-Chiang, Sirong Xin and Xu (John) Zhang. "A Proposal for Joint Marine Scientific Research Activities in the Disputed Maritime Areas of the South China Sea." *Coastal Management* 50, no. 3 (2022): 215–36.

Chau, Thompson and John Liu. "China Rolls Dice with Myanmar's Military, Sidelines Democratic NUG." Nikkei Asia, 16 Feb. 2022. https://asia.nikkei.com/Spotlight/Myanmar-Crisis/China-rolls-dice-with-Myanmar-s-military-sidelines-democratic-NUG.

Cheng, Bin. "Pre-emptive or Similar Type of Self-Defense in the Territory of Foreign States." *Chinese Journal of International Law* 12 (2013): 1–8.

Chesterman, Simon. *Just War or Just Peace? Humanitarian Intervention and International Law*. Oxford: Oxford University Press, 2001.

———. "Responsibility to Protect and Humanitarian Intervention: From Apology to Utopia and Back Again." In *The Oxford Handbook of the International Law of Global Security*, ed. Robin Geiß and Nils Melzer, pp. 808–20. Oxford: Oxford University Press, 2021.

Chimni, B.S. "Customary International Law: A Third World Perspective." *American Society of International Law* 112 (2018): 1–46.

Chinese Society of International Law. "The South China Sea Arbitration Awards: A Critical Study." *Chinese Journal of International Law* 17 (2018): 207–748.

Clancy, Pearce. "Neutral Arms Transfer and the Russian Invasion of Ukraine." *International and Comparative Law Quarterly* 72, no. 2 (2023): 527–43.

Clapham, Andrew. *War*. Oxford: Oxford University Press, 2021.

Clark, Roger S. "Nuremberg and the Crime against Peace." *Washington University Global Studies Law Review* 6 (2007): 527–550.

Cleary, Thomas. *The Japanese Art of War: Understanding the Culture of Strategy*. Boulder, CO: Shambhala Classics, 2005.

Cohen, David. "Seeking Justice on the Cheap: Is the East Timor Tribunal Really a Model for the Future?" *Analysis from the East-West Center* 61 (Aug. 2002): 1–8.

Cohen, Gal. "Mixing Oil and Water? The Interaction between *Jus ad Bellum* and *Jus in Bello* during Armed Conflicts." *Journal on the Use of Force & International Law* 9, no. 2 (2022): 352–90.

Conlan, Thomas. "The Nature of Warfare in Fourteenth Century Japan: The Record of Nomoto Tomoyuki." *Journal of Japanese Studies* 25 (1999): 299–330.

Convention for the Amelioration of the Condition of the Wounded and Sick in Armed Forces in the Field, 75 *United Nations Treaty Series* 31. Entered into force 21 Oct. 1950.

Convention for the Amelioration of the Condition of the Wounded, Sick and Shipwrecked Members of Armed Forces at Sea, 75 *United Nations Treaty Series* 85. Entered into force 21 Oct. 1950.

Convention for the Prevention and Punishment of the Crime of Genocide, 78 *United Nations Treaty Series* 277. Entered into force 12 Jan. 1951.

Convention Relative to the Protection of Civilian Persons in Time of War, 75 *United Nations Treaty Series* 287. Entered into force 21 Oct. 1950.

Convention Relative to the Treatment of Prisoners of War, 75 *United Nations Treaty Series* 135. Entered into force 21 Oct. 1950.

Cooper, Katrina. "Law and Diplomacy in the Compulsory Conciliation between Australia and Timor-Leste." In *Research Handbook on Law and Diplomacy*, ed. Margaret E. McGuiness and David P. Stewart, pp. 41–60. Cheltenham: Edward Elgar Publishing, 2022.

Corten, Olivier and Vaios Koutroulis. "The 2022 Russian Intervention in Ukraine: What Is the Impact on the Interpretation of *Jus contra Bellum*." *Leiden Journal of International Law* 36 (2023): 997–1022.

Cox, Brian. "United Nations Security Council Reform: Collected Proposals and Possible Consequences." *South Carolina Journal of International Law & Business* 6 (2009): 89–128.

Crocombe, Ron. *Asia in the Pacific Islands: Replacing the West.* Suva: IPS Publications, University of South Pacific, 2007.

Dascalopoulou-Livada, Phani. *Contemporary Issues in International Law.* The Hague: Eleven International Publishing, 2019.

Davenport, Tara. "Southeast Asian Approaches to Maritime Boundaries." *Asian Journal of International Law* 4 (2014): 309–357.

Davenport, Tara, Hao Duy Phan and Robert Beckman, eds. *The Timor-Leste/Australia Conciliation: A Victory for UNCLOS and Peaceful Settlement of Disputes.* Singapore: World Scientific, 2019.

Decision on the Prosecution's Request for a Ruling on Jurisdiction under Article 19(3) of the Statute, Case ICC-RoC46(3)-01/18, 6 Sept. 2018

Decision Pursuant to Article 15 of the Rome Statute on the Authorization of an Investigation into the Situation in the People's Republic of Bangladesh/Republic of the Union of Myanmar, No ICC-0-1/19, 14 Nov. 2019.

DeRosa, Mary B. "Lawyering and the Use of Force in Libya and Syria Operations." In *Research Handbook on Law and Diplomacy*, ed. Margaret E. McGuiness and David P. Stewart, pp. 74–81. Cheltenham: Edward Elgar Publishing, 2022.

Desierto, Diane A. "Enforcement Options and Paths to Compliance: Disputants and Global Stakeholders in *Philippines v. China*." *Asian Journal of International Law* 8 (2018): 64–75.

De Wet, Erika. "The (Im)permissibility of Military Assistance on Request during a Civil War." *Journal on the Use of Force & International Law* 7, no. 1 (2020): 26–34.

———. *Military Assistance on Request and the Use of Force*. Oxford: Oxford University Press, 2020.

Dinstein, Yoram and Arne Willy Dahl. *Oslo Manual on Select Topics of the Law of Armed Conflict: Rules and Commentary*. Cham: Springer, 2020.

Doherty, Ben and Kate Lamb. "West Papuan Independence Petition Is Rebuffed at UN." *The Guardian*, 30 Sept. 2017. https://www.theguardian.com/world/2017/sep/30/west-papua-independence-petition-is-rebuffed-at-un.

Dolzikova, Darya and Matthew Savill. "Why Iran May Accelerate Its Nuclear Program and Israel May Be Tempted to Attack It." *Bulletin of the Atomic Scientists*, 26 Apr. 2024. https://thebulletin.org/2024 /04 /why-iran-may-accelerate-its-nuclear-program-and-israel-may-be-tempted-to-attack-it/.

Drummond, Brian. "UK Nuclear Deterrence Policy: An Unlawful Threat of Force." *Journal on the Use of Force & International Law* 6, no. 2 (2019): 193–241.

Ebrahim, Nadeem. "Houthis Try to Assure Skeptics They Won't Seek Full Control of Yemen, as Saudis Eye Exit." CNN, 14 Apr. 2023. https://edition.cnn.com/2023/04/14/middleeast/yemen-saudi-houthi-interview-mime-intl/index.html.

Eritrea–Ethiopia Claims Commission—Final Award—Eritrea's Damages Claims, 17 Aug. 2009. R.I.A.A., vol. xxvi, pp. 505–630.

Eumsin, Payan. "Problems in International Relations from the Perspective of Thai Military Leaders Who Negotiated the Ban Romklao-Botaen Ceasefire Agreement of 1988." *Journal of Social Sciences* 51 (2021): 75–98.

Evans, Malcolm D. and Reese Lewis. *Islands, Law and Context: The Treatment of Islands in International Law*. Cheltenham: Edward Elgar Publishing, 2023.

Fairbank, John King, ed. *The Chinese World Order: Traditional China's Foreign Relations*. Cambridge, MA: Harvard University Press, 1968.

Farrar, Salim. "The Organisation of Islamic Cooperation: Forever on the Periphery of Public International Law." *Chinese Journal of International Law* 13 (2014): 787–817.

Fidler, David P. "Revolt against or from within the West—TWAIL, the Developing World, and the Future Direction of International Law." *Chinese Journal of International Law* 2 (2003): 29–76

Fleck, Dieter, ed. *The Handbook of International Humanitarian Law*. 3rd ed. Oxford: Oxford University Press, 2013.

Fraihat, Ibrahim. *Iran and Saudi Arabia: Taming a Chaotic Conflict*. Edinburgh: Edinburgh University Press, 2020.

Franchini, Daniel. "Extraterritorial Sanctions in Response to Global Security Challenges: Countermeasures as Gap-Fillers in the United Nations Collective Security System." *Cambridge International Law Journal* 12, no. 1 (2023): 129–48.

Gaggioli, Gloria, ed. *The Use of Force in Armed Conflicts: Interplay between the Conduct of Hostilities and Law Enforcement Paradigms*. Geneva: ICRC, 2013.

Ganor, Ben. "Defining Terrorism: Is One Man's Terrorist Another Man's Freedom Fighter?" *Media Asia* 29, no. 3 (2002): 123–33.

Garwood-Gowers, Andrew. "China and the Responsibility to Protect: The Implications of the Libyan Intervention." *Asian Journal of International Law* 2 (2012): 375–93.

Gates, Robert M. *Duty: Memoirs of a Secretary at War.* New York: Vintage Books, 2014.

Geiß, Robin and Nils Melzer, eds. *The Oxford Handbook of the International Law of Global Security.* Oxford: Oxford University Press, 2021.

General Assembly Human Rights Council. *Report of the Human Rights Council on its thirty-ninth session.* A/HRC/39/43, 23 Nov. 2018. https://www.ohchr.orgen/HRBodies/HRC/RegularSessions/Session39/Documents/A_HRC_39_2_EN.doc.

Gill, Terry D. and Kinga Tibori-Szabó. *The Use of Force and the International Legal System.* Cambridge: Cambridge University Press, 2023.

Ginsburg, Tom. "Eastphalia as the Perfection of Westphalia." *Indiana Journal of Global Legal Studies* 17, no. 1 (2010): 27–45.

Global Centre for Responsibility to Protect. "Libya." 2 Apr. 2022 https://www.globalr2p.org/countries/libya/.

———. "Atrocity Alert Number 325." 9 Nov. 2022.

———. *Summary of the 2023 UN General Assembly Plenary Meeting on the Responsibility to Protect.* 14 July 2023.

Goldthorpe, Chloe. "The Armed Attack Requirement and Customary International Law: Whose Views Count?" *Journal on the Use of Force & International Law* 10, no. 1 (2023): 49–73.

General Act of the Conference of Berlin concerning the Congo. Chapter VI, *American Journal of International Law Supplement* 1 (1909): 7–25

Great Britain, Prime Minister's Office. "Syria Action: UK Government Legal Position." 14 Apr. 2018. https://www.gov.uk/government/publications/syria-action-uk-government-legal-position/syria-action-uk-government-legal-position.

Green, James A. *Collective Self-Defence in International Law.* Cambridge: Cambridge University Press, 2024.

Haddah, Mohammed. "Infographic: Yemen's War Explained in Maps and Charts." Al Jazeera, 9 Feb. 2022 https://www.aljazeera.com/news/2022/2/9/yemens-war-explained-in-maps-and-charts-interactive.

Halevy, Nir and Yair Berson. "Thinking about the Distant Future Promotes the Prospects of Peace: A Construal-Level Perspective on Intergroup Conflict Resolution." *Journal of Conflict Resolution* 66, no. 6 (2022): 1119–43.

Hamilton, Tomas. *The Arms Trade and International Criminal Law: Reframing Accountability for Complicit Weapon Suppliers.* Oxford: Oxford University Press, 2025.

Hathaway, Oona A. "The Case for Creating an International Tribunal to Prosecute the Crime of Aggression against Ukraine (Part I)." *Just Security*, 20 Sept. 2022. https://www.justsecurity.org/83117/the-case-for-creating-an-internationaltribunal-to-prosecute-the-crime-of-aggression-against-ukraine/

———. "How the Erosion of U.S. War Powers Constraints Has Undermined International Law Constraints on the Use of Force." *Harvard National Security Journal* 14 (2023): 336–66.

Hathaway, Oona A. and Azmat Khan. "'Mistakes' in War." *University of Pennsylvania Law Review* 173 (2024): 1–88.

Hathaway, Oona A., Maggie M. Mills and Thomas M. Poston. "War Reparations: The Case for Countermeasures." *Stanford Law Review* 76 (2024): 971–1050.

Hathaway, Oona A., Maggie M. Mills and Heather Zimmerman. "Crisis and Change at the United Nations: Non-amendment Reform and Institutional Evolution." *Michigan Journal of International Law* 46 (2025): 1–67.

Hayton, Bill. "Claim-Making in the Paracel Islands 1802–1936." In *Peaceful Management of Maritime Disputes*, ed. James Kraska and Heecheol Yang, pp. 175–96. Abingdon: Routledge, 2023.

Heaton, William R. "China and the Southeast Asian Communist Movements: The Decline of Dual Track Diplomacy." *Asian Survey* 22, no. 8 (1982): 779–800.

Hegde, Venkatachala G. "India and International Settlement of Disputes." *Indian Journal of International Law* 56 (2016): 1–40.

Henderson, Christian. "The 25 February 2021 Military Strikes and the 'Armed Attack' Requirement of Self-Defence: From '*sina qua non*' to the Point of Vanishing?" *Journal on the Use of Force & International Law* 9 (2022): 55–77.

———. "A Reply to Brassat: The Lawfulness of Military Strikes against the Houthis in Yemen and the 'Fourth Problem' of Necessity and Proportionality." *EJIL Talk!*, 1 Apr. 2024. https://www.ejiltalk.org/a-reply-to-brassat-the-military-strikes-against-the-houthis-in-yemen-and-the-fourth-problem-of-necessity-and-proportionality/.

Henderson, Stacey. *Atrocity Crimes and International Law: Responsibility to Protect, Intercession, and Non-forceful Responses*. Abingdon: Routledge, 2022.

Hilpold, Peter. "Intervening in the Name of Humanity: R2P and the Power of Ideas." *Journal of Conflict and Security Law* 17, no. 1 (2012): 49–79.

Holler, Kevin Jon. "Creating a Special Tribunal for Aggression Against Ukraine Is a Bad Idea." *Opinio Juris*, 7 Mar. 2022. https://opiniojuris.org/2022/03/07/creating-a-special-tribunal-for-aggression-against-ukraine-is-a-bad-idea/.

Hornung, Josie. "Terrorism and Pillar Two Protection Assistance: The Yazidis on Mount Sinjar." *Global Responsibility to Protect* 14, no. 2 (2022): 232–56.

"Houthis Targeted 193 Ships Linked to Tel Aviv, US, UK in the past year." *Middle East Monitor*, 7 Oct. 2024. https://www.middleeastmonitor.com/20241007-houthis-targeted-193-ships-linked-to-tel-aviv-us-uk-in-the-past-year/.

Hsu, Aye Shan. "Myanmar Ethnic Armed Groups' Advances against Junta: State-by-State Breakdown." *Irrawaddy*, 14 May 2024. https://www.irrawaddy.com/opinion/analysis/myanmar-ethnic-armed-groups-advances-against-junta-state-by-state-breakdown.html.

Hu, Henan. "The Doctrine of Occupation: An Analysis of Its Invalidity under the Framework of International Legal Positivism." *Chinese Journal of International Law* 15 (2016): 75–138.

Ikeshima, Taisaku. "China's Dashed Line in the South China Sea: Legal Limits and Future Prospects." *Waseda Global Forum* 10 (2013): 17–50.

"India and China Troops Clash on Arunachal Pradesh Mountain Border." BBC, 13 Dec. 2022. https://www.bbc.com/news/world-asia-63953400.

Institute for Economics & Peace. *Global Peace Index 2024: Measuring Peace in a Complex World*. Sydney: IEP, 2024.

International Committee of the Red Cross. *International Humanitarian Law and the Challenges of Contemporary Armed Conflicts*. Geneva: ICRC, 2015.

———. *Arms Transfer to Parties to Armed Conflict: What the Law Says*. Geneva: ICRC, 2024.

———. *How Is the Term "Armed Conflict" Defined in International Humanitarian Law?* Geneva: ICRC Opinion Paper, 2024.

International Law Association. "Final Report on the Meaning of Armed Conflict in International Law." In *Report of the Seventy-Fourth Conference*, pp. 805–48. The Hague: ILA, 2010.

———. *Final Report on Aggression and the Use of Force*. 2018.

———. Resolution 3/2018 of the Committee on Recognition and Non-recognition in International Law. 78th Conference of the International Law Association, Sydney, Australia, 19–24 Aug. 2018.

Island of Palmas Case (Netherlands v. USA), Award of 4 Apr. 1928, 2 R.I.A.A. 829.

Jain, Vanshaj Ravi. "Broken Boundaries: Border and Identity Formation in Post-colonial Punjab." *Asian Journal of International Law* 10 (2020): 261–92.

Japan Ministry of Defense. *National Security, National Defense Strategy, and Defense Buildup Program (Outline)*. Dec. 2023. https://www.mod.go.jp/en/d_act/d_policy/pdf/english.pdf.

Jayakumar, S. and Tommy Koh. *Pedra Branca: The Road to the World Court*. Singapore: NUS Press, 2009.

Jitpiromsri, Srisompop, Paul Chambers and Napisa Waitoolkiat. "Special Issue: Quagmire of Violence in Thailand's Southern Borderlands Chapter 1: Introduction." *Asian Affairs: An American Review* 45, no. 2 (2018): 43–55.

Jöbstl, Hannes and Dean Rosenberg. "The Humanization of War Reparations: Combatant Deaths and Compensation in Unlawful Wars." *Michigan Journal of International Law* 45, no. 45.1 (2024): 39–91.

Johnsen, Gregory D. "The UAE's Three Strategic Interests in Yemen." Arab Gulf States Institute in Washington, 24 Feb. 2022.

Jones, Sidney. "Identity Conflicts in Southeast Asia: An Overview." In *The State of Conflict and Violence in Asia 2021: Identity-Based Conflict and Extremism*, ed. Asia Foundation, pp. 31–8. San Francisco: Asia Foundation, 2022.

Journal of Boundaries & Ocean Studies–Selected Papers. 1, no. 1 (Spring 2019).

Judah, Tim. *Kosovo: What Everyone Needs to Know*. New York: Oxford University Press, 2008.

Kampmann, Christoph. "The Treaty of Westphalia as Peace Settlement and Political Concept." In *International Law and Peace Settlement*, ed. Marc Weller, Mark Retter and Andrea Varga, pp. 64–85. Cambridge: Cambridge University Press, 2022.

Kanehara, Atsuko. "Double Aspects of Being a Sovereign State: Positive and Passive Aspects." https://cigs.canon/en/article/20240611_8159.html.

Kardon, Isaac B. *China's Law of the Sea: The New Rules of Maritime Order*. New Haven, CT: Yale University Press, 2023.

Karoubi, Mohammad Taghi. "Unilateral Use of Armed Forces and the Challenge of Humanitarian Intervention in International Law." *Asian Yearbook of International Law* 10 (2005): 95–124.

Kattan, Victor. "The Ghosts of the Temple of Preah Vihear/Phra Viharn in the 2013 Judgment." *Asian Journal of International Law* 5, no. 1 (2015): 16–25.

Katzenstein, Suzanne. "Hybrid Tribunals: Searching for Justice in East Timor." *Harvard Human Rights Journal* 16 (2003): 245–78.

Kaye, Stuart. "Conciliation in International Dispute Resolution: An Evaluation of the Timor Sea Dispute." In *Peaceful Management of Maritime Disputes*, ed. James Kraska and Heecheol Yang, pp. 156–72. Abingdon: Routledge, 2023.

Keesing's Contemporary Archives 34 (Nov. 1988): 26292.

Keesing's Record of World Events 8 (Mar. 1962): 18659.

Kendall, Elizabeth. "Jihadi Militancy and Houthi Insurgency in Yemen." In *Routledge Handbook of U.S. Counterterrorism and Irregular Warfare Operations*, ed. Michael A. Sheehan, Erich Marquardt and Liam Collins, pp. 83–94. Abingdon: Routledge, 2022.

Kent, Lia. "Interrogating the 'Gap' between Law and Justice: East Timor's Serious Crime Process." *Human Rights Quarterly* 34, no. 4 (2012): 1021–44.

Kiel, Hannah. *Arms Transfer to Non-state Actors: The Erosion of Norms in International Law*. Cheltenham: Edward Elgar Publishing, 2024.

Kilibarda, Pavle. *Recognition of States under International Law*. Oxford: Oxford University Press, 2024.

Kittichaisaree, Kriangsak. *Public International Law of Cyberspace*. Cham: Springer, 2017.

———. *International Human Rights Law and Diplomacy*. Cheltenham: Edward Elgar Publishing, 2020.

———. "International Humanitarian Law and the Asia-Pacific Struggles for National Liberation." In *Asia-Pacific Perspectives on International Humanitarian Law*, ed. Suzannah Linton, Tim McCormack and Sandesh Sivakumaran, pp. 139–55. Cambridge: Cambridge University Press, 2020.

———. *The Obligation to Extradite or Prosecute*. Oxford: Oxford University Press, 2018.

———. *The Rohingya, Justice and International Law*. Abingdon: Routledge, 2021.

Kleffner, Jann K. "Scope of Application of International Humanitarian Law." In *The Handbook of International Humanitarian Law*, 3rd ed., ed. Dieter Fleck, pp. 43–78. Oxford: Oxford University Press, 2013.

———. "The Legal Fog of an Illusion: Three Reflections on 'Organization' and 'Intensity' as Criteria for the Temporal Scope of the Law of Non-international Armed Conflict." *International Law Studies* 95 (2019): 161–78.

Kluge, Emma. "A New Agenda for the Global South: West Papua, the United Nations, and the Politics of Decolonization." *Humanity* 13, no. 1 (June 2022): 66–85.

Koh, Tommy. *Building a New Legal Order for the Oceans*. Singapore: NUS Press, 2020.

KontraS and International Center for Transitional Justice. *Derailed: Transitional Justice in Indonesia since the Fall of Soeharto*. 2011.

Kotova, Anastasiya and Ntina Tzouvala. "In Defense of Comparisons: Russia and the Transmutations of Imperialism in International Law." *American Journal of International Law* 116 (2022): 710–19.

Kraska, James and Heecheol Yang, eds. *Peaceful Management of Maritime Disputes*. Abingdon: Routledge, 2023.

Kress, Claus. "Some Reflections on the International Legal Framework Governing Transnational Armed Conflicts." *Journal of Conflict & Security Law* 15 (2010): 245–74.

Ku, Charlotte. "The Archipelagic States Concept and Regional Stability in Southeast Asia." *Case Western Reserve Journal of International Law* 23 (1991): 463–78.

Labuda, Patryk I. "Countering Imperialism in International Law: Examining the Special Tribunal for Aggression against Ukraine through a Post-colonial Eastern European Lens." *Yale Journal of International Law* 49, no. 2 (2024): 271–310.

Lackner, Helen. *Yemen in Crisis: Autocracy, Neo-Liberalism and the Disintegration of a State*. London: Saqi Books, 2017.

Lam, Sze Hong. "The Gentle Civilizer of the Far East—A Re-examination of the Encounter between 'China' and 'International Law'." *Journal of the History of International Law* 26 (2024): 1–45.

Landauer, Carl. "C.H. Alexandrowicz's India and the Kautilyan Moment." *Asian Journal of International Law* 14 (2024): 235.

Lasserre, Frédéric. "Maritime Borders in the South China Sea: Dynamics of Claims and Legal Basis." In *Assessing Maritime Disputes in East Asia: Political and Legal Perspectives*, ed. Barthélémy Courmont and Frédéric Lasserre, pp. 122–40. Abingdon: Routledge, 2017.

Lebow, Richard Ned. *Avoiding War, Making Peace*. Cham: Palgrave Macmillan, 2018.

Lee, Hee Eun and Seokwoo Lee. "Positivism in International Law: State Sovereignty, Self-Determination, and Alternative Perspectives." *Asian Yearbook of International Law* 16 (2010): 1–24.

Lee, Jaemin. *Artificial Intelligence and International Law*. Singapore: Springer, 2022.

Lemos, Miguel. "*Jus Cogens* Versus the Chapter VII Powers of the Security Council: With Particular References to Humanitarian Intervention and Terrorism." *Chinese Journal of International Law* 19, no. 1 (2020): 1–52.

Lessa, Francesca and Leigh Payne, eds. *Amnesty in the Age of Human Rights Accountability*. Cambridge: Cambridge University Press, 2012.

Lewis, Dustin A., Naz K. Modirzadeh and Gabriella Blum. "Quantum of Silence: Inaction and *Jus ad Bellum*." In *Annex HLS PILAC Catalogue of Communications to the Security Council of Measures Taken by United Nations Member States in Purported Exercise of the Right of Self-Defense: October 24, 1945 through December 31, 2018*. Cambridge, MA: Harvard Law School, 2019.

Li, Jianwei and Pingping Chen. "Joint Development in the South China Sea: Is the Time Ripe?" *Asian Yearbook of International Law* 22 (2016): 131–58.

Li, Lingqun. *China's Policy towards the South China Sea: When Geopolitics Meets the Law of the Sea*. Abingdon: Routledge, 2019.

Lieblich, Eliav. "Wars of Recovery." *European Journal of International Law* 34 (2023): 349–81.

Linton, Suzannah. "International Humanitarian Law in Indonesia." In *Asia-Pacific Perspectives on International Humanitarian Law*, ed. Suzannah Linton, Tim McCormack and Sandesh Sivakumaran, pp. 506–37. Cambridge: Cambridge University Press, 2020.

———. "International Humanitarian Law in Occupied East Timor: Displacement, Relocation and Famine." In *Asia-Pacific Perspectives on International Humanitarian Law*, ed. Suzannah Linton, Tim McCormack and Sandesh Sivakumaran, pp. 400–22. Cambridge: Cambridge University Press, 2020.

Linton, Suzannah, Tim McCormack and Sandesh Sivakumaran, eds. *Asia-Pacific Perspectives on International Humanitarian Law*. Cambridge: Cambridge University Press, 2020.

Liow, Joseph Chinyong. *Religion and Nationalism in Southeast Asia*. Cambridge: Cambridge University Press, 2016.

Lopes, Gutemberg P., Jr. "The Sino-Brazilian Principles in a Latin American and BRICS Context: The Case for Comparative Public Budgeting Legal Research." *Wisconsin International Law Journal* 33 (2015): 1–45.

Lott, Alexander. *Hybrid Threats and the Law of the Sea: Use of Force and Discriminatory Navigational Restrictions in Straits*. Leiden: Brill, 2022.

Lubell, Noam and Michael Wood. "The ILA's 2018 Report on Aggression and the Use of Force." *Journal on the Use of Force & International Law* 6, no. 1 (2019): 4–11.

Lupi, Sarah. "Is the Time Right to Make 'Provision of Weapons' an International Crime?" *Cambridge International Law Journal* 11 (2022): 75–95.

Lush, Emma. "The View through a Different Lens: Increasing Respect for International Humanitarian Law through the Use of International Human Rights Law

Framework." *Journal of International Humanitarian Legal Studies* 14, no. 1 (2023): 95–129.

Ma Jianying, *The United States Involvement in the South China Sea Disputes*. New York: Peter Lang Publishing, 2022.

"Malaysian PM Urges Diplomatic Engagement, Rejects External Interference on South China Sea." *Xinhua*, 7 June 2024. https://www.chinadaily.comcn/a/202406/07/WS6663083aa31082fc043cb88a.html.

Malik, Brigadier General S.K. *The Quranic Concept of War*. New Delhi: Himalayan Books, 1986.

Man, Wan Kadir bin Che. *Muslim Separatism: The Moros in Southern Philippines and the Malays in Southern Thailand*. PhD thesis, Australian National University, 1987.

Mani, V.S. "An Indian Perspective on the Evolution of International Law on the Threshold of the Third Millennium." *Asian Yearbook of International Law* 9 (2004): 31–77.

Martin, Craig. "What Was the International Legal Basis for the Strike on al-Zawahiri?" *Just Security*, 9 Aug. 2022. https://www.justsecurity.org/82605/what-was-the-international-legal-basis-for-the-strike-on-al-zawahiri/.

Marxsen, Christian. "Violation and Confirmation of the Law: The Intricate Effects of the Invocation of the Law in Armed Conflict." *Journal on the Use of Force & International Law* 5, no. 1 (2018): 8–39.

Mauri, Diego. *Autonomous Weapons Systems and the Protection of the Human Person: An International Law Analysis*. Cheltenham: Edward Elgar Publishing, 2022.

McDougall, Carrie. "The Imperative of Prosecuting Crimes of Aggression Committed against Ukraine." *Journal of Conflict and Security Law* 28, no. 2 (2023): 203–30.

McFarland, Tim. "Minimum Levels of Human Intervention in Autonomous Attacks." *Journal of Conflict and Security Law* 27, no. 3 (2022): 387–409.

McGibbon, Sarah. "The 'Unwilling or Unable' Doctrine Unmasked: A Case Study of ISIL in Syria." *Hague Yearbook of International Law* 32 (2021): 69–102.

McWhinney, Edward. "The Renewed Vitality of the International Law Principles of Peaceful Coexistence in the Post-Iraq Invasion Era: The 50th Anniversary of the China/India Pancha Shila Agreement of 1954." *Chinese Journal of International Law* 3, no. 2 (2004): 379–84.

Mietzner, Marcus. "Indonesia: The Military's Transformation from Praetorian Ruler to Presidential Coalition Partner." In *The Oxford Encyclopedia of the Military in Politics*, ed. William R. Thompson and Hicham Bou Nassif, n.p. New York: Oxford University Press, 2020.

Milanovic, Marko. "Intelligence Sharing in Multinational Military Operations and Complicity under International Law." *International Law Studies* 97 (2021): 1269–403.

———. "Revisiting Coercion as an Element of Prohibited Intervention in International Law." *American Journal of International Law* 117, no. 4 (2023): 601–50.

Mohammad, Talal. *Iranian–Saudi Rivalry since 1979: In the Words of Kings and Clerics*. London: I.B. Tauris, 2023.

Mori, Tadashi. "Collective Self-Defence in International Law and in the New Japanese Legislation for Peace and Security (2015)." *Japanese Yearbook of International Law* 60 (2017): 158–70.

Moynihan, Harriet. *Aiding and Assisting: Challenges in Armed Conflict and Counterterrorism*. London: Chatham House, 2022.

Mrázek, Josef. "The International Court of Justice and Its Power of Judicial Review of the United Nations Security Council Resolutions." *Lawyer Quarterly* 12 (2022): 393–407.

Müllerson, Rein. "Self-Defence against Armed Attacks by Non-state Actors." *Chinese Journal of International Law* 18 (2019): 751–75.

Murphy, Sean D., Won Kidane and Thomas R. Snider. *Litigating War: Arbitration of Civil Injury by the Eritrea–Ethiopia Claims Commission*. New York: Oxford University Press, 2013.

Musgrave, Thomas D. "An Analysis of the 1969 Act of Free Choice in West Papua." In *Sovereignty, Statehood and State Responsibility*, ed. Christine Chinkin and Freya Baetens, pp. 209–28. Cambridge: Cambridge University Press, 2015.

Nanda, Ved. "Self-Determination in International Law: The Tragic Tale of Two Cities—Islamabad (West Pakistan) and Dacca (East Pakistan)." *American Journal of International Law* 66, no. 2 (1972): 321–36.

Nanlohy, Sascha. "R2P, Terrorism, and the Protection of Civilians—Are All Humans Human? Or Are Some More Human than Others?" *Global Responsibility to Protect* 14, no. 2 (2022): 178–203.

Nasu, Hitoshi. "Revisiting the Principle of Non-intervention: A Structural Principle of International Law or a Political Obstacle to Regional Security in Asia?" *Asian Journal of International Law* 3 (2013): 25–50.

Nasu, Hitoshi and Donald R. Rothwell. "Re-evaluating the Role of International Law in Territorial and Maritime Disputes in East Asia." *Asian Journal of International Law* 4 (2014): 55–79.

National Institute of South China Sea Studies. "A Legal Critique of the Award of the Arbitral Tribunal in the *Matter of the South China Sea Arbitration*." *Asian Yearbook of International Law* 24 (2018): 151–293.

Newman, Edward. "Exploring the UK's Doctrine of Humanitarian Intervention." *International Peacekeeping* 28 (2021): 632–60.

Nguyen, Quoc Tan Trung. "Rethinking the Legality of Intervention by Invitation: Toward Neutrality." *Journal of Conflict and Security Law* 24, no. 2 (2019): 201–38.

Nguyen Hong, Thao. "Indonesia-Vietnam Maritime Delimitation: From a Single-Line to Double-Line." In *Asia and UNCLOS 30 Years' Implementation: An Assessment*, ed. Nguyen Hong Thao and Vu Hai Dang, pp. 267–93. Singapore: Springer, 2024.

Nishimoto, Kentaro. "The Obligation of Self-Restraint in Undelimited Maritime Areas." *Japan Review* 3 (2019): 28–38.

Nobile, Philip, ed. *Judgment at the Smithsonian: The Bombing of Hiroshima and Nagasaki*. Boston, MA: Da Capo Press, 1995.

Nordquist, Myron H. "UNCLOS Article 121 and Itu Aba in the South China Sea Final Award: A Correct Interpretation?" In *The South China Sea Arbitration: The Legal Dimension*, ed. S. Jayakumar, Tommy Koh, Robert Beckman, Tara Davenport and Hao Duy Phan, pp. 176–204. Cheltenham: Edward Elgar Publishing, 2018.

Nußberger, Benjamin K. *Interstate Assistance to the Use of Force*. Baden-Baden: Nomos, 2023.

Nyunt, General Khin. *Myanmar's Difficulty with the Western Gate: What the "Rohingya" Issue Poses*. N.P., 2019.

O'Connell, Mary Ellen. "Twenty Years of Drone Attacks." *EJIL Talk!*, 15 Nov. 2022. https://www.ejiltalk.org/twenty-years-of-drone-attacks/.

O'Meara, Chris. "February 2021 American Airstrikes in Syria: Necessary and Proportionate Acts of Self-Defence or Unlawful Armed Reprisals?" *Journal on the Use of Force & International Law 9*, no. 1 (2022): 78–98.

———. "Reconceptualising the Right of Self-Defence against 'Imminent' Armed Attacks." *Journal on the Use of Force & International Law 9*, no. 2 (2022): 278–323.

Ochs, Sara L. and Kirbi Walters. "Forced Justice: The Kosovo Specialist Chambers." *Duke Journal of Comparative & International Law 32* (2022): 239–85.

Office of the Historian, US Department of State. "A Guide to the United States' History of Recognition, Diplomatic, and Consular Relations, by Country, since 1776: Kosovo." Washington, DC: Department of State.

Office of the Staff Judge Advocate (USA). "Archipelagic States." *International Law Studies* 97 (2021): 12–17.

Office of the UN High Commissioner for Human Rights. "Situation of Human Rights in Myanmar since 1 February 2021." A/HRC/49/72 (15 Mar. 2022).

———. "Report of the Independent International Commission of Inquiry on the Syrian Arab Republic." A/HRC/51/45 (17 Aug. 2022).

Okimoto, Keiichiro. "The Cumulative Requirements of *Jus ad Bellum* and *Jus in Bello* in the Context of Self-Defence." *Chinese Journal of International Law* 11 (2012): 45–75.

Ong, David M. "The International Legal Obligations of States in Disputed Maritime Jurisdiction Zones and Prospects for Co-operative Arrangements in the East China Sea Region." *Asian Yearbook of International Law* 22 (2016): 109–30.

———. "Discerning the International Legal Threshold for Sovereignty over Islands: Implications for Judicial Settlement of International Disputes." In *Peaceful Management of Maritime Disputes*, ed. James Kraska and Heecheol Yang, pp. 1–26. Abingdon: Routledge, 2023.

Osawa, Toshiro. "On Pursuing UN Security Council Reform." Association of Japanese Institutes of Strategic Studies (AJISS) Commentary, 11 Dec. 2023.

"Over 900 Pieces of Relics Retrieved from Shipwrecks in South China Sea." *Xinhua* 13 June 2024. https://english.news.cn/20240613/60116daccfb74c65a764ae5f500f20a9/c.html.

Owada, Hisashi. "The United Nations and the Maintenance of International Peace and Security—The Current Debate in the Light of Reform Proposals." *Japanese Annual of International Law* 48 (2005): 1–25.

"Pakistan Summons Afghan Diplomat over Border Shelling." *Al Jazeera*, 16 Dec. 2022. https://www.aljazeera.com/news/2022/12/16/pakistan-summons-afghan-diplomat-over-border-clashes

Pan, Junwu. "Chinese Philosophy and International Law." *Asian Journal of International Law* 1 (2011): 233–48.

Pandiaraj, S. "Sovereignty as Responsibility: Reflections on the Legal Status of the Doctrine of Responsibility to Protect." *Chinese Journal of International Law* 15 (2016): 795–815.

Pawakapan, Puangthong R. *State and Uncivil Society in Thailand at the Temple of Preah Vihear.* Singapore: ISEAS-Yusof Ishak Institute, 2013.

Peace Research Institute Oslo. *Conflict Trends: A Global Overview, 1946–2023.* Oslo: PRIO, 2024.

Pedrozo, Raul (Pete). "Is a South China Sea Code of Conduct Viable?" *International Law Studies* 97 (2021): 937–55.

———. "Vietnam's Indisputable Sovereignty over the Paracel Islands." In *Peaceful Management of Maritime Disputes*, ed. James Kraska and Heecheol Yang, pp. 193–213. Abingdon: Routledge, 2023.

Pemmaraju, Sreenivasa Rao. "Optimum World Order beyond War: A Long View on Current Challenges." *Cambridge International Law Journal* 11 (2022): 154–79.

Peng, Nian. "India's Involvement in the South China Sea Disputes." *The Diplomat*, 10 Nov. 2023. https://thediplomat.com/2023/11/indias-growing-involvement-in-the-south -china-sea-disputes/.

Phan, Hao Duy. "Institutional Design and Its Constraints: Explaining ASEAN's Role in the Temple of Preah Vihear Dispute." *Asian Journal of International Law* 5 (2015): 7–15.

Phonprapai, Salinee. *Battlefield to Marketplace: Responses to Thailand's Major Foreign Policy Change.* Bangkok: International Studies Center, 2021.

Piatkowski, Mateusz. "War in the Air from Spain to Yemen: The Challenges in Examining the Conduct of Air Bombardment." *Journal of Conflict and Security Law* 26, no. 3 (2021): 493–524.

Pitlo III, Lucio Blanco. "Duty to Cooperate and Practical Cooperation in the South China Sea." *China & US Focus*, 10 Aug. 2022. https://www.chinausfocus.com/peace-security/duty-to-cooperate-and-practical-cooperation-in-the-south-china-sea.

Pobjie, Erin. *Prohibited Force: The Meaning of "Use of Force" in International Law.* Cambridge: Cambridge University Press, 2024.

Poling, Gregory B. *On Dangerous Ground: America's Century in the South China Sea.* New York: Oxford University Press, 2022.

Pompeo, Mike. *Never Give an Inch: Fighting for the America I Love.* Northampton, MA: Broadside Books, 2023.

Prosecutor v. Dusko Tadic, Decision on the Defence Motion for Interlocutory Appeal on Jurisdiction, International Criminal Tribunal for the former Yugoslavia (ICTY) Appeals Chamber, Judgment of 2 Oct. 1995.

Prosecutor v. Ljube Boškoski and Johan Tarčulovski, Case No. IT-04-82-T, ICTY Trial Chamber II, Judgment of 10 July 2008.

Prosecutor v. Jean-Pierre Bemba Gombo, ICC-01/05-01/08, Pre-Trial Chamber II, Judgment of 15 June 2009.

Protocol Additional to the Geneva Conventions of 12 Aug. 1949, and relating to the Protection of Victims of International Armed Conflicts (Protocol I), opened for signature June 8, 1977, 1125 U.N.T.S. 3 (entered into force 7 Dec. 1978).

Public International Law & Policy Group and Resonate! Yemen, *Policy Planning White Paper: The Southern Question.* Washington, DC: Public International Law & Policy Group, Apr. 2022.

Rabasa, Angel and John Haseman. *The Military and Democracy in Indonesia.* Santa Monica, CA: Rand, 2002.

Radpey, Loqman. *Towards an Independent Kurdistan: Self-Determination in International Law.* Abingdon: Routledge, 2023.

Rao, P.S. "Non-state Actors and Self-Defence: A Relook at the UN Charter Article 51." *Indian Journal of International Law* 56 (2016): 127–71.

Rather, Shaiba. "Falling through the Cracks: Kashmir's Resistance against Settler Colonialism and the Limits of International Law." *Harvard International Law Journal Online* 63 (2022): 1–22.

Redaelli, Chiara. *Intervention in Civil Wars: Effectiveness, Legitimacy, and Human Rights.* Oxford: Hart, 2021.

Report of the Office of the UN High Commissioner for Human Rights. A/HRC/50/68 (28 June 2022).

Report of the Special Committee on the Charter of the United Nations and on the Strengthening of the Role of the Organization, A/76/33 (25 Feb. 2021).

Report of the UN Secretary-General, Our Common Agenda. New York: United Nations, 2021.

Report of the UN Secretary-General on Justice and Reconciliation for Timor-Leste. S/2006/580 (26 July 2006).

"Responsibility to Protect: The Lessons of Libya." *The Economist,* 19 May 2011. https://www.economist.com/international/2011/05/19/the-lessons-of-libya.

Richter, Dagmar. "Judicial Review of Security Council Decisions—A Modern Vision of the Administration of Justice?" *Polish Yearbook of International Law* 32 (2012): 21–97.

Robles, Alfredo C., Jr. *The Defaulting State and the South China Sea Arbitration.* Singapore: Palgrave Macmillan, 2023.

Roscini, Marco and Riccardo Labianco. "The Intersections between the Arms Trade Treaty and the International Law of Foreign Intervention in Situations of Internal Unrest." *Israel Yearbook of Human Rights* 52 (2022): 365–93.

Roscini, Marco and Marco Longobardo. "Demilitarised Zones." In *Research Handbook on International Arms Control Law*, ed. Eric Myjer and Thilo Marauhn, pp. 467–80. Cheltenham: Edward Elgar Publishing, 2022.

Rossi, Christopher. "Interstitial Space and the High Himalayan Dispute between China and India." *Harvard International Law Journal* 62 (2021): 429–86.

Ruys, Tom. "Of Arms, Funding and 'Non-lethal Assistance'—Issues Surrounding Third-State Intervention in the Syrian Civil War." *Chinese Journal of International Law* 13 (2014): 13–53.

Ruys, Tom and Felipe Rodríguez Silvestre. "Illegal: The Recourse to Force to Recover Occupied Territory and the Second Nagorno-Karabakh War." *European Journal of International Law* 32, no. 4 (2021): 1287–97.

Salamat, Patchrathanyarasm. "The Quranic Concept of Peace and Humanity." *Manusya: Journal of Humanities* 11 (2008): 1–27.

Salter, Michael and Yinan Yin. "Analysing Regionalism within International Law and Relations: The Shanghai Cooperation Organisation as a *Grossraum*." *Chinese Journal of International Law* 13 (2014): 819–77.

Santos, Soliman M., Jr. "Jihad and International Humanitarian Law: Three Moro Rebel Groups in the Philippines." In *Asia-Pacific Perspectives on International Humanitarian Law*, ed. Suzannah Linton, Tim McCormack and Sandesh Sivakumaran, pp. 374–99. Cambridge: Cambridge University Press, 2020.

Sarkin, Jeremy Julian and Ross Callum Capazorio. "The Syrian Conflict as a Test Case for the Limits of the International Community and International Law: Global Politics and State Sovereignty Versus Human Rights Protection." *Human Rights Quarterly* 44, no. 3 (2022): 476–513.

Schaller, Christian. "Using Force against Terrorists 'Outside' Areas of Active Hostilities–The Obama Approach and the Bin Laden Raid Revisited." *Journal of Conflict & Security Law* 20 (2015): 195–227.

Scharf, Michael P. "Power Shift: The Return of the Uniting for Peace Resolution." *Case Western Reserve Journal of International Law* 55 (2023): 217–50.

Scharf, Michael P., Milena Sterio and Paul Williams. *The Syrian Conflict's Impact on International Law*. Cambridge: Cambridge University Press, 2020.

Schmitt, Michael N., ed. *Tallinn Manual 2.0 on the International Law Applicable to Cyber Operations*. Cambridge: Cambridge University Press, 2017.

———. "Ukrainian Symposium: Classification of the Conflict(s)." Lieber Institute -West Point, 14 Dec. 2022. https://lieber.westpoint.edu/classification-of-the-conflicts/

Schmitt, Michael N. and W. Casey Biggerstaff. "Aid and Assistance as a 'Use of Force' under the *Jus ad Bellum*", 100 *International Law Studies* (2023): 186–228.

Schmitt, Michael N. and Christopher M. Ford. "Assessing U.S. Justifications for Using Force in Response to Syria's Chemical Attacks: An International Law Perspective." *Journal of National Security Law & Policy* 9 (2017): 283–303.

Schultheiss, Christian. *Ocean Governance and Conflict in the East and South China Sea: Negotiating Natural Resources, Institutions and Power.* Amsterdam: Amsterdam University Press, 2024.

Schwelb, Egon. "Amendments to Articles 23, 27 and 61 of the Charter of the United Nations." *American Journal of International Law* 59 (1965): 834–56.

Scott, James W., ed. *A Research Agenda for Border Studies.* Cheltenham: Edward Elgar Publishing, 2020.

Seo, Youngmin. "Power Shift, the South China Sea Dispute, and the Role of International Law." *Michigan Journal of International Law* 45 (2024): 93–152.

———. *The South China Sea Dispute as International Law and Politics: Discovering the Role of Law in Times of Power Shift.* Leiden: Brill, 2024.

Seow, Colin. "Chasing the Frontier in Humanitarian Intervention Law: The Case for *Aequitas ad Bellum.*" *Asian Journal of International Law* 6, no. 2 (2016): 294–325.

Shah, Sikander Ahmed. *International Law and Drone Strikes in Pakistan: The Legal and Socio-political Aspects.* London: Routledge, 2015.

Shanny, Yuval. "Human Rights Norms Applicable in the Situation of Armed Conflict: Beyond the Lex Generalis/Lex Specialis Framework." *Japanese Yearbook of International Law* 66 (2023): 3–20.

Sharan, A. "From Non-intervention to R2P", *Indian Journal of International Law* 56 (2021): 81–94.

Sharma, Ashok. "India's Quest for UN Security Council Permanent Membership: A Holy Grail of Its Foreign Policy." *Times of India*, 1 Apr. 2024. https://timesofindia.indiatimes.com/blogs/ashoks-statecraft/indias-quest-for-un-security-council-permanent-membership-a-holy-grail-of-its-foreign-policy/.

Shi, Jiuyong. "Prohibition of Use of Force in International Law." *Chinese Journal of International Law* 17, no. 1 (2018): 1–14.

Shimazu, Naoko. *Japan, Race and Equality: The Racial Equality Proposal of 1919.* Abingdon: Routledge, 1998.

Sikkink, Kathryn. *Evidence for Hope: Making Human Rights Work in the 21st Century.* Princeton, NJ: Princeton University Press, 2017.

Singh, Prabhakar. "India before and after the *Right of Passage* Case." *Asian Journal of International Law* 5 (2015): 176–208.

Sinha, Nirmal C. "The Simla Convention 1914: A Chinese Puzzle." *Presidency College Magazine: Diamond Jubilee Number.* Calcutta, 1974.

Sivaramakrisnan, Arvind. "Kashmir Issue Clouds Indian View of Kosovo." *The Hindu,* 4 Apr. 2011. https://www.thehindu.com/news/the-india-cables/Kashmir-issue-clouds-Indian-view-of-Kosovo/article14670496.ece.

Smith, Josh. "New North Korea Law Outlines Nuclear Weapons Use, including Preemptive Strikes." *Japan Times*, 9 Sept. 2022. https://www.japantimes.co.jp/news/2022/09/09/asia-pacific/north-korea-nuclear-weapons-policy/.

Song, Yann-huei. "Peaceful Proposals and Maritime Cooperation between Mainland China, Japan, and Taiwan in the East China Sea: Progress Made and Challenges Ahead." *Asian Yearbook of International Law* 22 (2016): 20–49.

"South China Sea Archaeology Centre to Boost Beijing's Claims." *Bangkok Post*, 23 Feb. 2023. https://www.bangkokpost.com/world/2511704/south-china-sea-archaeology-centre-aims-to-boost-beijings-claims.

Sparks, Tom. *Self-Determination in the International Legal System: Whose Claim, to What Right?* Oxford: Hart, 2023.

"Special Issue on Jurisdiction and Admissibility of the South China Sea Arbitration." *Chinese Journal of International Law* 15 (2016): 217–487.

Starski, Paulina. "Silence within the Process of Normative Change and Evolution of the Prohibition on the Use of Force: Normative Volatility and Legislative Responsibility." *Journal on the Use of Force & International Law* 4 (2017): 14–65.

Steinberg, Guido. *The "Axis of Resistance": Iran's Expansion in the Middle East Is Hitting a Wall.* Berlin: German Institute for International and Security Affairs, 2021.

Sterio, Milena. *The Right to Self-determination under International Law: "Selfistants", Secession, and the Rule of the Great Powers.* Abingdon: Routledge, 2013.

Stockholm International Peace Research Institute. *SIPRI Yearbook 2022: Armaments, Disarmament and International Security Summary.* Stockholm: SIPRI, 2022.

Stranglio, Sebastian. "China Pledges Support for Myanmar's Junta 'No Matter How the Situation Changes'." *The Diplomat,* 4 Apr. 2022. https://thediplomat.com/2022/04/china-pledges-support-for-myanmars-junta-no-matter-how-the-situation-changes/.

Suh, Jiwon. *The Politics of Post-Suharto Transitional Justice in Indonesia.* PhD thesis, Ohio State University, 2012.

Svensson, Isak. "Conflict Resolution in Civil Wars." In *Routledge Handbook of Civil Wars*, ed. Edward Newman and Karl DeRouen, Jr., pp. 363–75. Abingdon: Routledge, 2014.

Syailendra, Emirza Adi. "China, Indonesia, and Malaysia Waltzing Around Oil Rigs." *The Diplomat,* 18 Aug. 2022. https://thediplomat.com/2022/08/china-indonesia-and-malaysia-waltzing-around-oil-rigs/.

Syrian British Consortium. *A Decade after the Daraya: Documenting a Massacre.* London: Syrian British Consortium, 2022.

Syukri, Ibrahim. *History of the Malay Kingdom of Patani.* Trans. Conner Bailey and John N. Miksic. Athens, OH: Ohio University Press, 1985.

Tacik, Przemysaw. *Deconstructing Self-Determination in International Law: Sovereignty, Exception, and Biopolitics.* Leiden: Brill/Nijhoff, 2023. https://doi.org/10.1163/9789004680265.

Talmon, Stefan. *The South China Sea Arbitration: Jurisdiction, Admissibility, Procedure.* Leiden: Brill, 2022.

Taylor, Isaac. "The Responsibility to Protect from Terror: The Ethics of Foreign Counter-terrorist Interventions." *Global Responsibility to Protect* 14 (2022): 155–77. https://doi.org/10.1163/1875-984X-14010013.

Terry, Patrick C.R. "The Recognition of New States in Times of Secession: Is State Recognition Turning into Another Means of Intervention?" *Asian Yearbook of International Law* 20 (2014): 53–114.

Thippimol, Onanong. *Review Histories of Pat(t)ani: Different Point of Views*. Bangkok: Thailand Science Research and Innovation, 2020.

Thompson, Shamala Kandiah, Karin Landgren and Paul Romita. "The United Nations in Hindsight: The Long and Winding Road to Security Council Reform." *Just Security,* 30 Sept. 2022. https://www.justsecurity.org/83310/the-united-nations-in-hindsight-long-winding-road-to-security-council-reform/.

"Timeline for Yemen's Seven Year Conflict." *Arab News*, 7 Apr. 2022. https://www.arabnews.com/node/2058946/middle-east.

Tinoco Claims Arbitration (Great Britain v. Costa Rica). 1923. 1 R.I.A.A. 369.

Trahan, Jennifer. "Legal Issues Surrounding Veto Use and Aggression." *Case Western Reserve Journal of International Law* 55 (2023): 93–146.

Tzimas, Themis. "Self-Defence by Non-state Actors in States of Fragmented Authority." *Journal of Conflict & Security Law* 24 (2019): 175–99

UN International Law Commission. "Identification and Legal Consequences of Peremptory Norms of General International Law (*Jus Cogens*)." *Yearbook of the International Law Commission*. Vol. II. Part Two (2022): 121–169.

———. "Peremptory Norms of General International Law (*Jus Cogens*)." A/77/10 (2022).

Untawale, Mukund G. "The Kutch-Sind Dispute." *International and Comparative Law Quarterly* 23, no. 4 (1974): 818–39.

van der Steenhoven, Nick. "Conduct and Subsequent Practice by States in the Application of the Requirement to Report under UN Charter Article 51." *Journal on the Use of Force & International Law* 6 (2019): 242–72.

Van Dyke Jon and Mark Valencia, "How Valid Are the South China Sea Claims under the Law of the Sea Convention?" *Southeast Asian Affairs* (2000): 47–63.

van Logchem, Youri. *The Rights and Obligations of States in Disputed Maritime Areas*. Cambridge: Cambridge University Press, 2021.

van Schaack, Beth. *Imagining Justice for Syria*. New York: Oxford University Press, 2020.

Venditti, Bruno. "Mapped: The World's Largest Armies in 2024." *Visual Capitalist,* 1 June 2024. https://www.visualcapitalist.com/mapped-the-worlds-largest-armies-in-2024/.

Visser, Laura. "Intervention by Invitation and Collective Self-Defence: Two Sides of the Same Coin?" *Journal on the Use of Force & International Law* 7 (2020): 292–316.

Voller, Yaniv. *Second-Generation Liberation Wars: Rethinking Colonialism in Iraqi Kurdistan and Southern Sudan.* Cambridge: Cambridge University Press, 2022.

Wahyuningroem, Sri Lestari. *Transitional Justice from State to Civil Society: Democratization in Indonesia.* Abingdon: Routledge, 2021.

Walker, J. Samuel. "Recent Literature on Truman's Atomic Bomb Decision: A Search for Middle Ground." *Diplomatic History* 29 (2005): 311–34.

Webster, Daniel. Letter to Henry Stephen Fox. In *The Papers of Daniel Webster: Diplomatic Papers*, ed. K.E. Shewmaker. Vol. 1, 1841–43. Hanover, NH: University Press of New England, 1983.

Wentker, Alexander. "The Armed Attack Exception to Neutrality in International Peace and Security Law." *International & Comparative Law Quarterly* 73 (2024): 963–96.

Wetter, J. Gillis. "The Rann of Kutch Arbitration." *American Journal of International Law* 65 (1971): 346–57.

Wheatley, Steven. "The Emergence of New States in International Law: The Insights from Complexity Theory." *Chinese Journal of International Law* 15 (2016): 579–606.

Wheaton, Henry. *Elements of International Law.* Boston: William Beach Lawrence, 1855.

Whomersley, Chris. "The Award on the Merits in the Case Brought by the Philippines against China relating to the South China Sea: A Critique." *Chinese Journal of International Law* 17 (2018): 387–423.

Wilson, Page. *Aggression, Crime and International Security.* Abingdon: Routledge, 2009.

Winter, Elliot. "The Compatibility of Autonomous Weapons with the Principles of International Humanitarian Law." *Journal of Conflict and Security Law* 27, no. 1 (2022): 1–20.

Wong, Meagan S. "Targeted Killings and the International Legal Framework: With Particular Reference to the US Operation against Osama Bin Laden." *Chinese Journal of International Law* 11 (2012): 127–63.

Wong, Tessa. "Philippine President Warns China against 'Act of War'." BBC, 1 June 2024. https://www.bbc.com/news/articles/c7223knz3ezo.

Wood, Michael. "International Law and the Use of Force: What Happens in Practice?" *Indian Journal of International Law* 53 (2013): 345–67.

Xu, Hong. "The Chair's Summary of the Colloquium on the Five Principles of Peaceful Coexistence and the Development of International Law Held in Beijing on May 27, 2014." *Chinese Journal of International Law* 13, no. 3 (2014): 501–6.

Xue, Hanqin. "China's Open Policy and International Law." *Chinese Journal of International Law* 4 (2005): 133–9.

———. "Chinese Observations on International Law." *Chinese Journal of International Law* 6 (2007): 83–93.

———. "Chinese Contemporary Perspectives on International Law: History, Culture and International Law." *Collected Courses of the Hague Academy of International Law* 355 (2011): 41–234.

———. "Meaningful Dialogue through a Common Discourse: Law and Values in a Multi-Polar World." *Asian Journal of International Law* 1, no. 1 (2011): 13–19.

Xue, Rue. "Humanitarianism in Chinese Traditional Military Ethics and International Humanitarian Law Training in the People's Liberation Army." In *Asia-Pacific Perspectives on International Humanitarian Law*, ed. Suzannah Linton, Tim McCormack and Sandesh Sivakumaran, pp. 93–106. Cambridge: Cambridge University Press, 2020.

Yanai, Shunji. "New Japanese Legislation for Peace and Security: Its Background and Salient Points." *Japanese Yearbook of International Law* 60 (2017): 136–57.

Yanev, Lachezar. "Syrian War Crimes Trials in the Netherlands: Claiming Universal Jurisdiction over Terrorist Offences and the War Crime of Outrages upon Personal Dignity of the Dead." *Netherlands Yearbook of International Law* 52 (2021): 301–26.

Yee, Sienho. "The Dynamic Interplay between the Interpreters of Security Council Resolutions." *Chinese Journal of International Law* 11 (2012): 613–22.

———. "Territory in the Work of the Institut de Droit International." *Chinese Journal of International Law* 21 (2022): 219–57.

Yip, Ka Lok. *The Use of Force against Individuals in War under International Law: A Social Ontological Approach.* Oxford: Oxford University Press, 2022.

Yoshihara, Toshi. "The 1974 Paracels Sea Battle: A Campaign Appraisal." *Naval War College Review* 69 (2016): 1–25.

Zamani, Masoud and Majid Nikouei. "Intervention by Invitation, Collective Self-Defence and the Enigma of Effective Control." *Chinese Journal of International Law* 16 (2017): 663–94.

Zawacki, Benjamin. "Politically Inconvenient, Legally Correct: A Non-international Armed Conflict in Southern Thailand." *Journal of Conflict and Security Law* 18, no. 1 (2013): 151–79.

Zhang, Xinjun and Xidi Chen. "China and the Settlement of Territorial Disputes." In *The Handbook of China and International Law*, ed. Ignacio de la Rasilla and Congyan Cai, pp. 522–47. Cambridge: Cambridge University Press, 2024.

Zhu, Yuan Yi. "Suzerainty, Semi-Sovereignty, and International Legal Hierarchies on China's Borderlands." *Asian Journal of International Law* 10 (2020): 293–320.

Zongze, Ruan. "Responsible Protection: Building a Safer World." *China Institute of International Studies* 34 (2012): 19–41.

National Courts

Reference by the Lord Advocate of Devolution Issues under Paragraph 34 of Schedule 6 to the Scotland Act 1998, UK Supreme Court [2022] UKSC 31.

Reference re Secession of Quebec, 2 Canada Supreme Court Rep. 217 (1998).

International Court of Justice (in chronological order)

Corfu Channel, ICJ Rep. 1949, p. 4.

Anglo-Norwegian Fisheries case, ICJ Rep. 1951, p. 116.

Case concerning the Temple of Preah Vihear (Cambodia v. Thailand), Preliminary Objections, ICJ Rep. 1961, p. 17.

Case concerning the Temple of Preah Vihear (Cambodia v. Thailand), Judgment, ICJ Rep. 1962, p. 6.

Certain Expenses of the United Nations (Article 17, Paragraph 2, of the Charter), Advisory Opinion, ICJ Rep. 1962, p. 151.

North Sea Continental Shelf Cases (Federal Republic of Germany/Denmark; Federal Republic of Germany/Netherlands), ICJ Rep. 1969, p. 3.

Legal Consequences for States of the Continued Presence of South Africa in Namibia (South West Africa) notwithstanding Security Council Resolution 276 (1970), Advisory Opinion, ICJ Rep. 1971, p. 16.

Western Sahara, Advisory Opinion, ICJ Rep. 1975, p. 12.

Military and Paramilitary Activities in and against Nicaragua (Nicaragua v. USA), ICJ Rep. 1986, p. 14.

East Timor (Portugal v. Australia), ICJ Rep. 1995, p. 90.

Legality of the Threat or Use of Nuclear Weapons, Advisory Opinion, ICJ Rep. 1996, p. 226.

Legality of Use of Force (Yugoslavia v. Belgium), Provisional Measures, Order of 2 June 1999, ICJ Rep. 1999, p. 124.

*Maritime Delimitation and Territorial Questions between Qatar and Bahrain (Qatar v. Bahrain), I*CJ Rep. 2001, p. 40.

Land and Maritime Boundary between Cameroon and Nigeria (Cameroon v. Nigeria: Equatorial Guinea intervening), ICJ Rep. 2002, p. 303.

Sovereignty over Pulau Ligitan and Pulau Sipadan (Indonesia/Malaysia), ICJ Rep. 2002, p. 625.

Legal Consequences of the Construction of a Wall in the Occupied Palestinian Territory, Advisory Opinion, ICJ Rep. 2004, p. 136.

Armed Activities on the Territory of the Congo (Democratic Republic of the Congo v. Uganda), ICJ Rep. 2005, p. 168.

Application of the Convention on the Prevention and Punishment of the Crime of Genocide (Bosnia and Herzegovina v. Serbia and Montenegro), ICJ Rep. 2007, p. 43.

Territorial and Maritime Dispute between Nicaragua and Honduras in the Caribbean Sea (Nicaragua v. Honduras), ICJ Rep. 2007, p. 659.

Sovereignty over Pedra Branca/Pulau Batu Puteh, Middle Rocks and South Ledge (Malaysia/Singapore), ICJ Rep. 2008, p. 12.

Accordance with International Law of the Unilateral Declaration of Independence in Respect of Kosovo, Advisory Opinion, ICJ Rep. 2010, p. 403.

Questions relating to the Obligation to Prosecute or Extradite (Belgium v. Senegal), ICJ Rep. 2012 (II), p. 422.

Territorial and Maritime Dispute (Nicaragua v. Colombia), ICJ Rep. 2012, p. 624.

Request for Interpretation of the Judgment of 15 June 1962 in the Case concerning the Temple of Preah Vihear (Cambodia v. Thailand) (Cambodia v. Thailand), Provisional Measures, Order of 18 July 2011, ICJ Rep. 2011, p. 537.

Request for Interpretation of the Judgment of 15 June 1962 in the Case concerning the Temple of Preah Vihear (Cambodia v. Thailand) (Cambodia v. Thailand), Judgment, ICJ Rep. 2013, p. 281.

Obligations concerning Negotiations relating to Cessation of the Nuclear Arms Race and to Nuclear Disarmament (Marshall Islands v. India), Jurisdiction and Admissibility, ICJ Rep. 2016, p. 255.

Obligations concerning Negotiations relating to Cessation of the Nuclear Arms Race and to Nuclear Disarmament (Marshall Islands v. Pakistan), Jurisdiction and Admissibility, ICJ Rep. 2016, p. 552.

Obligations concerning Negotiations relating to Cessation of the Nuclear Arms Race and to Nuclear Disarmament (Marshall Islands v. United Kingdom), Preliminary Objections, ICJ Rep. 2016, p. 833.

Legal Consequences of the Separation of the Chagos Archipelago from Mauritius in 1965, Advisory Opinion, ICJ Rep. 2019, p. 95.

Application of the Convention on the Prevention and Punishment of the Crime of Genocide (The Gambia v. Myanmar), Preliminary Objections, ICJ Rep. 2022, p. 477.

Armed Activities in the Territory of the Congo (DR Congo v. Uganda) Reparations, ICJ Rep. 2022, p. 13.

International Tribunal for the Law of the Sea (in chronological order)

M/V "SAIGA" (No. 2) (Saint Vincent and the Grenadines v. Guinea), ITLOS Rep. 1999, p. 10.

Delimitation of the Maritime Boundary in the Bay of Bengal (Bangladesh/Myanmar), ITLOS Rep. 2012, p. 4.

Case concerning the Detention of Three Ukrainian Naval Vessels (Ukraine v. Russian Federation), Provisional Measures, ITLOS Rep. 2019, p. 283.

Dispute concerning Delimitation of the Maritime Boundary between Mauritius and Maldives in the Indian Ocean (Mauritius/Maldives), Preliminary Objections, ITLOS Rep. 2021, p. 17.

Permanent Court of Arbitration (in chronological order)

Guyana/Suriname Arbitration, Award of 17 Sept. 2007, 30 R.I.A.A. 1 (2007).

Bay of Bengal Maritime Boundary Arbitration between Bangladesh and India (Bangladesh v. India). PCA Case Repository 2010–16, PCA, 2014.

South China Sea Arbitration (Philippines v. China), Award on Jurisdiction and Admissibility. PCA Case Repository 2013–19, PCA, 2015.

Arbitration regarding the Chagos Marine Protected Area between Mauritius and the United Kingdom of Great Britain and Northern Ireland, Award of 18 Mar. 2015, 31 R.I.A.A. 359 (2015).

South China Sea Arbitration (Philippines v. China), Award. PCA Case Repository 2013–19, PCA, 2016.

Dispute concerning the Detention of Ukrainian Naval Vessels and Servicemen, Award on the Preliminary Objections of the Russian Federation, 27 June 2022, PCA Case No. 2019–28.

Index

11 September 2001, 33, 195–9
1970 Declaration on Friendly Relations, 14, 16, 30–1, 34, 87, 103, 116, 122, 131–2, 133, 138, 157, 170, 253

Abdullah, Mohamad, 261
"absolute necessity" principle, 146
accession, 57, 58
accidental use of force, 102
Aceh, 124, 127
acquiescence, 44, 45
acquisition of territories, 80, *see also* annexation
Adachi, Mineichiro, 11
Ad Hoc Human Rights Court for Timor-Leste in Jakarta, 164–5
Afghanistan, 23, 97–8
African Union, 141, 177, 192, 195–6, 219, 238–9
aggression, definition of, 116, *see also* Definition of Aggression
Ahtisaari, Martti, 136
airspace, 109
airstrikes, 184, 196, 200, 204, 206, 215, 221, 242
Al-Assad, Maher, 261–2
Albania, 134, 259
al-Gharib, Eyad, 261
Algiers Agreement, 246
Al Qaeda, 44, 149, 195, 199, 225
Al Qaeda in the Arabian Peninsula (AQAP), 213, 215
ancient origins of the laws of war, 41
Andrews, Tom, 194
annexation, 130, 157–67
anticipatory self-defence, 32–3, 242
appeasements, 233, 266
Aquino III, Benigno, 97
Arab League, 177, 187–8
Arab League Charter, 23
Arab Spring, 177, 211
arbitral proceedings, 83–5, 86
arbitral tribunals, 72, 83–5, 86, 96–7, 99, 109, 112, 113
arbitration, 87–97, 217, 246
archaeology, 81n62
archipelagic state doctrine, 8
armed attack
- definition of, 30, 31, 33, 34, 42, 49
- frontier incidents versus "armed attacks," 97–103
- "imminent" versus "threat of," 198
- occupation as, 115–17

armed conflict
- definition of, 2–3, 144–5
- organisation of armed groups, 145

Armenia-Azerbaijan 44 day war, 115, 117
armies, top ten world's largest, 4
armistices, 116
Arms Trade Treaty (ATT) 2013, 250–1
arms trading, 160, 215, 227, 250–2

ARSIWA (UN International Law Commission's Articles on Responsibility of States for Internationally Wrongful Acts), 247–9, 252
Arthashastra, 9
Articles on the Protection of Persons in the Event of Disasters, 175–6
artificial intelligence (AI), 6
artificial islands, 85, 86
Art of War, The (Sun Tsu), 9
Arunachal Pradesh, 64, 65, 66, 67
ASEAN (Association of Southeast Asian Nations)
  Cambodia-Thailand dispute over Preah Vihear/Phra Viharn, 71–3
  code of conduct (COC), 107
  Declaration on the Conduct of Parties in the South China/East Sea, 104, 106
  disaster relief, 175
  East Timor, 161
  Five Point Consensus, 193
  Global Security Initiative (GSI), 20
  history of, 23
  Myanmar, 153–4, 192–3
  South China Sea, 89–90
  Timor-Leste, 165–6
  Vietnam invasion of Cambodia, 51, 52
Asia Foundation, 125
Asian-African Conferences, 14–16, 62, 119, 157
Asia-Pacific Economic Cooperation (APEC), 164
Asia-Pacific Roundtable, 89–90
Assad regime, 171, 179–80, 182–4, 187–8, 201, 204, 208, 260, 261, 262
asset freezing, 247
assisting states, liability of, 247–8
Australia
  East Timor, 160, 161, 162–3, 166
  Quadrilateral Security Dialogue, 22, 108
  South China Sea, 89
  Syria, 203
  Timor-Leste, 166
authoritarianism, 55
autonomous areas, 58, 61, 125, 135, 162
autonomous weapons ("drones"/"UAVs"), 6, *see also* drone strikes
Azerbaijan, 115

Balkans, 134–7
Balochistan, 125
Bandung Conference, Indonesia 1955, 14, 15, 16, 62, 119, 157
Bangladesh, 59, 96, 123–4, 130, 132–3, 153
Ban Romklao, 55, 67–8
Bay of Bengal, 96
Beijing colloquium, 18
Bharatiya Janata Party, 61
Bhutan, 64
bilateralism, 16, 59, 63, 65, 73, 93, 107, 109, 227
bin Laden, Osama, 198
Border Defence Cooperation Agreement, 65
border disputes, 54–5, *see also* sovereignty
Border Peace and Tranquility Agreement, 64
border securitisation, 55
Borneo, 94
boundary treaties, 62–3
Boutros-Ghali, Boutros, 14
BRICS, 24, 67, 265
British colonialism, 12, 55, 56, 91, 98, 192
Brunei, 83

Buddhist communities
Kashmir, 58, 61
Myanmar, 125
Thailand, 129–30
Tibet, 66
burden of proof, 100
Bush Doctrine, 33

Cambodia, 49–53, 55, 69–77, 171
Canada, 26, 32, 133, 138, 203
Cançado Trindade, Judge, 138–9
Caroline test, 32, 198
Case Concerning Right of Passage over Indian Territory (Portugal v. India), 60
ceasefires, 58, 68, 222, 224, 243
Chagos Marine Protected Area Arbitration (Mauritius v. United Kingdom), 113
chemical weapons, 182, 183–8, 237, 262
China
assistance to Myanmar, 175
boundary treaties, 62–3
China-India dispute over McMahon Line, 55, 62–7
Chinese embassy Belgrade bombing, 102
Coast Guard Law, 98
Confidence Building Measures (CBMs), 103
Confucianism, 13
cooperation MOU with Philippines, 106
Cultural Revolution, 18–19
customary international law, 81
Declaration on the Conduct of Parties in the South China/East Sea, 104
East Timor, 161
foreign policy, 14
Global Security Initiative (GSI), 19, 235, 240, 265
and Indonesia, 106
international dispute mechanisms, 13
joint development with Japan, 105
Libya, 178
McMahon Line, 55, 62–7, 242
Myanmar, 154–5, 190–1, 193
Nanking massacre, 12
nuclear weapons, 242, 244
"opening up," 13
permanent members of UNSC, 13, 236
and the Philippines, 111
Responsible Protection (RP) Concept, 188–9
and Russia, 240
San Francisco Conference 1945, 12
self-determination, 132
size of army, 4
South China Sea, 77, 78, 82–90, 97, 104–7
stance on the international order, 21
suzerainty, 63, 80
Syria, 180, 206–7, 208
Taiwan, 79, 138
"Ten Principles," 15
Tibet, 14
Timor-Leste, 166
tributary system, 9–10
and the Ukraine crisis, 21
Versailles Peace Conference, 11
Vietnam, 50, 63
Yemen, 227
China-UN Peace and Development Trust Fund, 19
Chinese Coast Guard (CCG), 88–9, 90, 98, 110, 111
Chinese Society of International Law, 16
civilian losses, 115, 144, 146, 147, 183, 185, 225
civil wars, 140, 187–8, 217, 218, 222, 225, 226, 227

climate change, 18
codes of conduct, 104, 107, 236–7
Cold War, 15, 160
collateral damage, 5–6
collective security, 111, 174
Collective Security Treaty Organization, 65, 186
collective self-defence, 25, 29–30, 32, 35, 42, 195, 198, 202–3, 210
colonialism
dispute settlements, 91
East Timor, 158, 159
and the international order, 10, 12
Myanmar, 192
occupation, 81–2
root of boundary disputes, 55
and self-determination, 120–2, 130, 132, 133, 146
and the UN Charter, 12
use of force in the name of self-determination, 120–2
Commission for Reception, Truth, and Reconciliation in East Timor, 164
Commission of Inquiry into Human Rights Violations in East Timor (KPP-HAM), 165
Commission on the Limits of the Continental Shelf, 96
Committee Against Torture, 151
Committee on Economic, Social and Cultural Rights, 151
Committee on Enforced Disappearance, 151
Committee on the Elimination of Discrimination against Women, 151
Committee on the Elimination of Racial Discrimination, 151
Committee on the Rights of the Child, 151
communism, 233
compensation for illegal use of force, 245–54
compromis (special agreement), 93–4
compromise, 233
conduct of hostilities paradigm, 146
Conference of the States Parties, 186–7
Conference on Interaction and Confidence Building Measures in Asia, 20
Conference on Security and Cooperation in Europe, 131
Confidence Building Measures (CBMs), 65, 66, 103–13
Confucianism, 13
consent, 210, 219
conspiracy to wage aggressive war, 12
Convention against Torture and Other Cruel, Inhuman or Degrading Treatment or Punishment, 151, 254
Convention concerning the Protection of the World Cultural and Natural Heritage, 74
Convention for the Suppression of Terrorist Bombings, 148
Convention on the Elimination of All Forms of Discrimination Against Women, 151
Convention on the Elimination of All Forms of Racial Discrimination, 151
Convention on the Prevention and Punishment of the Crime of Genocide, 152–3
Convention on the Prohibition of the Development, Production, Stockpiling and Use of Chemical Weapons and Their Destruction, 186–7
Convention on the Rights of the Child, 151
cooling-off periods, 102
cooperation arrangements, 106, 162, 166
Cooperation Council for the Arab States of the Gulf, 214
copper, 126
coral reefs, 86
Costa Rica, 217
Council of Europe, 259
countermeasures, 247

coups, 158, 192, 211, 219
crimes against humanity
  Responsibility to Protect (R2P) doctrine, 177, 179, 185
  and self-determination, 153
  state responsibility, 250, 251
  Syria, 262
  Timor-Leste, 164
  Tokyo War Crimes Tribunal (International Military Tribunal for the Far East) 1946, 11–12
  universal jurisdiction, 260, 263
  Yemen, 221, 225
crimes against peace, 11–12
critical date, 87, 112
cultural sensitivities, 90
customary international law
  annexation, 157
  chemical weapons, 185
  international regime, 30, 31–2
  recognition of states, 142
  Responsibility to Protect (R2P) doctrine, 174
  and self-determination, 122, 146
  South China Sea, 81
  sovereignty disputes, 115
  Syria, 181
  UN Security Council, 46
cyberattacks, 37–8
cyberspace, 18
Cyclone Nargis, 174–5
Czechoslovakia, 140

Declaration on the Conduct of Parties in the South China/East Sea, 104, 106
declarations of independence, 136–8, 139, 140, 164
decolonisation, 125, 127
de-escalation, 4, 68, 102, 192, 200
Definition of Aggression, 31, 116, 170, 256–7
demilitarised zones, 73, 135
Democratic Republic of Timor-Leste, 164
"dependent peoples," 120, 121
deprivation of liberty, 182, 261
diplomacy
  Arunachal Pradesh, 67
  Cambodia-Thailand dispute over Preah Vihear/Phra Viharn, 71
  East Timor, 160
  India-Pakistan dispute over Kashmir, 59
  Myanmar, 194
  and the necessity test, 34, 35
  Pakistan-Afghanistan, 98
  preventive, 252
  Responsibility to Protect (R2P) doctrine, 177
  Russia-Ukraine war, 259
  South China Sea, 89
  Syria, 183, 185, 187, 188
  terrorism, 208
  Yemen, 224, 227–8
diplomatic conferences, 130–1
disarmament agreements, 141
disaster relief, 174–6
discovery of unoccupied territories, 79–80
discrimination between combatants and civilians, 40
displacement camps, 181
dispute settlements
  and Asian cultural sensitivities, 90–1
  colonialism, 91
  Five Principles of Peaceful Coexistence, 18
  third-party dispute settlement mechanisms, 24–6
dissolution, 140
distinction principle, 6
domestic law, authorisation of use of force, 98
"do not escalate first," 89
"double standards," 92

DR Congo v. Uganda, 33, 34, 245–6, 253, 266
drone strikes, 199, 216, 225, 242
Droubi, Mohannad, 260
Durand Line, 98
Dutch colonialism, 126, 158
Duterte, Rodrigo, 97

"Eastphalian" world order, 16
East Timor, 124, 130, 157–67, 257–8
East Timor (Portugal v. Australia), 162, 166
Economic Community of West African States, 219
ecosystem protection, 86
Eide, Kai, 135
elections
  Cambodia, 52
  Kashmir, 58
  Kosovo, 136
  Tigray, 141
  Yemen, 212
Elements of International Law (Wheaton, 1836), 11
environment, 40, 41, 86
equality principle, 18
Eritrea, 140, 246, 247, 266
estoppel, 44
Ethiopia, 140–2, 246, 247, 266
ethnic armed groups, 155
ethnic cleansing, 134, 192, 205
ethno-nationalism, 125–6
Eurojust, 263
European Parliament, 206
European Peace Facility (EPF), 252
European Union (EU), 229, 243, 250, 252
exclusive economic zones, 25, 63, 82, 84–7, 90, 104, 106
extradition, 164
extremism, 125

face and honour, 90, 94
facilitating wrongful acts, 245–54
Falklands/Malvinas, 114, 116
federalism, 155
First World War, 10
fishing, 84, 85, 86, 106–7
Five Principles of Peaceful Coexistence, 13, 14, 15, 16, 17, 18, 24, 111
former Yugoslavia, 134–5, 169
France
  East Timor, 160
  Mali, 210, 219
  permanent members of UNSC, 13
  Responsibility to Protect (R2P) doctrine, 174
  Syria, 184, 203
  universal jurisdiction, 261–3
  Yemen, 216
freedom fighters, 148–9
Free Papua Movement, 126
French colonialism, 68, 69, 74, 75–6
FRETILIN (Revolutionary Front for an Independent East Timor), 158, 161
frontier incidents versus "armed attacks," 97–103

G4, 238
G20, 67, 260
Gaddafi, President, 177, 178, 179, 192
gas
  Confidence Building Measures (CBMs), 105
  cooperation arrangements, 106, 109–10
  East Timor, 166
  sovereignty disputes, 90
Gaza, 49, 228, 230
Geneva Conventions, 41, 130–1, 143–6, 147, 181, 246, 251, 254

genocide
East Timor, 164
Iraq, 255
nuclear weapons, 40
self-determination, 123
state responsibility, 250, 251
universal jurisdiction, 260, 262
Genocide Convention, 254
geographical scope of book, 3
Germany, 204, 243, 260–1
Global Centre for Responsibility to Protect, 224
globalisation, 16
Global Peace Index, 221
Global Security Initiative (GSI), 19–21, 235, 240, 265
Goa, 120–1
gold, 126
gravity threshold, 34, 35, 36, 256–7
Greater Sunrise field, 166
great powers (Western), 10
Group of 7, 224
Group of 77, 172
Group of Eminent Experts on Yemen, 221, 222
Group of Friends of R2P, 189
guerrilla warfare, 158
Gulf Cooperation Council (GCC), 23, 211, 212, 213, 222, 227, 244, 265
Guterres, António, 194, 234
Guterres, Eurico, 165
Guyana-Suriname, 98–100

Habibie, President, 162
Hadi, President, 211, 212, 213, 214, 215, 217, 220, 222, 223, 225, 226
Hague, The, 258, 263
Hague Regulations of 1907, 41
Harvard Law School, 44, 204
hegemonic powers, 18
Helsinki Final Act, 131, 135
Himalayas, 64
Hindu communities, 56, 58, 61
Hindu texts, 9
hinterland, theory of, 82
Hiroshima, 11, 12
Houthis, 211–19, 220, 222–7, 228, 229, 243, 244
Huber, Max, 79
humanitarian intervention, 154, 168–72, 192, 194, 220
humanitarian standards, 130–1
human rights abuses, *see also* humanitarian intervention
East Timor, 164–5
Responsibility to Protect (R2P) doctrine, 177
self-determination, 139, 150–1
state responsibility, 249
Yemen, 221–2, 224, 225
human rights law, *see also* international humanitarian law (IHL)
Bandung Conference, Indonesia 1955, 14
Kashmir, 61
nuclear weapons, 40
proportionality, 147
Responsibility to Protect (R2P) doctrine, 198–9
right to self-determination, 120
Yemen, 215
Human Rights Watch, 260
Hussein, Saddam, 157, 182, 255–6, 266
"hybrid" tribunals, 257–8

identity, 55
"illegal occupation," 114
immediacy requirement, 37, 114, 198
impunity, 165, 258
Independent International Commission of Inquiry on the Syrian Arab Republic, 181, 207

India
  "Act East Policy," 27
  Balochistan, 125
  China-India dispute over McMahon Line, 55, 62–7
  foreign policy, 14
  and the ICJ, 25
  India-Bangladesh maritime disputes, 96–7
  India-Pakistan 4 day conflict in May 2025, 200–1
  India v. Pakistan non-state actors, 199–201
  Indo-Pakistani war of 1971, 59, 123–4
  Kashmir, 55, 56–62, 138
  liberation of Goa, 120–1
  and Myanmar, 194
  nuclear weapons, 239, 241–2
  partition, 55, 56
  Quadrilateral Security Dialogue, 22, 27, 108
  Rann of Kutch dispute, 95–6
  self-determination, 131
  size of army, 4
  Tibet, 14
  UNSC, 238, 239
individual criminal responsibility, 254–64
Indonesia
  archipelagic state doctrine, 8
  and China, 106
  cooperation arrangements, 106
  East Timor, 157–67
  Ligitan and Sipadan, 94
  self-determination, 124, 131
  South China Sea, 88–9, 90
  West Papua, 126–7
Indonesian National Commission on Human Rights, 126–7
Indo-Pakistani war of 1971, 59, 123–4
insurgency, 125–7, 128, 133, 140, 147, 149, 218
intelligence information, 5
intensity of conflict, 144–5
intergroup conflict and peace, inherent paradox, 233–4
international aid, 174, 248, *see also* humanitarian intervention
International Alliance for Defending Rights and Freedom, 260
International Committee of the Red Cross, 146
International Convention for the Protection of All Persons from Enforced Disappearance, 151
International Convention for the Suppression of Terrorist Bombings (1997), 148
International Convention on the Elimination of All Forms of Racial Discrimination, 151
International Court of Justice (ICJ)
  1970 Declaration on Friendly Relations, 87, 122
  annexation, 157
  Armed Activities in the Territory of the Congo (DR Congo v. Uganda), 33, 34, 97, 245–6, 253, 266
  Cambodia-Thailand dispute over Preah Vihear/Phra Viharn, 72–4, 76
  Certain Expenses, 47
  China, 13
  colonialism, 91
  definition of "armed attack," 31–2
  East Timor, 162–3, 166
  evidentiary tests, 101–2
  Gabčíkovo-Magymaros Project (Hungary/Slovakia), 49
  humanitarian intervention, 169, 170
  India, 25
  intervention by invitation, 209

judicial review, 29
Kashmir, 60
Kosovo, 137, 138
Land and Maritime Boundary between Cameroon and Nigeria (Cameroon v. Nigeria: Equatorial Guinea intervening), 79–80
Laos-Thailand dispute over Ban Romklao, 68
Legality of the Threat or Use of Nuclear Weapons, 38–40, 240, 265
Malaysia-Indonesia maritime disputes, 94
Malaysia-Singapore maritime dispute, 93–4
Nicaragua v. USA (Military and Paramilitary Activities in and against Nicaragua), 30–1, 32, 34, 92, 97, 218, 252, 253
non-intervention principle, 218
nuclear weapons, 241
obligations *erga omnes partes*, 254
Oil Platforms (Iran v. USA), 34, 97, 100–1
predecessors of, 11
and pre-emptive self-defence, 33
Qatar-Bahrain, 91, 94–5
Responsibility to Protect (R2P) doctrine, 174
Rohingyas, 153
self-determination, 119, 132, 139
Temple of Preah Vihar, 68, 69, 73
Territorial and Maritime Dispute (Nicaragua v. Colombia), 80
third-party dispute settlement mechanisms, 25–6
and the UNSC, 240
use of force, 30, 99–100
international courts/tribunals as third-party dispute settlement mechanisms, 24–5
International Covenant on Civil and Political Rights (ICCPR), 60–1, 119, 131, 132, 133, 151
International Covenant on Economic, Social and Cultural Rights (IC-ESCR), 60–1, 119, 131, 132–3, 151
International Criminal Court (ICC), 153, 178, 222, 256–7
international criminal courts, 254–64
International Groups of Experts, 37–8
international humanitarian law (IHL)
defined, 6
European Peace Facility (EPF), 252
nuclear weapons, 39, 40
Responsibility to Protect (R2P) doctrine, 177
self-determination, 143–8
state responsibility, 246
Syria, 181
targeted killings of terrorists, 199
Yemen, 215
international human rights law, 6, 146, 149–56
international law
acquisition of territories, 80
China, 13, 16
and discovered areas, 79
European basis of, 11
Global Security Initiative (GSI), 19
India, 14
Japan, 10
and the use of force, 28–53
Western bias, 91
International Law Association (ILA), 2, 36, 37, 142, 171, 209, 218, 219
international legal order, 8–27
International Military Tribunal for the Far East (Tokyo War Crimes Tribunal) 1946, 11–12, 255, 266
international security presence, 135
International Syria Support Group (ISSG), 183

International Tribunal for the Law of the Sea (ITLOS), 96, 112, 113
intertemporal law, 79, 80
intervention by invitation, 43, 209–30
Iran
  and the ICJ, 26
  intervention by invitation, 211
  Iran-Pakistan cross-border missile attacks 2024, 4
  Iran-UAE dispute over islands in Strait of Hormuz, 54
  nuclear weapons, 240, 242–4
  Oil Platforms (Iran v. USA), 34, 97, 100–1
  San Francisco Conference 1945, 12
  state responsibility, 248
  and Syria, 187, 201, 204, 206
  Syria, 208
  Yemen, 216, 226–7, 228
Iraq, 12, 23, 160–1, 171, 176, 202, 204, 248, 255
Islamic State in Iraq and the Levant (ISIL), 37, 125, 149, 176, 183, 187, 195, 197–8, 201, 205–6, 225
island, definition of, 85
Island of Palmas Case (Netherlands v. USA), 79
Israel
  airstrikes on Syria, 201
  and the airstrikes on the Iranian embassy 2024, 4
  anticipatory self-defence, 33
  Hamas-Israel war, 4, 49, 228
  nuclear weapons, 242–3
  Six Day War, 114
  Yemen, 229–30

Jammu, 57, 58, 59, 60, 61, 199, 200–1
Japan
  and the ICJ, 25
  and the international order, 21–2
  joint development with China, 105
  "opening up," 10
  policy on collective self-defence, 35
  Quadrilateral Security Dialogue, 22, 108
  samurai tradition, 9
  South China Sea, 77, 78, 85
  Tokyo War Crimes Tribunal (International Military Tribunal for the Far East) 1946, 11–12
  UNSC, 238
Jaranilla y Jebución, Delfín, 12
Johor State, Malaysia, 93
Joint Comprehensive Plan of Action, 243
joint development in disputed land territory, 104
joint fish stock assessment, 106–7
joint marine scientific research, 106–7, 110
judicial review, 29
jus ad bellum, 6, 9, 44, 45
jus cogens, 46, 117–18, 119, 137, 218, 240
jus in bello, 6, 9, *see also* international humanitarian law (IHL)

"Kargil War," 59
Kashmir, 55, 56–62, 138, 199–201
Kenya, 195–6
Khin Nyunt, General, 192
Khmer Rouge, 50, 51
Koo, Wellington, 75
Korean War, 47–8
Koroma, Judge, 138
Kosovo, 132, 134–7, 139, 169, 170–1, 258–9, 266
Kosovo Specialist Chambers (KSC), 258
KPP-HAM (Commission of Inquiry into Human Rights Violations in East Timor), 165
Kurds, 124–5, 171, 201, 205, 255
Kuwait, 160–1, 216

L.69, 238
Ladakh, 61
land reclamation, 86
Laos, 55, 67–8, 132
law enforcement, 102–3, 113, 143–8, 196, 197
League of Arab States, 20, 23, 160–1, 187, 192, 213, 214, 216, 243
League of Nations, 10, 11
Lebanon, 12
legality/lawfulness versus legitimacy, 5
Liberation Tigers of Tamil Eelam armed group, 43
Libya, 177–88, 248–9
Ligitan and Sipadan, 91, 94
Line of Actual Control, 64, 65, 66, 103
Line of Control, 59, 60, 103, 199, 200
Louisa Reef, 83
low-tide elevations, 84

MacArthur, General Douglas, 12
Malacca Strait, 27, 191
Malay Peninsula, 127
Malaysia
  Ligitan and Sipadan, 91, 94
  Pedra Branca/Pulau Batu Puteh, 93
  South China Sea, 83, 88–9, 112
Mali, 210, 219
maps, 67, 69, 70, 74–5, 76, 79, 112
Marcos, Ferdinand R., 97
maritime area disputes, 55
maritime boundaries, 63, 83, 84–5, 104, 166
maritime cooperation zones, 162, 166
Marshall Islands, 240–1
martial law, 123
McMahon Line, 55, 62–7, 242
Mei Ju-ao, 12
memoranda of understanding, 106
Middle East Security Forum, 21
Middle Rocks, 93–4
militant rebels, 128
military aid/assistance, 30, 57, 218, 219, 248
military-to-military communications, 112
Milosevic, Slobodan, 134
Mischief Reef, 107
mistakes in war causing unintentional deaths/injuries/destructions, 6
misunderstandings, 22, 60, 111, 112, 233, 266
Modi, Prime Minister, 27, 67
Moro nationalism, 125
multilateralism, 19, 107, 189
multipolarisation, 16
Muslim Brotherhood, 223, 225
Muslim communities
  Kashmir, 56, 61
  Myanmar, 125, 126
  Philippines, 149
  protection against human rights abuses, 151–2
  Rohingyas, 153, 154–5, 192, 193
  Thailand, 127–30, 152
  Yemen, 211, 223, 226–7
Muslim-majority states, 22, 213, 226
Mustafa, Salih, 258
mutual assistance, 29
mutual benefit interests, 18
Mutual Defence Treaty, 108–10
Myanmar, 96, 125, 132, 152–5, 174–5, 190–4

Nagasaki, 11, 12
Nagorno-Karabakh war (2020), 115, 117
Nanda, Satya, 8
Nanking massacre, China, 12
Natalegawa, Marty, 71
national integrity, 130
nationalism, 55, 123, 125

NATO (North Atlantic Treaty Organization), 22, 134, 169, 170, 178
NATO Cooperative Cyber Defence Centre of Excellence, 37–8
Nazi Germany, 182
necessity criteria
  absolute necessity, 146–7
  Caroline test, 32, 198
  diplomacy, 34, 35
  Oil Platforms (Iran v. USA), 33–4
  self-defence, 33–4
  self-defence against non-state actors, 198
  use of force, 36
Nepal, 64
Netherlands, 229, 235, 263
neutral states, 40
new agenda for peace, 19, 234–5
new states, recognition of, 142–3
NGOs, 150, 224, 260, 261
Nguyen Phu Trong, 103
Nicaragua v. Colombia (Territorial and Maritime Dispute), 80
Nicaragua v. USA (Military and Paramilitary Activities in and against Nicaragua), 30–1, 32, 34, 92, 97, 218, 252, 253
"nine-dash line," 78, 79, 84, 88, 106, 112
no-fly zones, 178
non-aggression principle, 17
Non-Aligned Movement (NAM), 173–4
non-alignment, 15, 173–4
non-interference, 14, 17, 20, 153
non-intervention principle, 12, 14, 30, 31, 209, 218, 253–4
non-lethal assistance, 250
non-military responses to perceived threats, 35
non-state actors, 37, 195–208
non-use of force in response to humanitarian atrocities, 177
non-use of force to settle sovereignty disputes, 87–97
North Korea, 4, 46–7, 49, 244–5
nuclear bombs, 11
nuclear deterrence, 39–40, 41
nuclear weapons, 38–41, 237, 239, 240–5
Nuremberg Trials, 255, 266

observer missions, 72
occupation, 113–14, 115–17, 121, 132, 160, 205, 206
Oda, Judge, 39, 40
Office for the Coordination of Humanitarian Affairs of the United Nations, 220
official secrets, 5
oil
  cooperation arrangements, 109–10
  cooperation on development, 106
  Costa Rica, 217
  East Timor, 166
  South China Sea, 78, 88, 89, 94, 95, 99–101
  Yemen, 222
Oil Platforms (Iran v. USA), 33–4, 97, 100–1
Open-Ended Working Group on Developments in the Field of Information and Telecommunications in the Context of International Security, 38
Operation Aspides, 229
Operation Gibraltar, 58–9
Operation Linda Nchi, 195–6
Operation Praying Mantis, 100, 101
Operation Provide Comfort, 171
Operation Searchlight, 123
opinio juris, 30

Opium Wars, 62
Optional Protocol to the Convention against Torture, 151
Organisation for the Prohibition of Chemical Weapons, 187
Organisation of African Unity (OAU), 246
organisation of armed groups, 145
Organisation of Islamic Cooperation (OIC), 22–3, 113–14, 148, 151–2, 177, 187
Oslo Manual on Select Topics of the Law of Armed Conflict: Rules and Commentary, 197
Our Common Agenda, 19
outer space, 18, 234–5
Owada, Judge Hisashi, 174, 207, 208

Pakistan
- Balochistan, 125
- and the ICJ, 25–6
- India-Pakistan 4 day conflict in May 2025, 200–1
- India-Pakistan dispute over Kashmir, 55, 56–62
- India v. Pakistan non-state actors, 199–201
- Indo-Pakistani war of 1971, 59, 123–4
- "mere frontier incidents," 97–8
- nuclear weapons, 241–2
- partition, 55, 56, 125
- *Rann of Kutch* dispute, 95–6
- size of army, 4
- terrorism, 148

Pal, Radhabinod, 12
Palestine, 148–9, 228, 237
Paracels/Xisha Islands, 55, 78, 82, 112
Paris Peace Agreements, 51–2
Paris terrorist attacks 2015, 203
Paris Tribunal, 262
partition, 55, 56, 125
peace, 3, 233–5, 265–6
peaceful coexistence, 15, 19
peacekeeping, 226
Peace of Westphalia (1648), 9–10, 16
Peace Research Institute Oslo, 4
Pedra Branca/Pulau Batu Puteh, 93, 94
Permanent Court of Arbitration, 83
Permanent Court of International Justice, 11
Philippines
- archipelagic state doctrine, 8
- Confidence Building Measures (CBMs), 108–13
- cooperation MOU with China, 106
- and the ICJ, 26
- Moro nationalism, 125
- Muslim communities, 125 as well???, 149
- Mutual Defence Treaty, 108–10
- San Francisco Conference 1945, 12
- South China Sea, 83–6, 87, 97

philosophy, 41
poison, 41, *see also* chemical weapons
polar regions, 18
Political Statement on the Suppression of the Veto in Case of Mass Atrocities, 237
Pompeo, Mike, 242n19
populism, 55
Portuguese colonialism, 60, 120–1, 124, 158, 159, 162–3
positive peace, 3
postcolonialism, 55, 124–5, 138, 139
Prabowo Subianto, 106
Preah Vihear/Phra Viharn, 55, 69–77

precaution, 6, 147
precision-guided munitions, 229
pre-emptive self-defence, 33, 42
prohibition of aggression, 46
proportionality
  humanitarian intervention, 185
  IHL principle, 6
  international humanitarian law (IHL or *jus in bello*), 147
  nuclear weapons, 40
  Oil Platforms (Iran v. USA), 101
  self-defence, 30, 32, 33, 34, 35
  self-defence against non-state actors, 198
  use of force, 36
Protection of Victims of International Armed Conflicts Protocol (AP I), 146, 254
Protection of Victims of Non-international Armed Conflicts Protocol (AP II), 143, 145–6, 147, 254
protests against competing claims, 88
Protocol Additional to the Geneva Conventions of 12 August 1949 (1977), 143, 146
public domain information, reliance on, 5
Punjab, 55–6
Putin, Vladimir, 21

Qatar-Bahrain, 91, 94–5
Quadrilateral Security Dialogue, 22, 27, 107–8
qualified silence, 44–5
Quebec, 133
Quintana, Moreno, 75
Quran, 9

racial equality, 10
Radcliffe Line, 55
Rann of Kutch dispute, 95–6
Raslan, Anwar, 261
recognition of states, 142–3
reconciliation, 95, 164, 165, 193, 233, 234, 258, 266
Reference re Secession of Quebec, 133, 138
referenda, 58, 60, 126, 140, 163–7
refugees, 123, 179, 187–8
regional organisations, 22–4
religious boundaries, 55
Responsibility to Protect (R2P) doctrine, 172–94, 207
"responsible dialogue," 21
restraint, 88
riots, 144
Rohingyas, 153, 154–5, 192
Rome Statute (1988), 153, 180, 256, 258, 262
Russia
  and China, 240
  and Libya, 178
  and Myanmar, 193
  nuclear weapons, 245
  permanent members of UNSC, 13
  South China Sea, 78
  Syria, 180, 204, 206, 208, 219
Russia-Ukraine war, 20, 21, 48, 172, 240, 259

Sakhanh, Haisam Omar, 260–1
Saleh, President Ali Abdullah, 211, 214n9, 223, 225
samurai tradition, 9
sanctions, 152, 183, 185, 194, 213, 222, 229
San Francisco Conference 1945, 12
Saudi Arabia
  nuclear weapons, 240
  Qatar-Bahrain, 94–5

San Francisco Conference 1945, 12
UNSC, 237
war crimes, 260
and Yemen, 213, 215, 216, 223, 225, 227–8
Scarborough Shoal, 85–6, 110, 111
seabed/ocean floor, 18, 26, 84
Sea Isle City, 100–1
secession
former Yugoslavia, 134
legal right of, 138
Myanmar, 155
Pakistan, 59
recognition of states, 142–3
"remedial secession," 137, 139
rights to, 140–1
self-determination, 123, 132, 133, 136
Second World War, 11–12, 29
self-defence
anticipatory, 32–3, 242
Bush Doctrine, 33
cyberattacks, 37–8
extraterritorial actions, 37
frontier incidents versus "armed attacks," 97–103
international regime, 29–41
intervention by invitation, 220
Laos-Thailand dispute over Ban Romklao, 68
necessity criteria, 33–5
non-consensual, 197–8
non-state actors, 195–208
pre-emptive self-defence, 33, 42
proportionality, 34
qualified silence, 45
to recover territories, 113–18
reports to UNSC, 41–4
Yemen, 213
self-determination, 119–56
East Timor, 159, 160, 162
internal versus external, 138–9, 149–56
international legal order, 16, 17
Kashmir, 57, 60–1
sovereignty disputes, 118
separatism, 125, 149, 152
Serbia, 134, 136–7, 170, 259
Serious Crimes Panel, 164
"shadowing" of vessels, 89
Shanghai Cooperation Organisation (SCO), 20, 24, 65
Shangri-la Dialogue, 110
Shi Jiuyong, Judge, 32–3, 34, 39, 45, 169, 170–1
shipping, 78, 228–9
ships, stopping, 102
silence, and the use of force, 44–6
Simla Agreement, 59, 63–4
Singapore, 93, 127
Sino-Indian Confidence-Building Measures (CBM) Agreement in 1996, 65, 66
Sino-Pakistani Agreement 1963, 65
Six Day War (1967), 114
small-scale border attacks, 36
Somalia, 195–6
South China Sea, 22, 27, 55, 77–97, 104–13
South China Sea Arbitration aware, 87, 111, 112
Southern Movement, 223, 226
Southern Transitional Council (STC), 215, 221, 223, 226, 228
South Korea, 4, 77, 244–5
South Ledge, 93–4
South Sudan, 140
sovereign equality, 10, 14, 16, 40, 41
sovereign immunity, 98

sovereignty, 54–118
East Timor, 162
Five Principles of Peaceful Coexistence, 17–18
India, 124
India v. Pakistan non-state actors, 200
international legal order, 10, 13, 14
Kosovo, 137–8
recognition of, 137–8
Responsibility to Protect (R2P) doctrine, 192
self-determination, 130, 131
Syria, 202
UN Convention on the Law of the Sea (UNCLOS), 26
Soviet Union
Bandung Conference, Indonesia 1955, 15
dissolution of, 140
India-Pakistan dispute over Kashmir, 59
Indo-Pakistani war of 1971, 124
Laos-Thailand dispute over Ban Romklao, 68
UN Security Council, 46–7, 51
veto, 51, 122
special agreements, 93–4
special economic zones, 191
Special Tribunal for the Crime of Aggression against Ukraine, 259
Spender, Percy, 75
Spratlys/Nansha Islands, 55, 78, 82, 83, 85, 86–7, 111
Sri Lanka, 43
state-based conflicts, definition of, 4
Riyadh Summit for Cooperation and Development, 244
state of war, definition of, 1–2
state responsibility, 245–54
Stockholm International Peace Research Institute, 3
Strait of Hormuz, 54
Subaihi, Major-General Mahmoud al-, 215
subsoil, 18, 26, 84
Suharto, General, 126, 158, 162, 165
Sun Tsu, 9
surgical strikes, 200
sustainable development, 18
suzerainty, 63, 80
Sweden, 260–1
Symposium on the International Situation and China's Foreign Relations, 66
Symposium on the International Situation and China's Foreign Relations (Beijing, 2022), 18
Syria
airstrikes, 34–5, 171, 242
arms supply, 250
non-state actors, 201–8
Responsibility to Protect (R2P) doctrine, 177–88, 190
San Francisco Conference 1945, 12
terrorism and self-defence, 197–8
universal jurisdiction, 263–4
UNSC reform, 237
war crimes, 260–1
Yemen, 219

Taiwan, 79, 138
Taliban, 97–8
"Tanker War," 100
targeted killings of terrorists, 198
tariffs, 92
Tashkent Declaration, 59
Temple of Preah Vihar, 68, 69
temporality, 234
"Ten Principles," 14–16, 18, 119, 157
terra nullius, 81, 83
Territorial and Maritime Dispute (Nicaragua v. Colombia), 80
territorial disputes, 54, *see also* sovereignty

territorial integrity, 17, 77, 130–1, 134, 138–9, 146, 155, 169, 171, 192, 200
terrorism, 195–208
and the definition of armed conflict, 144–5
definitions of, 148
versus freedom fighters, 148–9
intervention by invitation, 43
Kashmir, 62
non-interference principle, 17
and pre-emptive self-defence, 33
Shanghai Cooperation Organisation (SCO), 24
Yemen, 222, 223, 229
Thaçi, Hashim, 258
Thailand
assistance to Myanmar, 175
Cambodia-Thailand dispute over Preah Vihear/Phra Viharn, 55, 69–77
ethno-nationalism, 125–6
foreign policy, 52
Laos-Thailand dispute over Ban Romklao, 55, 67–8
Muslim communities, 127–30, 152
self-determination, 127–9, 132
and Vietnam, 51, 52
third-party dispute settlement mechanisms, 24, 90–1, 93, 112–13
Tibet, 14, 63, 64, 66
Tigray War, 140–2
"Timor Gap" treaty, 162, 166
Timor-Leste, 163–7
Tinoco Claims Arbitration (Great Britain v. Costa Rica), 217
Tokyo War Crimes Tribunal (International Military Tribunal for the Far East) 1946, 11–12
trade, 78, 89, 92, 166, 190
treaties
China, 62
East Timor, 162, 163
human rights, 150, 151
Siam-France, 68
Treaty of Amity and Cooperation in Southeast Asia 1976, 23, 72
Treaty of Joint Arab Defence, 213
Treaty of Versailles, 11
Treaty on the Non-proliferation of Nuclear Weapons, 244, 265
Treaty on the Prohibition of Nuclear Weapons, 241–2
tribunals, 24–5, 83–5, 164, 255, 257–8, 259
tributary system, 10
truth commissions, 164
Tuna offshore gas field, 90
Türkiye, 115, 201–2, 205, 206, 207, 208

UAE, 54, 216, 223, 225, 228
Uganda, 253
Ukraine, 20, 21, 172, 240, 259
UN (United Nations)
Basic Principles on the Use of Force and Firearms by Law Enforcement Officials, 102–3
central role in international peace, 18
decolonisation committee, 127
Global Security Initiative (GSI), 19
membership of Asian states, 13
Office for the Coordination of Humanitarian Affairs of the United Nations, 220
Open-Ended Working Group on Developments in the Field of Information and Telecommunications in the Context of International Security, 38
Peacebuilding Fund and Peacebuilding Commission, 234–5, 266
peacekeeping, 226
Responsibility to Protect (R2P) doctrine, 172–7
United Nations Register of Conventional Arms (UNROCA), 251–2

UN Charter
Article 2(4), 29–30, 36, 38, 39, 48, 98, 115, 138, 169–70, 210
Article 2(5), 248
Article 24(1), 28
Article 27(3), 28, 239
Article 51, 29–30, 33, 34–5, 36–9, 41–3, 114, 116, 197, 201, 202, 204, 205, 213, 216, 219
Article 52(3), 239
Article 108, 236
Articles 2(4), 254
Chapter VI, 239
Chapter VII, 28–9, 134–5, 160–1, 171, 173, 177, 180, 184, 186, 194, 211, 214, 251
collective security, 28–9
cyberattacks, 38
definition of "armed attack," 116
drafting of, 12
Five Principles of Peaceful Coexistence, 14, 17
Global Security Initiative (GSI), 19
Goa, 121–2
humanitarian intervention, 172
human rights law, 150
and the ICC, 256
Laos-Thailand dispute over Ban Romklao, 67–8
military aid/assistance, 30
non-state actors, 37, 197
nuclear weapons, 39
obligation to settle disputes by peaceful means, 90
and the OIC Charter, 22
peaceful means for dispute resolution, 115
self-defence, 197
self-determination, 119, 120, 131
"Ten Principles," 14–16, 18, 119, 157
and the term "armed conflict," 2
Ukraine, 21
use of force, 29–30, 36, 99
UN Commission for India and Pakistan, 57–8
UN Convention on the Law of the Sea (UNCLOS), 8, 26, 79, 83–7, 96, 98–100, 104, 106, 108, 109, 112–13, 166
UN Educational, Scientific and Cultural Organization (UNESCO), 70, 74, 76
UN General Assembly
Declaration on Principles of International Law concerning Friendly Relations and Cooperation (1970 Declaration on Friendly Relations), 14, 16, 30–1, 34, 87, 103, 116, 122, 131–2, 133, 138, 157, 170, 253
Declaration on the Granting of Independence to Colonial Countries and Peoples, 119–20, 131, 159
Definition of Aggression, 31, 116, 170, 256–7
East Timor, 159, 160
emergency special sessions, 48–9
International, Impartial and Independent Mechanism to Assist in the Investigation and Prosecution of Persons Responsible for the Most Serious Crimes, 182
Kosovo, 137
Libya, 249
Peacebuilding Commission, 235, 266
on Peaceful and Neighbourly Relations among States, 16
reform of UNSC, 238

- Resolution 1236 of 1957 on Peaceful and Neighbourly Relations among States, 16
- Responsibility to Protect (R2P) doctrine, 189
- self-defence to recover territories, 114
- silence, 45
- Uniting for Peace Resolution, 47, 239
- UNSC deadlocks, 47
- Veto Initiative, 48–9

UN High Commissioner for Human Rights, 150
UN Human Rights Council (HRC), 150–1, 181, 207, 221, 222
UN International Law Commission (ILC), 175–6
UN International Law Commission's Articles on Responsibility of States for Internationally Wrongful Acts (ARSIWA), 247–9, 252
United Kingdom
- East Timor, 160
- humanitarian intervention, 169, 171, 192
- and the ICJ, 25
- and Iraq, 248
- Myanmar, 191–2
- nuclear weapons, 241
- permanent members of UNSC, 13
- Syria, 184, 185–6, 203
- Yemen, 216, 229

United States
- airstrikes, 34–5, 184, 185, 202
- Bandung Conference, Indonesia 1955, 15
- disaster relief, 174
- East Timor, 160, 161
- humanitarian intervention, 171, 176
- and the ICJ, 92
- India-Pakistan dispute over Kashmir, 59
- intervention to help suppress Al Qaeda, 44
- Iraq, 176, 182–3
- Kosovo, 171
- Kuwait, 161
- Laos-Thailand dispute over Ban Romklao, 68
- Libya, 249
- Mutual Defence Treaty, 108–10
- Myanmar, 154, 174–5
- nuclear weapons, 21, 243
- *Oil Platforms (Iran v. USA)*, 34, 97, 100–1
- permanent members of UNSC, 13
- Quadrilateral Security Dialogue, 22, 108
- Somalia, 196
- South China Sea, 89
- Syria, 184, 197–8, 203, 205, 206
- targeted killings of terrorists, 198–9
- West Papua, 126
- and the WTO, 92
- Yemen, 214, 216, 222, 229

United States—Certain Measures on Steel and Aluminium Products, 92
Uniting for Consensus, 238
Uniting for Peace Resolution, 47–8
unity of purpose, 29
Universal Declaration of Human Rights, 120, 150
universal jurisdiction, 260
universal periodic reviews (UPRs), 150
UN Mission in the Republic of South Sudan, 140
unnecessary suffering, 40
unoccupied territories, discovery of, 79–80
UN Register of Conventional Arms (UNROCA), 251–2

UN Security Council
Accountability, Coherence and Transparency Group (ACT), 236–7
annexation, 157
Article 51, 204–5
assessment of 'intensity' of conflict, 144
authorisation of humanitarian intervention, 169
authorisation of use of force, 36, 173
Cambodia-Thailand dispute over Preah Vihear/Phra Viharn, 70
"Chapter VII" measures, 184
Cold War freeze, 160
deadlocks, 46–9
determination of existence of threat to peace, 29
East Timor, 159, 160, 164
and failure to perform obligations set by ICJ, 92
Goa, 121
humanitarian intervention, 171
immediacy requirement, 114
India-Pakistan dispute over Kashmir, 60
Indo-Pakistani war of 1971, 124
Kashmir, 57–8, 59
Kosovo, 134–7
Kuwait, 160
lack of judicial review, 29
Libya, 177, 249
maintenance of international peace, 28
Mutual Defence Treaty, 108
Myanmar, 192–4
non-state actors, 37
overriding non-aggression principle, 17
Peacebuilding Commission, 235, 266
peacekeeping, 196, 226
permanent members, 13, 28, 236, 238, 239–40
proactive use of powers, 36
reform of, 236–40
reports to, 41–4
Resolution 1244 (1999), 139
Resolution 1973 (2011), 177, 178, 192
Resolution 2249 (2015), 203–4
Responsibility to Protect (R2P) doctrine, 190
Saudi Arabia, 237
self-defence, 204–5
self-defence to recover territories, 114
silence, 45
Syria, 179, 180, 183, 184, 186, 202, 204, 205
terrorism, 195
Ukraine, 21
veto, 45, 46, 48, 122, 169, 178, 180, 190, 191, 202, 237, 238, 239, 265
Yemen, 211–13, 214, 216, 217, 222, 227, 228
UN Transitional Administration in West New Guinea (West Irian), 126
UN Transitional Authority for East Timor (UNTAET), 164, 165
UN Transitional Authority in Cambodia (UNTAC), 52
use of force, 28–53
"accidental," 102
to avert humanitarian catastrophe, 171–2, 186
below threshold of "armed attack," 49
burden of proof, 100
frontier incidents versus "armed attacks," 97–103
humanitarian intervention, 185
international humanitarian law (IHL), 146–7
non-specificity of weapons, 38
to protect human rights, 182
silence, 44–6
state liability, 245–54
USS *Samuel B. Roberts*, 100–1
uti possidetis juris, 80

Vanuatu, 126
Versailles Peace Conference, 10
veto, 45, 46, 48, 122, 169, 178, 180, 190, 191, 202, 237, 238, 239, 265
victors' justice, 12, 256
Vienna Declaration and Progamme of Action, 131, 132
Vietnam
  and China, 63
  Confidence Building Measures (CBMs), 103
  invasion by China, 50
  invasion of Cambodia, 49–53, 171
  size of army, 4
  South China Sea, 78, 82–3, 87, 90

war, definition of, 1–2
war crimes
  East Timor, 164
  state responsibility, 250, 255
  Syria, 179, 185, 262
  Tokyo War Crimes Tribunal (International Military Tribunal for the Far East) 1946, 11–12
  universal jurisdiction, 260, 263
  Yemen, 221, 225
weapons of mass destruction, 182
Weeramantry, Judge, 39, 40–1
Western ideas, 9–10, 81, 91, 120–2, 130, 146, *see also* colonialism
West Papua, 124, 126–7
Westphalian system, 9–10, 16
Wheaton, Henry, 11
Whitsun Reef, 87
Wilson, Harold, 95
win-win cooperation, 18, 20
Working Mechanism for Consultation and Coordination on India–China Border Affairs, 66
World Conference on Human Rights, 131
World Heritage Sites, 70, 74, 76–7
World Summit (UN) 2005, 172, 173, 190
World Trade Organization (WTO), 13, 92

Xi Jinping, 21, 67, 103, 191
Xue Hanqin, Judge, 13, 62

Yazidis, 176
Yemen, 44, 209, 211–30, 244, 260
Yusuf, Judge, 138, 139

Zawahiri, Ayman al-, 199
zero-sum game thinking, 18
Zhou En-lai, 15, 62
zones of cooperation, 162, 166